STUDIA MISSIONALIA

Publication of the Faculty of Missiology, Gregorian University.

Publication de la Faculté de Missiologie de l'Université Grégorienne.

MARIASUSAI DHAVAMONY, S.J., *Director*.

GOD'S KINGDOM
AND MISSION

LE ROYAUME DE DIEU
ET LA MISSION

EDITRICE PONTIFICIA UNIVERSITÀ GREGORIANA
ROMA 1997

IMPRIMI POTEST

P. Giuseppe Pittau, S.I.
Rector Universitatis
Romae, die 24 martii 1997

IMPRIMATUR

Dal Vicariato di Roma, 22 aprile 1997
Sac. Luigi Moretti
Segretario Generale

ISBN 88-7652-741-9

© E.P.U.G. - Roma - 1997

Editrice Pontificia Università Gregoriana
Piazza della Pilotta, 35 - 00187 Roma, Italia

CONTENTS — SOMMAIRE

God's Kingdom and Mission
Le Royaume de Dieu et la Mission

Klemens Stock, Die Bergpredickt als Programm für das Reich Gottes	1
I. de la Potterie, Jésus, Témoin de la Vérité et Roi par la Vérité	21
Giuseppe Ferraro, Vedere il regno e nascere da acqua e da Spirito	43
Ugo Vanni, La Preghiera e il Regno	65
Earl C. Muller, The Trinity and the Kingdom	91
William Henn, The Church and the Kingdom of God	119
Philip J. Rosato, The Eucharist and the Kingdom of God	149
Jacques Servais, Il regno di Dio e la vita consacrata	171
Franz Josef van Beeck, Kingdom of God and Salvation	195
Lucien Legrand, Good News of the Kingdom or Good News of Jesus Christ?	211
Mariasusai Dhavamony, The Kingdom of God and Religious Pluralism	227
James A. Wiseman, The Kingdom of God in Monastic Interreligious Dialogue	251
John Fuellenbach, The Kingdom of God in Latin American Liberation Theology	267

FABC Theological Commission, The Kingdom of
    God and Evangelization in Asia 293

A. Emmanuel Orobator, The Idea of the Kingdom
    of God in African Theology 327

Rt. Rev. Peter K. Sarpong, Asante Culture and the
    Kingdom of God 359

CONTRIBUTORS — COLLABORATEURS

FRANZ JOSEF VAN BEECK, Professor of Dogmatic Theology, Loyola University, Chicago.

MARIASUSAI DHAVAMONY - Professor of Theology and Phenomenology of Religions, Gregorian University, Rome.

GIUSEPPE FERRARO, Professor of Biblical Theology, Gregorian University, Rome.

JOHN FUELLENBACH, Professor of Dogmatic Theology, Gregorian University, Rome.

WILLIAM HENN, Professor of Dogmatic Theology, Gregorian University, Rome.

LUCIEN LEGRAND, Professor of Biblical Theology, St. Peter's Seminary, Bangalore.

EARL C. MULLER, Professor of Dogmatic Theology, Gregorian University, Rome.

A. EMMANUEL OROBATOR, Research Scholar, Jesuit School of Theology at Berkeley.

I. DE LA POTTERIE, Professor of New Testament Exegesis, Pontifical Biblical Institute, Rome.

PHILIP J. ROSATO, Professor of Dogmatic Theology, Gregorian University, Rome.

RT. REV. PETER SARPONG, Bishop of Kumasi, anthropologist and Theologian.

JACQUES SERVAIS, Professor of Spiritual Theology, Gregorian University, Rome.

KLEMENS STOCK, Professor of New Testament Exegesis, Pontifical Biblical Institute, Rome.

UGO VANNI, Professor of New Testament Exegesis, Gregorian University, Rome.

JAMES A. WISEMAN, Professor of Theology at the Catholic University of America, Washington D.C., U.S.A.

Die Bergpredigt als Programm für das Reich Gottes

KLEMENS STOCK

Von den fünf Reden Jesu, die wir im Matthäusevangelium finden, ist die Bergpredigt (Mt 5-7) die erste und längste. Mit ihr beginnt Jesus sein öffentliches Wirken und in ihr entfaltet er programmatisch seine Botschaft. Diese ist zusammengefaßt in dem Wort: «Kehrt um! Denn das Himmelreich ist nahe» (Mt 4,17). In der Bergpredigt legt Jesus dar, wie die Umkehr zu vollziehen ist und was er unter dem Himmelreich versteht. Bei Matthäus wird besonders häufig vom Reich (Gottes) gesprochen (46 mal; Markus 14; Lukas 36) und er gebraucht vor allem den Ausdruck 'Himmelreich' (32 mal). Dieser entspricht der jüdischen Sprechweise, die den Namen Gottes vermeidet und dafür Ersatzausdrücke wie 'Himmel', 'Kraft', 'Wohnung' verwendet. 'Himmelreich' meint 'Reich Gottes', wobei der 'himmlische', überirdische und übermenschliche Charakter dieses Reiches betont sein mag.

Neben der Parabelrede (13,1-53) mit 11 Vorkommen spricht die Bergpredigt am häufigsten (8 mal) vom Reich (Gottes), und zwar in den Formen von 'Himmelreich' (5,3.10.19.19.20; 7,21), 'dein Reich' (6,10) und 'Reich Gottes' (6,33). Wie die Stellenangaben zeigen, kommt der Ausdruck besonders im Anfangsteil vor, ist aber strategisch über die ganze Rede verteilt.

1. DIE TEXTE VOM REICH UND IHR INHALT

Bei unserem Versuch herauszuarbeiten, was die Bergpredigt über das Reich Gottes zu sagen hat, wollen wir von den Versen ausgehen, die direkt vom Reich Gottes sprechen. Wir wollen den Text dieser Verse anführen, feststellen, was sie unmittelbar aussagen, und uns durch sie zu den anderen Teilen der Bergpredigt weiterführen lassen.

Die Bergpredigt (Bp) wird durch die acht Seligkeiten eröffnet. An deren Anfang und Ende heißt es: «Selig, die arm sind vor Gott; denn ihnen gehört das Himmelreich» und «Selig, die um der Gerechtigkeit willen verfolgt werden; denn ihnen gehört das Himmelreich» (5,3.10). Wo er von seiner eigenen Sendung spricht, sagt Jesus: «Wer auch nur eines von den kleinsten Geboten aufhebt und die Menschen entsprechend lehrt, der wird im Himmelreich der Kleinste sein. Wer sie aber hält und halten lehrt, der wird groß sein im Himmelreich» (5,19). In der Überleitung zu den Antithesen, die das Verhalten zum Nächsten behandeln, heißt es: «Darum sage ich euch: Wenn eure Gerechtigkeit nicht weit größer ist als die der Schriftgelehrten und Pharisäer, werdet ihr nicht in das Himmelreich kommen» (5,20). Im mittleren Teil der Bp (6,1-18) werden die Grundformen jüdischer Frömmigkeit aufgeführt und es geht um das Verhältnis zu Gott. Hier lehrt Jesus seine Hörer beten: «Vater unser im Himmel ... dein Reich komme» (6,9-10). Wo er von der Sorge um die materiellen Dinge spricht (6,19-34), sagt er gegen Ende: «Suchet aber zuerst das Reich Gottes und seine Gerechtigkeit; dann wird euch alles andere dazugegeben» (6,33). Den Schlußteil der Bp (7,21-27) beginnt Jesus mit der Feststellung: «Nicht jeder, der zu mir sagt: Herr! Herr! wird in das Himmelreich kommen, sondern nur, wer den Willen meines Vaters im Himmel erfüllt» (7,21).

Wenn wir auf den Inhalt dieser Verse achten, stellen wir fest, daß keiner sagt, was mit dem Himmelreich gemeint ist. Es wird vorausgesetzt, daß die Bedeutung dieses Ausdrucks bekannt ist. Eine Sonderstellung unter diesen Versen nimmt 6,10 ein, in dem um das Kommen des Reiches gebetet wird. Alle anderen Verse sind ähnlich aufgebaut und behandeln fast das gleiche Thema. Sie bestehen aus zwei Sätzen und sprechen von der Beziehung zum Reich Gottes. Dabei nennt der eine Satz diese Beziehung, während der andere angibt, von welcher Bedingung diese Beziehung abhängt. Die Bedingungen heißen: arm sein vor Gott (5,3), um der Gerechtigkeit willen verfolgt werden (5,10), die kleinsten Gebote halten und halten lehren (5,19), eine größere Gerechtigkeit haben (5,20), den Willen des Vaters im Himmel erfüllen (7,21).

Wenn diese Bedingungen erfüllt sind, sind die folgenden Beziehungen zum Reich gegeben: ihnen gehört das Himmelreich (5,3.10), er wird groß sein im Himmelreich (5,19), sie werden in das Himmelreich kommen (5,20; 7,21). Die Bedeutung dieser Beziehung wird am Anfang zweimal genannt: Diejenigen, denen das Himmelreich gehört, werden seliggepriesen (5,3-10); sein Besitz macht sie grenzenlos glücklich.

Den Stellen der Bp, die direkt vom Reich Gottes sprechen, können wir vor allem drei Feststellungen entnehmen: 1. Die Seligkeit des Menschen, der Sinn und die Erfüllung seines Lebens, hängt von seiner Zugehörigkeit zum Reich Gottes ab. 2. Diese Zugehörigkeit ergibt sich nicht von selber, sondern ist an Bedingungen geknüpft. 3. In beiden Bereichen ist Gott der Bestimmende. Es ist das Reich Gottes, das dem Menschen die Seligkeit schenkt, und es ist der Wille Gottes, der zu erfüllen ist, um in das Reich Gottes eingehen zu können. Von beiden Seiten her ist der Mensch ganz auf Gott verwiesen.

Wir wollen im Folgenden die Bp untersuchen, ob sie genauere Angaben über das Reich Gottes macht und ob sie die Bedingungen für die Zugehörigkeit mehr im einzelnen entfaltet. Entsprechend diesen Angaben und Bestimmungen wird sie sich als Programm für das Reich Gottes erweisen.

2. Das Reich Gottes nach der Bergpredigt

Wir finden weder in der Bp noch im übrigen Matthäusevangelium ausdrückliche Angaben, oder gar eine Definition, was mit Reich Gottes gemeint ist. Um seinen Sinn zu verstehen, wollen wir den Ausdruck selber untersuchen, ferner darauf achten, was die acht Seligkeiten, an deren Anfang und Ende er sich findet, als Kontext über ihn zu sagen haben, und schließlich in Betrachtung ziehen, was die Bp über das Handeln des himmlischen Vaters sagt.

a. *Das Wort «Reich (Gottes)»*

Der Ausdruck 'hē basileia tōn ouranōn' (Himmelreich) oder 'hē basileia tou theou' (Reich Gottes) spricht von Gott als König ('basileus') und bezieht sich auf sein Königtum, auf sein Handeln und Herrschen als König (Königsherrschaft) und auf den Bereich dieses Herrschens (Königreich). 'Königsherrschaft Gottes' unterscheidet sich von dem vergleichbaren Ausdruck 'Allmacht Gottes' dadurch, daß es nicht abstrakt und allgemein von der Macht und Herrschaft Gottes spricht, sondern die Beziehung zum Volk des Königs einschließt; der König hat Macht und herrscht für sein Volk. Das Alte Testament verwendet nicht den Ausdruck 'Königsherrschaft Gottes', aber es spricht oft davon, daß Gott König ist für sein Volk: «Der Herr ist König für immer und ewig» (Ex 15,18; vgl. Ps 146,10; Jes 6,5; 24,23). Als König setzt Gott seine Macht ein zugunsten seines Volkes. Das Vorbild für den König ist der Hirt. So wird auch Gott als Hirt seines Volkes gesehen (Ps 22; Ez 34), der seine Fürsorge und Macht aufbietet, damit sein Volk leben kann. Der Ausdruck 'Königsherrschaft Gottes' spricht also vom königlichen Herrschen Gottes, von der machtvollen und liebevollen Zuwendung Gottes zu seinem Volk.

b. *Die Seligpreisungen Mt 5,3-10*

Alle acht Seligpreisungen bestehen aus drei Teilen und haben denselben Aufbau. Am Anfang wird feierlich erklärt: 'Selig sind'. Dann wird angegeben, was die Menschen kennzeichnet, denen die Seligerklärung gilt. Im letzten Glied wird der Grund genannt, warum Menschen dieser Art für selig erklärt werden.

Die erste Seligpreisung richtet sich an Menschen, die arm sind vor Gott; als Grund dafür wird angegeben: «denn ihnen gehört das Himmelreich» (5,3). Ein Besitzverhältnis wird hier behauptet und die Armen vor Gott werden als die Eigentümer des Himmelreiches vorgestellt. Es wird nicht nur gesagt, daß sie zum Himmelreich gehören, sondern daß dieses ihnen gehört, ihr Eigentum ist. Das Himmelreich meint aber die machtvolle und liebevolle Zuwendung Gottes zu seinem Volk. Die Armen vor Gott haben also einen Anspruch auf die Macht und die Liebe Gottes, sie haben ein Recht darauf, von der Macht und der Liebe Gottes ganz durchdrungen und erfaßt zu werden. Und gerade das bedeutet für sie Seligkeit, vollkommene Freude, vollendetes Glück.

Die achte Seligpreisung wendet sich an die Menschen,

die um der Gerechtigkeit willen verfolgt werden. Sie gibt für deren Seligerklärung denselben Grund an wie die erste: «denn ihnen gehört das Himmelreich»; auch sie sind Eigentümer der Königsherrschaft Gottes. Die anderen sechs Seligpreisungen, die zwischen der ersten und der achten stehen, werden auf verschiedene Weise begründet: «denn sie werden getröstet werden» (5,4) usw. Für die erste Begründung «denn ihnen gehört das Himmelreich» ist es also eigentümlich, daß sie wiederholt wird, daß sie am Anfang und Ende steht und die anderen Begründungen wie eine Klammer umschließt und daß sie mit dem Ausdruck 'Himmelreich' über die Seligpreisungen hinausgreift und den Zusammenhang mit der übrigen Bp und dem Matthäusevangelium herstellt. Was das Verhältnis zu den anderen Begründungen angeht, darf man aus dem dargelegten Sachverhalt wohl schließen: Mit dem «denn ihnen gehört das Himmelreich» wird die fundamentale und umfassende Begründung der Seligkeit gegeben; sie besteht in der machtvollen und liebevollen Zuwendung Gottes. Auf der anderen Seite sprechen die übrigen Begründungen in konkreter Weise vom Handeln Gottes, und wir können sie verstehen als mehr ins einzelne gehende Beschreibung dessen, was mit 'Himmelreich' gemeint ist. Wie wir schon festgestellt haben, beschreibt das Evangelium nirgends den Inhalt von 'Himmelreich'. Diese Lücke können wir in etwa ausfüllen, wenn wir die weiteren Begründungen (5,4-9) genauer untersuchen.

Die zweite Seligpreisung «Selig die Trauernden» wird begründet: «denn sie werden getröstet werden (5,4). Hier wird, wie in insgesamt vier Seligpreisungen (5,4.6.7.9), die Passivform verwendet. Es wird Tröstung zugesagt, aber es wird nicht offen ausgedrückt, woher der Trost kommt. Dieses Sprechen im Passiv folgt einem Brauch der Zeit Jesu. Aus Ehrfurcht vor Gott haben die Juden den Namen Gottes 'Jahwe' und das Wort 'Gott' nicht gebraucht. Eines der Mittel, um dennoch von Gott sprechen zu können, war der Gebrauch des Passivs. «Sie werden getröstet werden» bedeutet also «Gott wird sie trösten». Auch die folgenden Passivformen sprechen vom Handeln Gottes.

Wie Gott tröstet, wird in der Apokalypse ausgeführt: «Er wird in ihrer Mitte wohnen, und sie werden sein Volk sein; und er, Gott, wird bei ihnen sein. Er wird alle Tränen von ihren Augen abwischen: Der Tod wird nicht mehr sein, keine Trauer, keine Klage, keine Mühsal. Denn was früher war, ist vergangen. Er, der auf dem Throne saß, sprach: Seht, ich mache alles neu» (21,3-5). Gott wird nicht mit Worten trösten, sondern durch sein Tun. Er wird nicht innerhalb der Verhältnisse der gegenwärtigen Welt handeln, sondern wird diese überwinden durch seine schöpferische Kraft, durch die er alles neu macht. Er wird die Trauernden trösten, indem er alle Ursachen der Trauer beseitigt, vor allem den Tod. Kennzeichnend für das Verhalten Gottes ist seine ständige Gegenwart bei den Menschen, seine offene Zuwendung zu ihnen. In Jes 66,13 hat Gott angekündigt: «Wie eine Mutter ihren Sohn tröstet, so werde ich euch trösten». Der allmächtige Schöpfer, der alles neu schafft, verhält sich wie eine Mutter. Die neue Welt Gottes ist nicht eine kalte Konstruktion, in die wir Menschen hineingezwungen werden, sie ist bestimmt von der personalen Gegenwart Gottes, der seine grenzenlose Macht in Liebe, nach Art einer Mutter, einsetzt. Für die Königsherrschaft Gottes wird hier also deutlich, daß sie alle Ursachen des Leids überwindet und daß sie die Gegenwart Gottes in liebevoller, mütterlicher Zuwendung schenkt.

An die dritte Seligpreisung: «Selig, die keine Gewalt anwenden» schließt sich die Begründung an: «denn sie werden das Land erben» (5,5). Ähnlich heißt es in Ps 37,11: «Die Sanftmütigen werden das Land erben und froh sein über die Fülle des Heils». Derselbe Psalm sagt, daß diejenigen, die Böses tun, aus dem Land verschwinden und das Leben verlieren. Das Land ist die Grundlage für das Leben; wenn es genutzt wird, gibt es die Mittel zum Leben. Das Land ist auch der Raum, in dem sich das Leben eines Volkes in Freiheit und Sicherheit entfalten kann. Für das Alte Testament steht im Mittelpunkt, daß Gott seinem Volk das Land verheißen und geschenkt hat. Darin vor allem zeigt sich die Fürsorge Gottes für sein Volk. Land bedeutet Leben, Grundlage und Raum für das Leben. Die Menschen, die keine Gewalt anwenden, werden das Land nicht erkämpfen oder erobern, es wird ihnen als Erbschaft zufallen. Das 'Erben' setzt eine bestimmte Beziehung voraus. Gewöhnlich sind es Eltern, die den Besitz ihren Kindern vererben. In der Seligpreisung ist es Gott, der die Sanftmütigen als seine Kinder behandelt und ihnen das Land zuteilt. Damit ist nicht gemeint, daß Gott das Land auf dieser Erde neu verteilen wird. Wo Jesus an anderen Stellen vom 'Erben' spricht, nennt er 'das ewige Leben' (Mt 19,29) oder 'das Reich Gottes' (Mt 25,34). Auch 'das Land' meint keint irdisches, sondern ein endzeitliches Gut. Es ist eine weitere Seite der Königsherrschaft Gottes, daß Gott das Leben seiner Getreun auf eine absolut sichere Grundlage und in einen Raum der ungehindert freien Entfaltung stellt.

In der vierten Seligpreisung heißt es: «Selig, die hungern und dürsten nach der Gerechtigkeit; denn sie werden gesättigt werden» (5,6). Das Passiv verweist wieder auf Gott. Gott wird sie sättigen. Bei Hunger und Durst und Sättigung geht es um das Leben. In Hunger und Durst drückt sich das elementare Verlangen nach dem aus, was zum Weiterführen des Lebens notwendig ist. Bei der Sättigung ist aller Mangel überwunden, und das Leben kann ruhig und freudig weitergehen. Der natürliche Hunger und Durst gehen auf Speise und Trank. Jesus spricht vom Hunger und Durst nach der Gerechtigkeit. Mit 'Gerechtigkeit' ist das rechte Handeln des Menschen gemeint, das dann recht ist, wenn es sich am Willen Gottes orientiert und das Gebot Gottes erfüllt. Denen, die aus innerstem Streben heraus den Willen Gottes erfüllen wollen, ist die Sättigung zugesagt. Aus der Verbindung mit Gott kommt das Leben. Eine der intensivsten Weisen der Verbindung mit ihm ist die Erfüllung seines Willens. Den, der sich Gott in dieser Weise verbindet und sein ganzes Verlangen auf die Gerechtigkeit richtet, wird Gott sättigen; er wird ihm Leben in Fülle schenken. Leben braucht 'Land', d.h. eine sichere Grundlage und einen Raum der Entfaltung; Leben braucht auch 'Sättigung', d.h. das volle Maß der Nahrung. Es ist ein Kennzeichen der Königsherrschaft Gottes, daß sie lebensfreundlich ist und in jeder Hinsicht Leben in Fülle und voller Entfaltung schenkt.

Die fünfte Seligpreisung «Selig die Barmherzigen» wird so begründet: «denn sie werden Erbarmen finden» (5,7). Im griechischen Text treffen wir wieder das Passiv an, und wieder ist der Sinn: Gott wird sich ihrer erbarmen. Auf Erbarmen sind die Menschen angewiesen, die in einer Notlage sich befinden und sich selber nicht helfen können. Erbarmen zeigen die Menschen, die die Notlage ihres Nächsten sehen, ihr Herz nicht verschließen, sondern dem anderen nach Kräften helfen (Mt 25,31-46; Lk 10,30-37). Wie vor allem das Gleichnis vom unbarmherzigen Knecht zeigt, erweist sich das Erbarmen Gottes besonders darin, daß er dem Menschen auch sehr große Schuld vergibt. Allerdings wird diese Vergebung erst voll wirksam, wenn auch der Mensch barmherig ist und denen, die ihm gegenüber in Schuld sind, verzeiht. Dieser Zusammenhang zwischen menschlichem und göttlichem Vergeben, zwischen menschlichem und göttlichem Erbarmen wird auch an anderer, zentraler Stelle von Jesus betont (Mt 6,12.14-15). Wir Menschen sind Sünder und hängen für die Vergebung von Gott ab. Alle anderen Seligpreisungen würden ihren Wert verlieren, wenn wir nicht auf das Erbarmen und die Vergebung Gottes hoffen dürften. Die Königsherrschaft Gottes erweist sich dem schuldigen Menschen gegenüber als Erbarmen und Vergebung. Gott ist der barmherzige Vater, der seine verlorenen Söhne und Töchter voll Freude bei sich aufnimmt (Lk 15,11-32).

In der nächsten Seligpreisung heißt es: «Selig, die ein reines Herz haben; denn sie werden Gott schauen» (5,8). Auf den ersten Blick wird hier nur von einem menschlichen Tun gesprochen 'Gott schauen'. Von der Sache her ist es klar, daß damit ein Tun Gottes verbunden sein muß. Die Schau Gottes, die unmittelbare Begegnung mit Gott, kann von keinem Geschöpf her erreicht oder gar erzwungen werden. Gott ist verborgen, er ist der, «der in unzugänglichem Licht wohnt» (1 Tim 6,16). Von ihm gilt, was das Ende des Johannesprologs sagt: «Niemand hat Gott jemals gesehen; der einzige Sohn, der Gott ist und der am Herzen des Vaters ruht, er hat Kunde gebracht» (Joh 1,18). In diesem irdischen Leben können wir Gott nicht schauen, aber Jesus bringt uns Kunde von Gott. Zu dieser Kunde gehört es, daß in der Vollendung die Schau Gottes geschenkt sein wird. 'Königsherrschaft Gottes' meint die Zuwendung Gottes zu uns Menschen. Wie weit diese Zuwendung geht, zeigt diese Seligpreisung. Gott ist nicht derjenige, der in ungestörter und erhabener Verborgenheit bleibt, der uns zwar große Gaben schenkt, uns aber mit diesen auch abfertigt und direkt und unmittelbar mit uns nichts zu tun haben will. Gott bringt sich selber ins Spiel, läßt uns zu ihm selber kommen und gibt uns Anteil an seinem eigenen Leben. Die folgende Seligpreisung spricht das noch deutlicher aus.

Bei der vorletzten Seligpreisung «Selig die Frieden stiften» sagt die Begründung: «denn sie werden Söhne Gottes genannt werden» (5,9). Das Passiv verweist wieder auf Gott und hat den Sinn: Sie sind nicht nur Söhne Gottes, sondern Gott wird sie öffentlich als seine Söhne anerkennen. Hier berühren wir den Kern der Kunde von Gott, die erst Jesus bringt und die nur er bringen kann. Von Jesus gilt: «Mir ist von meinem Vater alles übergeben worden; niemand kennt den Sohn, nur der Vater, und niemand kennt den Vater, nur der Sohn und der, dem es der Sohn offenbaren will» (Mt 11,27). Jesus allein ist der Sohn (vgl. Mt 3,17; 17,5); er allein kennt Gott als den Vater und er allein kann ihn als den Vater offenbaren. So zeigt er seinen Hörern, in welchem Verhältnis sie zu Gott stehen, und lehrt sie beten: «Unser Vater im Himmel» (6,9). Auch bei dem letzten und bleibenden Auftrag, den der auferstandene Herr für alle Zeiten seinen Aposteln gibt, steht dieses Verhältnis im Mittelpunkt: «Geht zu allen Völkern und macht alle Menschen zu meinen Jüngern; tauft sie auf den Namen des Vaters und des Sohnes und des heiligen Geistes, und lehrt sie, alles zu befolgen, was ich euch geboten habe» (28,19-20). Durch die Taufe sollen die Apostel alle Menschen unter den Namen des Gottes stellen, von dem Jesus Kunde gebracht hat und den er als Vater, Sohn und Heiligen Geist geoffenbart hat. Durch die Taufe werden die Menschen in den Macht- und Schutzbereich dieses Gottes aufgenommen und treten in die Gemeinschaft mit ihm ein. Diese Gemeinschaft ist das Kennzeichen der Jünger Jesu, der Christen. Sie wird in der Taufe grundgelegt und ist das ganze Leben hindurch zu bewähren im Hören und Tun des Wortes Jesu, durch das er den Willen seines Vaters mitgeteilt hat. Bei der Vollendung wird diese Gemeinschaft von Gott öffentlich anerkannt und wird dann ihrer ganzen Wirklichkeit nach gelebt. Auf Erden sind wir Kinder Gottes, die ihren Vater nicht sehen, aber an ihn glauben. Bei der Vollendung werden die

Kinder ihrem Vater begegnen und die Brüder und Schwestern ihrem Bruder Jesus Christus; sie werden aufgenommen in die 'Familie' Gottes und werden hineingenommen in das Leben, das der Vater mit dem Sohn in der Einheit des Heiligen Geistes lebt. Dieses Leben, das im vollkommenen gegenseitigen Erkennen und Lieben besteht, ist vollendete Seligkeit. Damit erreicht das Himmelreich, die Königsherrschaft Gottes, seine volle Entfaltung, sein Ziel und seinen unvergänglichen und unüberbietbaren Höhepunkt.

Was 'Himmelreich' genauerhin bedeutet, können wir tatsächlich den Zusagen der Seligpreisungen entnehmen. Sie liegen alle auf der Linie dessen, was 'Himmelreich' anspricht: Gott in seiner Liebe setzt seine ganze Macht für das Leben seines Volkes ein. Dies äußert sich darin, daß alles Negative, das dem Leben entgegensteht, es mindert oder nimmt, überwunden wird: Leid und Tod sind aus der neuen Schöpfung ausgeschlossen («sie werden getröstet werden») und die Schuld, die von Gott, dem Quell allen Lebens, trennt, wird vergeben («sie werden Erbarmen finden»). Das Leben ist in seiner freien Entfaltung («sie werden das Land erben») und in seiner Fülle («sie werden gesättigt werden») gesichert. Der Inhalt dieses Lebens besteht im freien Zugang zu Gott («sie werden Gott schauen»), der die Lebensgemeinschaft mit Gott möglich macht, die Teilnahme an dem Leben, das dem Vater und dem Sohn in der Einheit des Heiligen Geistes eigen ist («sie werden Söhne Gottes genannt werden»). Alles, was Jesus so über das Himmelreich sagt, führt er an, um sein achtmaliges 'Selig' zu begründen. Das Kennzeichen des Reiches Gottes ist die Seligkeit. Wer in das königliche Handeln Gottes einbezogen ist, erfährt dies als Seligkeit, als überströmendes Glück, als unendliche Freude.

c. *Das Handeln des himmlischen Vaters*

Neben dem Ausdruck 'Reich, Herrschaft' ('basileia') ist in der Bp und bei Matthäus nur noch der Ausdruck 'Vater' ('patēr') mit 'Himmel' verbunden. So wird neben dem 'Himmelreich' (32 mal) vom 'Vater im Himmel' (13 mal) und vom 'himmlischen Vater' (7 mal) gesprochen. Das Himmelreich ist das Reich des himmlischen Vaters (vgl. 6,10; 13,43; 26,29). Wie wir gesehen haben, meint das Himmelreich das königliche Herrschen Gottes, des Vaters. Wir wollen noch feststellen, was die Bp über das Handeln des Vaters sagt, um eventuell den Sinn von 'Himmelreich' noch etwas mehr zu bestimmen.

Die Bp spricht von Gott als Vater 15 mal und von ihm als Gott 5 mal; es steht also im Vordergrund, daß er der Vater ist. Sein Handeln wird in verschiedener Weise beschrieben. Es bezieht sich teilweise auf das irdische Geschehen und schaut auch darüber hinaus. Er läßt seine Sonne aufgehen über Böse und Gute und läßt regnen über Gerechte und Ungerechte (5,45). Er nährt die Vögel (6,26) und kleidet die Pflanzen (6,30) und weiß, daß wir Menschen Speise, Trank und Kleidung brauchen (6,32).

Von seinem künftigen Tun wird gesprochen, wenn es heißt, daß er das Verborgene sieht und das rechte Almosengeben, Beten und Fasten vergelten wird (6,4.6.18); es wird aber nicht ausgeführt, worin diese Vergeltung besteht. Ebenso wird im Futur gesagt, daß er uns verzeihen wird oder nicht, je nachdem wir unseren Mitmenschen vergeben haben oder nicht (6,14-15).

Ganz allgemein heißt es im Vergleich mit dem Tun irdischer Väter: «wieviel mehr wird euer Vater im Himmel denen Gutes geben, die ihn bitten» (7,11). In dem Gebet, das Jesus seine Hörer lehrt, will er ihnen gerade zeigen, um welches Handeln sie den Vater im Himmel bitten sollen. An erster Stelle sollen 'die Dinge Gottes' verwirklicht werden: 'dein Name, dein Reich, dein Wille'; in der Mitte steht das Reich, um dessen Kommen zu beten ist. An zweiter Stelle soll sich der Vater 'unserer Dinge' annehmen: 'unser Brot, unsere Schulden, die Versuchung und das Böse, die uns betreffen'. Was das Himmelreich angeht, wird hier deutlich, daß sein Kommen vom Vater im Himmel abhängt; er wird darum gebeten. Für unsere Frage, worin es genauerhin besteht, erhalten wir keine weitere Antwort. Die zwei Seiten an ihm, daß zu ihm die Vergebung der Schuld gehört und daß unser Sinn vor allem Irdischen auf das Himmelreich und die Gerechtigkeit Gottes ausgerichtet sein muß (5,6; 6,32-33), werden bestätigt. Es bleibt also dabei, daß die acht Seligkeiten am meisten darüber sagen, worin das königliche Handeln Gottes zugunsten seines Volkes besteht.

3. Das notwendige menschliche Handeln

Am Anfang, als wir den Bestand der Aussagen über das Himmelreich aufnahmen, haben wir festgestellt, daß fast alle von einer Beziehung zum Himmelreich sprechen und diese an eine Bedingung knüpfen: Das Himmelreich gehört nur dem, der arm ist vor Gott (5,3) usw. Das Himmelreich kann nicht von den Menschen her geplant, aufgebaut und verwirklicht werden. Als das königliche Herrschen Gottes kommt es von Gott her und es kommt dann, wann Gott es will. Das bedeutet aber keineswegs, daß wir Menschen untätig auf das Kommen des Reiches warten sollen oder daß es gleichgültig ist, was wir tun. Wie wichtig unser Handeln ist, zeigt allein schon der Schluß der Bp, der nur vom Hören und Tun der Worte Jesu spricht und dieses nachdrücklich einschärft (7,24-27). Von unserem Handeln nach dem Willen Gottes hängt unsere Zugehörigkeit zum Himmelreich ab. Jesus spricht nur an wenigen Stellen der Bp direkt vom Handeln Gottes; dieses können wir ruhig Gott überlassen. Er spricht aber durch die ganze Bp hindurch ausführlich davon, was wir Menschen nach dem Willen Gottes tun sollen; das ist mit der Hilfe Gottes unsere Aufgabe, und darauf sollen wir unser ganzes Mühen richten. Wir wollen nach dem Hauptinhalt der Worte Jesu fragen und dabei dem Aufbau der Bp folgen.

a. *Das menschliche Tun nach den Seligpreisungen*

Der unlösbare Zusammenhang zwischen dem menschlichen Tun und der Zugehörigkeit zum Himmelreich zeigt sich sofort am Anfang der Bp, in den acht Seligkeiten (5,3-10). Wie wir schon erwähnten, haben alle den gleichen Aufbau aus drei Teilen, wobei der zweite Teil immer eine menschliche Haltung oder ein menschliches Tun nennt. Die erste Seligkeit sagt: «Selig, die arm sind vor Gott; denn ihnen gehört das Himmelreich» (5,3). Armsein vor Gott ist die Bedingung für den Besitz des Himmelreichs, der seinerseits die Seligkeit mit sich bringt. Wir wollen kurz beschreiben, was Jesus in diesen zweiten Teilen der Seligpreisungen ausführt.

Wer vor Gott arm ist, anerkennt Gott als seinen Schöpfer und Herrn. Er weiß es und er steht dazu, daß er aus sich selber nichts hat und daß er alles, von seinem Leben und seinem Leib angefangen, von Gott erhalten hat. Weil ihm alles geschenkt wurde, weiß er, daß er nicht ein unabhängiger Herr ist, sondern Gott Rechenschaft schuldet. Er nimmt aber auch das, was ihm Gott geschenkt hat und schenkt, dankbar an und hat wie ein Kind offene Hände, um sich weiter von Gott beschenken zu lassen. Das Armsein vor Gott ist die erste und grundlegende Haltung des Menschen. In ihr gibt er der Grundwahrheit seiner Existenz die Ehre, daß er nämlich ein Geschöpf Gottes ist, das seinem Schöpfer alles verdankt.

Ursachen der Trauer sind nach der Heiligen Schrift vor allem der Tod (Gen 23,2; 50,3) und die Sünde (1 Kor 5,1-2; Jak 4,8-10) und das Leiden der Mitmenschen (Ps 34,13-14; Sir 7,34). In der Trauer nehme ich teil am Unglück und Leid, das andere getroffen hat. Sie ist eine Form der Nächstenliebe; ich kann dem anderen nicht aktiv helfen, ich lasse ihn aber auch nicht in seinem Schmerz allein, sondern teile diesen mit ihm. Es ist eine Form des Egoismus, sich gegen das Leid der anderen und die Hinfälligkeit unseres irdischen Lebens zu verschließen und die Trauer zu verweigern. Das große Beispiel dafür ist die Hure Babylon (Offb 18,7). Bei dieser Haltung will ich in Ruhe das irdische Leben genießen und ausschöpfen und will mich vom Leid anderer und vom Blick auf die menschliche Ohnmacht und Vergänglichkeit nicht stören lassen. Wir haben nur ein Herz. Wenn wir es gegenüber dem Leid und der Vergänglichkeit hart gemacht haben, wird es auch für den Trost Gottes nicht offen und empfänglich sein. In der ersten Seligkeit wurde unsere Grundhaltung gegenüber Gott als unserem Schöpfer und Herrn angesprochen. Auch hier geht es um eine umfassende Grundhaltung, und zwar gegenüber der Situation unserer Hinfälligkeit und Vergänglichkeit im gegenwärtigen irdischen Leben.

Die Erklärung «Selig die Sanftmütigen» oder «Selig, die keine Gewalt anwenden» nennt die Grundhaltung gegenüber den Mitmenschen, besonders bei Spannungen und in Konfliktfällen. Das Neue Testament erwähnt die Sanftmut zusammen mit der Demut (Mt 11,29; Eph 4,2), der Selbstbeherrschung (Gal 5,23) und der Großmut (Eph 4,2; Kol 3,12). Es kommt nicht zuerst darauf an, was wir für unsere Mitmenschen tun, sondern was wir ihnen gegenüber unterlassen (vgl: keine Gewalt anwenden). In seinem Hohenlied der Liebe führt Paulus vor allem an, was die Liebe nicht tut (1 Kor 13,4-7). Sanftmut meint die beherrschte, respektvolle Güte gegenüber den Mitmenschen. Der Sanftmütige gibt dem Mitmenschen Raum, läßt ihn gelten in seiner persönlichen Eigenart und anerkennt ihn als gleichwertig. Er begegnet dem anderen mit Wohlwollen und Anerkennung und weiß seine negativen Emotionen zu beherrschen. Paulus zählt die Sanftmut zu den Gaben des Heiligen Geistes (Gal 5,23). Sie erscheint als die Haupteigenschaft Jesu (Mt 11,29; 21,5; 2 Kor 10,1).

Gerechtigkeit meint das rechte Handeln des Menschen in allen Bereichen und Beziehungen, in denen er steht. Unser Handeln ist gerecht, wenn es sich am Willen Gottes ausrichtet. In der Bp und in seinem ganzen Wirken will Jesus den Willen des Vaters bekannt machen. Die vierte Seligpreisung spricht also nicht von einem abgegrenzten Bereich, sondern vom rechten menschlichen Handeln insgesamt. Jesus sagt, daß wir nicht nebenbei und hin und wieder, sondern spontan und radikal, wie in Hunger und Durst, ständig und aus der innersten Natur heraus auf das rechte Handeln aus sein sollen. Wenn wir in der rechten Weise arm sind vor Gott, unsere Abhängigkeit von ihm und unsere Verantwortung vor ihm anerkennen, läßt uns diese Haltung danach fragen, was der Wille unseres Schöpfers und Herrn ist, und treibt sie uns dazu an, diesen Willen aus der innersten Natur heraus zu tun.

Als Arme im Geiste anerkennen wir unsere Abhängigkeit von Gott. Als Barmherzige gehen wir in der rechten Weise um mit den Mitmenschen, die von uns abhängen und auf unsere Hilfe oder Verzeihung angewiesen sind. Wie die Trauer ist auch die Barmherzigkeit Anteilnahme am Leid und an der Not des anderen. Zur Trauer gehört die Erfahrung der menschlichen Ohnmacht, zur Barmherzigkeit aber die tatkräftige Hilfe. Mit dem barmherzigen Samariter (Lk 10,30-37) gibt Jesus ein Vorbild und zeigt, wie ein barmherziger Mensch handelt. Für ihn ist es kennzeichnend, daß er offene Augen hat und die Not seiner Mitmenschen sieht, daß er ein Herz hat und von Mitleid gerührt wird und daß er wirksam hilft. Gott will ganz besonders, daß wir barmherzig sind (Mt 9,13; 12,7; 23,23 vgl. Hos 6,6). Wie das Gleichnis vom unbarmherzigen Knecht zeigt (Mt 18,23-35), äußert sich die Barmherzigkeit vor allem auch im Verzeihen. Gott verzeiht uns unsere Schuld, wenn wir unseren Schuldnern verziehen haben (Mt 6,12).

In der Sprache der Heiligen Schrift ist das 'Herz' der Ursprungsort von Denken, Wollen und Fühlen; es enthält das ganze bewußte Leben des Menschen und bestimmt sein ganzes Handeln. 'Unrein' ist alles, was sich gegen das Gebot Gottes und damit gegen den Willen Gottes richtet (Mt 15,19-20). Dementsprechend ist das 'rein', was mit dem Willen Gottes übereinstimmt. Wer ein reines Herz hat, stimmt schon im Bereich des Denkens, Wollens und Fühlens und nicht erst im Bereich des Handelns mit dem Willen Gottes überein (vgl. Mt 5,21-22.27-28). Auch ohne böse Taten kann das Herz böse sein. Wenn uns daran liegt, gerecht zu handeln, dann müssen wir uns um ein reines Herz bemühen und schon in unseren inneren Haltungen und Überzeugungen mit Gott im Einklang sein. Wie die Seligpreisung derer, die hungern und dürsten nach der Gerechtigkeit, so bezieht sich auch die Seligpreisung derer, die ein reines Herz haben, auf den gesamten Bereich des menschlichen Handelns. Dieses soll nicht nur in seiner Ausführung, sondern auch in seiner Vorbereitung, von der Wurzel her, an Gott und seinem Willen ausgerichtet sein.

Der Friede auf allen Ebenen der menschlichen Beziehungen ist ein hohes und gefährdetes Gut. Er schließt nicht nur das erbitterte Gegeneinander aus, sondern geht auch über ein kühles Nebeneinander hinaus und meint ein aktives, verständnisvolles Miteinander. Das Friedenstiften, der aktive Einsatz für den Frieden, setzt die in den anderen Seligpreisungen genannten Haltungen und Handlungen voraus. Sie alle sind notwendig, um den Frieden zu erhalten oder ihn wiederherzustellen. Nicht umsonst ist diese Seligpreisung die letzte von denen, die sich auf ein Tun beziehen. Das Mühen um gelungene Gemeinschaft, um Ausgleich und Versöhnung ist mühsam und kann nur von echter Nächstenliebe getragen werden. Der Friede, die Harmonie, das herzliche und lebendige Miteinander charakterisiert aber das Leben Gottes, die Gemeinschaft zwischen Vater und Sohn im Heiligen Geist.

Daher ist es gerade den Friedenstiftern zugesagt, daß Gott sie als seine Söhne anerkennen wird (vgl. Mt 5,43-48).

Wer hungert und dürstet nach der Gerechtigkeit (5,6), wird zwar von Jesus seliggepriesen, er darf aber nicht damit rechnen, daß er von allen Menschen anerkannt wird. Jesus selber, der am vollkommensten Gerechte, ist verfolgt und gewaltsam getötet worden. Er bereitet auch seine Hörer auf die Verfolgung vor. Sie sollen sich mit allen Kräften um den Frieden bemühen (5,9); sie dürfen aber nicht Jesus und seinem Wort untreu werden, um den Menschen zu gefallen und mit ihnen im Frieden zu sein (vgl. Mt 13,21). Wenn es nicht anders geht, müssen sie Ablehnung und Verfolgung auf sich nehmen. Um jeden Preis ist an Jesus und an seinem Wort festzuhalten, weil nur in der Verbindung mit ihm das Leben gewonnen wird (Mt 16,25). Die Seligpreisung der Verfolgten um der Gerechtigkeit willen gilt denen, die Jesus und seinem Wort unter allen Umständen treu bleiben.

Jesus beginnt seine Unterweisung über das rechte, dem Himmelreich gemäße menschliche Handeln nicht mit Einzelvorschriften. Am Anfang der Bp nennt er fundamentale umfassende Haltungen, die das Verhalten gegenüber Gott und gegenüber den Mitmenschen bestimmen sollen. Alle diese Haltungen sind darauf ausgerichtet, daß der Mensch aus seiner egoistischen Isolation heraustritt und die Übereinstimmung mit Gott und die Gemeinschaft mit seinen Mitmenschen sucht. Vier Seligpreisungen sind auf die Übereinstimmung mit Gott bezogen und vier auf die Gemeinschaft mit den Mitmenschen. Durch die Armut im Geiste anerkenne ich meine totale Abhängigkeit von Gott als meinem Schöpfer und Herrn. Daraus folgt, daß ich nach dem Willen Gottes frage und mich an ihm ausrichte in meinem äußeren Tun (Hunger und Durst nach der Gerechtigkeit), in meinen inneren Bewegungen (Reinheit des Herzens), in unbedingter Treue, auch bei großen Nachteilen (Verfolgung um der Gerechtigkeit willen). Trauer, Sanftmut, Barmherzigkeit, Bemühen um Frieden gelten der lebendigen und harmonischen Gemeinschaft mit den Mitmenschen. Wenn wir uns diese Haltungen zu eigen machen und nach ihnen zu handeln suchen, unterstellen wir uns Gott und setzen uns ein gemäß den Absichten Gottes. Die königliche Herrschaft Gottes ist ausgerichtet auf die Fülle des Lebens für sein Volk, die gegeben ist in der vollendeten Gemeinschaft mit Gott und den Menschen. Indem all unser Mühen auf die Übereinstimmung mit Gott und auf die Gemeinschaft mit den Menschen ausgerichtet ist, haben wir uns der königlichen Herrschaft Gottes unterstellt und sind ganz offen, von der Fülle seines königlichen Herrschens und Handelns erreicht zu werden.

b. *Das menschliche Tun nach der übrigen Bergpredigt*

Durch die ganze Bp hindurch unterweist Jesus seine Hörer darin was sie nach dem Willen Gottes tun sollen. Wir können nicht auf die einzelnen Unterweisungen eingehen und wollen nur die Hauptabschnitte entsprechend dem Aufbau der Bp angeben.

In Mt 5,21-48 spricht Jesus vom Verhalten gegenüber dem Mitmenschen und erwähnt dabei verschiedene Konfliktbereiche, vom Töten und Zürnen bis zur Feindesliebe. Seine Unterweisung gipfelt in der Aufforderung: «Seid ihr also vollkommen, wie euer himmlischer Vater vollkommen ist» (5,48). Das Handeln nach dem Willen Gottes wird zum Handeln nach dem Vorbild Gottes. Es bezieht sich zunächst auf das Verhalten gegenüber den Feinden und folgt dem, «der seine Sonne aufgehen läßt über Bösen und Guten, und regnen läßt über Gerechte und Ungerechte» (5,45). Es gilt dann aber insgesamt für alles Verhalten gegenüber den Mitmenschen, das, wie das Verhalten Gottes, allein von der Liebe bestimmt sein soll (vgl. Mt 7,12; 22,37-40).

Der nächste Abschnitt (6,1-18) befaßt sich mit den klassischen Formen der jüdischen Frömmigkeit: Almosengeben, Beten und Fasten, also mit Handlungen, die sich direkt an Gott wenden. Gleich am Beginn nennt Jesus die Grundnorm für dieses Handeln: «Hütet euch, eure Gerechtigkeit vor den Menschen zur Schau zu stellen; sonst habt ihr keinen Lohn von eurem Vater im Himmel zu erwarten» (6,1). Entscheidend ist also, daß diese Handlungen allein um Gottes willen geschehen und daß wir in keiner Weise auf eine Wirkung bei den Menschen aus sind. Besonders ausführlich spricht Jesus vom Beten (6,5-15) und hier, im wirklichen Zentrum der Bp, lehrt er seine Hörer das 'Vater unser' als ihr Gebet.

In 6,19-34 geht es um das Verhältnis zu den materiellen Dingen, vor allem auch zu Essen, Trinken und Kleidung, auf die wir Menschen für unser irdisches Leben angewiesen sind. Hier wehrt Jesus aller Anhänglichkeit des Herzens und allem ängstlichen Sorgen und nennt als Grundhaltung: «Suchet zuerst das Reich Gottes und seine Gerechtigkeit; dann wird euch alles andere dazugegeben» (6,33).

In diesen drei Abschnitten sagt Jesus, wie wir uns, nach dem Willen Gottes, in den drei wichtigsten Beziehungen, in denen wir stehen, verhalten sollen: in der Beziehung zu den Mitmenschen, in der Beziehung zu Gott und in der Beziehung zur materiellen Welt. In allen drei Bereichen geht es immer auch um Gott, und sollen wir uns von Gott bestimmen lassen. In unserem Verhalten zum Nächsten sollen wir dem Vorbild des himmlischen Vaters folgen, der sich in seinem Handeln nur von seiner Liebe leiten läßt. Bei unseren Handlungen, die sich an Gott richten, soll es uns allein um Gott gehen. Unser Herz darf nie den materiellen Dingen, sondern muß immer Gott gehören, auf den wir all unser Vertrauen setzen. Unsere Aufgabe gegenüber der Herrschaft Gottes besteht darin, daß wir unser Denken, Wollen und Handeln in allen Bereichen dem Willen Gottes unterstellen, uns von Gott durchherrschen lassen. Was wir so, im Vertrauen auf die Autorität Jesu, anstreben und vollziehen, wird vollendet, wenn Gott seine königliche Herrschaft endgültig durchsetzt und sichtbar macht.

Der letzte Teil der Bp (7,1-23) ist weniger geschlossen und beschäftigt sich mit verschiedenen Themen. Am Schluß richtet Jesus den Blick auf das Ergehen des Hauses, das auf Felsen gebaut ist, und des anderen Hauses, das auf Sand errichtet ist. Damit will er seinen Hörern nachdrücklich einschärfen, daß das bloße Hören nicht genügt, sondern daß das Tun dessen, was sie gehört haben, absolut notwendig ist (7,24-27). Noch einmal ist deutlich, daß die Königsherrschaft Gottes, ihre Offenbarung und Verwirklichung, die Sache Gottes ist. Genauso deutlich ist es aber auch, daß der einzelne Mensch von dieser Herrschaft und ihren Wirkungen nicht erreicht wird, wenn er sich nicht in seinem ganzen Sein und Verhalten von ihr bestimmen läßt, d.h. dem durch Jesus geoffenbarten Willen des himmlischen Vaters folgt.

4. Die Bergpredigt als Programm

In der Bp entwirft Jesus eine Gesamtsicht von unserem menschlichen Leben und seinem Sinn. Er zeigt, was das Ziel unseres Lebens ist und er zeigt den Weg, wie es voll entfaltet und verwirklicht werden kann. Im Mittelpunkt steht Gott. Alles wird von ihm bestimmt, geht von ihm aus und ist auf ihn ausgerichtet, hängt von seinem Willen, von seiner Macht und Güte ab.

Nach dem, was Jesus ausführt, hat Gott uns Menschen für die Seligkeit bestimmt, für die Fülle des Lebens und der Freude. Von Gott, unserem Schöpfer und Herrn, haben wir, ohne jedes Zutun unsererseits, das irdische Leben empfangen, als Geschenk und Aufgabe. Von Gott sollen wir auch die Fülle des Lebens und der Freude, das ewige Leben, empfangen, das von allen Schatten der Not und Vergänglichkeit frei ist. Auch dieses Leben ist Geschenk Gottes, verdankt sich dem königlichen und väterlichen Herrschen und Handeln Gottes in allen seinen Ausprägungen. Wir erhalten es aber nicht ohne unser eigenes Zutun. Nur wenn wir unser jetziges Leben entsprechend dem von Jesus verkündeten Willen Gottes gestalten, sind wir für das Geschenk des ewigen Lebens bereit. Damit uns die königliche Herrschaft Gottes, seine väterliche Zuwendung, voll erreichen kann, ist es notwendig, daß wir unser gegenwärtiges Leben nicht im Widerspruch zu Gott führen, sondern uns möglichst vollständig vom Willen Gottes bestimmen lassen. Dann wird Gott die Gemeinschaft mit ihm, die wir jetzt schon suchen und leben, zur vollen Entfaltung bringen.

In der Bp, am klarsten und nachdrücklichsten in den Seligkeiten (achtmalige Wiederholung), zeigt Jesus diese Struktur und diese Zusammenhänge auf. Er gibt ein Programm der königlichen Herrschaft Gottes, indem er ausführt, was Gott mit uns Menschen vorhat und wie er uns zu diesem Ziel bringen will. Jesus zeigt aber nicht nur die Struktur, sondern nennt auch viele Einzelheiten, besonders was unser menschliches Handeln nach dem Willen Gottes betrifft. So ist die Bp nicht nur eine Grundsatzerklärung, sondern ein Programm, das die wichtigsten Bereiche des menschlichen Lebens mit konkreten Ausführungen anspricht.

Wo Jesus, der auferstandene und mit aller Vollmacht ausgestattete Herr, seinen Aposteln den universalen Missionsauftrag gibt, da befiehlt er ihnen als Letztes: «Lehrt sie alles halten, was ich euch geboten habe» (28,20). Was Jesus ihnen geboten hat, steht vor allem auch in der Bp. Sie gehört zu der Botschaft, die die Apostel durch ihr Lehren zu allen Völkern bringen sollen. In der Bp selbst hatte Jesus bereits eine andere Form der Mission und Verkündigung angegeben. Er nannte seine Hörer 'Salz der Erde' und 'Licht der Welt' (5,13.14) und er sagte ihnen: «So soll euer Licht vor den Menschen leuchten, damit sie eure guten Werke sehen und euren Vater im Himmel preisen» (5,16). Mit den 'guten Werken' ist das Leben und Handeln nach der Bp gemeint. Dadurch werden die Hörer Jesu zum Licht der Welt und dadurch vor allem können sie die Menschen mit dem Vater im Himmel bekannt machen, den Jesus verkündet hat. Zu Gott, dem Vater, führen war das Ziel der Sendung Jesu und ist das Ziel jeder Sendung, die von ihm herkommt.

Literaturauswahl zur Bergpredigt

H.B. Betz, *The Sermon on the Mount*. Minneapolis, 1995.
I. Boer, *Die Seligpreisungen der Bergpredigt*. Königstein/Ts., 1986.
F. Comacho, *La proclama del Reino*. Madrid, 1986.
T.L. Donaldson, *Jesus on the Mountain*. Sheffield, 1985.
M. Dumais, *Le Sermon sur la Montagne*. Paris, 1995.
R.A. Guelich, *The Sermon on the Mount*. Waco, 1982.
M.D. Hamm, *The Beatitudes in Context*. Wilmington, 1989.
J. Lambrecht, *«Eh bien! Moi, je vous dis»* (Mt 5-7; Lc 6). Paris, 1986.
F.M. López-Melús, *Las Bienaventuranzas*. Salamanca, 1988.
S.A. Panimolle, *Il discorso della montagna*. Cinisello Balsamo, 1986.
G. Strecker, *Die Bergpredigt*. Göttingen, 1984.
K. Syreeni, *The Making of the Sermon on the Mount*. Helsinki, 1987.
H. Weder, *Die «Rede der Reden»*. Zürich, 1985.

*Jésus, Témoin de la Vérité et Roi par la Vérité**

I. DE LA POTTERIE

La plupart des traits que l'on peut dégager pour l'expression μαρτυρεῖν τῇ ἀληθείᾳ à propos du Baptiste (Jn 5,33) reparaissent avec plus de netteté dans l'application que le Christ s'en fait à lui-même. Quand Pilate, durant la Passion, demande à Jésus s'il est vraiment roi, celui-ci répond: «*Toi*, tu dis que je suis roi. *Moi*, c'est à cette fin que je suis né et que je suis venu dans le monde: pour rendre témoignage à la vérité; quiconque est de la vérité écoute ma voix» (Jn 18,37)[1].

Le contraste ici marqué par Jésus entre la façon de voir du magistrat romain, qui songe à une royauté politique, et la sienne propre, laisse déjà entendre, que, dans sa réponse, il va expliquer *le sens véritable de sa royauté*. Cette réponse se compose de deux parties; dans la première Jésus indique le but de sa venue en ce monde: *rendre témoignage à la vérité*; le second membre de la phrase nous montre le comportement d'un groupe d'hommes, ceux qui sont de la vérité: ces hommes-là écoutent la voix de Jésus. Bien que les deux parties du verset soient simplement juxtaposées (il y a asyndète),

---

* Ceci est le texte remanié d'un chapitre de notre ouvrage *La vérité dans Saint Jean* I (An. Bib. 71), Roma 1977, pp. 100-116.

[1] Remarquons l'emploi emphatique des pronoms (BLASS-DEBRUNNER, § 277) et leur opposition (σὺ ... ἐγὼ ...); nous avons tâché de garder ces nuances dans notre traduction. La réponse σὺ λέγεις (comp. Mt 27,11 par.; Mt 26,64: σὺ εἶπας et Lc 22,70: ὑμεῖς λέγετε) n'est pas équivalente à un simple «oui» (contre Bultmann); elle exprime une certaine réserve, une restriction dans l'affirmation: Jésus ne récuse pas sa qualité de roi, mais il l'entend tout autrement que Pilate; aussi ne reprend-il pas le mot βασιλεύς dans sa réponse. Sur la portée de σὺ λέγεις, cf. BLASS-DEBRUNNER, § 441,3, et les commentaires de Bernard et Barrett; voir aussi les études de O. MERLIER, Σὺ λέγεις ὅτι βασιλεύς εἰμι (*Jean 18,37*), RÉtGr 46 (1933) 204-209 (la formule a le sens d'une réponse évasive ou même négative) et de J. IRMSCHER, Σὺ λέγεις (*Mk. XV.2; Mt. XXVII,11; Lk. XXIII,3*), Studii clasice (Bucarest) 2 (1960) 151-158 (formule affirmative, mais non sans restriction).

et que leur lien logique ne soit pas directement apparent, elles se réfèrent certainement l'une à l'autre et forment un tout, comme le montre le mot-crochet «vérité»:

> ... ἵνα μαρτυρήσω τῇ ἀληθείᾳ ·
> ὁ ὢν ἐκ τῆς ἀληθείας ...

Ces deux membres, pris ensemble, permettent de comprendre comment Jésus conçoit sa *royauté*:

— lui-même *témoigne pour la vérité*;
— ceux qui *sont de la vérité* l'écoutent.

Par cette structure, on voit que, du point de vue du thème de la *royauté*, le second membre, incontestablement, est le plus important; là Jésus explique quelle est la vraie nature de sa royauté: elle consiste dans la soumission et la docilité envers lui de la part des hommes qui sont de la vérité[2]. Le premier membre, dès lors, indique le présupposé et le fondement de cette souveraineté de Jésus: c'est le fait qu'il est venu comme témoin de la vérité; par cette vérité qu'il communique aux hommes, il désire régner sur eux. Mais sa royauté ne devient une réalité concrète que par la docilité et l'obéissance des siens[3].

Il nous faut maintenant étudier de plus près ce témoignage de Jésus; nous verrons ensuite en quel sens il faut considérer ce témoignage comme le véritable fondement de sa royauté.

---

[2] Nous voudrions attirer l'attention sur l'expression πᾶς ὁ ὢν ἐκ τῆς ἀληθείας (nous l'examinerons en détail au chap. VIII): il est remarquable que, lorsque cette tournure (πᾶς suivi d'un participe) est appliquée aux disciples de Jésus, elle décrit toujours une attitude de *foi*: la formule la plus usuelle est πᾶς ὁ πιστεύων (3,15.16; 6.40; 11,26; 12,46); en 3,8, πᾶς ὁ γεγεννημένος ἐκ τοῦ πνεύματος a pratiquement le même sens (cf. ScEccl 14 [1962] 417-443, surtout 435-439 [= *La Vie selon l'Esprit*, 31-63, surtout 53-57]); enfin, en 4,13, πᾶς ὁ πίνων ἐκ τοῦ ὕδατος τούτου (l'eau du puits) est opposé au début du v. 14 («celui qui boira de l'eau que *moi* je lui donnerai»), qui décrit, lui aussi, l'acte de foi: boire l'eau vive = accueillir la parole de vérité de Jésus et donc, croire en lui.

[3] La plupart des commentateurs omettent de montrer le lien étroit qui unit la seconde partie de la réponse de Jésus (ἐγὼ εἰς τοῦτο ...) à la première (σὺ λέγεις ὅτι βασιλεύς εἰμι). Westcott et surtout Godet l'ont fort bien indiqué. Ce dernier écrit: «C'est son œuvre de prophète qui est le fondement de sa *royauté*»; Westcott également voit dans le témoignage que Jésus rend à la vérité «the foundation ... of His *sovereignty*».

1. *Jésus, témoin de la vérité*

Témoigner en faveur de la vérité est indiqué par Jésus comme le grand but de sa venue en ce monde: εἰς τοῦτο ἐλήλυθα εἰς τὸν κόσμον. On le constate une fois de plus: le mystère de l'Incarnation commande toute la pensée de Jean.

Mais il est significatif que, pour désigner le but et le sens de ce moment capital dans l'histoire du salut, il utilise le verbe ἔρχεσθαι de deux façons différentes. Parfois, Jésus emploie le verbe à l'aoriste (ἦλθον), et considère donc sa venue comme un fait du passé; mais dans ce cas, le but envisagé est un but à venir, le *but final* de sa mission: l'accomplissement de l'œuvre du salut au moment de «l'heure» (12,27), la réalisation du salut du monde (12,47), le don de la vie aux hommes (10,10)[4]. Dans une seconde série — c'est à elle qu'appartient notre texte de 18,37 — le verbe se trouve au parfait-présent (ἐλήλυθα), qui est presque équivalent à «je suis parmi vous» (cf. 16,28). Cette fois, il n'est plus question d'un but dernier, mais de l'*activité continue* de Jésus tout au long de son existence, c'est-à-dire du sens même de sa *présence* parmi nous, donc du sens de l'Incarnation[5]. Or, quand le sens de cette présence est indiqué, il s'agit toujours de la révélation apportée par Jésus: il est présent dans le monde comme envoyé du Père qui est «véridique» (7,28); il est dans le monde comme «maître» (διδάσκαλος, 3,2), comme «lumière» (12,46; 3,19), afin que les hommes comprennent son «langage» de vérité[6] et écoutent sa «parole» (8,42-43); il est dans le monde au nom du Père, mais les hommes refusent de l'ac-

---

[4] Exception apparente en 9,39: εἰς κρῖμα ἐγὼ εἰς τὸν κόσμον τοῦτον ἦλθον, où κρῖμα désigne la discrimination opérée par la présence du Christ (voir Westcott); mais, ici encore, le but assigné à la venue du Christ n'est pas tant son activité durant sa vie terrestre que le terme auquel elle aboutit: l'option de l'homme devant le Christ. On voit donc que, dans chacun de ces cas, le but de l'Incarnation est ce dernier stade à atteindre: par rapport au moment *passé* de l'Incarnation (indiqué par ἦλθον), ce but est projeté dans l'*avenir*.

[5] En d'autres termes, le but envisagé dans ces textes se réalise au cours même de la vie de Jésus: d'où le parfait ἐλήλυθα qui souligne la *présence* de Jésus parmi les hommes. Le but de cet ἐλήλυθα n'est plus l'œuvre de salut qu'il aurait à accomplir plus tard; il s'agit plutôt du sens même de sa *présence* parmi les hommes: c'est une *présence révélatrice*.

[6] En 8,43, D remplace λαλιάν par ἀλήθειαν: comme interprétation du verset cette leçon est intéressante, car le «langage» de Jésus que les Juifs ne comprennent pas est certainement un langage de révélation, une communication de la *vérité*.

cueillir et de croire en lui (5,43-44). Dans la même ligne de pensée vient aussi notre texte de 18,37: Jésus est (venu) dans le monde pour rendre témoignage à la vérité, afin que ceux qui sont de la vérité écoutent sa voix. Pour les deux membres de ce verset, on trouve donc deux séries de formules correspondantes dans les textes que nous venons de citer:

à ἀλήθεια correspondent   διδαχή (cf. 3,2: διδάσκαλος)
                                      λαλιά (8,43)[7]
                                      λόγος (*ibid.*)
                                      φῶς (3,19; 12,46)

à ἀκούει μου τῆς φωνῆς   (οὐ) λαμβάνετέ με (5,43)
correspondent   τὴν λαλιὰν τὴν ἐμὴν (οὐ)
                                      γινώσκετε (8,43)
                                      ἀκούειν τὸν λόγον τὸν ἐμόν
                                      (*ibid.*)
                                      ἔρχεται πρὸς τὸ φῶς (3,20)
                                      ὁ πιστεύων εἰς ἐμέ
                                      (12,46; cf. 16,27-28)

Par ces différents parallèles, on saisit déjà comment il faudra comprendre cette «vérité» à laquelle Jésus vient rendre témoignage: étant pratiquement équivalente à l'«enseignement» que Jésus transmet de la part de Dieu, à la «parole» révélatrice qu'il est lui-même, la vérité ne peut désigner rien d'autre que la *révélation* en faveur de quoi il témoigne et qui en fait s'identifie à sa propre personne. Par là même est exclu tel essai d'explication d'après lequel «la vérité» dans notre texte signifierait, comme dans l'A.T., la fidélité de Dieu à l'Alliance[8]; il faut également écarter l'interprétation largement répandue, qui voit ici dans l'ἀλήθεια la «réalité du divin»: le Christ se présente, disent plusieurs commentateurs, comme un témoin du monde céleste, comme le révélateur *de Dieu* dans le monde[9]. Mais nous avons déjà souligné plus

---

[7] Voir la note précédente.

[8] Cf. M.-É. BOISMARD, *La royauté universelle du Christ-Roi*, dans *La fête du Christ-Roi* (Assemblées du Seigneur, 88), 1966, 33-45.

[9] Cette interprétation, de type grec (platonicien) ou gnostique, est acceptée par de nombreux auteurs: Westcott, DODD (*The Interpretation*, 176), BARRETT («wit-

d'une fois que le mot ἀλήθεια dans S. Jean n'est *jamais* appliqué à Dieu lui-même; et dans le cas présent, l'analyse que nous venons de faire montre que le terme «vérité» n'est pas à rapprocher de quelque attribut divin; il est mis en parallèle aux mots «enseignement», «parole», «langage» et «lumière»; il doit donc s'entendre de *la révélation comme telle*, apportée historiquement par le Christ et réalisée en lui.

Il faut toutefois indiquer avec plus de précision encore sur quoi porte concrètement cette révélation dont Jésus témoigne. Rappelons-nous tout d'abord ce que nous avons exposé au début de ce chapitre: quand Jésus se présente comme témoin, il indique parfois comme objet de son témoignage ce qu'il a vu et entendu au ciel (3,11.32), mais le plus souvent il témoigne au sujet de *lui-même* (5,31; 8,13.14.18). Cela suggère que, si la vérité dont Jésus témoigne est ce qu'il a vu et entendu auprès du Père, cette révélation doit être liée d'une manière toute spéciale à *sa propre personne (qui est venue d'auprès du Père), et à sa propre mission (de révélation) parmi nous*.

Une comparaison avec le témoignage du Précurseur (cf. μεμαρτύρηκεν τῇ ἀληθείᾳ, 5,33) nous oriente dans le même sens. Plusieurs différences sautent aux yeux. Premièrement, pour ce qui est du lien entre le témoignage et la mission: la «venue» pour le témoignage est exprimée différemment dans le cas du Baptiste et dans celui de Jésus; pour Jean-Baptiste, nous trouvons: ἦλθεν ... ἵνα μαρτυρήσῃ (1,7); pour Jésus: ἐλήλυθα ... ἵνα μαρτυρήσω (18,37). La différence des temps, ici encore, a sa raison d'être: l'aoriste, utilisé pour le Baptiste, indique que son témoignage était une tâche précise, à accom-

---

nessing ... to the eternal reality which is beyond and above the phenomena of the world»), Bultmann, Lauck, Schick; de même H. SCHLIER (*Die Zeit der Kirche*, Freiburg i. Br., 1956, 64; *L'État selon le Nouveau Testament*, LumVie n. 49 [1960] 102: «la vérité, c'est la réalité divine...»; 103: «la Réalité de Dieu»), A. AUGUSTINOVIĆ (*'Αλήθεια nel IV Vangelo*, 186: «le cose divine, il divino, quell'assoluta realtà di cui Cristo è la viva incarnazione e rivelatore»), J. BLANK (*Die Verhandlung vor Pilatus [Joh 18,28-19,16] im Lichte Johanneischer Theologie*, BZ 3 [1959] 70), E. HAENCHEN (*Jesus vor Pilatus*, ThLZ 85 [1960] 100, n. 31: «Bultmann wird — religionsgeschichtlich gesehen — recht haben, wenn er ... hier bei Johannes ἀλήθεια im gnostischen Sinne gebraucht findet als Offenbarung der göttlichen Wirklichkeit und als diese selbst»). En voit avec stupéfaction combien de confusion règne encore au sujet du sens de ce mot «vérité» dans S. Jean: décidément, l'influence de Bultmann a du mal à mourir.

plir en des circonstances déterminées (ce serait en fait la délégation juive, venue de Jérusalem au début de la vie publique, cf. 1,19-34; 5,33). Le témoignage du Christ, au contraire, n'était pas une mission à remplir à tel ou tel moment: toute son existence, *toute sa présence ici-bas* (ἐλήλυθα), était un témoignage. Deuxième différence: Jésus, et lui seul, met son témoignage en relation directe avec son Incarnation, avec sa venue en ce monde et sa présence parmi les hommes; ceci montre qu'il ne témoigne pas seulement, comme le Précurseur, par sa prédication, mais aussi par sa présence, *par le mystère même de sa personne*. Dernière différence enfin, et peut-être la plus importante de toutes: Jean n'était qu'un instrument; par lui (δι' αὐτοῦ, 1,7), les hommes seraient amenés à la foi, mais celui auquel il rendait témoignage était *un autre*, à savoir le Messie, qui se présentait à lui. Dans le cas de Jésus, il en va tout autrement: le but de son témoignage n'est pas de conduire à un autre; c'est que les hommes écoutent *sa propre voix* (18,37), c'est qu'ils croient *en lui*, qu'ils se montrent dociles *envers lui*. Cette obéissance envers lui, à laquelle il les invite par son témoignage, montre de nouveau que la vérité dont il est le témoin doit d'une façon mystérieuse s'identifier à sa personne. Cela était d'ailleurs déjà suggéré par le témoignage de Jean-Baptiste lui-même: en rendant témoignage à la vérité, ce n'est pas pour un système de doctrine, c'est en faveur de la personne de Jésus-Messie qu'il témoignait, pour que les hommes crussent *en lui*. Quand le Christ, à son tour, déclare qu'il témoigne pour la vérité, c'est en réalité *de lui-même* et *pour lui-même* qu'il témoigne.

Ainsi apparaît la signification exacte et nuancée qu'il faut donner à la déclaration solennelle de Jésus devant Pilate: «Je suis né et je suis venu dans le monde, afin de *rendre témoignage à la vérité*». Au sens formel, ces mots signifient que Jésus se présentait comme un témoin de la révélation messianique: la raison d'être de sa présence parmi les hommes était de leur apporter la révélation, de les amener à accueillir cette vérité. Mais on ne peut s'arrêter là. Sinon on semblerait mettre une opposition entre Jésus et «la vérité», comme si celle-ci était un donné objectif existant déjà avant lui, et auquel lui-même viendrait rendre témoignage. Les textes au contraire nous obligent à *identifier* Jésus et la révélation: si Jésus apporte la plénitude de la révélation, il le fait en dévoilant son propre mystère; en témoignant pour la vérité, il témoigne donc pour lui-même. Il est essentiel, croyons-nous, sous peine de gauchir la vraie portée de cette parole de Jésus, de maintenir fermement l'un et l'autre de ces deux points de vue, et de les unir synthétiquement: d'une part, — et c'est de là qu'il faut partir — le mot ἀλήθεια désigne bien *la révélation* comme telle: il a donc un sens plus fonctionnel que substantiel; d'autre part, cette révélation ne se réduit pas simplement à des paroles et à une doctrine, ni même aux œuvres de Jésus: sa doctrine et ses œuvre conduisent à la révélation *de ce qu'il est lui-même*; dès lors la vérité en vient à désigner en fait *la révélation du mystère de Jésus*. C'est ce qu'Apollinaire de Laodicée a su exprimer en une formule remarquablement dense: ἀλήθειαν λέγει τὸ ἑαυτὸν ἀποδεῖξαι τοῖς ἀνθρώποις καὶ διὰ τῆς ἑαυτοῦ γνώσεως τὴν σωτηρίαν αὐτοῖς χαρίσασθαι[10]. Si l'analyse des textes nous oblige à dépasser pour notre formule le sens simplement fonctionnel de «vérité-révélation» et à voir aussi dans la vérité une désignation de Jésus, la raison en est qu'il nous apporte cette révélation *dans sa propre personne*: l'explication, en dernière analyse, est donc à chercher dans le mystère même de l'Incarnation (εἰς τοῦτο εἰς τὸν κόσμον ἐλήλυθα).

Constatons en terminant que les deux aspects du mot ἀλήθεια que nous venons de dégager sont ceux que l'on rencontre, plus ou moins nettement, dans les interprétations anciennes de Jn 18,37; mais on ne les y trouve malheureusement que séparés l'un de l'autre: les Grecs, en général, ont tendance à réduire la vérité dont Jésus témoigne à l'*enseignement* qu'il apporte (Chrysostome, Théoodore de Mopsueste, la *Chaîne*, Euthymius; citons ce dernier: διὰ τοῦτο ἦλθον εἰς τὸν κόσμον ἵνα διδάξω τὴν ἀλήθειαν); les Latins (Augustin, Bède, Thomas d'Aquin) identifient d'emblée la vérité à *Jésus*: «ut testimonium perhibeam veritati, scilicet mihi qui sum veritas» (S. Thomas, n. 2359). Il faut croyons-nous, joindre en synthèse ces deux interprétations: en rendant té-

---

[10] CORDERIUS, *Cat. graec. Patr.*, 430 (pour la traduction, voir plus loin la n. 31); M. ZERWICK, «*Veritatem facere*», VD 18 (1938) 376: «Christi de *veritate* testimonium est Christi *de se ipso* testimonium».

moignage à la vérité, Jésus, sans doute, témoigne pour sa doctrine, pour la *révélation* qu'il transmet; mais sa propre personne est au cœur de son message: car pour le Christ, révéler, c'est avant tout *se révéler lui-même*, comme celui qui est venu en ce monde. Cette interprétation a été formulée en termes excellents par un théologien orthodoxe, A. Scrima: dans ce passage, dit-il, «la question de l'identité [la question 'Es-tu roi?'] devient la question de l'origine: d'où vient? d'où est celui qui témoigne de la vérité? ... la vérité ... apparaît ... comme la révélation ou *le dévoilement* — par la venue dans le monde de Jésus-Christ — *de son origine mystérieuse* qui n'est pas de ce monde. Ce dont témoigne le Christ, c'est *ce qu'il est*, c'est-à-dire *d'où il vient*, et la consommation de ce témoignage dans le temps constitue l'économie du salut»[11].

2. *Jésus est roi par sa vérité*

1. La déclaration de Jésus en Jn 18,37 est une réponse à la question de Pilate: «Donc tu es roi?» Il y indique le vrai sens de sa royauté. Comment comprendre que la vérité dont Jésus témoigne puisse être le fondement de sa *royauté*?

Rappelons ce que nous avons établi au début de cette section[12]: l'explication formelle de la royauté de Jésus doit se chercher dans les mots de la fin du verset: «Quiconque est de la vérité écoute ma voix (ἀκούει μου τῆς φωνῆς)». Quand le verbe avec le génitif est appliqué aux hommes, il signifie soit «écouter avec attention, écouter et comprendre» (1,37; 7,32.40; 10,3; 19,13), soit, en un sens plus théologique, «écouter, obéir» (cf. 3,29; 6,60)[13]; dans l'allégorie du bon Pasteur,

---

[11] A. SCRIMA, *La resurrection comme centre de l'économie du salut*, dans *Resurrexit. Actes du symposium international sur la Résurrection de Jésus (Rome 1970)*, édition préparée par É. Dhanis, Libreria Editrice Vaticana, 1974³, 546-553 (cf. 548-549).

[12] Voir plus haut pp. 21 ss. On peut donc s'étonner que M.-É. BOISMARD, lorsqu'il commente *La royauté universelle du Christ* dans notre passage (cf. note 8), ne fasse aucune mention des derniers mots du v. 37; ce sont les mots essentiels; cf. encore A. DAUER, *Die Passionsgeschichte im Johannesevangelium. Eine traditionsgeschichtliche und theologische Untersuchung zu Joh 18,1-19,30*, München, 1972, 259; lui non plus n'a pas remarqué que la véritable réponse de Jésus se trouve dans la dernière partie du verset.

[13] ABBOTT, *Johannine Vocabulary*, n. 1614; BLASS-DEBRUNNER, § 173, 2: «ἀκούειν φωνῆς bei Joh. im Sinn des Gehorchens ... ἀκ. φωνήν von der Wahrnehmung».

cette construction sert à décrire la docilité attentive des brebis à l'égard du Pasteur: elles «écoutent sa voix» (10,8.16.27). Lorsque le contexte est directement sotériologique, la nuance de soumission est plus nettement marquée: c'est en «écoutant la voix» du Fils de Dieu, dit Jésus, que les morts (spirituels) vivront (5,25.28)[14]. Dans le dialogue avec Pilate, la nuance est la même: Jésus veut laisser entendre que sa royauté n'est pas comme celle des rois de ce monde: elle consiste dans la soumission des siens à sa parole, à sa vérité; s'il règne sur les siens, ce n'est pas par l'emploi de la force ou de la puissance, c'est *par la vérité* dont il témoigne, et que tous ceux «qui sont de la vérité» accueillent avec foi[15].

2. Ceci pose un problème: la royauté de Jésus, on le sait, est un thème de prédilection dans S. Jean. Mais est-elle, comme ici, toujours fondée sur la «vérité»? Et si ce n'est pas le cas, c'est-à-dire si l'on trouve dans le IVe évangile des conceptions différentes sur la royauté du Christ, est-il encore possible de les ramener à une vision fondamentalement une?

Le IVe évangile marque un intérêt tout particulier pour le titre βασιλεύς: en plus des parallèles aux passages synoptiques, on trouve huit textes où ce mot ne se lit que chez Jean[16]. Ce titre «roi» indique la dignité du Roi-Messie (cf.

---

[14] Voir encore 1 Jn 4,6: ὃς οὐκ ἔστιν ἐκ τοῦ θεου, οὐκ ἀκούει ἡμῶν (obéissance à ceux qui enseignent), et Jn 12,47: ἀκούειν τῶν ῥημάτων μου, qui n'est pas encore identique à l'observation de ces paroles (φυλάττειν), mais implique quand même qu'on les a «écoutées» avec attention; comparer également 19,8 (ἤκουσεν ... τοῦτον τὸν λόγον) et 19,13 (ἀκούσας τῶν λόγων τούτων).

[15] Comparer CYR. D'ALEX.: ἵνα ... βασιλεύουσαν τῶν ὅλων ἐπιδείξῃ τὴν ἀλήθειαν (PUSEY, III, 55,22-24; PG, 74, 621); EUTHYMIUS: βασιλεὺς ὢν εἰς τὸ βασιλεύειν ἐνηνθρώπησα, καὶ διὰ τοῦτο ἦλθον εἰς τὸν κόσμον ἵνα διδάξω τὴν ἀλήθειαν, ὅτι βασιλεὺς ὢν ἀΐδιος ἐνηνθρώπησα εἰς τὸ βασιλεύειν τῶν πιστευόντων εἰς ἐμέ (PG, 129, 1461). Ce texte d'Euthymius paraphrase avec bonheur le verset de saint Jean: le Christ est venu pour enseigner la vérité et pour régner (par elle) sur ceux qui croient en lui. Quant au texte de Cyrille, il fait ressortir clairement que l'instrument de la royauté du Christ, c'est bien la vérité: βασιλεύουσαν ... τὴν ἀλήθειαν. Le lien entre la vérité révélée et la royauté du Christ est aussi fort bien marqué par S. THOMAS: «In quantum manifesto *me veritatem*, in tantum regnum mihi paro» (n. 2359); cf. C.H. DODD, *The Interpretation*, 435: «Here we have the evangelist's definition of true kingship: it is essentially the sovereignty of ἀλήθεια»; F.-M. BRAUN, *La seigneurie du Christ dans le monde selon saint Jean*, RTh 67 (1967) 357-386 (378): «La βασιλεία qui n'est pas de ce monde ... (a) pour objet l'unification des hommes dans la vérité».

[16] Jn 1,49; 6,15; 18,37 (*bis*); 19,14.15.21 (*bis*). Cf. V. TAYLOR, *The Names of Jesus*, London, 1954, 76.

1,49). Comment Jésus la concevait-il? Sa fuite dans la montagne, lorsque la foule songeait à «l'enlever pour le faire roi» (6,15), montre qu'il ne voulait à aucun prix se voir investir d'un pouvoir politique. La façon dont le IVe évangile a compris cette royauté de Jésus apparaît dans la scène de l'entrée messianique à Jérusalem, le jour des Rameaux. A la fin du récit, Jean est le seul évangéliste qui rapporte ce mot amer des Pharisiens: «Voilà le monde (ὁ κόσμος) parti après lui!» (12,19)[17]; c'était pour Jean une sorte de prophétie inconsciente, car aussitôt après il décrit la venue des Grecs auprès de Jésus. L'expression (ἀπ)έρχεσθαι ὀπίσω τινός signifie souvent: marcher à la suite de quelqu'un pour se faire son disciple (cf. Mc 1,17.20; 8,34). Jean semble avoir voulu insinuer ici ce que serait en réalité la *royauté du Christ*: non pas la domination temporelle d'un roi de ce monde, mais le pouvoir d'un *maître* qui accueille des *disciples*, et qui désire *voir venir à lui* tous les hommes. Ces deux traits reparaîtront plus loin: le Roi-Messie *groupe autour de lui des disciples*, non pas des sujets; et il veut donner à cette royauté qui sera la sienne une portée *universelle*.

Le récit de la Passion est la section de l'évangile où le titre «roi» revient le plus souvent (douze fois)[18] et avec le plus de résonances théologiques; c'est ici également que se trouve notre texte de 18,37, où la royauté de Jésus est liée à son témoignage pour la vérité. Dans les scènes suivantes, plusieurs détails ont de toute évidence une portée symbolique et soulignent fortement la dignité royale de Jésus. Ce ne peut être un hasard si le couronnement d'épines (19,1-3) se trouve exactement au centre des sept scènes qui se succèdent au prétoire[19].

---

[17] De nombreux témoins lisent ὁ κόσμος ὅλος, expression juive pour dire «tout le monde»; cette leçon pourrait être primitive. Mais, même alors, Jean doit avoir compris cette réflexion des Pharisiens en un sens plus profond, étant donné la connexion qu'il met entre cette phrase et la venue des Grecs immédiatement après. Voir Loisy, Lagrange, Hoskyns, Bultmann, Barrett, et surtout Lightfoot (250-251).

[18] Il est beaucoup moins fréquent dans les sections correspondantes des synoptiques (Mc: 6 fois; Mt et Lc: 4 fois).

[19] Pour la portée théologique du procès devant Pilate, voir: H. SCHLIER, *Jesus und Pilatus nach dem Johannesevangelium*, dans *Die Zeit der Kirche*, 56-74; J. BLANK, *Die Verhandlung vor Pilatus Joh 18,28-19,16 im Lichte johanneischer Theologie*, BZ 3 (1959) 60-81; E. HAENCHEN, *Jesus vor Pilatus (Joh. 18,28-19,15) (Zur Methode der Auslegung)*, ThLZ 85 (1960) 93-102; I. DE LA POTTERIE, *Jésus roi*

Dans la scène de l'«Ecce Homo», Jésus est présenté aux Juifs, portant les insignes royaux, la couronne et la pourpre (19,5); et Jean, contrairement aux synoptiques (Mt 27,31 et Mc 15,20), omet de dire qu'ils lui furent enlevés. Au Lithostrotos, Pilate déclare aux Juifs: «Voilà votre roi» (19,14). Tous les détails de ce passage concourent à donner à cette déclaration du procurateur un poids extraordinaire: le fait qu'en ce moment précis Jésus est *assis au tribunal* devant les Juifs[20], l'indication du lieu (Gabbatha) et de l'heure (la sixième heure, le jour de la préparation de la pâque), font de cette scène une véritable intronisation royale de Jésus[21]. Quant à la crucifixion de Jésus, elle est considérée par Jean comme une exaltation (3,14; 8,28; 12,32); quatre versets ne lui sont pas de trop pour parler de l'inscription de la croix (19,19-22), car elle proclame que Jésus de Nazareth est *le roi des Juifs*; et s'il est le seul à mentionner les trois langues de l'écriteau, c'est que ce détail donne à la royauté de Jésus une portée universelle. On constate donc que, pour saint Jean, la royauté du Christ est étroitement liée à sa Passion et à sa croix: c'est au Calvaire que le Fils de l'Homme devient pleinement roi[22].

---

et juge d'après Jn 19,13: Ἐκάθισεν ἐπὶ βήματος, Bibl 41 (1960) 217-247; *La Passion selon saint Jean. Jn 18,1-19,42*, dans *Le Triduum Pascal* (Ass. du Seign., 21), Cerf, 19693, 21-34; A. DAUER, *op. cit.*, 249-269.

[20] Du moins si l'on admet le sens transitif de ἐκάθισεν, qui semble bien s'imposer, cf. *Jésus roi et juge*, 221-233.

[21] «La croix est devenue un trône», M. DIBELIUS, *La signification religieuse des récits évangéliques de la Passion*, RHPhRel 13 (1933) 41; «Er kennzeichnet das Kreuz als den Thron dieses Königs», W. THÜSING, *Die Erhöhung*, 31.

[22] Nous disons: dans l'évangile. Car dans l'Apocalypse, «le grand livre inspiré traitant de cette Royauté [du Christ]» (H.-M. FÉRET, *L'Apocalypse de saint Jean. Vision chrétienne de l'histoire*, Paris, 1946, 91), le thème apparaît sous un angle tout différent. La «victoire» du Christ et sa «royauté» y sont étroitement unies: l'établissement de sa royauté y est avant tout considéré comme un triomphe sur les puissances ennemies. Alors que dans l'évangile toute idée de domination temporelle était exclue pour l'établissement du royaume messianique, elle réapparaît nettement dans l'Apocalypse: dès le début du livre, le Christ est appelé «le Prince des rois de la terre» (1,5); il possède gloire et puissance (1,6); Dieu et son Christ détiennent «la royauté sur le monde» (11,15); cette domination est acquise parce que l'accusateur de nos frères a été jeté bas (12,10); les rois de la terre, qui ont lié leur cause à celle de la Bête, seront vaincus par l'Agneau, et les nations païennes, frappées par celui qui s'appelle le Verbe de Dieu: celui-ci est donc proclamé solennellement Roi des rois et Seigneur des seigneurs (17,14; 19,16). Sans doute, l'aspect positif et salvifique n'est pas absent: le cantique de l'Agneau montre tous les païens qui viennent se prosterner devant le Roi des nations (15,3-4), et dans ce contexte de soumission et d'adoration, les thèmes de la victoire et de la royauté sont plutôt excep-

Comment concevoir cette royauté du Christ en croix? Jésus y est-il considéré comme roi parce qu'il triomphe de *ses adversaires*, ou plutôt par la royauté qu'il exerce sur *les siens*? Deux fois, à l'approche de la Passion, Jésus avait parlé de sa victoire sur le monde ou sur le prince de ce monde (12,31; 16,33); dans 12,31-32, ce thème est voisin de celui de l'exaltation de Jésus; mais nulle part dans le IVe évangile, la royauté de Jésus n'est expliquée *directement* et *formellement* par son triomphe sur les forces du mal[23]. Elle est uniquement considérée dans une perspective positive de salut, par rapport aux *croyants*: au moment de sa mort, Jésus «livra l'Esprit» (19,30)[24]; pour Jean, le Crucifié est le véritable Agneau pascal (19,33.36); le sang et l'eau qui coulent de son côté sont le signe du salut qui s'accomplit en cette heure; et tout le récit se termine sur un texte d'Écriture (19,37 = Zach 12,10) qui décrit les hommes *regardant avec foi* vers le Christ en croix. Aucun doute possible: pour Jean, si Jésus sur la croix est véritablement *roi*, c'est en tant que *Sauveur* du monde; c'est

---

tionnels; ils ne reparaissent plus dans la description finale de la Jérusalem céleste. Ainsi, comme l'a fort bien noté le P.H.-M. FÉRET, «l'Apocalypse, au terme de la révélation néo-testamentaire, reprend-elle brusquement et avec une insistance manifestement intentionnelle les grands thèmes traditionnels du messianisme et de la domination du Messie sur les nations de la terre» (*loc. cit.*).

L'important pour nous était de marquer la différence d'orientation de l'Apocalypse et du quatrième évangile, en ce qui concerne la royauté du Christ: l'Apocalypse reprend les grands motifs traditionnels du messianisme terrestre, pour marquer que la seigneurie de Jésus doit s'imposer à tous les hommes. Le quatrième évangile par contre laisse tomber tout ce scénario apocalyptique et politique, pour montrer en quoi réellement consiste la royauté de Jésus et par quels moyens *spirituels* elle s'établit: elle est *le règne de la vérité*; et les hommes accèdent à ce royaume par *la foi*. Par la force des choses, dans ce contexte tout spirituel, la royauté de Jésus n'est plus considérée que sous l'angle positif: pour se réaliser, elle suppose comme condition essentielle la libre soumission de la foi. La *royauté* du Christ sur *les siens* et sa *victoire* sur le monde sont donc, dans l'évangile, deux thèmes nettement différents, et même, en un certain sens, antithétiques. Voir cependant 1 Jn 5,4.

[23] Nous nous séparons ici de V. TAYLOR, *Jesus and his Sacrifice. A Study of the Passion-Sayings in the Gospels*, London, 1955, 260-261; ID., *The Names of Jesus*, London, 1955, 76-77; l'auteur n'a pas remarqué combien le thème de la royauté de Jésus reçoit une orientation foncièrement différente dans le quatrième évangile et dans l'Apocalypse.

[24] Le sens spirituel de l'expression est admis actuellement par un bon nombre d'auteurs (Hoskyns, Barrett, Lightfoot, Mollat, etc.). La preuve de ce sens double est dans la formule même employée par Jean, παρέδωκεν τὸ πνεῦμα, nulle part attestée dans l'Antiquité en dehors des écrits johanniques pour décrire le simple fait de la mort physique. Par ailleurs, d'après Jn 7,39, l'Esprit serait donné au moment de la glorification du Christ: c'est ce qui s'accomplit en 19,30.

parce que du haut de sa croix Jésus *attire à lui tous les hommes* (12,32).

3. Le problème signalé plus haut apparaît maintenant dans toute son acuité: d'une part, Jésus déclare qu'il est roi par la *vérité*; d'autre part, il devient pleinement roi par sa *croix*[25]. Aurions-nous là deux théologies différentes, deux conceptions inconciliables? Rien n'est moins probable dans un écrit comme le IVe évangile, que nous savons si fortement unifié autour de quelques idées fondamentales. Mais si synthèse il y a entre les deux points de vue, il semble qu'elle ne pourra consister que dans un lien très étroit et organique entre la *vérité* et la *croix*. Et c'est bien à cela que nous aboutirons.

Partons de l'explication fournie par Jésus en 18,37: s'il est roi sur les siens, c'est qu'ils «écoutent sa voix», avec docilité et foi. Mais cette foi elle-même doit être en progrès constant, elle est une découverte continue. Une adhésion enthousiaste, comme celle de ces Juifs qui avaient été gagnés par les miracles (2,23), ou les discours (8,30) de Jésus, ne suffit pas encore pour faire de véritables disciples: il faut «demeurer» dans la parole de Jésus, pour découvrir progressivement toute la vérité (8,31-32). Or, précisément, la croix est ici un sommet: «d'un mouvement continu, tout au long de l'évangile, la foi monte vers cette découverte» du Fils de l'homme élevé de terre[26]. Jésus l'avait déjà déclaré à Nicodème (3,15), et il répéterait le même enseignement avant sa passion: ce n'est qu'une fois élevé de terre que le Fils de l'homme pourra *attirer tout à lui* (12,32). Aussi comprend-on que la scène du Calvaire se termine sur un texte de Zacharie qui exprime la foi des croyants: «Ils regarderont celui qu'ils ont transpercé» (19,37)[27].

---

[25] La même dualité d'aspects apparaît dans la liturgie. La préface de la messe du Christ-Roi parle du «regnum *veritatis*» (le texte d'évangile, pour ce jour, était naguère Jn 18,33-37; il se termine par ces mots: «omnis qui est ex veritate, audit vocem meam»). Par contre, aujourd'hui encore la liturgie du Vendredi-Saint célèbre le triomphe du Christ par la *croix*: «regnavit a ligno Deus» (hymne «*Vexilla Regis*»).

[26] D. MOLLAT, *La foi dans le quatrième Évangile*, 96.

[27] Schlatter a fort bien marqué le lien interne des trois textes que nous venons de citer (3,14-15; 12,32; 19,37): «Dieses Ziehen [en 12,32] bekommt durch 3,14 die Erläuterung, da dort die Erweckung des Glaubens als das genannt wird, was Jesus durch sein Kreuz bewirkt» (p. 272).

Si le Christ «élevé de terre» est comme un terme auquel doit aboutir la foi chrétienne, c'est qu'il constitue le point culminant de la révélation: le Christ qui meurt sur la croix comme victime de propitiation est, précisément par cette mort, la grande manifestation de l'amour de Dieu pour les hommes (1 Jn 4,9-10; cf. Jn 3,16).

La solution du problème paraît donc être la suivante: si Jésus est roi par la *vérité* mais aussi par la *croix*, c'est tout juste que la vérité du Christ s'accomplit à la croix[28]. Jésus est le témoin par excellence de la révélation; il l'est non seulement par son enseignement, mais aussi par les œuvres qu'il accomplit au nom de son Père (5,36; 10,25), et il l'est surtout par la grande œuvre du salut pour laquelle il est venu; c'est donc dans son «élévation» sur la croix et par sa mort, que la révélation de l'amour du Père atteint son point culminant. Probablement est-ce pour cette raison que l'élévation de la croix constitue aussi pour saint Jean une victoire sur le monde, une exaltation, la pleine réalisation de la royauté de Jésus.

Il est vrai que la révélation devra encore recevoir un dernier complément. Nous rencontrons ici un schème fondamental de la théologie johannique, celui des deux temps de la révélation: après le témoignage de *Jésus* en faveur de la vérité, il faudra encore, dans l'Église, le témoignage de l'*Esprit* de vérité (15,26); si d'après 18,37 Jésus est le grand témoin de la vérité, l'action de l'Esprit demeure pourtant nécessaire, pour conduire les croyants vers la vérité tout entière (16,13); c'est pourquoi, dans 1 Jn 5,6-8, avec le témoignage de l'eau et du sang, est également mentionné le témoignage de l'Esprit. Mais du point de vue historique et de l'œuvre terrestre de Jésus lui-même, le point culminant de la révélation doit se chercher indubitablement à la croix, au moment de l'Heure de Jésus.

---

[28] Le problème que nous touchons ici a été examiné, d'un autre point de vue, par Th. MÜLLER, *Das Heilsgeschehen im Johannesevangelium. Eine exegetische Studie, zugleich der Versuch einer Antwort an R. Bultmann*, Zürich, 1961; en réponse à Bultmann, il cherche à montrer qu'une synthèse est possible entre les deux lignes de pensée que l'on trouve dans S. Jean: l'une voit toute l'œuvre de Jésus à la lumière de l'Incarnation et considère même sa mort comme une *révélation*; l'autre conception, plus traditionnelle, voit cette mort comme un *sacrifice d'expiation*. Nous n'oserions pas dire que l'effort de synthèse ici tenté soit parfaitement réussi. Voir la recension de E. HAENCHEN, ThLZ 88 (1963) 116-118.

4. Résumons brièvement les résultats de nos analyses et tâchons de montrer que, si Jean semble à première vue avoir deux théologies de la royauté de Jésus — d'après l'une il serait roi par sa *croix*, d'après l'autre par la *vérité* — c'est en définitive l'aspect «vérité» qui fait l'unité et la synthèse des deux conceptions.

D'après Jn 18,37, Jésus est témoin de la vérité et règne sur les siens par cette vérité qu'ils accueillent avec foi. D'autre part, Jésus devient pleinement roi par sa croix; et la foi chrétienne véritable n'est pas seulement l'adhésion à la parole de Jésus, elle est la foi dans le Fils de l'homme élevé de terre et mourant sur la croix pour le salut du monde. Mais cette mort salvifique ne peut devenir objet de notre foi que si le sens qu'elle a pour les hommes nous est *révélé* et si nous en connaissons le mystère; le simple fait matériel de cette mort considérée en elle -même, l'événement brut dans sa pure objectivité, ne sauve pas le monde; il faut que le monde en perçoive la signification et qu'il s'y ouvre par la foi. Autrement dit, la Passion et la mort de Jésus ne constituent l'œuvre du salut que parce que Dieu s'y *révèle* en son Fils et que les hommes *croient* en lui (3,16). La mort de Jésus peut nous sauver et devenir effectivement l'instrument de sa royauté dans la mesure où elle nous est *révélée* comme telle, dans la mesure où elle devient pour nous *parole* et *vérité*[29]. Alors, la foi peut s'ouvrir à cet acte rédempteur; et c'est par cette foi des hommes que le Christ peut vraiment régner sur eux.

Ainsi donc, comme nous le disions tout à l'heure, seule *la vérité* dont Jésus témoigne constitue en définitive le fondement de sa royauté, comme il le déclarait lui-même à Pilate. Mais cette vérité de Jésus, loin de s'opposer à la croix, y conduit; car le sommet de la révélation précisément est atteint au moment de l'Heure du salut. La vérité de Jésus n'est pas seulement celle de sa parole; c'est aussi «la vérité de la Croix»[30].

---

[29] C'est ce qu'il y a de vrai dans la théorie de Bultmann: «Der Tod Jesu ist unter den Offenbarungsgedanken gestellt; in ihm handelt Jesus selbst als der Offenbarer...» (*Theologie*, 406); mais il ne s'ensuit pas que l'aspect sacrificiel ne soit pas johannique; nous dirions plutôt que, dans S. Jean, même l'aspect sacrificiel de l'œuvre du Christ devient révélation et vérité.

[30] Cette formule nous est inspirée par un passage d'une ancienne homélie, attribuée à l'évêque Athanase, mais qui contient d'importants fragments de Méliton de Sardes; elle vient d'être publiée par M. VAN ESBROECK, *Nouveaux fragments de*

En esquissant cette synthèse, n'aurions-nous pas dépassé les données de l'évangile pour aboutir dans le domaine de la théologie spéculative? Nous ne le pensons pas. Les textes johanniques eux-mêmes nous ont contraint à voir dans la *vérité* dont Jésus est le témoin, à la fois la révélation qu'il apporte et sa propre personne, ou plutôt, la révélation qu'il apporte *par* et *dans* sa personne. Et comme, par ailleurs, cette révélation culmine dans sa mort propitiatoire (1 Jn 4,9-10), la *vérité* par laquelle Jésus est roi, atteint sa plénitude à la *croix*. C'est bien là, sans doute, la théologie johannique de la mort du Christ dans ce qu'elle a de plus spécifique. Dès lors si, pour saint Jean, le Christ en croix *règne* sur les hommes en les *attirant* tous à lui, c'est parce qu'il y est roi par le rayonnement de sa vérité[31].

3. *Témoignage et jugement*

Un mot reste à dire d'une autre connexion du thème. Nous avons constaté ci-dessus que, dans l'apocalyptique juive et à Qumrân, le thème du témoignage était étroitement lié à celui du jugement eschatologique. Mais pour le témoignage de Jean-Baptiste en faveur de la vérité, une transformation radicale s'est manifestée: d'eschatologique dans les textes préchrétiens, le témoignage devenait directement messianique; Jean n'était plus un témoin à charge: il témoignait «en faveur» du Messie (3,26), il venait pour faire connaître et accueillir le Messie en Israël (1,31). Du coup, la relation entre son témoignage et le jugement s'en trouvait modifiée: le jugement dans S. Jean étant essentiellement lié au *refus* de la lumière, on ne peut plus dire que le témoignage du Baptiste

---

Méliton de Sardes dans une homélie géorgienne sur la Croix, Analecta bollandiana 90 (1972) 63-99; en voici le début, en traduction latine (cf. p. 73): «Lectio. Sermo sancti Athanasii episcopi *de veritate sanctae crucis* ... Audite *verba veritatis* et parabolas doctrinarum et voces prophetarum ...». La reprise de *veritas sanctae crucis* dans *verba veritatis* montre que l'auteur songe ici au *sens* de la Croix, à la *vérité* qui s'en dégage pour les chrétiens; ce message, cette révélation de la Croix, constitue l'objet des «paroles de vérité» qu'il adresse à ses auditeurs.

[31] Rappelons ici le beau texte d'Apollinaire de Laodicée cité plus haut p. 27: «La vérité dont il parle, c'est la *manifestation de lui-même* aux hommes, et le don du salut qu'il leur confère par cette connaissance de lui-même». La royaume du Christ est un «regnum *veritatis*» (voir la note 25).

était ordonné à ce jugement, puisqu'il témoignait *en faveur de* la vérité. Les deux thèmes du témoignage et du jugement demeuraient cependant connexes, quoique d'une façon différente; le jugement de condamnation devenait désormais une simple conséquence du *refus* de la vérité.

Qu'en est-il dans le cas de Jésus? Pour mieux nous en rendre compte, voyons rapidement, dans les autres discours du IVe évangile, la nature du lien qui unit les notions de témoignage, de vérité et de jugement.

Dans les discussions avec les Juifs, le thème du *témoignage* de Jésus est régulièrement rapproché de celui du *jugement*[32]. En 3,11-19, la chose est claire: Jésus témoigne de ce qu'il a vu, et les Juifs *refusent* d'accepter son témoigne (v. 11), c'est-à-dire de croire; mais aussitôt après il ajoute que quiconque «ne croit pas est déjà *condamné*» (v. 18); le jugement de condamnation est donc la conséquence immédiate de la prise de position négative des Juifs devant le témoignage de Jésus. Dans la section 5,22-40, l'ordre est inverse: Jésus parle d'abord du jugement (vv. 22-30), puis du témoignage (vv. 31-40); quoique de façon plus indirecte, ici aussi le lien des deux thèmes est encore apparent: celui qui écoute la parole de Jésus n'est pas soumis au jugement (v. 24), mais les Juifs refusent de croire en Jésus et dans les témoignages qui authentiquent sa mission (vv. 37-40). En 8,13-19, l'ordre est de nouveau celui du chapitre 3: le thème du témoignage précède. Jésus vient de se déclarer la lumière du monde: ceux qui le suivent ne marchent pas dans les ténèbres (8,12); Jésus concède alors aux Pharisiens qu'il se rend témoignage à lui-même (v. 14); et cette idée amorce aussitôt le thème du jugement (vv. 15-16).

Pareillement, on peut dire que la notion de *vérité*, elle aussi, est liée à celle de *jugement*[33]. Car l'instrument de la discrimination entre les hommes, c'est la lumière de Jésus: «Le jugement, le voici: la lumière est venue dans le monde et les hommes ont mieux aimé les ténèbres que la lumière» (3,19); de même, dans la section sur l'aveugle-na (9,1-41), Jésus se

---

[32] Sur la notion de jugement dans le IVe évangile, on consultera surtout: D. MOLLAT, art. *Jugement*, SDB, IV, 1379; R. BULTMANN, *Theologie*, 379-386: «Die κρίσις der Welt»; A. CORELL, *Consummatum est*, NY, 1959.

[33] «... ove c'è la verità (ἀλήθεια), quivi c'è un giudizio (cfr. 3,18-21 e 9,13-41)», G. DANESI, dans *Introduzione alla Bibbia*. IV: *I Vangeli*, Marietti, 1959, 543.

déclare «la lumière du monde» (9,5); mais c'est parce que les Pharisiens se ferment à la lumière que le Christ leur adresse cette parole terrible: «Votre péché demeure» (9,41). Mais en 3,19-21, ce thème de la lumière appelle immédiatement celui de la vérité, qui en est très proche[34]. «Celui qui fait la vérité vient à la lumière» (v. 21); refus de la lumière et refus de la vérité sont pratiquement équivalents. Ailleurs encore, ce refus est rapproché du jugement: «Qui me rejette et ne reçoit pas mes paroles a son juge: la parole que j'ai proclamée, c'est elle qui le jugera au dernier jour» (12,48; cf. 5,24). Le jugement, pour S. Jean, c'est donc bien le rejet de la lumière, le refus d'accueillir la parole de vérité, *le refus de croire*[35]. Le jugement implique condamnation, la κρίσις devient κατάκρισις; mais c'est l'homme lui-même, par son refus, qui prononce sa condamnation[36].

Reprenons maintenant notre texte de 18,37 sur le témoignage de Jésus en faveur de la vérité. Existe-t-il encore quelque rapport entre ce *témoignage* et le *jugement*? Les mots κρίνειν ou κρίσις, c'est un fait, ne paraissent pas dans cette partie du procès. Pourtant, le thème est implicitement présent, et il sera même accentué davantage dans la suite du récit de la Passion, comme nous allons le voir. En 18,37 même, Jésus décrit l'un des deux comportements possibles devant la vérité, celui de ceux «qui sont de la vérité»: ils croient et écoutent la voix de Jésus. Mais ce qui constitue le jugement, c'est précisément la position contraire: le refus de la vérité, le rejet du Christ. Or, les scènes suivantes vont décrire concrètement cette attitude des Juifs. Jésus lui-même, d'ailleurs, avait déclaré quelques jours avant: «C'est *maintenant* le jugement (κρίσις) du monde» (12,31); «le prince de ce monde est condamné (κέκριται)» (16,11). Dans ces deux textes est indiqué par anticipation le sens de l'«*Heure*» *de Jé-*

---

[34] Voir le tome II, chap. VI, § III, B, à propos de Jn 3,19; nous y analyserons en détail le rapport exact entre les notions de lumière et de vérité.

[35] Cf. A. CORELL, *op. cit.*, 163: «The crucial test in judgement is faith».

[36] Certains textes cependant (5,29; 12,48; 1 Jn 4,17) présentent le jugement comme futur, donc comme une réalité plus strictement eschatologique, conformément à la conception des synoptiques; mais ce jugement futur ne sera que la manifestation au grand jour d'une décision qu'auront déjà prise les croyants pendant leur vie, dans leur confrontation avec le Christ (voir surtout 12,48: le rapport des présents ἀθετῶν ..., λαμβάνων..., ἔχει...., et du futur κρινεῖ); cf. A. CORELL, *op. cit.*, 164-165.

sus, l'heure de sa Passion et de son exaltation: elle est aussi l'*heure du jugement du monde*.

Où s'accomplit concrètement ce jugement? En fait, à la croix. Il semble cependant que, sur le plan symbolique, il soit déjà anticipé dans l'épisode du Lithostrotos ou de Gabbatha; car Jean, très consciemment, a mis en parallèle la scène de Gabbatha et celle du Golgotha[37]. De part et d'autre nous avons exactement les mêmes thèmes théologiques: la proclamation de la *royauté* de Jésus, et le refus des Juifs, qui constitue leur *jugement*. Au prétoire, Pilate fait asseoir Jésus au tribunal[38] et proclame solennellement: «Voici votre roi» (19,13); l'importance unique de ce moment est fortement soulignée par saint Jean: «C'était la préparation de la Pâque, dit-il, environ la sixième heure» (v. 14). Mais à la proclamation de Pilate les Juifs répondent par ce seul cri: «Enlève, enlève! Crucifie-le!» (v. 15). *C'est ce choix qui les juge*. On voit donc tout ce qu'il y a de saisissant dans cette scène: Jésus est installé par Pilate ἐπὶ βήματος, «*pro tribunali*»; au moment même où les Juifs rejettent leur Roi-Messie, Jésus est là, en silence devant eux, dans l'attitude du juge. *Il est leur juge, parce qu'ils ne veulent pas qu'il soit leur roi*.

La scène du Calvaire a exactement le même sens: le titre de la croix publie en trois langues que Jésus de Nazareth est le *roi* de Juifs (19,19-22); et Jean ajoute que beaucoup de Juifs lurent cet écriteau; mais ici encore tout se conclut par un *refus*; ils protestent officiellement auprès du magistrat romain pour qu'il change ce titre de la croix.

On voit donc que, dans ces deux scènes parallèles, les thèmes de la *royauté* de Jésus et celui de sa fonction de *juge* sont étroitement connexes. Or, le verset de 18,37 sur le témoignage de Jésus en faveur de la vérité était précisément l'explication qu'il donnait à Pilate sur le sens véritable de sa royauté. On s'aperçoit maintenant en quel sens on peut dire que le témoignage de Jésus est encore lié au thème du jugement. Ce que nous avons expliqué ci-dessus pour Jean-Bap-

---

[37] Sur ce qui suit, cf. notre article *Jésus roi et juge d'après Jn 19,13*: Ἐκάθισεν ἐπὶ βήματος, Bibl 41 (1960) 217-247.

[38] Du moins si l'on admet que le verbe ἐκάθισεν doit être pris au sens transitif, comme plusieurs raisons le font penser (cf. *art. cit.*, 221-233). A. Dauer (*op. cit.*, 269-277) a contesté cette interprétation, mais d'une manière peu convaincante.

tiste vaut également dans le cas présent: si Jésus se présente comme témoin de la vérité, ce n'est plus *pour* un jugement de condamnation, comme dans l'apocalyptique; son seul désir, au contraire, est que les hommes accueillent son témoignage et que «ceux qui sont de la vérité écoutent sa voix». En fait, cependant, les hommes *rejetèrent* son témoignage, ils se refusèrent à le reconnaître pour Messie: ce fut là leur condamnation[39]. Le jugement des hommes n'est donc pas le *but* du témoignage de Jésus; il est la *conséquence* de leur refus; ils se condamnent eux-mêmes, parce qu'ils ont rejeté le témoignage de Jésus et qu'ils n'ont pas accueilli sa vérité.

D. Conclusion

Jetons un regard en arrière. Si nous comparons les deux textes johanniques sur le témoignage rendu à la vérité (5,33, pour Jean-Baptiste; 18,37, pour Jésus) avec le milieu apocalyptique d'où dérive le thème, nous pouvons mieux mesurer tout le chemin parcouru.

Dans les textes juifs, le témoignage des justes était directement orienté vers la condamnation des impies à l'heure du jugement. Dans S. Jean, au contraire, le témoignage vise un but positif, salvifique: l'adhésion des hommes à la vérité messianique. S'il est encore question d'un «jugement» des hommes, celui-ci est uniquement dû à leur propre choix; il est une conséquence de leur refus de la vérité.

Entre les deux textes johanniques eux-mêmes (5,33; 18,37), la différence n'est pas moins grande. Quand Jean-Baptiste témoigne en faveur de la vérité, c'est en fait *pour Jésus*, c'est pour le Messie qu'il témoigne. Mais quand le Christ lui-même se déclare témoin de la vérité, il n'est plus au service d'un autre: il témoigne en faveur de la révélation messianique, mais il apporte celle-ci dans sa propre personne; il té-

---

[39] Cf. ce qu'écrit G. Bornkamm, à propos de l'inscription de la croix: «Sie verkündet das Gericht über Israel, das jetzt seinen Messias verworfen hat. Darum der Protest der Juden, die vom Pilatus eine Korrektur fordern», *Jesus von Nazareth*, Stuttgart, 1956, 152; on trouve également chez les Pères de l'Église cette idée que la passion et la mort du Christ constituent le jugement de condamnation du monde: «O admirabilis potentia Crucis! o ineffabilis gloria Passionis! in qua et *tribunal Domini*, et *judicium mundi*, et potestas est Crucifixi», S. Léon, *Serm. VIII de Pass. Domini*, VII (PL, 54, 341 A).

moigne donc en définitive *pour lui-même*. Par là s'explique qu'il puisse présenter son témoignage comme le fondement immédiat de sa *royauté*.

A diverses reprises, dans ce chapitre et dans le précédent, nous avons constaté une tendance du IVe évangile à identifier l'ἀλήθεια à la personne de Jésus[40]; de plus en plus apparaît que la vérité, dans S. Jean, est essentiellement *christologique*. Nous pouvons maintenant aborder les deux grands textes qui disent explicitement tout ce qui demeurait jusqu'ici plus ou moins implicite: le Verbe fait chair est *plein de la grâce de la vérité* (Jn 1,14). *Jésus lui-même est la Vérité* (Jn 14,6).

---

[40] Dans 3 Jn 12 se rencontre une expressione assez inattendue, où la vérité, à première vue, semble également personnifiée; les termes μαρτυρεῖν et ἀλήθεια y sont rapprochés, comme dans les deux textes de l'évangile que nous avons étudiés dans ce chapitre: Δημητρίῳ μεμαρτύρηται ὑπὸ πάντων καὶ ὑπὸ αὐτῆς τῆς ἀληθείας, mais il s'agit ici d'un témoignage rendu *par* la vérité, ce qui est très différent de μαρτυρεῖν τῇ ἀληθείᾳ, rendre témoignage *en faveur de* la vérité. Nous expliquerons ce passage de 3 Jn 12 dans le tome II (chap. XI, § II, E), quand nous traiterons du rôle de la vérité dans la vie chrétienne.

N.B. — Notre texte était à l'impression quand nous avons pris connaissance de l'étude structurale de J. ESCANDE, *Jésus devant Pilate. Jean 18,18-19,24*. Foi et vie 73 (1974) 66-81 (cfr. p. 80 s. et n. 12). Détachons-en quelques remarques importantes, qui vont tout à fait dans la ligne de ce que nous avons développé ci-dessus: en raison de la structure narrative utilisée, la question de la Vérité (18,38) a ici une place centrale. Puisque la question de la vérité est soulevée dans un procès, il faut admettre que le récit vise tôt ou tard à résoudre ce problème. Il s'agit au fond du procès de la vérité: en 19,16, ce procès n'est pas clos; ce n'est qu'à la croix que les trois langues du *titulus* manifesteront l'éclat de la Vérité.

Vedere il regno e nascere da acqua e da spirito

GIUSEPPE FERRARO

Il tema del «regno» in connessione con lo Spirito, nel vangelo giovanneo è presente nel dialogo tra Gesù e Nicodemo nel terzo capitolo. Questo capitolo dal punto di vista del contenuto, si articola in tre parti: la prima (3,1-21) narra l'incontro di Gesù con Nicodemo e ne riferisce il colloquio; la seconda (3,22-30) propone la testimonianza di Giovanni Battista su Gesù; la terza (3,31-36) prosegue i temi iniziali[1]. Consideriamo qui il tema del regno in rapporto allo Spirito.

Nicodemo si presenta a Gesù di notte: la notte offre una ambientazione caratteristica; durante la notte avvenivano le discussioni dei maestri della legge e la notte era raccomandata come tempo opportuno per lo studio della Scrittura[2]. Nel quarto vangelo la notte per la sua oscurità ha valore di simbolo delle tenebre in contrapposizione alla luce. La pericope 3,1-21, infatti, è inquadrata dalla contrapposizione di questi due simboli: la notte e la luce; l'inizio presenta il venire di Nicodemo nella notte (3,2), la fine presenta il venire dell'uomo alla luce (3,21)[3]. L'evocazione della notte come simbolo della tenebra ricorre in altri momenti del vangelo[4]. Il perso-

---

[1] Sono state proposte varie ricostruzioni del capitolo, nel commentari di R. Bultmann, di R. Schnackenburg, e altri; tali rifacimenti, se risolvono alcuni problemi ne creano altri; perciò teniamo la composizione letteraria del testo attuale.

[2] Cf Str -Bill II, 419-420.

[3] Cf F. ROUSTANG, *L'entretien acvec Nicodème*, Nouvelle Revue Théologique 78 (1956) 352-353. Sant'Agostino rilevava a questo proposito: «Nicodemo si recò dal Signore, ma ci andò di notte; e anche questo particolare è degno di nota. Si reca dal Signore e si reca di notte; si accosta alla luce ma la cerca nelle tenebre» (Sant'AGOSTINO, *Commento al Vangelo di san Giovanni*, 11,4; Introduzioni e indici a cura di Agostino Vita, traduzione e note di Emilio Gandolfo, revisione di Vincenzo Tarulli, Roma 1968, p 257).

[4] Cf 9,4-5; 11,9-10; 13,30.

naggio che entra in scena, Nicodemo era membro del Sinedrio in qualità di dottore della legge; nel seguito del vangelo sarà menzionato altre due volte (7,50; 19,39) sempre in atteggiamento di buona disposizione d'animo verso Gesù.

Nel dialogo che avviene le parole di Gesù offrono una sequenza di rivelazioni di fronte alle quali Nicodemo manifesta la sua incomprensione. Nel discorrere di Gesù è presente a ogni ripresa l'espressione: ἀμὴν ἀμὴν λέγω σοι (3,3.5.10) che pone un forte accento sulla missione rivelatrice di Gesù. L'ultima battuta del dialogo è un discorso esteso (3,10-21) che ha come tema la persona di Gesù, Figlio dell'uomo, Figlio di Dio, Luce. La conversazione, che può essere divisa in vari modi, nella prima parte tratta del regno e della nascita da acqua e da Spirito (3,3-9), nella seconda parte espone la manifestazione di Gesù (3,10-21)[5].

I. Il regno

1. «Il regno di Dio», «Il mio regno», «Re» nel quarto vangelo

Le affermazioni sul «regno» e sullo «Spirito» (3,5-8) sono intrecciate con quelle sulla rigenerazione; esse pongono in rapporto regno, acqua e Spirito, carne e Spirito. Il termine «regno» ricorre cinque volte nell'intero vangelo, due volte nel colloquio con Nicodemo con l'espressione: «Il regno di Dio» e tre volte nel racconto della passione con l'espressione «Il mio regno». Il tema della regalità viene illustrato inoltre con il titolo di «Re» dato a Gesù, quattro nella prima parte del vangelo e dodici nel racconto della passione.

Per esporre il significato del «regno», partendo dalle due menzioni presenti nel nostro brano, ricerchiamo i passi affini nei vangeli sinottici, veniamo poi agli altri detti contenenti il termine «re» e l'espressione «il mio regno», osservando la progressiva concentrazione cristologica del tema del regno; il

---

[5] Per la struttura della pericope cf I DE LA POTTERIE, *Structura primae partis Evangelii Iohannis; Ad dialogum Iesu cum Nicodemo; Iesus et Nicodemus;* Verbum Domini 47 (1969) 130-140; 193-214; 257-283. G. GAETA, *Il dialogo con Nicodemo. Per l'interpretazione del capitolo terzo dell'evangelo di Giovanni*, Brescia 1974; R. SCHNACKENBURG, *Il vangelo di Giovanni*, prima parte, Brescia 1973, 517-521.

fatto poi che il regno è proposto come oggetto del verbo «vedere», confermando il suo significato cristologico, estende la sua connessione a Dio Padre e allo Spirito.

Nel colloquio con Nicodemo, Gesù menziona il «regno di Dio» nel discorso sulla nuova generazione: «Se uno non nasce dall'alto non può vedere il regno di Dio» (3,3); «Se uno non nasce da acqua e da Spirito non può entrare nel regno di Dio» (3,5). Questi detti risentono della tradizione sinottica ove il tema del «regno» è molto frequente e caratteristico[6]. Anche nei sinottici si parla di «vedere il regno» e di «entrare nel regno». Gesù dice: «In verità vi dico: vi sono alcuni qui presenti che non moriranno senza avere visto il regno di Dio venire con potenza» (Mc 9,1; Lc 9,27). Il testo parallelo nel primo vangelo suona: «Vedranno il Figlio dell'uomo venire nel suo regno» (Mt 16,28), trasformando il tema del regno di Dio in senso cristologico nel regno del Figlio dell'uomo. L'affermazione: «In verità vi dico: chi non accoglie il regno di Dio come un bambino non entrerà in esso» (Mc 10,15; cf Lc 18,17)[7] indica la disposizione interiore che occorre avere nei confronti del regno: convertirsi e diventare progressivamente come fanciulli; è un concetto simile a quello della nuova nascita. Nel terzo vangelo leggiamo: «Non c'è nessuno che abbia lasciato casa o moglie, fratelli o genitori o figli per il regno di Dio» (Lc 18,29), il passo parallelo nel secondo vangelo suona: «Non c'è nessuno che abbia lasciato casa o fratelli o sorelle o madre o padre o figli o campi a causa di me e a causa del vangelo» (Mc 10,29); e nel primo vangelo: «Chiunque avrà lasciato case o fratelli o sorelle o padre o madre o figli o campi per il mio nome» (Mt 19, 29); il termine e il tema del regno di Dio si trasforma nel tema «di me», «del vangelo» «del nome di me», cioè nella realtà della persona di Gesù. Nei sinottici osserviamo così una connessione molto stretta tra la realtà del regno e la persona del Signore.

Questo aspetto cristologico si intensifica nei passi del vangelo di Giovanni. Ciò appare nei testi contenenti il titolo «Re» attribuito a Gesù, e soprattutto nella espressione: «Il

---

[6] Nel nuovo Testamento il termine regno ha le seguenti presenze: Mt 55; Mc 20; Lc 46; Gv 5; At 8; Paolo 14 Gc 1; 2 Pt 1; Ap 9; complessivamente 162 ricorrenze.

[7] Il passo corrispondente nel primo vangelo ha «Regno dei cieli» (Mt 18,3). Cf C.H. DODD, *Historical Tradition*, 358-359.

mio regno». Natanaele dice a Gesù: «Tu sei il Figlio di Dio, tu sei il Re di Israele» (1,49); tale dichiarazione significa, nella mente di chi la pronuncia, la dignità messianica. Dopo la moltiplicazione del pane la folla cerca Gesù per proclamarlo re; egli rifiuta di assumere il titolo come era inteso dalla gente, secondo la concezione del messianismo terreno[8]. Nell'ingresso di Gesù a Gerusalemme la folla gli va incontro acclamando: «Benedetto colui che viene nel nome del Signore, il Re di Israele» (12,12-13). Il titolo «Re di Israele» designa Gesù come il messia, destinato a regnare sul popolo eletto. Il racconto dell'ingresso prosegue con una nuova attribuzione del titolo: «Ecco il tuo Re viene a te seduto sopra un puledro di asina» (12,14-15). La citazione libera di Zaccaria 9,9 sottolinea il carattere umile e pacifico del Re messianico[9]. Nel racconto della passione il titolo «Re» insieme con il termine «regno» si trova nel processo davanti al governatore romano e nell'atto della crocifissione, ove leggiamo: «Pilato compose l'iscrizione e la fece porre sulla croce: vi era scritto: Gesù il Nazareno, il Re dei Giudei (...). Era scritta in ebraico, in latino e in greco. I sommi sacerdoti dei Giudei dissero allora a Pilato: non scrivere il Re dei Giudei, ma che egli ha detto: Io sono il Re dei Giudei. Pilato rispose: ciò che ho scritto ho scritto» (19, 19-22). Le tre lingue, nelle quali viene scritto il titolo di «Re» per Gesù, esprimono i tre universi; la lingua ebraica l'universo religioso, la lingua latina l'universo politico dell'impero romano, la lingua greca l'universo della cultura. L'universalità del titolo «Re» che costituisce la causalità della morte di Gesù non poteva essere più insistentemente sottolineata[10].

Veniamo ora alla espressione: «il mio regno» ricorrente all'inizio dell'interrogatorio: «Pilato (...) chiamò Gesù e gli disse: Tu sei il Re dei Giudei? (...). Rispose Gesù: Il mio re-

---

[8] Cf J. C. O'NEILL, *The silence of Jesus*, New Testament Studies 15 (1969) 153-167.
[9] Cf M.-E. BOISMARD, *La Royauté du Christ dans le quatrième évangile*, Lumière et Vie 11 n 57 (1962) 46-63, 46-49.
[10] Anche il rifiuto di Pilato di acconsentire alla richiesta delle autorità giudaiche e la sua decisione di lasciare l'iscrizione già stabilita, è una accentuazione del titolo regale. Nella mentalità del governatore l'appellativo «Re dei Giudei» scritto sulla croce per Gesù era un segno del disprezzo dei Romani nei confronti dei Giudei; secondo la rappresentazione dell'evangelista invece è una rivelazione dell'autentica dignità di Gesù.

gno non è di questo mondo; se il mio regno fosse di questo mondo, i miei servitori combatterebbero perché non fossi consegnato ai Giudei; dunque il mio regno non è di quaggiù. Pilato gli disse: Dunque tu sei Re? Rispose Gesù: Tu lo dici; io sono Re. Io per questo sono nato e per questo sono venuto nel mondo: per rendere testimonianza alla verità. Chiunque è dalla verità, ascolta la voce di me» (18,33.36-37). Questa dichiarazione collocata al centro del racconto della passione, nel terzo atto[11], costituisce il punto culminante della rivelazione della regalità di Gesù. Tre volte ricorre ἡ βασιλεία ἡ ἐμή. Il possessivo «mio» è sottolineato, e sta in corrispondenza allo «Io» di Gesù: «Il mio regno»-«Io sono Re». Osserviamo il parallelismo tra il regno di Gesù e la persona di Gesù. Per Gesù: «Il mio regno non è di questo mondo; il mio regno non è di quaggiù» (18,36) esprime la conseguenza della rivelazione che egli ha dato di se stesso nel corso del vangelo, dicendo: «Io non sono del mondo» (8,23; 17,14.16) e qualificandosi come «Colui che viene dall'alto. Colui che viene dal cielo». Il regno di Gesù ha gli stessi caratteri di Gesù, il quale ha origine da Dio, viene dal cielo, è di lassù; il regno di Gesù ha la stessa natura di Gesù. Il termine possessivo «mio» che Gesù unisce al termine «regno» accentua il valore cristologico del regno stesso confermando la convergenza tra la realtà del regno e la persona del Signore; del regno di Gesù si possono predicare le stesse caratteristiche che appartengono alla persona di Gesù. Tale il valore del possessivo «mio» congiunto con la realtà e il mistero del «regno». E poiché per Gesù la rivelazione che egli non è del mondo, che egli è dall'alto, che egli viene, è disceso, è dal cielo significa la sua origine divina, la sua origine dal Padre, la sua missione dal Padre, la sua appartenenza alla stessa sfera del Padre, per il regno il possessivo «mio» che lo riferisce direttamente a Gesù contiene il riferimento anche a Dio Padre.

---

[11] Il processo davanti a Pilato, terzo atto dei cinque nei quali si sviluppa il racconto della passione, è costruito in sette scene di cui la dichiarazione sul «mio regno» si trova nella seconda. Per la struttura letteraria del racconto della passione nel vangelo di Giovanni cf A. JANSSENS DE VAREBEKE, *La structure des scènes du récit de la passion en Joh XVIII-XIX*, Ephemerides Theologicae Lovanienses 38 (1962) 504-522.

Così il regno di Dio (3,3.5) è il regno di Gesù (18,36), che confonde i suoi lineamenti con la persona stessa di Gesù.

La convergenza fino alla identificazione tra Gesù e «il mio regno» con il riferimento al Padre, viene confermata se consideriamo che nella prima risposta di Gesù a Nicodemo il regno è oggetto del verbo «vedere». Tale verbo, oltre a confermare il valore cristologico e teologico del regno, opera il collegamento anche con il suo valore pneumatologico.

2. *Vedere il regno*

L'abbondanza dei vocaboli di visione è caratteristico del quarto vangelo; Giovanni usa vari verbi che indicano differenti modi e gradi di vedere: semplice percezione, visuale fisica, osservazione attenta e scrutatrice, contemplazione, penetrazione profonda dell'oggetto, infine comunione con la realtà veduta e contemplata[12]. L'oggetto, il termine principale del «vedere» è la persona di Gesù da parte degli uomini; in lui è termine di visione anche Dio Padre e così pure lo Spirito.

Vedere Gesù in alcuni testi è soltanto una azione naturale, un esercizio degli occhi del corpo[13]; vedere Gesù tuttavia non rimane allo stadio corporeo, non è un puro vedere fisico, esso tende a superare l'esteriorità e l'apparenza, la superficie fenomenica, e procede in profondità, alla realtà presente in lui, è esercizio di fede; Gesù dice: «Questa è la volontà del Padre mio che chiunque vede (θεωρῶν) il Figlio e crede in lui abbia la vita eterna e io lo risusciterò» (6,40); vedere e credere stanno in coordinazione, riferiti alla vita eterna e alla risurrezione; vedere il Figlio è apprendere che in lui Dio offre agli uomini la salvezza, che devono accogliere con la fede in Gesù. Di fronte allo scandalo di molti dei suoi discepoli per il discorso sul pane disceso dal cielo, Gesù risponde con una nuova rivelazione provocante che annuncia il momento della

---

[12] Cf D. MOLLAT, *Jean l'évangéliste (saint)*, DS, VIII, 217. C. TRAETS, *Voir Jésus et le Père en lui selon l'évangile de Saint Jean*, Roma 1967, 7-9.

[13] I contemporanei di Gesù, che sono vissuti accanto a lui, le folle, i discepoli hanno visto l'uomo Gesù in modo naturale. I concittadini della donna samaritana sono invitati da lei: «Venite a vedere (ἴδετε) un uomo che mi ha detto tutto quello che ho fatto» (4,29); il precursore «vede (βλέπει) Gesù che viene» (1,29.34); i discepoli dalla loro barca «vedono (θεωροῦσιν) Gesù che cammina sul mare» (6,19); le folle vedono i segni che egli compie (2,23; 6,2), vedono le opere che egli fa (7,3; 15,24).

salita al cielo: «E se vedeste (θεωρῆτε) il Figlio dell'uomo salire là dove era prima?» (6,62). Il tema, l'oggetto del vedere è il Figlio dell'uomo che sale dove era prima; Gesù ha parlato per la prima volta di ascesa al cielo nel colloquio con Nicodemo (3,13)[14]. Il vedere esprime di più che il fatto di trovarsi di fronte all'evento di Gesù ascendente al cielo; è una visione che viene dalla fede e tende alla fede.

Nei discorsi di addio Gesù annuncia un non vedere e un vedere a suo riguardo; nella prima enunciazione sono contrapposti il mondo e i discepoli: «Ancora poco e il mondo non mi vedrà più; voi invece mi vedrete perché io vivo e voi vivrete» (14,19). Nella seconda vengono distinti i tempi: «Ancora un poco e non mi vedrete; un po' ancora e mi vedrete» (16,16.17.19). Il non vedere annunzia un periodo di assenza, che inizia con la morte di Gesù; il vedere di nuovo riguarda un tempo in cui lo si incontrerà vivente. Per il mondo il non vedere Gesù sarà definitivo poiché per il mondo il non vedere è il segno e la conseguenza della sua incredulità, del suo rifiuto nei riguardi di Gesù; per i discepoli il non vedere Gesù è il segno del suo ritorno al Padre: «Vado al Padre e non mi vedrete più» (16,10), e costituisce per loro la prova della fede. Quando lo vedranno vivente i discepoli comprenderanno che la sua vita è la stessa vita del Padre, alla quale anch'essi sono chiamati a partecipare[15].

Il nuovo esercizio del vedere Gesù è costituito dalle esperienze pasquali. Maria Maddalena vede (θεωρεῖ) Gesù che stava in piedi, ma non sa che è lui (20,14); dopo che lo ha ricono-

---

[14] Il verbo salire (ἀναβαίνω) indica il cammino ascensionale glorificante di Gesù, il mistero della esaltazione glorificazione in corrispodenza correlativa con il verbo discendere (καταβαίνω) che indica la sua venuta nel mondo. Discesa dal cielo e ascesa al cielo esprimono il ciclo completo di Gesù; qui si parla della ascesa; essa richiama per corrispondenza il discorso immediatamente precedente della discesa del pane vivo e di Gesù dal cielo (6,33.41.50-51.38.42). Il Signore parlerà della sua ascesa anche dopo la risurrezione: «Non sono ancora salito al Padre; io salgo al Padre mio e Padre vostro, Dio mio e Dio vostro» (20,17). Gesù parla per la prima volta di ascesa al cielo nel colloquio con Nicodemo (3,13); con la Maddalena parla di ascesa al Padre; in 6,62 di ascesa dove era prima. Il punto di arrivo della ascesa di Gesù è il luogo dove era prima, il cielo, Dio Padre.

[15] Il futuro vedere dei discepoli non sarà limitato alla esperienza delle apparizioni, ma si prolungherà al di là di esse, nella consapevolezza della unità tra il Figlio e il Padre della quale verranno resi partecipi, e continuerà nel tempo della chiesa; cf C. TRAETS, *Voir Jésus et le Père en lui selon l'évangile de Saint Jean*, o. c., 175-176.

sciuto ne dà l'annuncio: «ho visto (ἑώρακα) il Signore (20,18); alla sua venuta in mezzo ai discepoli, essi gioirono «vedendo (ἰδόντες) il Signore» (20,20) e ne danno l'annuncio a Tommaso: «Abbiamo visto (ἑωράκαμεν) il Signore» (20,25). Il culmine dell'uso del verbo vedere in rapporto alla fede si ha per Tommaso; ricevuto l'annuncio egli dice: «Se non vedo (ἴδω) nelle sue mani il segno dei chiodi e non metto le mani nel suo costato, non crederò» (20,25); Gesù, venuto otto giorno dopo, gli dice: «Metti qui il tuo dito e vedi (ἴδε) le mie mani, stendi la tua mano e mettila nel mio costato, e non essere incredulo ma credente» (20,27). Allora viene pronunciata la più alta professione di fede in Gesù: «Signore mio e mio Dio» (20,28). La visione di Gesù in Tommaso suscita la professione della sua fede in lui Signore e Dio, presente e vivente; l'apostolo riconosce e proclama l'identità di Gesù. Il vedere implica l'opzione di fede. La frase con cui Gesù risponde alla professione di fede dell'apostolo che prima non aveva creduto: «Perché mi hai veduto hai creduto, beati quelli che pur non avendo visto crederanno» (20,29) non è però una critica dei segni, delle apparizioni del Risorto, né un avvertimento a intendere i racconti finali del vangelo non come fatti reali ma come simboli destinati a orientare la fede genuina priva di appoggi sensibili[16].

---

[16] Cf R. BULTMANN, *Das Evangelium des Johannes*, 539-540. Il rimprovero di Gesù a Tommaso «Non essere più incredulo ma credente» (20,27) non riguarda il fatto che la fede dell'apostolo proviene dalla percezione sensibile della venuta del risorto, ma il fatto che aveva differito l'atto di fede determinandone egli stesso le condizioni e rifiutando la testimonianza degli altri che avevano già avuto l'esperienza della venuta di Gesù e avevano già veduto i segni. L'esperienza sensibile visuale dei discepoli della persona di Gesù risuscitato nel racconto evangelico delle apparizioni pasquali è presentata come il fondamento per la loro fede nella risurrezione; tale fede, a sua volta, diviene il fondamento per quella dei futuri credenti, i quali si affideranno alla testimonianza di coloro che hanno veduto. Lungi dall'essere svalutate, le venute pasquali del Risorto e l'esperienza sensibile che ne hanno i discepoli, sono presentate come normative per la fede. Quanto ai credenti futuri possiamo dire: come i discepoli, che erano presenti alla venuta del Signore e l'hanno percepita in modo sensibile visivamente, non sono stati dispensati dall'atto di fede che segue la visione, così coloro che crederanno sulla base dei primi testimoni, senza averne l'esperienza, non saranno privati di un loro incontro personale, di un loro contatto esistenziale con la venuta di Gesù risorto, di una loro penetrante intelligenza del suo mistero. Coloro che hanno visto il Signore risuscitato e coloro che credono senza avere veduto saranno in una situazione tale per cui i secondi non saranno meno favoriti dei primi; il contatto vivente con il Signore glorioso non sarà loro rifiutato; tale contatto con la venuta di Gesù accadrà nella nella liturgia, che caratterizza il racconto della venuta pasquale di Gesù.

Consideriamo infine i detti: «Gesù allora gridò con grande voce: chi crede in me non crede in me ma in colui che mi ha mandato; chi vede (θεωρῶν) me vede (θεωρεῖ) colui che mi ha mandato» (12,44-45). «Chi ha visto me ha visto il Padre (ὁ ἑωρακὼς ἐμὲ ἑώρακεν τὸν πατέρα)» (14,9). L'affermazione introdotta dal verbo gridare (κράζω) che è usato per esprimere una rivelazione solenne, contiene un parallelismo tra il verbo credere e il verbo vedere; viene così accentuata la connessione tra fede e visione; il vedere e il credere qui ha come punto di arrivo il Padre; questo vedere attinge il Padre approfondendo la fede[17]. Ci troviamo di fronte alla trasparenza di Gesù nel suo mistero di Figlio in unità con il Padre, colto nella visione di fede[18].

La possibilità di vedere il Padre in Gesù ha il suo fondamento nella derivazione e missione di Gesù dal Padre; per il mistero della unione e unità tra Gesù e il Padre è prima di tutto Gesù che vede il Padre, e vedendolo lo rivela: «Solo colui che viene da Dio ha visto il Padre» (6,46). «Dio non l'ha mai visto nessuno: l'Unigenito Figlio che è nel seno del Padre, lui lo ha rivelato» (1,18). L'uomo è radicalmente incapace di vedere Dio in se stesso, il Figlio Gesù che vede il Padre in se stesso con visione immediata diretta, che è unito a lui nella stessa vita divina, può condurre anche gli uomini alla visione del Padre nella propria persona, nella propria luce, che è la trasparenza della luce di Dio[19].

Da Gesù al Padre allo Spirito.

---

[17] «Poiché la fede non si arresta su Gesù o piuttosto, positivamente, poiché la fede riconosce Gesù come mandato, l'uomo percepisce il Padre nel Figlio (...); la percezione visuale perviene, attraverso la fede, a un possesso più totale del suo oggetto» (C. TRAETS, *Voir Jésus et le Père en lui selon l'évangile de Saint Jean*, o. c., 203).

[18] «L'uomo vede il Padre guardando Gesù, la sua persona e la sua azione, oggetto di percezione visuale; lo percepisce come mandato dal Padre che è presente nel Figlio nell'esecuzione della sua missione, ultimo affinamento della percezione che si trasforma in visione di fede (...). Percependo Gesù come Figlio unito al Padre, si vede in lui il Padre. Certo non si percepisce il Padre come un secondo oggetto, dotato di contorni propri, situato dietro Gesù. Non si tratta di due atti successivi di vedere, né di due oggetti visivi consecutivi, ma di una sola e unica percezione che approfondendosi attinge Gesù nel suo mistero totale. Ma questo vedere è un vedere reale, se è vero che vedere, nell'uomo, significa più che una reazione fisica della retina oculare, perché questo atto è essenzialmente, in questo vedere, interpretazione» (*Ibid*, 204).

[19] Cf 3,11.32; 5,37; 6,46; 8,38; 1 Gv 3,6; 4,20.

Anche lo Spirito è termine di visione; ciò avviene per esperienza del Precursore nell'incontro con Gesù: «Giovanni rese testimonianza dicendo: ho visto (τεθέαμαι) lo Spirito discendere come una colomba dal cielo e rimanere su di lui; e io non lo conoscevo, ma colui che mi ha mandato a battezzare con acqua mi aveva detto: Colui sul quale vedrai (ἴδῃς) lo Spirito scendere e rimanere su di lui, questi è il battezzatore in Spirito Santo; e io ho visto (ἑώρακα) e ho reso testimonianza che questi è il Figlio di Dio» (1,32-34). Oggetto dei verbi che indicano vedere è qui il discendere dello Spirito dal cielo in forma di colomba e il suo rimanere su Gesù; così al Precursore è concessa la rivelazione della unione intima tra lo Spirito e Gesù, visione che entra a costituire e manifestare, nella terstimonianza del Battista, i suoi titoli: battezzatore in Spirito Santo e Figlio di Dio[20].

Nella prima promessa sul Paralito Gesù afferma che il mondo non può ricevere lo Spirito «perché non lo vede e non lo conosce»; in contrapposizione dice dei discepoli: «voi lo conoscete» (14,17). Il mondo non vede lo Spirito della verità. Questo «non vedere», coordinato al «non conoscere», non è dovuto alla natura invisibile dello Spirito, che è la stessa del Padre, ma è dovuta alla scelta negativa operata dal mondo nei confronti di Gesù. Come tale scelta si prolunga nei confronti di Dio Padre, così si prolunga nei confronti dello Spirito; Gesù, il Padre, lo Spirito costituiscono lo stesso unico mistero. Il fatto di non vedere lo Spirito è presentato come motivazione della impossibilità totale da parte del mondo di accoglierlo e di riceverlo[21]. Questa opzione, com-

---

[20] «θεᾶσθαι qui significa un vedere spirituale, ma si riferisce piuttosto alla forma (discendere come colomba) della visione, mentre ἑώρακα si riferisce al suo significato interiore» (E.A. ABBOTT, *Johannine Grammar*, London 1906, n 2572). Cf M.-E. BOISMARD, *Les traditions johanniques concernant le Baptiste*, Revue Biblique 70 (1963) 5-42; B. VAN IERSEL, *Tradition and Redaktion in John 1,9-36*, NT 5 (1962) 245-267.

[21] «Il vedere giovanneo stabilisce un legame essenziale e dinamico tra la percezione visuale e la visione di fede mediante la quale si attinge il mistero della persona di Gesù. Il vedere si dirige come percezione visiva reale su una persona e su avvenimenti, sulla persona di Gesù impegnata negli avvenimenti della sua esistenza terrena. Questa persona e questi avvenimenti sono rivelatori del mistero di Gesù; egli è il Figlio unito al Padre (...). Lo sguardo dell'uomo che si posa sulla persona di Gesù e attinge in lui il Figlio, percepisce il Padre non come una immagine visiva sovrapposta ma come colui che dà al Figlio la sua dimensione totale (...). Il vedere è

piuta per la visione del Figlio, si estende al Padre e allo Spirito. Il mondo, che si è deliberatamente rifiutato allo sguardo di fede davanti a Gesù, si rifiuta deliberatamente alla fede nello Spirito; non lo vede perché si è reso volontariamente cieco. Tale cecità è la causa dell'impossibilità per il mondo di accogliere lo Spirito. Vedere lo Spirito è cogliere nella realtà della persona di Gesù la presenza del terzo autore divino della salvezza, che è disceso in Gesù, rimane in lui (1,32-33), gli è dato senza misura (3,34), e da lui si effonde e comunica a chi guardando con fede il Signore vede e coglie in lui il Padre e il Paraclito. Non vedere lo Spirito costituisce la ragione della impossibilità di accoglierlo non avendo guardato Gesù con fede e avendolo respinto.

Vedere il regno di Dio (a cui sta in parallelismo: entrare nel regno di Dio) significa dunque nel colloquio con Nicodemo essere in relazione a Gesù, credere in lui, accoglierlo, e mediante la fede essere resi partecipi della comunione di vita con lui, e in lui avere relazione con il Padre e con lo Spirito. La relazione con lo Spirito, come fonte di questa comunione di vita è esplicitata da Gesù nella enunciazione sulla nascita da acqua e da Spirito quale condizione necessaria per la partecipazione al regno.

II. LO SPIRITO

1. *La nascita da acqua e da Spirito*

Alla prima risposta di Gesù segue l'incomprensione di Nicodemo; egli comprende le parole del Signore su un piano

---

più che una semplice registrazione di immagini visuali, è essenzialmente una interpretazione (...). L'approfondimento della percezione visuale è opera divina che richiede la fede dell'uomo (...). In ragione della funzione ecclesiale la fede si realizza ora nell'uomo per la testimonianza della chiesa (...). Questo vedere va situato nel quadro del messaggio essenziale del vangelo giovanneo: Dio si rivela definitivamente ed esclusivamente nel suo Figlio Gesù offrendo in quanto Padre la salvezza al mondo e ponendo l'uomo di fronte a una opzione che, positiva o negativa, decide della sua sorte finale. Attraverso il suo vedere l'uomo prende coscienza dell'opzione di fronte a cui è posto. Optando per l'accoglienza egli percepisce il Padre in Gesù, mentre il rifiuto lo conduce all'accecamento. Così si opera la grande separazione tra coloro che sono salvati e coloro che si condannano» (C. TRAETS, *Voir Jésus et le Père en lui selon l'évangile de Saint Jean, o. c.*, 244-246).

naturale, come una ripetizione della nascita corporea e pone una nuova domanda. Gesù nel rispondere spiega dichiarando la nascita dall'alto come nascita da acqua e Spirito e svolgendo il tema dello Spirito in rapporto alla generazione: ἐὰν μή τις γεννηθῇ ἐξ ὕδατος καὶ πνεύματος, οὐ δύναται εἰσελθεῖν εἰς τὴν βασιλείαν τοῦ θεοῦ (3,5)[22].

Troviamo anzitutto il verbo γεννάω. In generale esso significa generare, procreare. È detto del Padre per la concezione, e della madre sia per la concezione che per il parto. Nel quarto vangelo il verbo oltre a ricorrere otto volte nella nostra pericope, si trova nel prologo: «A quanti però l'hanno accolto ha dato il potere di diventare figli di Dio, a quelli che credono nel suo nome, i quali non da sangue né da volere di carne né da volere di uomo, ma da Dio sono stati generati» (1,12-13). Il termine designa la generazione da Dio di coloro che hanno creduto nel Verbo di Dio; la generazione e rispettivamente la filiazione divina è dono di Dio concesso gratuitamente e accolto credendo in Gesù. In seguito il termine ricorre per designare la generazione naturale dell'uomo (cf 9,2.19.20.32.34; 16,21). Nel dialogo con Pilato Gesù dice di sé: ἐγὼ εἰς τοῦτο γεγέννημαι καὶ εἰς τοῦτο ἐλήλυθα εἰς τὸν κόσμον, ἵνα μαρτυρήσω τῇ ἀληθείᾳ (18,37) per indicare il mistero della sua venuta nel mondo, il mistero cioè dell'incarnazione e della propria missione salvifica come regalità consistente nella testimonianza della verità. Nella prima lettera giovannea leggiamo: «Chiunque crede che Gesù è il Cristo è generato da Dio» (1 Gv 5,1). «Tutto ciò che è generato da Dio vince il mondo; e questa è la vittoria che ha vinto il mondo: la nostra fede. Chi è che vince il mondo se non chi crede che Gesù è il Figlio di Dio? « (1 Gv 5,4-5).

In questi passi la nascita del cristiano da Dio è connessa con la fede. Questa unione intima tra generazione da Dio e fede viene dal fatto che il credere mette il credente in comu-

---

[22] La presenza nel testo delle parole: ὕδατος καὶ dal punto di vista critico è sicura poiché tutti i testimoni sono concordi nel riportare questa lezione; la discussione riguarda il problema se esse sono contenute nella tradizione primitiva oppure sono state aggiunte in seguito sotto l'influsso della pratica sacramentale del battesimo nella chiesa. Dal punto di vista della critica letteraria l'espressione viene confermata; cf G. GAETA, *Il dialogo con Nicodemo*, o. c., 66. 110-111 nota 19; F.M. BRAUN, *Jean le théologien, Sa Théologie. Le Christ notre Seigneur*, Paris 1972, 139-141.

nione con Cristo, nella partecipazione alla sua filiazione divina, nel possesso della vita eterna di Dio. Con il tema della nascita nella generazione da Dio per i credenti, Giovanni porta a compimento il processo di rivelazione dell'Antico Testamento sulla paternità di Dio e sulla filiazione da Dio che riguardava la comunità del popolo eletto e i suoi membri.

Nel discorso con Nicodemo la generazione di cui parla Gesù avviene da acqua e da Spirito. La congiunzione di acqua e Spirito non è nuova; si trova nell'antico Testamento e nella letteratura giudaica.

Il rinnovamento del popolo eletto viene così annunciato: «Dice il Signore: Io farò scorrere acqua sul suolo assetato, torrenti sul terreno arido. Spanderò il mio spirito sulla tua discendenza, la mia benedizione sui tuoi posteri; cresceranno come erba in mezzo all'acqua, come salici lungo acque correnti» (Is 44,2-4). È la profezia della fine della schiavitù in Babilonia. L'effusione dello Spirito su tutto il popolo appare come una novità; nella tradizione israelitica il dono dello Spirito era elargito ai capi, non a tutta la comunità. Effetto di tale dono è il ritorno al culto autentico del vero Dio che si esprime come appartenenza a lui. Ezechiele tocca il vertice del suo messaggio nell'annuncio della nuova alleanza mediante il dono dello Spirito: «Vi aspergerò con acqua pura e sarete purificati; io vi purificherò da tutte le vostre sozzure e da tutti i vostri idoli. Vi darò un cuore nuovo, metterò dentro di voi uno spirito nuovo, toglierò da voi il cuore di pietra e vi darò un cuore di carne. Porrò il mio Spirito dentro di voi e vi farò vivere secondo i miei statuti e vi farò osservare e mettere in pratica le mie leggi. Abiterete nella terra che io diedi ai vostri padri. Voi sarete il mio popolo e io sarò il vostro Dio» (Ez 36,24-28)[23]. Spirito e acqua sono congiunti, l'acqua per indicare la purificazione, lo Spirito per indicare il principio della vita nuova interiore[24].

---

[23] Il testo ha valore cultuale, cf G. BETTENZOLI, *Geist der Heiligkeit, Traditionsgeschichtliche Untersuchung des qds-Begriffs im Buch Ezechiel*, Firenze 1979, 193-194.

[24] Cf P. VAN IMSCHOOT, *L'esprit de Jahvé et l'alliance nouvelle*, Ephemerides Theologicae Lovanienses 13 (1936) 219. Altri testi profetici che annunciano il dono dello Spirito usano il verbo «effondere» o «versare» tradotto nella lingua greca dei Settanta con ἐκχέω: «Non nasconderò più loro il mio volto perché effonderò il mio Spirito sulla casa di Israele» (Ez 39,29). «Io effonderò il mio Spirito sopra ogni uo-

Il testo evangelico nella congiunzione di acqua e Spirito è chiaramente battesimale. L'insieme di acqua e Spirito nella vita della chiesa primitiva designa l'atto sacramentale del battesimo. San Paolo aveva spiegato il senso di questo atto vitale come una misteriosa immersione nello Spirito: «Noi tutti siamo stati battezzati in un solo Spirito per formare un solo corpo, Giudei e Greci, schiavi e liberi, e tutti ci siamo abbeverati a un solo Spirito» (1 Cor 12,13). Il credente immerso nell'acqua riceve il dono dello Spirito come principio di vita nuova: «Dio ci ha salvati (...) mediante un lavacro di rigenerazione e di rinnovamento nello Spirito Santo effuso da lui su di noi abbondantemente per mezzo di Gesù Cristo» (Tt 3,5-6). Il quarto vangelo nel presente testo evoca questa dottrina e questa prassi corrente nella chiesa. Nel sacramento del battesimo chi agisce operando la rigenerazione è lo Spirito; l'acqua costituisce il segno; essa è paragonabile al seno materno di cui lo Spirito è il principio di fecondità; si percepisce l'evocazione primordiale: «Il pnema aleggiava sulle acque» (Gn 1,2) con significato di atto creatore.

La nascita, la generazione da acqua e Spirito di Gv 3,5 non è la rinnovazione del processo fisico corporale, non è rientrare nel seno della madre terrena come capisce Nicodemo; essa è di natura diversa superiore, è opera dello Spirito di Dio, mediante una azione sacramentale. La nuova vita non viene data per virtù dell'acqua, ma per la forza dello Spirito che agisce attraverso l'acqua. L'espressione «nascere dall'acqua e dallo Spirito» indica un nuovo essere escatologico del credente, nel quale appare la presenza e l'azione dello Spirito nel sacramento primo e fondamentale dell'esistenza cristiana[25].

---

mo (...); anche sopra gli schiavi e le schiave in quei giorni effonderò il mio Spirito» (Gl 3,1-2). «Effonderò sopra la casa di Davide e sopra gli abitanti di Gerusalemme uno Spirito di grazia e di consolazione» (Zc 12,10). Questo verbo è usato nel nuovo Testamento per indicare il dono dello Spirito; At 2,17-18 cita il testo ora riferito di Gioele; nel discorso di Pentecoste Pietro proclama: «Gesù innalzato alla destra di Dio, dopo avere ricevuto dal Padre lo Spirito Santo che egli aveva promesso, lo ha effuso» (At 2,33). Il verbo rappresenta la donazione dello Spirito con l'immagine del versare l'acqua. Cf J. BEHM, ἐκχέω, Grande Lessico del Nuovo Testamento III, 377-378.

[25] Cf H. KLOS, *Die Sakramente im Johannesevangelium. Vorkommen und Bedeutung von Taufe, Eucharistie und Busse im vierten Evangelium*, Stuttgart 1970, 69-74.

2. La carne e lo Spirito

Il discorso di Gesù a Nicodemo continua: τὸ γεγεννημένον ἐκ τῆς σαρκὸς σάρξ ἐστιν, καὶ τὸ γεγεννημένον ἐκ τοῦ πνεύματος πνεῦμά ἐστιν (3,6). Troviamo qui una espressione caratteristica del dualismo che ha il suo terreno vitale non nello gnosticismo e nella cultura ellenistica, ma nella Bibbia. La parola «carne» designa l'esistenza terrena e naturale dell'uomo in quanto transitoria, corruttibile, vana e destinata alla morte, incapace di procurare da sé la salvezza[26].

Mediante la generazione naturale il vivente che nasce riceve la natura di chi lo genera; perciò una generazione fisica e terrena dà origine all'uomo terreno, denominato «carne». La generazione da Dio invece, per virtù dello Spirito comunica una esistenza della sua stessa qualità, una esistenza divina nel suo principio, non sottomessa alla caducità e alla corruzione, non soggetta all'ignoranza e alla incapacità di comprendere le cose di Dio. Questa vita data in dono viene denominata «spirito» in contrapposizione a «carne». Dallo Spirito di Dio viene generato e nasce l'uomo spirituale.

L'evento della nascita dallo Spirito resta misterioso e incomprensibile. Gesù ricorre al paragone della realtà naturale del vento per poi ritornare allo Spirito: τὸ πνεῦμα ὅπου θέλει πνεῖ καὶ τὴν φωνὴν αὐτοῦ ἀκούεις, οὐκ οἶδας πόθεν ἔρχεται καὶ ποῦ ὑπάγει. οὕτως ἐστὶν πᾶς ὁ γεγεννημένος ἐκ τοῦ πνεύματος (3,8). Il testo greco gioca sul fatto che il vento e lo Spirito vengono indicati con lo stesso vocabolo; all'inizio della frase «pneuma» significa il vento, al termine significa lo Spirito[27]; con il suo aspetto misterioso il vento si presta a questo paragone; il mistero del vento consiste nel fatto che non se ne conosce l'origine e la destinazione, di dove viene e dove va, la sua corsa non sembra regolata da

---

[26] «σάρξ è la sfera terrena perfettamente idonea a valutare cose terrene ma inadeguata a giudicare chi viene da un'altra sfera (...). È la sfera umano terrena che non ha alcuna conoscenza di Dio e quindi non ne può dare comunicazione» (E. Schweizer, σάρξ, Grande Lessico del Nuovo Testamento XI, 1365).

[27] «Ludit Christus analogice in voce spiritus: prius enim per spiritum accipit ventum, deinde accipit ipsum Spiritum Sanctum, quia ventus index et symbolum est Spiritus Sancti, ut patet Actorum 2,1 ubi Spiritus Sanctus per speciem venti validi descendit in apostolos» (Cornelii A Lapide, *Commentarius in S. Joannis evangelium*, secunda editio veneta, Typis Hieronymi Albritii, Venetiis 1717 p. 217).

alcuna legge. Del vento però si esperimentano gli effetti e se ne sente la voce molteplice di mormorio o di tempesta, e perciò nessuno mette in dubbio l'esistenza del vento[28]. Ciò che vale del vento sul piano naturale serve in questo paragone a descrivere la nascita dallo Spirito e il suo frutto. In chi è nato dallo Spirito è presente, agisce e vibra una forza che sfugge alla comprensione naturale e quindi alle previsioni umane e al potere di controllo dell'uomo e si esercita con indescrivibile libertà, con sconcertante autonomia ed energia: «L'uomo che lo Spirito ha generato ad una vita nuova è al pari del vento, libero di muoversi a suo piacimento»[29].

Anche lo Spirito, come il vento, può essere conosciuto ed esperimentato nei suoi effetti. L'evangelista scriveva questi testi mentre la comunità primitiva viveva una intensa animazione dello Spirito; l'aspetto carismatico qualificava e penetrava profondamente la vita dei credenti. Di questi animati dallo Spirito si può dire: «Vi sono tali uomini, ma il fatto che vi siano non è una possibilità umana. La loro esistenza è un enigma per l'uomo carnale, proprio come la persona stessa del Rivelatore, la cui origine e la cui direzione rimane nascosta agli occhi del mondo»[30].

Notiamo che dello pneuma vengono fatte nel nostro testo affermazioni simili a quelle che troviamo per Gesù; i temi della provenienza «di dove viene (πόθεν ἔρχεται)» e della destinazione «dove va (ποῦ ὑπάγει)» sono fondamentali nella cristologia giovannea[31]. In questo uso delle stesse espressioni per Gesù e per lo pneuma vediamo confermato l'intimo legame tra Cristo e lo Spirito, e quindi tra la cristologia e la pneumatologia; il tema della «voce» poi, nel quarto vangelo, si riferisce a tutti tre gli autori divini della salvezza: a Gesù[32],

---

[28] Un'affermazione simile si legge nell'antico Testamento: «Come ignori per quale via lo spirito entra nelle ossa dentro il seno di una donna incinta, così ignori l'opera di Dio che fa tutto» (Si 11,5). Si tratta in questo detto del mistero della vita nel suo processo naturale come termine di paragone per il mistero dell'agire di Dio.

[29] G. GAETA, *Dialogo con Nicodemo*, o.c., 59.

[30] R. BULTMANN, *Das Evangelium des Johannes*, Göttingen 1953, 101-102.

[31] «So di dove vengo e dove vado; voi invece non sapete di dove vengo e dove vado» (8,14); cf 7,27-28; 9,29-30; 19,9; sul tema della destinazione cf 13,36; 14,5; 16,5. Si tratta di espressioni che indicano in modo sintetico il mistero della persona di Gesù.

[32] Il termine «voce» viene quasi sempre usato per la voce di Gesù: voce dello sposo (3,29); voce di colui che chiama alla vita (5,25.28; 11,43), voce del buon pastore (10,3.4.5.16.27); voce della verità (18,37).

al Padre[33] e nel nostro testo al vento come immagine dello Spirito. Si ripropone così l'unità nel mistero della salvezza. Alla rivelazione sul vedere il regno, essere generati da acqua e da Spirito, ascoltare la voce dello Spirito soggiace una profonda connessione tra il regno, Dio Padre, il Figlio Gesù Cristo, lo Spirito .

III. LA TESTIMONIANZA DI GESÙ

L'incomprensione da parte di Nicodemo e la sua domanda: «Come può accadere questo?» (3,9) dà occasione a un discorso che si presenta come testimonianza solenne di fronte al mondo a favore della dignità trascendente di Gesù e del valore salvifico della sua opera; la testimonianza, positiva in sé, viene resa con tono polemico contro coloro che non credono. Il discorso è una sintesi del cherugma giovanneo che diviene testimonianza della chiesa: «Noi parliamo di quello che sappiamo e testimoniamo quello che abbiamo veduto, ma voi non accogliete la nostra testimonianza» (3,11). Nel passaggio dall'«Io» del discorso precedente al «noi» di quello attuale avviene il fondersi della testimonianza di Gesù con quella dei discepoli; l'«Io» di Gesù è presente nel «noi» della comunità come nel suo prolungamento nel tempo dello Spirito. Insieme con la cristologia e la pneumatologia si trova in questo brano una ecclesiologia, che si esprime come esperienza vissuta relativa a Gesù e animata dallo Spirito quale fonte della rinascita dall'alto.

Nella serie di affermazioni su Gesù che seguono si delineano i cenni di tre linee cristologiche sulla base di tre titoli e dei temi che essi radunano attorno a sé. Non entriamo nell'esegesi del testo, indichiamo soltanto l'emergere di queste tre rappresentazioni di Gesù: Figlio dell'uomo, Figlio di Dio, Luce. Nella contemplazione e rivelazione del Signore il testo trascorre quasi inavvertitamente dall'uno all'altro titolo; si hanno come tre cerchi concentrici attraverso i quali la rivelazione avanza in un procedimento a spirale con sintesi sempre

---

[33] «Voi non avete mai udito la sua voce né avete visto il suo volto» (5,37); «Padre glorifica il tuo nome. Venne una voce dal cielo: l'ho glorificato e di nuovo lo glorificherò (...) Gesù disse: questa voce non è venuta per me ma per voi» (12,28.30).

più condensata; vi è comunicazione di proprietà tra il Figlio dell'uomo e il Figlio di Dio e la Luce; tale ricchezza, che rende affascinante la manifestazione della persona di Gesù, con grande gusto per il contemplativo, rende difficile all'interprete delimitare con precisione i confini dei tre titoli.

1. *Il Figlio dell'uomo*

La testimonianza sul Figlio dell'uomo si svolge in due momenti riguardanti il primo la sua ascesa discesa, il secondo la sua esaltazione.

«Nessuno è mai salito al cielo fuorché il Figlio dell'uomo che è disceso dal cielo» (3,13). Questo movimento, come abbiamo già accennato, comprende tutto l'itinerario dalla terra al cielo, cioè tutta la vicenda della passione morte risurrezione e ascensione; il mistero di ascesa suppone quello della discesa dal cielo alla terra che ha preceduto l'ascesa. La sequenza ascesa-discesa è caratteristica della teologia del Figlio dell'uomo nel quarto vangelo[34]. Egli viene presentato come l'essere di origine divina che al cielo ritorna dopo esserne disceso, portatore della rivelazione perfetta delle cose celesti, cioè di Dio Padre: è da lui che egli proviene ed è a lui che ritorna: «Sono uscito dal Padre e sono venuto nel mondo, ora lascio di nuovo il mondo e vado al Padre» (16,28). Il Figlio dell'uomo è egli stesso mistero celeste. Questo carattere penetra tutta l'attività salvifica di Gesù rendendola trascendente, divina. Spettatrice di questo mistero nella storia è la chiesa, sono i discepoli che ne diventano i testimoni davanti al mondo. «Testimoniamo quello che abbiamo veduto» (3,11) L'unione di ascesa-discesa è frutto dell'intelligenza della fede

---

[34] «Lo schema cristologico giovanneo di discesa-ascesa (innalzamento alla croce e alla gloria) appare in questi versetti nella forma più perfetta. È lo sviluppo teologico più completo dei detti sinottici sul "Figlio dell'uomo" legati all'escatologia futura (cf Gv 5,27) ed alla predizione della passione sullo sfondo del quarto carme di Is 52,13, dove sono uniti insieme i verbi "innalzare" e "glorificare". Mentre per la discesa dal cielo si può fare ricorso all'apocalittica giudaica e alla discesa dal cielo della Sapienza (Bar 3,29-30) e alla discesa della parola di Dio (Is 55,10-11) per l'ascesa al cielo invece non si trova nessun vero parallelo. Ciò dipende dal fatto che questo secondo elemento dello schema proviene dall'esperienza nuova della risurrezione ascensione» (G. SEGALLA, *Giovanni*, Roma 1976, 179).

che si è servita di questi termini per esprimere e definire l'itinerario di Gesù. Questo stesso mistero riceve una nuova raffigurazione nel momento successivo dell'esaltazione: «Come Mosè innalzò il serpente nel deserto, così bisogna che sia innalzato il Figlio dell'uomo perché chiunque crede in lui abbia la vita eterna» (3,14-15). Il cammino del Figlio dell'uomo contiene il suo innalzamento espresso dal verbo ὑψόω. Nel nuovo Testamento esso indica generalmente il passaggio da uno stato di umiliazione o di bassa condizione a uno stato di glorificazione[35]. Così Gesù dopo la sua morte è stato elevato alla signoria divina, alla destra del Padre[36]. Nel quarto vangelo l'esaltazione di Gesù è già immanente alla sofferenza e alla morte in croce: «Quando avrete innalzato il Figlio dell'uomo allora saprete che Io sono» (8,28). «Io quando sarò innalzato da terra attirerò tutti a me» (12,32). L'evangelista stesso in quest'ultimo testo dà il significato del verbo innalzare aggiungendo: «Questo diceva per indicare di quale morte doveva morire» (12,33). La novità di questa concezione sta nel fatto che la morte di Gesù non è soltanto la condizione necessaria per l'esaltazione, ma è già in se stessa l'inizio dell'esaltazione. Tale è il mistero di Gesù: la morte è trasfigurata come innalzamento; la finalità di tutto è la salvezza, presentata in termini di fede e di vita; chiunque crede in lui ha la vita eterna; il mistero di esaltazione come parte dell'ascesa del Figlio dell'uomo è realtà salvifica.

2. Il Figlio di Dio

Il Figlio dell'uomo in profondità confonde i suoi lineamenti con il Figlio di Dio nel suo duplice rapporto verso il Padre dal quale è donato, e verso gli uomini ai quali si rivolge la sua opera salvifica: «Dio ha tanto amato gli uomini che ha dato il suo Figlio unigenito perché chiunque crede in lui non muoia ma abbia la vita eterna» (3,16). Il Figlio di Dio è per i credenti espressione dell'agape del Padre. Il nome «Figlio», «Figlio di Dio» indica di natura sua la relatività al Padre. Proveniente dall'antico Testamento, in cui era attribuito sia al po-

---

[35] Cf Mt 23,12; Lc 1,52; 14,11.
[36] Cf At 2,33; 5,31; 13,17; Fil 2,9.

polo eletto sia al suo re con significato di eletto da Dio per compiere una missione, questo nome viene applicato a Gesù con un valore nuovo, inaudito, con caratteristiche tali che fanno esplodere l'idea veterotestamentaria, e ne rivelano la realtà in una sfera trascendente. L'aspetto della elezione divina per la filiazione divina di Gesù diviene la sua intimità unica e totale con il Padre; questa intimità si esprime ora con la terminologia del dono e, nella frase successiva, con la terminologia della missione: Dio ha dato, Dio ha mandato il suo Figlio. L'unicità del rapporto tra il Figlio e il Padre è indicato dalla qualifica: «Figlio unigenito». Per comprendere questa relazione intima e misteriosa è necessario entrarvi con la fede: chi crede in lui ha la vita eterna. Così si entra nel regno. La discesa del Figlio dell'uomo si trasforma nella missione del Figlio unigenito di Dio. Compito della sua missione è la salvezza, che viene espressa ancora in termini di fede: «Dio non ha mandato il Figlio nel mondo per giudicare il mondo, ma perché il mondo si salvi per mezzo di lui. Chi crede in lui non è condannato, ma chi non crede è già stato condannato perché non ha creduto nel nome dell'unigenito Figlio di Dio» (3,17-18). Il mondo si autocondanna perché rifiuta di accogliere il Figlio di Dio con fede; il credente invece è salvato[37]. La presentazione di Gesù nei suoi titoli è sempre in ordine alla nostra salvezza. Ora il Figlio unigenito di Dio entra nella descrizione della Luce.

3. *Gesù Luce*

Il terzo aspetto con cui viene presentato Gesù è quello della Luce, mediante termini che riecheggiano i temi del prologo del vangelo, benché nel presente testo non appaia il titolo di Logos. Il concetto che opera la connessione e il passaggio tra il titolo di Figlio di Dio e il tema della luce è quello della crisi, cioè giudizio negativo di condanna: «Il giudizio è questo: la luce è venuta nel mondo, ma gli uomini hanno preferito le tenebre alla luce, perché le loro opere erano malvage. Chiunque infatti fa il male odia la luce e non viene alla luce

---

[37] La duplice attività del Figlio, operare la crisi e dare la vita, qui appena enunciata, troverà il suo svolgimento nel discorso sull'opera comune del Padre e del Figlio (5,19-30).

perché non siano svelate le sue opere. Ma chi opera la verità viene alla luce perché appaia chiaramente che le sue opere sono state fatte in Dio» (3,19-21).

Nell'enunciazione: «la luce è venuta nel mondo», risuona un compendio del prologo, nella figura del Figlio di Dio si intravvede la folgorazione del Verbo-Luce: «In lui era la vita e la vita era la luce degli uomini; la luce splende nelle tenebre e le tenebre non l'hanno accolta» (1,45). Il rifiuto di accoglienza nei confronti della Luce costituisce il giudizio di Dio, la crisi che discerne gli uomini fra di loro, la condanna. Anche questa testimonianza rivelante che riporta ai vertici del prologo la presenza e l'attività di Gesù Luce è efficacemente salvifica; in modo positivo per coloro che accolgono la Luce credendo e ne compiono le opere, in modo negativo per coloro che rifiutano la luce e restano nelle tenebre. L'apparizione sulla scena del mondo del Verbo Luce è discriminante[38].

La domanda di Nicodemo: «Come può accadere questo?» (3,9) ha ottenuto risposta nella rivelazione su Gesù. La domanda si riferiva alla nascita dallo Spirito. La risposta anticipa gli svolgimenti successivi del vangelo. L'ascensione e l'esaltazione del Figlio dell'uomo, la missione del Figlio di Dio in ordine alla vita eterna, l'apparizione discriminante della Luce rendono possibile il dono dello Spirito il quale opera la misteriosa generazione.

L'episodio che aveva avuto inizio con l'ingresso in scena di Nicodemo che va da Gesù nella notte, nelle tenebre, si conclude con il giungere dell'uomo alla Luce, che è la persona stessa di Gesù. Al termine Nicodemo è perduto di vista, chi domina in piena luminosità è Gesù rivelato come Figlio dell'uomo asceso al cielo perché disceso dal cielo, come Figlio unigenito di Dio donato e mandato dal Padre per la vita degli uomini che credono in lui, come Luce che illumina e dissipa le tenebre.

Il regno e lo Spirito: vedere il regno, il quale converge fino alla identificazione con Gesù, è vedere Gesù con la visione della fede, e in lui il Padre e lo Spirito Santo; rinascere dal-

---

[38] In questo testo è implicita una cristologia di Gesù Giudice, cf G. GAETA, *Il dialogo con Nicodemo*, o.c., 97.

l'acqua e dallo Spirito è essere divinamente generato con il dono della fede e del battesimo, così da poter entrare nel regno, nella comunione con Gesù, il Padre e lo Spirito. Questa visione e ingresso nel regno fa nascere, come risposta di chi è rinato dall'acqua e dallo Spirito, il canto della gioia e del ringraziamento: «Con gioia rendiamo grazie al Padre che ci ha messi in grado di partecipare alla sorte dei santi nella luce; è lui infatti che ci ha liberati dal potere delle tenebre e ci ha trasferiti nel regno del suo Figlio diletto» (Col 1,12-13).

La Preghiera e il Regno

UGO VANNI

1. INTRODUZIONE

La preghiera più esplicita riferita al regno ci viene attestata nella pericope del «Padre nostro» di Matteo e di Luca.

Anche se le due redazioni differiscono sensibilmente tra di loro[1], la richiesta concernente il regno presenta la stessa formulazione:

ἐλθέτω ἡ βασιλεία σου, «venga il tuo regno» (Mt 6,10; Lc 11,2).

Questa richiesta precisa costituisce il nostro punto di partenza.

L'espressione, però, nella sua concisione lapidaria, suppone che la comunità cristiana primitiva — la quale diede indubbiamente una sua impronta alle due formulazioni, anche se è difficile precisarla[2] — si rendesse conto del valore della

---

[1] La redazione di Matteo (6,9b-13), la più lunga, è quella usata nella liturgia. Un confronto sinottico tra le due mette in risalto i seguenti aspetti: Luca omette alcune espressioni che si trovano in Matteo: in luogo di Πάτερ ἡμῶν ὁ ἐν τοῖς οὐρανοῖς Luca ha soltanto Πάτερ; l'espressione γενηθήτω τὸ θέλημά σου ὡς ἐν οὐρανῷ καὶ ἐπὶ γῆς è omessa completamente da Luca; l'espressione di Matteo riferita al pane δὸς ἡμῖν σήμερον appare variata in Luca: δίδου ἡμῖν τὸ καθ' ἡμέραν; l'espressione καὶ ἄφες ἡμῖν τὰ ὀφειλήματα ἡμῶν, ὡς καὶ ἡμεῖς ἀφήκαμεν τοῖς ὀφειλέταις ἡμῶν di Matteo appare variata in Luca: καὶ ἄφες ἡμῖν τὰς ἁμαρτίας ἡμῶν καὶ γὰρ αὐτοὶ ἀφίομεν παντὶ ὀφείλοντι ἡμῖν; finalmente non troviamo in Luca l'espressione conclusiva di Matteo: ἀλλὰ ῥῦσαι ἡμᾶς ἀπὸ τοῦ πονηροῦ. Questo confronto è significativo: ci dice subito che il "Padre nostro" non è una formula stereotipa, ma semplicemente una griglia di preghiera. Anche la richiesta della venuta del regno si situa in questa griglia e deve essere ripensata mentre viene formulata, come le altre richieste che sono indicate.

[2] La formulazione matteana mostra un colorito più giudaico e appare ambientata in una comunità giudeo-cristiana; la formulazione di Luca potrebbe risentire dell'influsso paolino, specialmente per il fatto che il semplice Πάτερ posto all'ini-

richiesta e che quindi comprendesse il senso sia di regno che di venuta. Occorrerà esplicitare tale senso.

Inoltre, come altri studi hanno documentato[3], il «Padre nostro», «breviarium totius evangelii» come lo qualifica Tertulliano[4], esplica una funzione di sintesi e di sviluppo ulteriore di molti elementi presenti nei vangeli sinottici e nel Nuovo Testamento in generale. Viene da chiedersi: quali sono gli elementi che si sono condensati nella richiesta del regno spingendo le due comunità sinottiche soggiacenti al vangelo di Matteo e di Luca, a formularla o, quanto meno, ad accoglierla? Inoltre: si trova una richiesta della venuta del regno, magari espressa in forma diversa, negli altri scritti del NT? E ancora: oltre alla preghiera di richiesta, esiste qualche altra forma di preghiera riferita al regno e alla sua venuta?

Da tutto questo emerge una trafila di ricerca. Preciseremo anzitutto il concetto di regno e di venuta e esamineremo la preghiera di richiesta così come la troviamo formulata in Matteo e Luca. In un secondo passo studieremo la preghiera riferita al regno nell'ambito delle Lettere Paoline. In un terzo passo ci sposteremo in avanti e studieremo la preghiera riguardante il regno e la venuta nell'Apocalisse. Questo campionario variato di ricerca ci permetterà di delineare, in uno sguardo di insieme, i tratti fondamentali della preghiera del regno come appare nel NT: sarà la conclusione.

---

zio fa ripensare all'invocazione *'abbá* che, tipica di Gesù nella sua vita terrena (cf Mc 14,34), viene poi fatta propria audacemente anche dai cristiani quando prendono coscienza di essere guidati nella loro preghiera dallo Spirito di Gesù (cf Gal 4,6; Rom 8,15 e, per tutta la questione, W. MARCHEL, *Abba, Père! La prière du Christ et des chrétiens.* Roma, 1971²). È proprio l'azione dello Spirito che trasforma la griglia di preghiera in una preghiera viva.

[3] Cfr. U. VANNI, «*Il Padre Nostro* I, II», in «La Civiltà Cattolica», 144 (1993) 345-358; 447-490.

[4] «Neque enim propria tantum orationis officia complexa est, venerationem Dei aut hominis petitionem, sed omnem paene sermonem Domini, omnem commemerationem disciplinae, ut revera in oratione breviarium totius evangelii comprehendatur», Tertulliano, *De oratione*, 1.

2. La richiesta esplicita della venuta del regno e il suo contesto in Matteo e Luca

2.1. «Venga il tuo regno»

Il concetto sia di regno che di venuta abbracciano un arco teologico-biblico esteso. Hanno le loro radici nell'AT ma trovano nel Nuovo Testamento uno sviluppo particolare e caratteristico[5].

L'uno e l'altro sono stati ampiamente oggetto di studio[6]. Il presente numero di *Studia Missionalia* è una spinta in avanti su questa linea anche sotto il profilo strettamente biblico.

Rimandando quindi a questi studi per un approfondimento di dettaglio esponiamo in sintesi ciò che sembra soggiacente sia al «regno» che alla «venuta» nella richiesta del Padre nostro.

Il «regno di Dio», il «tuo regno» come troviamo nella invocazione al Padre, potremmo tentare di definirlo come la risultante spazio-temporale che si determina dall'incrocio di due linee, una discendente da parte di Dio e una ascendente che invece parte dall'uomo. Precisiamo. La linea discendente è costituita da un'iniziativa specifica che, presa da Dio, raggiunge l'uomo con l'offerta dell'alleanza nell'Antico Testamento, con l'offerta di Cristo nel Nuovo. La linea ascendente parte dall'uomo. Se questi, quando è raggiunto dalla iniziativa di Dio, reagisce positivamente con un'accoglienza disponibile, allora le due linee si incontrano e si determina una situazione nuova. La situazione di popolo di Dio, di ἐκκλησία nell'AT. Tale situazione ha un suo sviluppo cronologico che coincide con la storia del popolo di Dio dell'AT; ha an-

---

[5] Ciò si vede anche da uno sguardo statistico alla terminologia. Prendendo come referente i LXX, la "Bibbia Cristiana" usata dagli autori del NT, notiamo che βασιλεία τοῦ θεοῦ vi ricorre solo in Sal 17,3 mentre ricorre 28 volte nel NT; βασιλεία τῶν οὐρανῶν non ricorre mai nei LXX, mentre lo troviamo 24 volte nel NT. Il termine che corrisponde al regno nei LXX è sempre piuttosto ἐκκλησία dove ricorre 114 volte.

[6] Cf R. SCHNACKENBURG, *Gottes Herrschaft und Reich. Eine biblisch-theologische Studie*, Freiburg 1965; H. GIESEN, *Herrschaft Gottes - heute oder morgen? Zur Heilsbotschaft Jesu und der synoptischen Evangelien*, Regensburg 1995 (con ampia bibliografia a pp. 139-160); TORIBIO CUADRATO, *«El viniente». Estudio exegético y teológico del verbo ἔρχεσθαι en la literatura joánica*, Zaragoza 1993.

che un certo sviluppo spaziale: il popolo occupa la terra «proprietà di Dio» che Dio stesso gli assegna.

Nel Nuovo Testamento si ha una maggiorazione, documentata anche dalla frequenza delle ricorrenze specifiche le quali presentano un salto notevole nelle statistiche di frequenza. Si parla sempre di più di «regno di Dio», «regno dei cieli» o semplicemente di «regno», con significato di fondo preciso: è la situazione che si determina quando la linea discendente con cui il Padre offre il dono di Cristo si incontra e si incrocia con quella ascendente dell'accettazione di fede. Nasce una nuova realtà chiamata appunto «regno di Dio», «regno dei cieli» o semplicemente «regno» che si sviluppa destinata a svilupparsi nel tempo e nello spazio. Lo sviluppo nello spazio è a raggio universale e tende a raggiungere «l'estremità della terra» (Atti 1,8)[7]. Lo sviluppo nel tempo terminerà con la seconda venuta di Cristo (cf Atti 1,11) e allora si avrà la conclusione di tutto lo sviluppo del regno.

Il regno dei cieli attuale — che nei vangeli coincide con la realtà della chiesa — diventerà il regno escatologico, quando il dono di Cristo e la sua accoglienza si saranno realizzati con tutte le loro implicazioni. Paolo riserverà alla situazione attuale il nome di ἐκκλησία e chiamerà questa situazione terminale semplicemente «il regno»: sarà il regno che Cristo Figlio offrirà definitivamente proprio al Padre (cf 1 Cor 15,24).

Quando rivolgendosi al Padre si chiede la venuta del suo regno ci si muove in questo complesso contesto di valori. Ci si riferisce alla situazione altamente positiva che è emersa nella storia dall'accoglienza di Cristo offerto dal Padre, situazione in movimento verso una pienezza. La comunità cristiana, soggetto della preghiera, sa di esserne parte. E sa che lo sviluppo in avanti nel tempo come quello in estensione nello spazio si concluderanno con la realizzazione del regno escatologico.

Del regno in divenire viene richiesta la venuta: «venga».

Non si tratta di una prima venuta, di un inizio. La linea discendente quando viene insegnata la preghiera ha già raggiunto l'uomo e si è anche avuta una prima risposta.

---

[7] Tutto il brano 1,6-8 degli Atti è riferito al divenire del regno che sotto la pressione dello Spirito gli apostoli annunceranno con la loro testimonianza.

Il regno, già iniziato, si sta realizzando in crescendo: la preghiera che riguarda la «venuta» si riferisce proprio a questo sviluppo. Parte dal presente e fa pressione sul futuro.

E il futuro sarà, rispetto al soggetto che prega — la comunità cristiana — anzitutto un futuro immediato. La forma grammaticale dell'imperativo aoristo indica una puntualizzazione. Lo potremmo parafrasare con «venga adesso»[8].

Visto che il segmento di regno che si realizza nel presente è come un passaggio obbligato che porta alla realizzazione piena, si ha anche un riferimento al compimento futuro. Ma è quel futuro che è implicito in un presente in divenire, orientato verso una meta precisa.

Ma in che consiste propriamente la venuta che si chiede? Non è la prima e non è neppure direttamente la venuta conclusiva, ma è una venuta intermedia tra le due, che interessa la comunità cristiana nel presente. È un di più di regno che viene chiesto a effetto immediato: una maggiore presenza di Cristo e una maggiore accoglienza nei suoi riguardi, magari stimolata dalla constatazione del «vuoto» dei valori di Cristo nell'ambito della storia in cui si vive.

Infine la richiesta è fatta direttamente al Padre e si riferisce esplicitamente a un regno che è «suo». Non ci si limita a dire «venga il regno» ma si insiste sul fatto che il regno che si vuole è proprio del Padre a cui si chiede. C'è una dimensione filiale nella richiesta e c'è una dimensione paterna-filiale anche nel suo oggetto.

2.2 Il contesto globale della richiesta.

Una richiesta così intensa non si può pensare improvvisata. Ci aspettiamo di trovare, nei due vangeli sinottici che ce la riportano, elementi significativi che portino ad apprezzare il regno, fino a farne un oggetto di preghiera. Troviamo in effetti sia in Matteo che in Luca riferimenti significativi che portano ad un apprezzamento appassionato del regno. Ci limitiamo a qualche esempio indicativo.

---

[8] «Der Imp. Präs. ist durativ oder iterativ, der Imp. Aor. ist momentan», F. BLASS - A. DEBRUNNER - F. REHKOPF, *Grammatik des neutestamentlichen Griechisch*, Göttingen, 1975[14], p. 274.

Cominciamo da Matteo. Il regno dei cieli viene fatto desiderare. Se ne annuncia l'imminenza, «si è avvicinato», ἤγγικεν (Mt 3,2; 4,7; 10,7). È un valore tale da far proclamare beati i poveri (cf Mt 5,3), qualunque sia il senso specifico da attribuire alla categoria[9], e i perseguitati a causa della giustizia (cf Mt 5,10).

L'insegnamento di Gesù e le parabole che lo spiegano contribuiscono a rendere il regno vicino, comprensibile e soprattutto desiderabile: non si può rimanere indifferenti quando si sente che il regno dei cieli «è simile a un tesoro nascosto in un campo: e l'uomo che l'ha trovato lo nascose e per la *gioia che deriva da esso* — ἀπὸ τῆς χαρᾶς αὐτοῦ — va e vende tutti i suoi averi e compra quel campo» (Mt 13,44). È la passione gioiosa per il tesoro, come pure per la perla preziosa (cf Mt 13,45-46), che spinge il mercante ad agire.

Il regno è un dono che deve essere non solo accolto, ma anche cercato e sviluppato ulteriormente con tutto l'impegno: «Cercate come prima cosa — πρῶτον — il regno e la sua giustizia, e tutte queste cose vi saranno aggiunte» (Mt 6,33).

Il regno desiderato e oggetto di una ricerca talmente coinvolgente da avere una priorità su tutto il resto, diventa spontaneamente oggetto di preghiera: il cristiano che ne prende coscienza si sente spinto a chiederlo al Padre celeste.

Anche in Luca — in parallelo con Matteo — il regno è oggetto di apprezzamento, ricercato e desiderato. Appare come un valore così grande da relativizzare qualunque altro valore, anche gli affetti e i legami familiari[10]. Esige il coraggio della irreversibilità[11].

---

[9] L'esegesi oscilla tra un significato prevalentemente sociologico — e allora «il regno dei cieli», la presenza di Gesù accolto farebbe cambiare anche la storia superando la povertà e la miseria — a un senso spirituale, suggerito dall'aggiunta di τῷ πνεύματι, «nello spirito» che Matteo fa rispetto al semplice πτοχοί della fonte Q e di Luca. Allora il significato sarebbe quello di un esproprio personale da praticare in vista dell'accoglienza piena del Cristo offerto dal Padre e che, realizzato, apre le porte alla nuova situazione di regno che così si verifica. Sembra preferibile questa seconda interpretazione che comporta, ma in un secondo tempo, i benifici sociali della prima. Cf per tutta la questione U. Luz, *Das Evangelium nach Matthäus*, I (Mt 1-7), Zürich - Neukirchen-Vluyn, 1985, pp. 204-208.

[10] «Lascia che i morti seppelliscano i loro morti. Tu vai e annuncia il regno di Dio» (Lc 9,60). Questo detto è proprio di Luca.

[11] «Nessuno che ha messo mano all'aratro e si volge indietro è adatto al regno di Dio», Lc 9,62. Anche questo detto è proprio di Luca.

Il regno apprezzato diventa spontaneamente oggetto di preghiera. Ciò che si apprezza si chiede. Troviamo documentato questo passaggio importante nella preghiera che uno dei due crocifissi con lui rivolge a Gesù: «Signore ricordati di me quando verrai nel tuo regno» (Lc 23,42)[12].

Concludendo: la richiesta «venga il tuo regno» ricorrente nel Padre nostro condensa la bramosia appassionata e la stima del regno espressa in tutto il grande contesto dei due sinottici, Matteo e Luca. Ha davvero ragione Tertulliano.

E qui sorge spontantea una domanda: questo fenomeno di un passaggio dall'apprezzamento alla preghiera si verifica anche in altri settori del NT? Una risposta a questa domanda porta a prendere in considerazione anzitutto il «Corpus Paulinum» che in parte precede e in parte è parallelo alla redazione dei Vangeli.

3. La preghiera e il regno nelle Lettere Paoline

Paolo pone sempre la preghiera in primo piano. La pratica personalmente, la pratica nel gruppo dei suoi collaboratori immediati, la pratica con la sua comunità. Prega per loro e richiede, con un'insistenza che sorprende, la loro preghiera per lui e per la realizzazione dei suoi progetti di apostolato. In questa sinfonia di preghiera c'è posto per una preghiera riguardante il regno?

A prima vista si direbbe di no. Il regno come lo intende Paolo è — lo abbiamo osservato — strettamente escatologico. La richiesta della venuta del regno invece, pur puntando verso la conclusione escatologica, comincia espressamente nel presente. Se c'è in Paolo una richiesta o una preghiera riguardante il regno come lo intendiamo sulla scorta del «Padre nostro» dovrà essere espressa — ci aspettiamo — con un'altra terminologia.

Pur riservando il termine βασιλεία alla conclusione escatologica, Paolo non solo non ignora ma mette particolarmente in luce lo sviluppo antecedente dovuto alla presenza attiva

---

[12] Pur con tutti i problemi esegetici che comporta, il brano indica fondamentalmente una richiesta di partecipazione al regno di Dio realizzato da Gesù. Il regno di Dio diventa sulla croce il suo regno (cfr. Gv 19,19-23). Per la problematica della pericope Lc 23,42-43 cf I.H. MARSHALL, *The Gospel of Luke*, Exeter, 1978, pp. 872-873.

di Cristo risorto e la esprime proprio con βασιλεύειν, un termine che appartiene allo stesso campo semantico di βασιλεία, regno. Vediamo più da vicino un testo importante a questo proposito dove troviamo abbinati e coordinati tra di loro i due termini βασιλεύειν e βασιλεία:

> «Quindi la conclusione (τὸ τέλος) quando consegnerà il regno a Dio e Padre (ὅταν παραδιδῷ τὴν βασιλείαν τῷ θεῷ καὶ πατρί), quando avrà disattivato ogni principio e potestà e potenza. È necessario infatti che egli regni (αὐτὸν βασιλεύειν) fino a quando ponga tutti i nemici sotto i suoi piedi» (1 Cor 15,25).

Il regno da consegnare al Padre appare subito come il regno realizzato in tutte le sue implicazioni e proprio del livello escatologico. Prima di raggiungere questo livello e in funzione del raggiungimento troviamo il regnare di Cristo. Si tratta di un impegno attivo da parte di Cristo il quale, attuando il progetto di Dio[13], regna vincendo gli elementi antagonisti. Regna adesso preparando il regno escatologico da offrire al Padre alla fine. È, questo, un fatto di importanza fondamentale per la situazione del cristiano nel presente la quale appare, in ultima analisi, come una preparazione del regno escatologico[14].

Data la dimensione onnicomprensiva sopra rilevata della preghiera in Paolo ci aspettiamo che lo sviluppo attuale della storia della salvezza in vista del regno ne divenga l'oggetto.

Ciò di fatto si verifica tutte le volte che Paolo sollecita preghiere a suo favore. Egli non lo fa per se stesso, per la sua salute malferma come sarebbe naturale e comprensibile, ma proprio in vista dell'attività di apostolato che sta svolgendo

---

[13] Il progetto di Dio viene qui espresso in δεῖ «è necessario» che non indica un determinismo fisico ma la logica infallibile e trascendente con cui Dio organizza il divenire della storia.

[14] La pericope 1 Cor 15,24-25 è stata fatta oggetto di studio e di ricerca. Cf U. HEIL, «Theologische Interpretation von 1 Kor 15,23-28», *ZeitNTWiss* 84 (1993) 27-35; A. LINDEMANN «Parusie Christi und Herrschaft Gottes; zur Exegese von lKor 15,23-28», *WDienst* 19 (1987), 87-107; W. SCHMITHALS, «The Pre-Pauline Tradition in 1 Corinthians 15:20-28», *PerspRelStud* 20 (1993) 357-380. Di particolare interesse per il nostro tema è il contributo di C.E. HILL, «Understanding of Christ's Kingdom in I Corinthians 15:20-28», *NovTest* 30 (1988), 297-320.

(cf Rom 15,30b; 2 Cor 1,11; Col 4,12). E l'apostolato di Paolo è detto da Lui «ministero di riconciliazione» (2 Cor 5,17) non nel senso banale della composizione di una lite, ma in riferimento all'azione che Dio svolge per mezzo di Cristo per trasformare il mondo dallo stato attuale a quello di regno[15].

Il cammino dalla situazione presente a quella futura e definitiva diventa anche esplicitamente oggetto di preghiera di richiesta. Troviamo questo in 1 Tes 5,23. Paolo, rivolgendosi alla giovane comunità di Tessalonica, esprime un coinvolgimento in crescendo: prima prega (ἐρωτῶμεν ὑμᾶς: 5,12. La preghiera si protrae fino a 5,13), poi esorta (παρακαλοῦμεν: 5,14: l'esortazione si sviluppa in ben tredici imperativi fino a 5,22) e finalmente affida tutto a Dio, sfociando in una preghiera:

> «Lui stesso, poi, Iddio della pace vi santifichi completamente (ἁγιάσαι ὑμᾶς ὁλοτελεῖς) e che il vostro spirito integro (ὁλόκληρον) e l'anima e il corpo senza rimprovero (ἀμέμπτως) sia custodito (τηρηθείη) in vista della venuta (ἐν τῇ παρουσίᾳ) del Signore nostro Gesù Cristo»[16].

C'è sullo sfondo l'ultima venuta di Cristo (παρουσίᾳ) che coincide con la realizzazione del regno escatologico. È difficile precisare, a livello della prima Lettera ai Tessalonice-

---

[15] Come indica il movimento letterario di 2 Cor 5,16-21, è in atto uno sviluppo di convergenza di tutte le cose verso Dio in forza della «nuova creazione» (5,17) in rapporto con Cristo. Lo sviluppo parte dalla situazione attuale degli uomini e punta, tramite un rinnovamento continuato, a raggiungere una omogenità perfetta con Dio e con Cristo. Sarà la situazione di regno escatologico.

[16] Il brano è notoriamente discusso per quanto riguarda la concezione antropologica soggiacente: si è parlato di una tricotomia: ψυχή, πνεῦμα, σῶμα (cf J. O'Callaghan, «¿Una nueva interpretación de 1 Tes 5,23?», *Studia Papirologica* 4, 1965, 7-25), di una dicotomia, considerando ψυχη e πνεῦμα come sinonimi (è la interpretazione di S. Agostino: «...constat inter nos sic eam etiam proprie spiritum noncupari, ut non sit universa anima sed aliquid eius», Migne, PL, 44,545). Più probabilmente, sulla linea delle osservazioni sempre valide di A. van Stempvoort («Eine stilistische Lösung einer alten Schwierigkeit in 1 Thess 5,23», *New Testament Studies*, 7, 1960s, 262-265), Paolo mantiene qui la visione globale di tutto l'uomo che normalmente presenta. Abbiamo da una parte lo πνεῦμα dell'uomo al quale appartiene una completezza di funzioni e che quindi viene qualificato come ὁλόκληρον; dall'altra il σῶμα e la ψυχή come espressione della vita concreta di tutta la persona e che deve essere condotta «senza rimprovero», ἀμέμπτως. I due aspetti sono posti in parallelismo sinonimico e sono oggetto insieme dell'azione di mantenimento richiesta a Dio con τηρηθείη.

si, se Paolo aspettava la venuta come imminente o se almeno lo desiderava. Ma, qualunque possa essere il tratto di tempo che Paolo poneva tra il presente, suo e dei Tessalonicesi, e la realizzazione definitiva del regno, si occupa di fatto proprio di questo tratto intermedio e lo fa in chiave di preghiera. Domanda a Dio di santificare con tutte le implicazioni la comunità di Tessalonica e di custodirne — τηρηθείη è un «passivo teologico»[17] — i singoli componenti in tutto ciò che comporta una piena funzionalità della personalità cristiana per tutto l'arco di tempo che li separa dalla venuta e li prepara ad essa. In altri termini, Paolo chiede a Dio di seguire passo passo la comunità cristiana nel suo cammino attuale verso il regno.

Ma è soprattutto nella Lettera agli Efesini e ai Colossesi[18] che emerge la preghiera riferibile alla storia della salvezza in divenire collegata col regno escatologico. Cristo, presente nella chiesa, la spinge verso il compimento escatologico che qui — nelle due Lettere — viene denominato πλήρωμα, «la pienezza realizzata»[19].

A questo proposito troviamo un testo importante nella Lettera agli Efesini. Nel contesto di una comprensione sempre maggiore dell'influsso che il Cristo κύριος, risorto e intronizzato «sopra tutte le cose» (1,22), esercita sugli uomini, l'autore afferma:

«E tutto sottopose sotto i suoi piedi e lo donò come capo sopra tutte le cose alla chiesa, la quale è il suo corpo,

---

[17] Il soggetto attivo del passivo τηρηθείη è manifestamente Dio, come appare anche dal parallelismo sinonimico tra le due parti del versetto. All'espressione «Iddio della pace vi santifichi completamente...» corrisponde «e l'anima e il corpo senza rimprovero sia custodito». L'unica conclusione di tutte e due le parti, quella attiva e quella passiva, che si ha con l'espressione «in vista della venuta» conferma l'unità di fondo del versetto e il parallelismo notate tra le due parti che lo compongono.

[18] Come è noto l'autenticità delle due Lettere è tuttora oggetto di discussione. A prescindere dall'autore reale, possiamo notare che il materiale di fondo è paolino. Si rileva in tutte e due le Lettere una accentuazione della dimensione liturgico-ecclesiale e questo le rende paticolarmente interessanti a proposito di preghiera.

[19] Πλήρωμα che ricorre 12 volte in Paolo implica sempre, per il suffisso -μα un agente attivo che produce un risultato di pienezza. Può essere una pienezza che già è stata realizzata — è il caso di Rom 15,29; 1 Cor 10,26; Gal 4,4; Col 1,19; 2,9 —, può essere invece una pienezza che ancora deve realizzarsi — Rom 11,12.25; 13,10; Ef 1,10.23; 3,19; 4,13 —, ma vista sempre sotto la spinta attiva di un agente che la determina. È il caso della pienezza tipica del regno escatologico collegata col Βασιλεύειν del regno in divenire, come appare nella Lettera agli Efesini.

la pienezza risultante (τὸ πλήρωμα) di colui che sta portando alla pienezza tutte le cose in tutti» (τοῦ τὰ πάντα ἐν πᾶσιν πληρουμένου: Ef 1,22-23).

Si tratta di Cristo morto e risorto: il Padre gli ha data la responsabilità di tutto e di tutti e, in questa prospettiva, lo ha donato[20] capo alla chiesa. Come tale Cristo influirà vitalmente su di essa. E la chiesa, nella prospettiva di un'animazione vitale da parte di Cristo capo, costituisce il suo corpo, la sua concretezza relazionale[21], il campo spazio-temporale in cui Cristo realizza e attua se stesso. L'influsso di Cristo sulla chiesa è dinamico anche nel senso di uno sviluppo nel tempo. Tende a una pienezza da realizzare e la realizzazione sarà completa quando si avrà il regno offerto dal Figlio al Padre (cf 1 Cor 15,27).

L'autore della Lettera sottolinea l'ampiezza e la forza di questo influsso di Cristo che sta «portando alla pienezza tutto quanto»[22] sotto tutti gli aspetti possibili.

L'impegno di Cristo teso alla realizzazione di una pienezza da raggiungere ha per oggetto la chiesa.

Siamo in pieno contesto di regno: la pienezza verso cui l'azione continua di Cristo spinge la chiesa costituirà, una volta raggiunta, il «regno» vero e proprio secondo la terminologia tipica di Paolo. La presenza compenetrante di Cristo nella chiesa attuale fa capire l'implicazione più importante della situazione presente. Dall'incrocio delle due linee, discendente e ascendente, dall'accoglienza di Cristo offerto dal

---

[20] Ἔδωκεν non sembra avere la valenza di «costituì» come potrebbe far pensare una ipotetica soggiacenza ebraica, ma, come ritiene oggi la larga maggioranza dei commentatori (Cf R. PENNA, *Lettera agli Efesini*, Bologna, 1988, p. 119), conserva la sua forza espressiva greca e va tradotto: «diede in dono». È il dono di Cristo da parte di Dio che, accettato, fa scattare il regno, come abbiamo osservato più sopra.

[21] Paolo elabora un proprio concetto di σῶμα che va aldilà sia del dualismo greco sia dell'indeterminatezza ebraica e che può essere espresso come la «concretezza relazionale della persona». Cf per un approfondimento e una documentazione U. VANNI, «Due città nella formazione di Paolo: Tarso e Gerusalemme», in *Atti del I Simposio di Tarso su S. Paolo Apostolo*. Roma, Ateneo Antoniano, 17-29.

[22] Si è discusso sulla valenza precisa di πληρουμένου che, grammaticalmente medio-passivo, può, proprio come tale, essere interpretato in senso attivo, passivo o riflessivo. Ciascuna di queste interpretazioni appare componibile col contesto. Ma l'espressione parallela che troviamo poco dopo in Ef 4,10 ἵνα πληρώσῃ τὰ πάντα, riferita a Cristo come soggetto attivo, induce a preferire il senso attivo. Cf PENNA, *Efesini*, 121-122.

Padre, è nata la chiesa, nella quale il Cristo accolto per mezzo della fede agisce in permanenza e come Signore la vivifica in tutto. Nessuna meraviglia che tutta la vita della chiesa si svolga in un rapporto strettissimo «con Cristo», ἐν Χριστῷ[23].

La chiesa in divenire appare allora chiaramente come protagonista di regno, dando a questo termine il significato vasto che abbiamo presentato più sopra. Questo rapporto tra Cristo e la chiesa — e così ritorniamo al nostro tema specifico — in chiave di regno è situato in un contesto esplicito di preghiera. Il testo di 1,22-33 che abbiamo esaminato dipende da 1,15-16:

> «Per questo anch'io per parte mia avendo sentito la fede nel Signore Gesù e l'amore verso tutti i santi che avete, non cesso di ringraziare per voi ricordandovi nelle mie preghiere perchè Iddio del Signore nostro Gesù Cristo, il Padre della gloria, vi dia uno spirito di conoscenza e di rivelazione in una conoscenza approfondita di Lui, illumini gli occhi del vostro cuore in modo che voi possiate conoscere...».

L'autore afferma di ringraziare Dio per la fede e l'amore che si sono realizzati nella comunità destinataria. Prosegue poi dicendo che si sente impegnato a pregare per tutti loro giorno e notte. Specifica anche l'oggetto di questa preghiera di richiesta: i cristiani ricevendo una illuminazione particolare nella loro interiorità — «gli occhi del cuore illuminati» —, potranno rendersi conto dell'impegno che Dio mette nel portare avanti tutta la storia della salvezza (Ef 1,17-23).

La preghiera, qui, non ha per oggetto l'attuazione del regno, ma la comprensione del suo divenire. C'è in campo la forza di Dio e l'energia di Cristo risorto. E la comprensione che Paolo chiede si sviluppa pregando.

Πλήρωμα nel senso indicato di una pienezza da raggiungersi anche se non copre tutta l'estensione del concetto di regno, ne costituisce l'aspetto più importante perché si riferisce alla fase conclusiva. La pienezza che viene raggiunta è l'ulti-

---

[23] È un'espressione tipicamente paolina, indicante un rapporto con Cristo che poi il contesto immediato specifica, e ricorrente 73 volte, distribuita in tutte le Lettere.

mo sviluppo di quella situazione nuova, determinata dalla presenza accolta di Cristo, nella quale consiste il regno. Quando troviamo menzionata la pienezza siamo nel contesto del regno. È il caso, ad esempio, di Ef 1,10:

«... per la programmazione (οἰκονομίαν) della pienezza da realizzarsi (πληρώματος) dei tempi, sintetizzare (ἀνακεφαλαιώσασθαι)[24] in Cristo tutte le cose, quelle sui cieli e quelle sulla terra».

C'è una pienezza da realizzare secondo la sua programmazione che abbraccia tutti i vari periodi della storia, i quali si susseguono in crescendo come i gradini di una scalinata in ascesa. Il punto di arrivo che coincide con la pienezza è una confluenza di tutta la realtà in Cristo come punto di sintesi suprema. È il punto di arrivo di un movimento ascendente, che ha luogo adesso. È davvero il contesto del regno con quel dinamismo cristologico e cristogenico che abbiamo rilevato. Cristo, in altri termini, costituisce il punto di partenza e il punto di arrivo del divenire del regno. Il punto di partenza perchè la situazione anche iniziale di regno è determinata da Lui, dalla sua presenza accettata; è il punto di arrivo perchè tutto lo sviluppo tende proprio a una compenetrazione piena, senza più ostacoli antagonistici né approssimazioni, senza più diaframmi, tra la sua vitalità di risorto, i suoi valori e tutto il creato, a cominciare dall'uomo (cf 1 Cor 15,20-28).

Ora questo sviluppo di regno dalla situazione attuale alla pienezza come si intravede in Ef 1,10 viene celebrato in un inno liturgico, difficile a ricostruire in tutti i dettagli, ma che

---

[24] Il verbo ἀνακεφαλαιώσασθαι è di difficile interpretazione. Una prima indicazione in proposito ci viene dall'analisi delle sue componenti: c'è anzitutto ἀνα- che indica un movimento ascendente, un certo sviluppo in crescendo; il verbo poi è riferito senz'altro a un sostantivo, ma si tratta di κεφαλή, «testa», oppure di κεφάλαιον «sintesi, sommario, punto centrale»? Si può intendere riferito a κεφαλή e allora si dovrà tradurre «portare a Cristo come a capo tutte le cose», oppure, secondo R. PENNA (*Efesini*, pp. 98-100) «intestare tutte le cose nel Cristo»; si può intendere riferito a κεφάλαιον e allora la traduzione sarà «far arrivare a una sintesi, a una ricapitolazione in Cristo tutte le cose». Questa seconda alternativa appare più aderente alla formazione grammaticale del verbo che direttamente è collegato proprio con κεφάλαιον. Lo stesso valore di una sintesi effettuata è riscontrebile nell'altra ricorrenza del verbo ἀνακεφαλαιόω in Paolo: ...ἐν ἑνὶ λόγῳ ἀνακεφαλαιοῦται (Rom 13,9).

appare chiaramente soggiacente alla grande benedizione di Ef 1,3-14[25]. Siamo in un contesto di preghiera celebrativa. Lo ritroviamo esplicitamente — ed è una conferma di quanto stiamo vedendo — anche in un brano in certo senso parallelo[26] che ricorre nella Lettera ai Colossesi, molto vicina sotto tanti aspetti a quella agli Efesini.

Il riferimento al regno diventa esplicito. Dopo aver dichiarato il suo impegno nella preghiera a favore dei destinatari perchè possano fruttificare in ogni opera buona, l'autore si associa ai suoi destinatari:

«ringraziando insieme (εὐχαριστοῦντες) il Padre che ci rese idonei a partecipare alla sorte dei santi nella luce, Lui che ci sottrasse dal potere delle tenebre e ci trasportò nel regno (εἰς τῆν βασιλείαν) del Figlio del suo amore» (Col 1,13).

Il cristiano sa di trovarsi nella situazione di regno che è quella determinata da Cristo come Figlio dell'amore continuo del Padre. Lo sa, il cristiano, e lo dice esprimendo coralmente la sua gioia in una celebrazione liturgica. La preghiera del regno diventa qui rendimento di grazie.

Un rapporto particolare con Dio come Padre emerge in un altro brano della Lettera agli Efesini nel quale la preghiera diventa di nuovo di richiesta ed è situata nel contesto del re-

---

[25] Il brano suggerisce anche a una prima lettura una certa struttura innica che però riesce difficile precisare fin nei dettagli. Le quasi innumerevoli suddivisioni strofiche proposte hanno tutte il vantaggio di mettere in risalto un aspetto del brano, ma nessuna è riuscita persuasiva: «Ciascuno di essi — i tentativi di strutturazione — fa notare un elemento importante, che però da solo non basta. Il motivo sta nel fatto che il peso strutturale maggiore non consiste nella pura forma letteraria quanto nel suo contenuto tematico» (PENNA, *Efesini*, pp. 83-84). Per una presentazione aggiornata delle posizioni principali rimandiamo a Penna, *Efesini* p. 83. Si deve osservare tuttavia che questo «canto in prosa» (PENNA, *Efesini*, p. 83) ha un indubbio aggancio liturgico, come indica già la sua appartenenza al genere della benedizione. Anche se non ci si può spingere, con Grelot (P. GRELOT, «La structure d'Éphésiens 1,3-14», *Revue Biblique* 96 (1989), 193-209) a identificare un ritmo di lettura liturgica a strofe del testo presente, si dovrà almeno ammetterne la lettura nell'ambito dell'assemblea.

[26] A questo punto, dopo un inizio epistolare normale — indirizzo e ringraziamento — il testo decolla, acquistando un tono lirico e celebrativo. Ciò inizia in 1,12 e si mantiene fino a 1,20. Il salto di tono ha fatto giustamente pensare a un inno primitivo incorporato poi nella Lettera. Avremmo in Colossesi lo stesso fenomeno letterario che riscontriamo in forma più ampia ed elaborata in Ef 1,3-14.

gno. Si tratta di Ef 3,14-21, un testo che si presenta esplicitamente conclusivo di tutto l'ampio contesto che precede, a cominciare da Ef 1,15. La preghiera di Paolo, già iniziata esplicitamente allora e protratta virtualmente senza interruzioni, emerge qui di nuovo in primo piano:

> «A motivo di tutto questo piego le mie ginocchia al Padre dal quale ogni famiglia (πᾶσα πατριά)[27] nei cieli e sulla terra prende nome» (Ef 3,14-15).

È un atteggiamento accentuato di preghiera rivolta esplicitamente al Padre, facendo pressione proprio sulla paternità. È un tratto caratteristico: come nel Padre nostro la preghiera del regno è sempre rivolta al Padre.

L'oggetto della preghiera riguarda tutta la struttura del cristiano in quanto tale: guidato dallo Spirito sarà sempre più consolidato «nell'uomo interiore» (Ef 3,16). Cristo abiterà nel suo cuore, dirigendo dal didentro tutte le sue scelte. E così, trovando nell'amore la sua radice e il fondamento di tutto se stesso, il cristiano sarà in grado di orientarsi e di impegnarsi nella sua storia e di avere dell'amore di Cristo nei suoi riguardi una comprensione che sempre si auto-supera. In questa situazione il cristiano è orientato a realizzare personalmente «tutta la pienezza di Dio» (Ef 3,19), programmata proprio da Lui. È la pienezza tipica che costituisce l'ultima fase del regno, come abbiamo più volte osservato. Ne segue che anche il contesto che qui precede il riferimento alla pienezza sarà da riferire al regno nella fase di adesso che prepara la pienezza finale. Il quadro suggestivo che Paolo ci presenta in Ef 3,16-19a sarà allora da riferirsi alla situazione presente del cristiano. Il cristiano, in altri termini, condotto dallo Spirito, che ha Cristo per centro della sua vita, che trova nell'amore di Cristo la sua radice e il suo fondamento, che cerca di comprendere un amore di

---

[27] Esiste una discussione sul valore preciso da attribuire al termine πατριά: da una parte si intravede che la frase a cui appartiene vuole sottolineare la paternità infinita di Dio che da la sua impronta a ogni forma di paternità creata; dall'altra il termine ha una chiara valenza concreta, come indica la documentazione reperibile nella letteratura greca. Nei vari codici della *Vetus Latina* troviamo «paternitas» — come nella Volgata — e anche «cognatio, familia, congregatio» (Cf R. SCHNACKENBURG, *Der Brief an die Epheser*, Zürich-Neukirchen-Vluyn, 1982, p. 149). Potremmo parafrasare «ogni forma di paternità realizzata».

Cristo sempre più grande di lui, il cristiano qui tratteggiato è in cammino verso la pienezza del regno di cui farà parte. Tutto questo è oggetto della preghiera di Paolo.

Il quale poi conclude:

«A Colui che ha la forza di fare al di sopra di tutto con un'abbondanza maggiore rispetto a ciò che chiediamo o pensiamo, secondo l'energia che è operante in noi, a lui la gloria nella chiesa e in Cristo Gesù per tutte le generazioni del secolo dei secoli, amen» (Ef 3,20-21)[28].

Emerge la chiesa, emerge l'energia di Dio, emerge la pienezza verso la quale l'energia in atto sta spingendo. È tutto in una preghiera di glorificazione che si salda spontaneamente a quella di richiesta. Chiedendo al Padre la situazione di regno per il cristiano in modo da arrivare alla pienezza, Paolo sente di essere esaudito. E allora da una parte ringrazia, dall'altra si sente rapito dalla potenza operante di Dio. Avverte che il regno attuato supererà ogni sua aspettativa.

Se diamo ora uno sguardo riassuntivo a questi esempi di preghiera in rapporto col regno che abbiamo presi dal *Corpus Paulinum*, si impone la constatazione di una continuità e insieme di un allargamento rispetto alla prospettiva dei sinottici. Il regno, sia nella sua fase conclusiva («regno» nel senso proprio di Paolo) sia nella sua fase attuale è oggetto di un apprezzamento appassionato che sfocia in vari tipi di preghiera. Non si trova in Paolo la richiesta esplicita della venuta del regno nella forma che troviamo nei sinottici. La concezione articolata di regno propria di Paolo ha forse impedito una formulazione del genere: «venga il tuo regno» in un contesto paolino avrebbe significato la richiesta, magari a effetto immediato, della conclusione finale, mentre anche nei sinottici, come abbiamo già rilevato, la richiesta della venuta ha per oggetto un segmento immediato di regno.

L'attenzione di Paolo si concentra sulla fase attuale. Visto in questa prospettiva, il regno in divenire assume una dimen-

---

[28] Cf. C. CASALE-MARCHESELLI, *La preghiera in S. Paolo*, Napoli 1975, 145-146. La dossologia, articolata in tre frasi (A: A Dio ... chiedere o pensare; B: secondo la potenza che opera in noi; C: A Lui la gloria... amen) è indirizzata al Padre.

sione squisitamente antropologica, passa tutto attraverso l'uomo: vengono messi in risalto gli elementi costitutivi dell'uomo che interessano il regno: il cuore, l'anima, il corpo, lo spirito.

Inoltre il regno nella fase attuale si trova in movimento nella storia. Questo aspetto viene sottolineato e dettagliato: lo sviluppo nella storia è dialettico, si svolge in un confronto serrato tra bene e male. Dio stesso per mezzo di Cristo porta avanti il confronto e ne garantisce l'esito finale positivo.

Lo sviluppo nella storia si concluderà con la pienezza, che costituisce il punto di saldatura tra la fase di adesso e quella definitiva. Con la pienezza attuata si avrà il regno vero e proprio — sempre secondo la terminologia Paolina — nella sua realizzazione ottimale.

La preghiera abbraccia tutta la fase attuale dello sviluppo del regno. Paolo prega intensamente il Padre perché tutte le componenti antropologiche esplichino il loro funzionamento migliore in vista della venuta. Insiste sul cuore e sull'uomo interiore.

Paolo si affaccia anche sullo sviluppo verso la pienezza. Qui la sua preghiera diventa spontaneamente lode, ringraziamento e celebrazione.

Al salto qualitativo che si ha come esplicitazione teologica in fatto di regno, corrisponde una preghiera più approfondita e dettagliata nei suoi elementi di richiesta e la fioritura di altri tipi di preghiera. Troveremo un fenomeno analogo nell'Apocalisse.

4. La preghiera e il regno nell'Apocalisse

Quello che abbiamo visto a livello dei vangeli sinottici e di Paolo trova uno sviluppo interessante nell'Apocalisse.

Il sostantivo «regno», βασιλεία, vi ricorre ben nove volte distribuite in tutto l'arco del libro. Sette volte vi ricorre il verbo «regnare», βασιλεύειν e 21 il termine βασιλεύς.

Il gruppo semantico βασιλεία-βασιλεύς-βασιλεύειν ha un suo rilievo ed è stato fatto ripetutamente oggetto di studio[29].

---

[29] Cf U. Vanni, «Regno 'non da questo mondo' ma 'regno del mondo'. Il regno di Cristo dal IV Vangelo all'Apocalisse», in *Studia Missionalia* 33 (1984) 207-240; «La promozione del regno come responsabilità sacerdotale dei cristiani secondo l'Apocalisse e la Prima Lettera di Pietro» *Gregorianum* 68 (1987).

I cristiani sono già regno di Dio e di Cristo. La loro accettazione per fede di Cristo crocifisso che inaugura sulla croce la sua regalità nei riguardi del nuovo popolo di Dio li ha posti in una situazione nuova, quella appunto di regno[30]. In tale situazione i cristiani hanno una responsabilità precisa: oltre che «regno», i cristiani, sono anche sacerdoti. Come tali dovranno mediare tra il progetto di Dio e la concretezza della storia in vista della realizzazione ulteriore del regno stesso. La celebrazione di Cristo agnello, fatta dai viventi e dai presbiteri in Ap 5,9-10, si riferisce proprio a loro:

«Tu sei in grado di prendere il libro
e di aprirne i sigilli
poiché fosti ucciso
e acquistasti a Dio nel tuo sangue
persone provenienti da ogni tribú e lingua e popolo e nazione
e li facesti (ἐποίησας αὐτούς) al nostro Dio
regno
e sacerdoti
e stanno regnando sulla terra (βασιλεύουσιν[31] ἐπὶ τῆς γῆς)» (Ap 5,9-10).

---

[30] È quanto troviamo affermato esplicitamente in Ap 1,5a-6. Rispondendo al saluto benedicente del lettore, il gruppo di ascolto dell'assemblea liturgica esprime una celebrazione appassionata dell'opera di Cristo nei suoi riguardi. Tra le azioni di Cristo in favore dei cristiani emerge — messo in risalto anche da un accorgimento stilistico che scioglie grammaticalmente la frase dal contesto che precede e che segue — il fatto che Egli li ha costituiti regno: «A Colui che ci ama e ci sciolse dai nostri peccati nel suo sangue — e fece noi regno (καὶ ἐποίησεν ἡμᾶς βασιλείαν), sacerdoti a Dio e Padre suo — a Lui la forza e la gloria per i secoli. Amen». Applicando loro quanto era espresso potenzialmente nella regalità attribuitagli con tanta solennità nel IV Vangelo (Cf Gv 18,36-38; 19,14; 19,19-22) Cristo realizza il suo regno nei cristiani, ma li fa nello stesso tempo sacerdoti conferendo loro una resposabilità di mediazione tra il progetto di Dio sul regno e la sua realizzione. Il cristiano dell'Apocalisse è e si sente particolarmente legato al regno e al suo divenire. La piccola dossologia di 1,5a-6 indirizzata esplicitamente a Cristo è anche, implicitamente, una celebrazione liturgica del regno.

[31] Esiste una importante questione di critica testuale riguardante proprio questo verbo. Il presente βασιλεύουσιν è documentato da A 046 1006 1611 e da alcune versioni; il futuro βασιλεύσουσιν appare documentato in ℵ P svariati minuscoli e molte versioni. L'autorità del codice A, il più importante codice dell'Apocalisse, sarebbe decisiva se proprio A in Ap 20,6 dove il contesto di futuri non ponesse βασιλεύσουσιν al presente. Per questo «a majority of the Committee, noting that in 20.6 codex Alexandrinus mistakenly reads βασιλεύουσιν for the future tense, pre-

Come svolgeranno i cristiani sacerdoti la loro mediazione in vista del regno da realizzare? Lo faranno innanzitutto con la preghiera esplicita. Introducendo la glorificazione di Cristo-agnello, l'autore sente il bisogno di metterle accanto le «preghiere dei santi» (Ap 5,8), cioè dei cristiani che ancora si trovano sulla terra.

Tali preghiere sono poste in un turibolo e sono identificate con l'incenso che però, sorprendentemente, non si trova in un turibolo ma in coppe d'oro:

«... aventi ciascuno — sono i presbiteri — una cetra e delle coppe d'oro ripiene di incensi, che sono le preghiere dei santi» (Ap 5,9).

Le preghiere-incenso hanno una potenzialità ascendente e tendono a raggiungere Dio e ci riescono davvero. In 8,3 le «preghiere di tutti i santi» sono situate su un altare d'oro situato nella trascendenza, vengono incensate da un angelo e così «salí il profumo degli incensi dato alle preghiere dei santi dalla mano dell'angelo fino davanti a Dio» (Ap 8,4).

E Dio non fa tardare la sua risposta. Si hanno, proprio in conseguenza delle preghiere, «tuoni e voci e lampi e un terremoto», simbolo tutto questo di un intervento di Dio nella storia tendente a superare il male e a potenziare il bene[32].

Nell'Apocalisse, accanto alla richiesta, troviamo altre forme di preghiera collegate con la realizzazione del regno. Il regno non è pensato soltanto in divenire ma, con la finalità evidente di animare i cristiani in cammino, viene presentato come realizzato.

Troviamo un primo esempio di questa realizzazione nella solenne celebrazione dossologica di 11,15-18.

---

ferred βασιλεύσουσιν here, as more suitable to the meaning of the context» (B.M. METZGER *Textual Commentary on the New Testament*, Stuttgart, 1994², p. 667). Ma il ragionamento non è persuasivo: il contesto può esigere il futuro solo se si dà a βασιλεύω il senso di «possedere il regno»; se invece si mantiene il senso usuale di «procurare il regno» il presente quadra perfettamente col contesto ed appare quindi preferibile, anche perché dal presunto errore di A in 20,6 non segue necessariamente che si abbia qua l'errore inverso.

[32] Cfr. per un approfondimento e una documentazione ulteriori U. VANNI, *La struttura letteraria dell'Apocalisse*, Brescia, 1980², pp. 141-148.

La celebrazione comincia con un'affermazione profetica particolarmente solenne:

«Divenne (ἐγένετο) il regno del mondo
del Signore nostro e del suo Cristo
e regnerà per i secoli dei secoli» (Ap 11,15).

La realtà particolare che nasce dall'incontro della linea discendente di Dio che offre Cristo e quella ascendente dell'uomo che accoglie, è denominata «il regno» (ἡ βασιλεία) e assume qui le proporzioni sociali del «mondo» degli uomini. La piena compenetrazione dei valori di Cristo realizzata in tutti gli spazi dell'uomo rende il regno del mondo «regno di Cristo». Il divenire, qui particolarmente sottolineato (ἐγένετο), si realizza mediante il superamento del sistema terrestre, come viene spiegato nel seguito della celebrazione:

«Rendiamo grazie a te, Signore Dio onnipotente
che sei e che eri
poiché hai preso la potenza tua quella grande
e regnasti (καὶ ἐβασίλευσας).
E le genti si adirarono
e venne la tua ira
e il tempo di giudicare i morti
e di dare la ricompensa ai tuoi servitori
ai profeti e ai santi e a coloro che temono il tuo nome,
quelli che sono piccoli e grandi[33]
e di mandare in rovina coloro che mandano in rovina la terra» (11,17-18).

Nella celebrazione, con un'anticipazione di stile profetico, il regno viene visto come già realizzato. È un regno suggestivo: comporta il superamento definitivo e irreversibile di tutto il male che si è verificato sulla terra nella storia degli uomini.

---

[33] C'è un problema grammaticale particolare: l'espressione τοὺς μικροὺς καὶ τοὺς μεγάλους all'accusativo sorprende: ci aspetteremmo il dativo, in consonaza con quanto precede: καὶ τοῖς ἁγίοις καὶ τοῖς φοβουμένοις τὸ ὄνομά σου. Si può forse spiegare come un fenomeno grammaticale di attrazione rispetto all'espressione immediatamente seguente: καὶ διαφθεῖραι τοὺς διαφθείροντας τὴν γῆν. I «piccoli e i grandi» sarebbe quindi da collegarsi con la capacità di Dio di distruggere il male, espressa da διαφθεῖραι, che raggiunge tutti indiscriminatamente a prescindere dalla loro qualifica sociale.

Il «sistema terrestre», una specie di anti-regno costruito dagli uomini sotto l'influsso del demoniaco[34], viene disattivato e ad esso succede il regno di Dio e di Cristo.

Questo fatto è talmente importante da meritare una celebrazione liturgica solenne, quella che abbiamo indicato. La preghiera, messa così in rapporto esplicito col regno, si fa qui lode ammirata e rendimento di grazie. Alle prese quotidianamente col male concretizzato nel sistema terrestre, assuma o no proporzioni persecutorie, la chiesa-assemblea guarda con gioia e gratitudine al momento in cui essa, per intervento di Cristo-agnello sul filo della storia della salvezza, si sentirà e sarà completamente liberata.

La preghiera del regno diventa preghiera di celebrazione e di ringraziamento.

Troviamo un contesto analogo in un altro brano dell'Apocalisse, anch'esso rapportato direttamente al regno e che merita un'attenzione particolare. Si tratta di Ap 19,6-8.

Il brano fa parte della grande celebrazione dossologica di 19,1-8, tutta improntata sulle ricorrenze tipiche di ἀλληλουϊά. Questo termine squisitamente liturgico[35] costituisce, date le sue quattro ricorrenze in 19,1-8, quasi un ritornello di tutto questo brano celebrativo. Oggetto della celebrazione in una prima fase (Ap 19,1-4) è l'eliminazione dell'anti-regno, simboleggiato dalla figura di Babilonia[36]. Dio realizza tale elimina-

---

[34] È un sistema di vita tutto immanente e chiuso alla trascendenza. La sua espressione più completa è data dalla figura di Babilonia, la convivenza consumistica, che assolutizza il presente, sostenuta dallo stato che si fa adorare, basata sullo sfruttamento di uomini da parte di altri uomini. L'Apocalisse ne fa una presentazione completa nel dramma liturgico di 18,1-24. Cf. C. BEDRIÑAN, *La dimensión socio-política del mensaje teológico del Apocalipsis*, Roma, 1996, 227-280.

[35] L'Apocallisse è l'unico libro del NT dove il termine è documentato e ciò contribuisce a evidenziare il carattere liturgico di tutto il libro. L'alleluia inserita nel brano si stacca grammaticalmente dal testo, costituendo come una seconda voce che fa da sfondo a tutta la celebrazione.

[36] Il simbolismo di Babilonia è complesso e discusso. Il punto di partenza è costituito dalla Babele-Babilonia biblica e dalla Roma imperiale. Ma l'autore rielabora creativamente secondo il suo stile i dati da cui parte facendo così di Babilonia una delle figure più importanti del suo mondo teologico. Babilonia — per limitarci ai tratti essenziali — rappresenta per lui la città convivenza costruita dall'uomo sfruttando le sue risorse e assolutizzandole, strumentalizzando altri uomini, con una chiusura totale alla trascendenza. Insieme allo stato che si fa adorare e alla propaganda che gli da vita, Babilonia costituisce il sistema terrestre, contrapposto al sistema di Cristo. Cf. per un approfondimento dei diversi aspetti implicati in tutto

zione tramite una mediazione storica complessa che comporta l'intervento attivo di Dio, di Cristo-agnello e dei cristiani.

In una seconda parte la celebrazione riguarda invece la realizzazione del regno. La celebrazione si fa particolarmente coinvolgente: un invito derivante direttamente dalla trascendenza, dal trono[37], esorta a ripetere l'alleluia ma sostituendo al termine il suo significato: «Lodate il nostro Dio»[38]. Sono invitati ad esprimere questa lode «tutti i suoi servitori, quelli che temono il suo nome, piccoli e grandi» (Ap 19,5b): è l'universalità del popolo di Dio, situato sia nella trascendenza, da dove esce la voce, sia sulla terra, come indica l'espressione «quelli che temono» (οἱ φοβούμενοι)[39].

Infatti la voce che esprime la celebrazione è «come di una folla numerosa e come voce di molte acque e come voce di tuoni potenti» (19,6a). Alla moltitudine sterminata degli uomini si associa, in certo modo[40], Dio stesso. L'importanza della celebrazione che segue è senza precedenti.

---

il processo di simbolizzazione A. CASALEGNO, «A ciudade entre realidade e símbolo: Duas perspectivas do Apocalipse», *PerspTeol* 27 (1995) 7-26; Ch. H. DYER, «The Identity of Babylon in Revelation 17-18», *BS* 144 (1987), 305-316.433-449; T.R. EDGAR «Babylon: Ecclesiastical, Political, or What?», *JournEvangTheolSoc*, 25 (1982), 333-341; M. RISSI, *Die Hure Babylon und die Verführung der Heiligen. Eine Studie zur Apokalypse des Johannes*, Stuttgart-Berlin-Cologne 1995; A. YARBRO COLLINS, «Oppression from Without: the Symbolisation of Rome as Evil in Early Christianity», *Concilium* 200 (1988), 66-74.

[37] Il trono costituisce un simbolo particolarmente importante in tutto il libro dell'Apocalisse. Indica la capacità di influsso di Dio trascendente sulla storia che si sta svolgendo. Tale influsso esercitato nella concretezza dei fatti tramite Cristo e i cristiani porterà il progetto di Dio sulla storia al livello di regno realizzato. Cf per tutto questo G. KOOTTAPPILLIL, *The Symbolism of* θρόνος *and its Biblical-Theological Implications in the Apocalypse*, Roma 1996.

[38] L'espressione αἰνεῖτε τῷ θεῷ ἡμῶν è un equivalente aderente di alleluia, propriamente «lodate Yahveh». Invece del nome proprio Dio usava dire *'adonay*, *'adonenu*, «il mio Signore, il nostro Signore», proprio come nel testo dell'Apocalisse. È importante e significativo che qui l'alleluia venga interpretata. Nell'Apocalisse non è un termine logorato dall'uso: il suo significato viene avvertito pienamente mentre il termine viene pronunciato.

[39] È un'espressione ricorrente in tutto l'ambito del NT ed esprime il senso del numinoso di Dio che si ha sulla terra. Non avrebbe un significato pieno riferita alla trascendenza.

[40] Il riferimento alle molte acque e ai tuoni potenti ci pone al livello di Dio alla cui voce queste immagini sono riferite. La particella ὡς «come» posta prima relativizza il riferimento, come del resto accade anche per la «folla». L'a. non ci da una descrizione realistica della voce che esprime la celebrazione, ma suggerisce dei punti di riferimento per aiutare il lettore a farsene un'idea elaborando il simbolo: qualunque assemblea liturgica terrestre che esprimerà la celebrazione dovrà sentirsi

E la celebrazione riguarda la realizzazione del regno:

A «Alleluia (lodate il Signore)
poiché (ὅτι ἐβασίλευσεν) regnò il Signore
il nostro Dio, l'onnipotente![41]

B Gioiamo ed esultiamo
e diamo a Lui gloria
poiché (ὅτι) vennero le nozze dell'Agnello
e la sua sposa si preparò
e le fu dato di rivestirsi
di un lino puro e luminoso» (19,6-8).

Notiamo anzitutto il parallelismo progressivo tra le due strofe (A e B) della pericope celebrativa. Il regno attuato di cui si parla nella prima diventa la situazione nuziale tra Cristo-agnello e il suo popolo nella seconda. Si tratta, qui, del regno giunto al massimo del suo sviluppo, oltre la dialettica che si è realizzata nella storia. La realtà che scaturisce dall'accettazione di Cristo e che ha costituito i cristiani come regno iniziale diventa, a regno attuato, l'amore paritetico tra due sposi, tra Cristo-agnello e i cristiani.

Questo culmine di regno viene celebrato nella preghiera liturgica dell'alleluia. La preghiera comincia con la lode, espressa dall'alleluia e motivata dall'avvento del regno. Dato che tra coloro che esprimono con tanta solennità la celebrazione ci sono, come abbiamo visto, i cristiani ancora sulla terra, l'attuazione del regno è per loro ancora futura. Ma la presenza di Dio e di Cristo nell'alveo della storia rende certa

---

interprete della «grande folla» di tutto il popolo di Dio, «come» se parlasse al suo nome e dovrà essere consapevole che Dio stesso in certo modo vi si associa, «come» se parlasse lui personalmente. La celebrazione del regno è sempre anche una celebrazione di Dio e che raggiunge Dio.

[41] C'è un problema di riferimento all'interno della pericope 19,6-8 che ne determina l'interpretazione. Ponendo la virgola dopo παντοκράτωρ di 19,6 come fa il *The Greek New Testament*, (Stuttgart, ⁴1993, p. 876), si mette in relazione la instaurazione del regno con la gioia di 19,7a («poiché — ὅτι — regnò il Signore... rallegriamoci»), con l'inconveniente di lasciare sospeso il secondo ὅτι della pericope che ricorre in 19,7b. Se invece — e sembra decisamente preferibile — diamo a ἀλληλουϊά di 19,6 non il valore di un grido di gioia, ma quello esplicito di «lodate il Signore», come suggerito da 19,5, il testo scorre senza intoppi, armonizzando in un parallelismo significativo i due ὅτι: «alleluia (lodiamo il Signore) poiché (ὅτι) il Signore regnò... rallegriamoci ed esultiamo... poiché (ὅτι) giunsero le nozze dell'agnello».

questa conclusione che, allora, viene considerata come realizzata: ἐβασίλευσεν è un aoristo profetico.

La lode a caldo si sviluppa ulteriormente nella strofa B. Come il regno raggiunge il suo vertice più alto nella situazione nuziale, così la celebrazione — rimanendo sempre sostanzialmente di lode — viene tutta pervasa dalla gioia.

L'autore quasi non trova parole per esprimerla adeguatamente e allora ricorre ai sinonimi: χαίρωμεν «gioiamo» indica una gioia intensa ma che si situa soprattutto nell'interiorità della persona, ἀγαλλιῶμεν «esultiamo» invece indica la gioia che si manifesta nel movimento e che quindi passa dall'interno all'esterno: è la gioia partecipata nell'ambito della assemblea liturgica.

Riassumendo: la dossologia di 19,6-8 invita i cristiani alla presa con le difficoltà quotidiane che comporta la realizzazione del regno in cui sono coinvolti a guardare arditamente in avanti, verso la conclusione. Il regno si realizzerà davvero, anche per il contributo che essi stanno dando e supererà ogni aspettativa. C'è davvero da lodare Dio: è la gioia della speranza. Siccome la collaborazione dei cristiani in vista del regno avviene soprattutto mediante la preghiera di richiesta, la gioia per il regno realizzato è anche la gioia di una preghiera esaudita.

Come nell'ambito paolino, la preghiera suscita nell'Apocalisse un interesse particolare proprio in riferimento al regno. Proprio perchè sono già, incoativamente, regno loro stessi, i cristiani avvertono il bisogno e il ruolo di portarne avanti la realizzazione fino in fondo. Lo fanno con la loro mediazione sacerdotale che trova nella preghiera di richiesta la sua principale forma di realizzazione. E quando il cristiano-regno pensa a se stesso e agli altri nella situazione di regno definitiva, la sua preghiera assume spontaneamente il tono della lode celebrativa, della gioia, del ringraziamento. Notiamo infine che, dato che il protagonista di fondo di tutto il libro è l'assemblea liturgica, quanto viene detto del cristiano assume una dimensione liturgico-comunitaria: il cristiano è divenuto regno iniziale mediante il battesimo proprio nell'assemblea liturgica. La preghiera di richiesta per il regno che lo impegna personalmente viene portata insieme a quella «di tutti i santi sull'altare d'oro davanti a Dio» (8,3). E anche la preghiera di ringraziamento e di lode è essenzialmente comunitaria.

5. Riflessioni conclusive

Possiamo ora, dopo aver seguito lo sviluppo della preghiera per il regno in tre grandi settori del Nuovo Testamento, raccogliere a fattor comune alcune impressioni conclusive.

Notiamo anzitutto la varietà della preghiera in rapporto al regno. Indirizzata al Padre, esplicitamente o implicitamente come avviene nell'Apocalisse, la preghiera rapportata al regno è richiesta, lode, celebrazione, ringraziamento.

Nei vangeli sinottici l'apprezzamento entusiasta nei riguardi del regno si condensa nella richiesta della sua venuta come la troviamo formulata nel Padre nostro. La richiesta della venuta del regno appare, così, inserita nel paradigma di preghiera proposto a tutti i cristiani. L'invito a pregare secondo quel paradigma — «Voi pregherete così...» Mt 6,9 — sarà raccolto ben presto nella chiesa. A parte la risonanza riscontrabile nelle comunità paoline[42], l'uso liturgico del Padre nostro ci è già testimoniato dalla *Didaché*[43]. Il fatto che la richiesta della venuta del regno si trovi nel paradigma fondamentale della preghiera cristiana le confereisce una importanza talmente rilevante da renderla imprescindibile. Il cristiano non potrà mai esimersi dal pregare per la venuta del regno.

Negli scritti paolini appare un allargamento di prospettiva. La preghiera per il regno è contestualizzata nello sviluppo globale della storia della salvezza al quale essa è riferita: si prega in effetti in riferimento diretto alla chiesa in divenire.

Protagonisti di tale preghiera sono Paolo e la comunità. Il ruolo di quest'ultima decolla e si impone all'attenzione soprattutto in quelle forme letterarie che mostrano un inno soggiacente. La preghiera in rapporto con la chiesa-regno diventa allora un'attenzione collettiva al divenire del regno, concretizzato nel cammino della chiesa verso la pienezza. Ne deriva un senso di stupore, di gioia, di ammirazione e di lode per la bontà divina che ha preso e prende l'iniziativa di tutto il divenire del regno. L'assemblea liturgica celebra la «lode della gloria della sua grazia» (Ef 1,6).

---

[42] Le due volte che Paolo usa il termine αββα (Gal 4,6; Rom 8,15) lo inserisce in un contesto di invocazine con grido (Gal 4,6 κρᾶζον; Rom 5,15 ἐν ᾧ κράζομεν). Ciò ha fatto pensare con fandamento all'assemblea liturgica in atto.
[43] *Didaché*, 8, 1-3.

Troviamo nell'Apocalisse la gioia prorompente per il regno attuato. Al «venga» ἐλθέτω, implicito o esplicito, della preghiera di richiesta corrisponde il «venne», ἦλθεν della conclusione. Venne l'ira che distrugge l'anti-regno, venne la festa nuziale di Cristo agnello che costituisce il vertice del regno realizzato. La preghiera allora si fa ringraziamento.

Le tre aree neotestamentarie che abbiamo esaminato ci mostrano come la preghiera segue tutto lo sviluppo del regno: ne chiede la venuta e lo sviluppo, lo contempla con gioia e attenzione nel suo divenire, ne celebra l'attuazione. Appare quindi come un elemento irrinunciabile per la comprensione del regno: non si può parlare del regno senza evidenziare la preghiera che lo accompagna in tutti gli aspetti che esso assume.

Una volta che il dono di Cristo è accolto dall'uomo e il regno è iniziato, lo sviluppo ulteriore è opera di Dio e di Cristo, ma dipende anche dall'uomo. Dio e Cristo ne sollecitano la collaborazione in forme svariate: la preghiera rimane la prima.

The Trinity and the Kingdom

EARL C. MULLER

One does not often find the themes of the kingdom of God and the Trinity treated together. There are several reasons for this. One has to do with the character of the biblical witness. The notion of a kingdom, whether of God or otherwise, is found embedded in the Old Testament witness to the great deeds of Yahweh on behalf of his people. That witness is monotheistic and not, as such, trinitarian in shape.

Secondly, even when one turns to the New Testament one finds that Jesus himself, in proclaiming the coming kingdom of God, tied that kingdom very closely to the God of the Old Testament, his Father. The Lord's Prayer makes the point explicitly — "Our Father ... your kingdom come." It is true that exegetes customarily link the advent of the kingdom in some manner to Jesus' own ministry, and indeed to the person of Christ himself. Jesus, in his proclamation and exorcisms and healings, causes the kingdom to be present. To the extent that the Son is thus brought into central focus vis-à-vis the kingdom of God, to that extent the exposition is moved in a trinitarian direction. Still, what tends to be overlooked in such discussions is the central role of the Holy Spirit even if it is never denied[1]. There is, for instance, only a handful of references to the Spirit throughout Rudolf Schnackenburg's expansive work, *God's Rule and Kingdom*, in spite of fairly clear passages such as Jn. 3:5 linking the Spirit to the kingdom[2]. The situation has not noticeably altered in the in-

---

[1] This is a situation that JAMES D.G. DUNN, in his opening remarks in his seminal work, "Spirit and Kingdom", *The Expository Times* 32 (1970-71): 36-40, finds regrettable since the relation to the Spirit "is the key to understanding much of the Kingdom proclamation in the Synoptics".

[2] 2nd enlarged ed. (New York: Herder and Herder, 1968), trans. JOHN MURRAY from *Gottes Herrschaft und Reich*, 4th ed. (Freiburg: Herder, 1965).

tervening thirty years as witnessed to by a similar paucity of references in Dennis Duling's recent article in the *Anchor Bible Dictionary*[3]. Of course, when the role of the Spirit is peripheralized it is hard to avoid reducing the discussion of any topic to monotheistic rather than to trinitarian terms.

A third reason for the sparsity of treatments of the theme of the Trinity and the kingdom of God is the tendency to understand kingship or the related lordship in essentialist rather than personalist categories. Power is a concept, for instance, which quickly comes to mind when one thinks of a kingdom; but this is understood principally as an attribute of the Godhead in traditional theology.

---

[3] "Kingdom of God, Kingdom of Heaven", in *Anchor Bible Dictionary*, vol. 4, DAVID NOEL FREEDMAN, et al., eds. (New York: Doubleday, 1992), pp. 49-69. The same could be said of any number of studies on the kingdom. See, for example BRUCE D. CHILTON, *God in Strength: Jesus' Announcement of the Kingdom*, The Biblical Seminar (Sheffield: JSOT Press/Sheffield Academic Press, 1987); RICHARD H. HIERS, *The Kingdom of God in the Synoptic Tradition*, University of Florida Humanities Monograph 33 (Gainesville: University of Florida Press, 1970) and *The Historical Jesus and the Kingdom of God*, University of Florida Humanities Monograph 38 (Gainesville: University of Florida Press, 1973); GEORGE ELDON LADD, *Jesus and the Kingdom: The Eschatology of Biblical Realism* (London: SPCK, 1966); BENEDICT T. VIVIANO, O.P., *The Kingdom of God in History* Good News Studies 27 (Wilmington, Delaware: Michael Glazier, 1988). E.P. SANDERS included an extensive section on the kingdom in *Jesus and Judaism* (Philadelphia: Fortress, 1985), pp. 123-241, but his focus on Jesus within Judaism seemed to have precluded any reference to the Spirit. JACQUES SCHLOSSER, *Le Règne de Dieu dans les dits de Jèsus*, Études bibliques (Paris: J. Gabalda, 1980) knows of Stephen Smalley's and J.D.G. Dunn's work (both cited below) but the Spirit's relation to the kingdom is never treated in more than a passing fashion. In the last decade or so one finds only a few references to the theme of the Spirit and the kingdom. Dunn's "Spirit and Kingdom" has already been mentioned. This awareness of the interconnectedness of the Spirit and the kingdom likewise inspires his *Jesus and the Spirit: A Study of the Religious and Charismatic Experience of Jesus and the First Christians as Reflected in the New Testament* (Philadelphia: Westminster, 1975). Also useful is G.R. BEASLEY-MURRAY, "John 3:3, 5: Baptism, Spirit and the Kingdom", *The Expository Times* 97 (6, 1986): 167-70. His book, *Jesus and the Kingdom of God* (Grand Rapids, Mich.: William B. Eerdmans, 1987), is so narrowly focused on the present and future of the kingdom, on the Son of Man sayings, and on the Parousia that Jn. 3:3, 5 is simply never cited nor is there anywhere a discussion of the role of the Spirit. Also notable is STEPHEN S. SMALLEY, "Spirit, Kingdom and Prayer in Luke-Acts", *Novum Testamentum* 15 (1973): 59-71, following up on Dunn's article and the dynamic character of the tension between the presentness and futurity of the kingdom. See also H. BLOCHER, "The Kingdom of God and Evil", *Evangelical Review of Theology* 16 (1992): 435-44 and CHRISTOPH WREMBEK, "Der Heilige Geist und das Reich Gottes: Neue Gedanken zu einem alten Thema" *Geist und Leben* 64 (1991): 167-83.

These reasons are not exhaustive but do suffice to indicate the sort of problems one encounters when approaching this theme and to underscore the importance and relative novelty of the approach taken by Jürgen Moltmann in his book, *The Trinity and the Kingdom of God: The Doctrine of God*[4]. Moltmann set out explicitly to develop a social understanding of the Trinity in contrast to previous approaches proceeding from a substance metaphysics or from the more recent philosophy of the absolute subject. One of his key insights was the observation that "Jesus did not proclaim the kingdom of God *the Lord*, but the kingdom of God *his Father*. ... It is not that lordship is the mark of God's fatherhood, but the very reverse: God's fatherhood towards Jesus the Son is the mark of the lordship and kingdom which Jesus preaches"[5]. The history, in which the "divine rule was given by the Father to the Son through Christ's resurrection" and which will be completed in the final consummation when that rule is transferred back to the Father, marks the doctrine of the kingdom as fundamentally trinitarian. "*God's triunity precedes the divine lordship*" and so "it is not the doctrine of the Trinity which interprets the rule of God ... the rule of God in the form of the rule of the Son and in the form of the lordship of the Father interprets the eternal life of the divine Trinity"[6]. This "history of the Son" leads naturally to the "history of the Trinity" which provides the basis on which he reconstructs trinitarian doctrine prior to applying it to the notion of the kingdom of God.

Moltmann makes a number of compelling points which are worth exploring within Catholic theology even if it is not possible to import his thought directly into that context. His rejection of monotheism is so extreme that he verges on tritheism. His relatively extensive rejection of the Western theological tradition is not easily integrated into a Catholic theology faithful to that tradition. The judgment that the papacy is a form of clerical monotheism that is to be rejected in favor of a synodal understanding of the Church and the vari-

---

[4] Translated by MARGARET KOHL (London: SCM, 1981) from the German, *Trinität und Reich Gottes* (Munich: Christian Kaiser, 1980).
[5] Ibid., p. 70. He faults Karl Barth on this point. Cf. p. 143.
[6] Ibid., pp. 92-93.

ous reasonings that lead him to that conclusion are likewise not compatible with authentic Catholic theology[7].

In the remainder of this article, then, I would propose to do two things. First, some redress needs to be made highlighting the role of the Spirit with respect to the kingdom of God in the New Testament. This will aid in addressing the problem of an exclusively monotheistic conception of the kingdom. Second, in part following up on material developed in the first part of the article, Moltmann's conception of the social Trinity will be reworked and integrated with other approaches to provide a fuller vision of the trinitarian character of the kingdom of God and its relationship to the Church.

I. The Spirit and the Kingdom in the New Testament

The "kingdom of God" as a concept already presupposes the presence of a realm, a creation, over which God is king. This realm or creation is "peopled" since kingship is primarily understood as personal rather than impersonal power[8]. These two considerations alone suggest that the

---

[7] There is no particular need to rehearse these issues here; there have already been a number of reviews exploring these problems from a Catholic perspective. The most trenchant criticism under Catholic auspices is provided by George Hunsinger's review in *The Thomist* 47 (1983): 129-39. Other negative reviews include John H. Wright, S.J.'s review in *America* 146 (Feb. 20, 1982): 139-40; James R. Pambrun's in *Église et Théologie* 18 (1987): 376-79; and the bibliographical essay of Jean-Hervé Nicolas, O.P., "Le discours sur Dieu", *Revue Thomiste* 85 (1985): 635-57, esp. pp. 645- 51. Other essays, while critical of certain of Moltmann's positions, seek to provide a positive Catholic counterpart. See, for instance, GIOVANNI MARCHESI, S.J., "Il mistero di Dio nella riflessione teologica di J. Moltmann ed E. Jüngel" La Civilta Cattolica 136 (3-17 agosto, 1995): 254-66 or PAUL D. MOLNAR, "The Function of the Trinity in Moltmann's Ecological Doctrine of Creation", *Theological Studies* 51 (1990): 273-97. Gerald O'Collins's review in *Gregorianum* 63 (1982): 158 and John J. O'Donnell's bibliographical article, "The Trinity in Recent German Theology", The Heythrop Journal 23 (1982): 153-67, esp. pp. 160-66, are more completely appreciative of Moltmann's work. O'Donnell provides an extented discussion of Moltmann's "history of the Trinity" in the works prior to *The Trinity and the Kingdom of God* in *Trinity and Temporality: The Christian Doctrine of God in the Light of Process Theology and the Theology of Hope* (Oxford: The University Press, 1983).

[8] This personal power may at some point, particularly in its origins, have been grounded in physical prowess — the brute ability to guarantee protection, for instance. God's kingship is grounded in a similar fashion in his power to protect and bless Israel, ultimately in his power over creation. This does not change the fact, however, that kingship, as such, is personal.

kingdom of God is most appropriately understood in terms of the economic relations of the divine persons to those who are, accordingly, ruled. The fundamental pattern of those relations, especially as reflected in the New Testament material, is found in the expression "the Father sends the Son to give the Spirit." That Jesus, in point of fact, comes preaching the imminent coming of the kingdom of God suggests, at the very least, that the coming of that kingdom and the giving of the Spirit are very tightly interwoven[9].

In the Preaching of John and the Early Ministry of Jesus

The preaching of John the Baptist is included here for three reasons: first, that preaching provides the context for the beginning of Jesus' own ministry and for this reason alone needs to be taken into consideration; each of the evangelists uses the preaching of John to sound key themes within their respective Gospels; finally, only Matthew has the Baptist himself preaching the imminence of the kingdom — this circumstance needs to be explored.

Mark reduces John's preaching to two points. The first is the "baptism of repentance for the forgiveness of sins" (1:4); the second is that after him one mightier than him will come who "will baptize you with the Holy Spirit" (1:7, 8). Jesus' own baptism reflects this pattern. He was baptized by John; on coming out of the water the Holy Spirit descended on him and the voice of the Father proclaimed him the beloved Son. Finally Jesus, in his own preaching, urged the people to "repent, and believe in the gospel" (1:14). Thematic repetitions make it clear that that gospel has to do especially with the baptism with the Holy Spirit first announced by John. The point of the repentance preached by Jesus is that "the time is fulfilled,"which is to say, "the kingdom of God is at hand." It is hard to avoid the conclusion, although it is not as such explicitly stated, that the kingdom of God has very much to do with the baptism with the Holy Spirit which is equally "at hand."

Luke expands considerably on the ministry of John who is described as "filled with the Holy Spirit, even from his

---

[9] DUNN, "Spirit and Kingdom", pp. 37-39.

mother's womb" (1:15) and having a mission "to turn the hearts" of the people, preparing them for the Lord" (1:16-17). The angel tells Mary that her son will be given "the throne of his father David" and will reign forever, though the theme of salvation is at least as strong as (and not incompatible with) that of kingship in what follows (1:54, 68-73, 77; 2:11, 30). This will be made possible because "the Holy Spirit will come upon you [Mary], and the power of the Most High will overshadow you" (1:32, 35)[10]. Through the Spirit's agency all of this is recognized (1:41-43; 2:26-30). The Holy Spirit thus prepares the way, provides knowledge of, and makes possible the coming of the kingdom[11].

John, for his part, comes "preaching a baptism of repentance" (3:3) and to that end points not to the imminent kingdom of God but to the imminent wrath of God (3:7). Like Mark, in addition to the preaching of repentance, Luke has John testifying that the one who follows him "will baptize you with the Holy Spirit" (3:16). Luke adds the note of a purifying fire as a complement to the wrath just mentioned. Those who do not repent "will burn with unquenchable fire"; those who do "shall see the salvation of God" (3:6, 17). Luke identifies this proclamation as "good news" (3:18 - εὐηγγελίζετο τὸν λαόν).

Jesus returns to Galilee "in the power of the Spirit" (4:14) and in the first teaching that Luke records he announces that the Scripture from Isaiah — "The Spirit of the Lord is upon me, because he has anointed me to preach good news to the poor" — has been fulfilled in the hearing of his audience (4:18-21). This is noteworthy because these verses are the only instance of a positive message in Luke's Gospel prior to the notice at the end of the chapter (4:43) that he must "preach the good news of the kingdom of God" elsewhere as well[12]. Insofar as Luke has provided us with any content for this "good news of the kingdom of God" it is to be identified with this announcement that the Spirit of God

---

[10] SMALLEY, "Spirit, Kingdom and Prayer", pp. 64-65.

[11] DUNN, "Spirit and Kingdom", p. 36.

[12] Vv. 22-29 narrate his rejection by his fellow countrymen; vv. 31-37 narrate an exorcism; vv. 38-41 narrate various healings. No further positive teaching is provided by Luke prior to v. 43.

is now active in Jesus' preaching. The appropriate conclusion would seem to be that "the kingdom of God is at hand" means that "the Spirit of God is now active" in some new and decisive way.

These two themes are again brought into conjunction with each other at the beginning of Acts. There Luke tells us that after his resurrection Jesus appeared to the disciples "speaking of the kingdom of God" (1:3). Again, the only positive content that Luke provides of what Jesus said during that time has to do with the Holy Spirit: the disciples were to wait in Jerusalem "for the promise of the Father, which, he said, 'you heard from me, for John baptized with water, but before many days you shall be baptized with the Holy Spirit'" (1:4-5)[13].

Matthew highlights the kingdom of God from the very beginning. Jesus is identified as the son of David in the very first verse. Joseph, himself identified as a son of David, is informed that the child conceived by Mary is "of the Holy Spirit" (1:20) and that he will "save his people from their sins" (1:21). The kingship of Christ is the motivating force which drives the narrative through the visit of the magi and the flight into Egypt. It is not surprising, then, that the evangelist puts into the mouth of the Baptist the proclamation of the imminence of the kingdom of heaven in addition to the motif of repentance found in the other Synoptic Gospels. Matthew also has John warning of the imminence of the wrath of God (3:7) as well as the purifying fire to come (3:12). What is constant in all of the Gospels is the notice that the one to follow John will "baptize you with the Holy Spirit" (3:11).

Jesus himself preaches repentance because, in an expression unique to Matthew, "the kingdom of heaven is at hand" (4:17). He goes everywhere "teaching in their synagogues and preaching the gospel of the kingdom and healing every disease and every infirmity among the people" (4:23). The Sermon on the Mount follows where a number of equivalences to the "kingdom of heaven" are established: "they

---

[13] DUNN, "Spirit and Kingdom", p. 38, dwells on this point. Cf. also SMALLEY, "Spirit, Kingdom and Prayer", pp. 63-64.

shall be comforted"; "they shall inherit the earth"; "they shall be satisfied [with righteousness]"; "they shall obtain mercy"; "they shall see God"; "they shall be called sons of God"; "your reward is great in heaven" (5:3-11).

John, in his Gospel, expands considerably on the testimony of the Baptist to Jesus even while constricting the Baptist's own role. There is no mention that John's baptism is for repentance for the forgiveness of sins, only that it is a baptism with water (1:26). Jesus own preeminence with respect to John is underscored (1:15, 27, 30). Insofar as a purpose for John's baptism is indicated it is in order "that he [Jesus] might be revealed to Israel" (1:31). John himself did not know him; Jesus is recognized because the Spirit descends and remains on him and by this he is recognized as the one "who baptizes with the Holy Spirit" (1:33). At this point John does not use any regal title for Jesus beyond "Son of God"; Jesus is rather "the Lamb of God" (1:34, 36). Still, the regal connotations are contained in the title "Messiah" and made explicit by Nathanael — "You are the Son of God! You are the King of Israel" (1:49). The connection between the Spirit and the kingdom is made explicit in John in Jesus' conversation with Nicodemus: "Unless one is born anew, he cannot see the kingdom of God ... unless one is born of water and the Spirit, he cannot enter the kingdom of God" (3:3,5).

Signs of the Kingdom

Schnackenberg notes that "statements about the kingly reign of God are not as frequent in late Jewish writers as might have been expected from the evidence in the gospels"[14]. This, combined with the relative absence of any kingdom proclamation in the preaching of the Baptist[15], suggests that the emphasis on the kingdom that one finds in the New Testament is to be attributed to Jesus himself. Schnackenberg develops several points in conjunction with Jesus' proclamation that are worth examining with a view to their relationship to the Spirit.

---

[14] *God's Rule*, p. 41.
[15] The sole instance, Mt. 3:2, fits in too neatly with Matthew's overall emphasis on the kingdom, as noted above, to be reliably traced back to the Baptist.

He notes from the first the eschatological character of that proclamation. In this Jesus carried over the perspectives of the prophets and later Judaism. There were distinctive features of that proclamation. Among the first that are mentioned is the insistence "that God's eschatological kingship was very close!"[16] Further, it is eschatological not simply because it incorporates the notion of the final age "but because it bears the mark of an eschatological event"[17]. Herein lies the importance of the exorcisms, healings, and miracles: Jesus did not simply talk about the kingdom of God; in his actions he made it present.

It was expected that anyone claiming to be annointed with God's Spirit, either in a properly messianic capacity or as a prophet, would provide appropriate signs supporting that claim[18]. This underlay the demand of the scribes and Pharisees for a sign (Mt. 12:38-42, 16:1-4; Mk. 8:11-2; cf. Lk. 11:29-32; Jn. 6:30). Jesus refused to give them any except that of Jonah but, in point of fact, he provided any number of signs: "'Go and tell John what you hear and see: the blind receive their sight and the lame walk, lepers are cleansed and the deaf hear, and the dead are raised up, and the poor have good news preached to them" (Mt. 11:2-6; Lk. 7:18-23; cf. Jn. 10:25, 31, 37-42). These signs and the preaching of the kingdom as such are consistently linked in the Gospels — "And he went ... preaching the gospel of the kingdom and healing every disease and every infirmity among the people"

---

[16] Ibid., p. 80.

[17] Ibid., p. 82.

[18] Qumran refers to prophets also as "anointed ones" (CD 5:21-6:1; 1QM 11:7, 8; CD 2:12). Cf. Marinus de Jonge, "Messiah", in *Anchor Bible Dictionary*, vol. 4, David Noel Freedman, et al., eds. (New York: Doubleday, 1992), p. 782. Expectations were quite varied at this time and intertestamental documents say very little about signs as such. Ibid., pp. 777-788. Still, when Simon, in First Maccabees, is made the leader and high priest of the Jews forever "until a trustworthy prophet should arise" the question arises how such a prophet was to be recognized. The examples of Theudas, who claimed "that at his command the river [Jordan] would be parted" and "the Egyptian" who claimed that "at his command Jerusalem's wall would fall down" speak to this generalized expectation of signs. Cf. Richard A. Horsley, "Messianic Movements in Judaism", in *Anchor Bible Dictionary*, vol. 4, p. 796. The signs need not be miraculous. "Great physical stature and military prowess" served to remind people of the biblical "tradition of the anointed king as a mighty warrior." Simon bar Giora may have gone to considerable trouble to reinforce the Davidic prototype. Ibid., p. 794.

(Mt. 4:23; cf. also Mt. 9:35, Mk. 1:14-39, Lk. 9:11). This conjunction between the performance of signs and the kingdom is presupposed in the expectation of those who work such signs that they will, perforce, enter the kingdom (Mt. 7:21-23). It is also presupposed that similar signs will accompany the disciples as they in their turn preach the coming kingdom (Mt. 10:1, 7-8; Mk. 3:13-15; 6:7, 12-13; 16:15-18; Lk. 9:1-2; 10:9; Acts 8:12-13). Paul explicitly identifies such signs as manifestations of the activity and power of the Spirit (Gal. 3:5; I Cor. 12:7-11) but such an identification is also found in at least the Gospel of Matthew — "if it is by the Spirit of God that I cast out demons, then the kingdom of God has come upon you" (Mt. 12:28; Luke's reference to the "finger of God" in 11:20 is likewise a reference to the Spirit)[19].

Although the kingdom is not explicitly mentioned in the testimony which the disciples will have to give when they are brought before the synagogues, rulers and authorities, governors and kings, it is a continuation of the mission given to them by Jesus to preach the kingdom. They are not to worry about such times because "the Holy Spirit will teach you in that very hour what you ought to say" (Lk. 12:12; cf. also Mt. 10:20, Jn. 14:26). The proclamation of the kingdom is accomplished in the power of the Spirit (Mt. 7:29, Mk. 1:22, Lk. 4:32, Jn. 7:46).

Entrance into the Kingdom

John's Gospel makes it clear that reception of the Spirit is the sine qua non for entrance into the kingdom and this is understood in the context of baptism — "unless one is born of water and the Spirit" (3:3-5)[20]. The rule of the connection between water baptism and the Spirit is confirmed in the exception provided by Cornelius. The Spirit comes on that household while Peter is preaching and he concludes that water baptism cannot be withheld from them (10:47-48). The implication this has is expressed eighteen verses later — "then to the Gentiles also God has granted repentance unto

---

[19] DUNN, "Spirit and Kingdom", p. 38; *Jesus and the Spirit*, pp. 44-53.
[20] See BEASLEY-MURRAY, "John 3:3, 5", p. 168, for some of the different ways this can be understood.

life" (11:18). The life in question is entrance into the kingdom of God on the day of the Lord (cf. Mt. 19:23-29; Mk. 10:23-30; Lk. 18:24-30)[21].

But the performance of the signs attendant on the proclamation of the kingdom, and the possession of the Spirit that this implies, is not enough for entrance into the kingdom on the day of the Lord. Many will have worked these signs but the Lord will say to them "I never knew you" (Mt. 8:23). If reception of the Spirit is essential for entrance this reception must be accompanied by appropriate fruit of the Spirit, preeminently by a conversion of heart. The one attitude that Jesus, and John before him, insists on as preparation for the coming kingdom is repentance (Mt. 3:2; 21:28-32; Mk. 1:15; Lk. 18:9-14). This much is implied in Matthew's parable of the eschatological marriage feast where the king asks the guest lacking the appropriate garb "how did you get in here without a wedding garment?" and has him thrown out (22:12).

There are, however, a number of attitudes that are named as essential for entrance into the kingdom throughout the Gospels: righteousness (Mt. 5:19-20), doing the will of the Father (Mt. 7:21), love (Mk. 12:28-34), becoming childlike (Mt. 18:3; 19:14; Mk. 10:14-15; Lk. 18:16-17), mercy and forgiveness (Mt. 18:23- 35), acceptance of the cross (Mt. 10:38-39; 16:24-26; 20:21-23; Mk. 8:34-37; 10:35-40; Lk. 9:23-25; 14:27). To these one could add the attitudes indicated in the Sermon on the Mount mentioned above in the initial discussion of Matthew's Gospel. Although the Gospels themselves do not develop the link between these attitudes and the Spirit of God explicitly this is nonetheless implied in the various names for the Spirit and his activity. He is named the "Holy Spirit" some twenty-five times in the Gospels, forty in Acts (cf. also Lk. 1:35). His descent on Christ occasions the revelation of Jesus as the "beloved Son" (Mt. 3:16; Mk. 1:10; Lk. 3:22, cf. 1:35) and the disciples are told that they will receive the Spirit of the Father, implying their own sonship (Mt. 10:20). The Spirit is active in testing and will be with the disciples in times of tribulation (Mt. 4:1; Mk. 1:12; 13:11). The

---

[21] Ibid., p. 169.

servant on whom the Spirit descends proclaims judgment (Mt. 12:18; cf. also Jn. 16:7-11); he is also sent to the poor and oppressed (Lk. 4:18). The Spirit opposes the flesh (Jn. 3:6, 6:63). Authentic worship of God is in spirit and truth (Jn. 4:23-24) but the Spirit is the Spirit of truth (Jn. 14:17, 15:26; 16:13) who inspires the prophets (Mt. 22:43; Mk. 12:36; Lk. 1:15, 17, 41, 67; Jn. 3:34; 16:13). Knowledge of the mysteries of the kingdom have been given to the disciples (Mt. 13:11, 19, 52; Mk. 4:11-12; Lk. 8:10) but it is the Spirit who will teach them what to say (Mt. 10:20; Lk. 12:12), indeed, who will teach them all things (Jn. 14:26). The Spirit is the Paraclete (Jn. 14:26, 15:26). Jesus breathes the Spirit on the disciples and in the same "breath" gives them the power to forgive sins.

Many of these points are made explicit by Paul[22]. The Spirit opposes the flesh. If those who do the works of the flesh will not inherit the kingdom of God, those who walk by the Spirit will. They have crucified the flesh with its passions and desires. The fruits of the Spirit are love, joy, peace, and so forth (Gal. 5:16-26). Through the Spirit by faith Christians wait for the hope of righteousness, for the new creation (Gal. 5:5-6, 6:15) — they are "re-elementized" by the Spirit (Gal. 5:25; compare 4:9). "God's love has been poured into our hearts through the Holy Spirit which has been given to us" (Rom. 5:5). "All who are led by the Spirit of God are sons of God"; we "have received the spirit of sonship. When we cry, 'Abba! Father'" (Rom. 14-16)! "For the kingdom of God is not food and drink but righteousness and peace and joy in the Holy Spirit" (Rom. 14:17). "Now we have received not the spirit of the world, but the Spirit which is from God, that we might understand the gifts bestowed on us by God" (2:12). Christians are the temple of God in whom dwells the Spirit of God (I Cor. 3:12). The examples from Paul could be multiplied. The point is that all of the requirements for entrance into the kingdom of God are realized for those who allow the Spirit to guide their lives. There is no other way to inherit eternal life, to inherit the kingdom.

---

[22] DUNN, "Spirit and Kingdom", p. 36.

The Multivalent Character of the Kingdom

When one surveys the various references to the kingdom in the New Testament one is struck by the variety of temporal locations envisioned for the kingdom. Complicating the issue further the kingdom is variously described as Christ's own kingdom or the kingdom of God. This has, understandably, given rise to a number of theories about the relationship of these various "kingdoms" to each other and to the Church[23].

Matthew provides a series of parables of the kingdom in chapter thirteen. In the second parable the kingdom of heaven is compared to a man who sowed good seed in his field but while he was sleeping an enemy came and sowed weeds among the wheat (Mt. 13:24-30, 36-43). They will be allowed to grow together until the harvest time. The temporal viewpoint is clearly the present world order; the harvest is the eschatological judgment or harvest at the end of that world order. "Evil-doers are now members of the community of salvation, that is, the Church. Eventually they will be cut off from the 'kingdom of the Son of man' which is distinct from the 'kingdom of the Father'"[24]. The parable of the mustard seed which follows, oriented as it is to the growth of the kingdom, likewise presumes a temporal location in the present as does the parable of the leaven which is hidden in the dough (cf. also Mk. 4:26-29). The eschatological kingdom will not be hidden; only the kingdom as a present reality is thus undiscernible except for its "leavening" effect in the present. The same sentiment underlies Jesus response to the Pharisees asking about the time of the coming of the kingdom in Luke's Gospel. There are no observable signs; rather, "the kingdom of God is in the midst of you" (Lk. 12:20-21). The final parable in this chapter in Matthew, the net which gathers "fish of every kind," likewise has a dual focus even if the emphasis is on the latter phase of judgment. There is a

---

[23] MOLTMANN, *The Trinity and the Kingdom*, pp. 202-12, provides several examples by way of developing his own trinitarian history of the kingdom. NORMAN PERRIN, *The Kingdom of God in the Teaching of Jesus*, The New Testament Library (London: SCM, 1963) and WENDELL WILLIS, *The Kingdom of God in 20th-Century Interpretation* (Peabody, Ma.: Hendrickson, 1987) provide surveys.

[24] SCHNACKENBERG, *God's Rule*, p. 159.

present gathering of a mixed harvest; at the fullness of time, when the net is full, the fish are separated. Paul's consistent focus is on the kingdom that is to come which will be inherited by the disciples who follow the Spirit, but even he (assuming the authenticity of Colossians) will speak of a present transfer into "the kingdom of his beloved Son" (Col. 1:13).

In the parable of the wheat and the weeds the kingdom in the present world order is identified as the "kingdom of the Son"; the kingdom that is entered at the end of time is identified as the "kingdom of the Father." This distinction is held with mixed consistency. The application of Zech. 9:9, "your king comes to you ... humble and riding on an ass, on a colt the foal of an ass," to Jesus in Mt. 21:4-5 (cf. also Mk. 11:10; Lk. 19:38-40; Jn. 1:29; 12:12-15) identifies a kingdom, no longer as coming in the future, but as present in the person of Jesus. Revelation identifies Jesus as the King of Kings who has even now made a kingdom for himself but in such a way that opens out to eternity (Rev. 1:5-6; 17:14; 19:16). The parable of the marriage feast likewise has a dual focus. The invitations are being sent out in the present time; the marriage feast is in the future (as it is in the parable of the ten virgins in Mt. 25:1-13); the Father is the king. At the Last Supper Jesus tells his disciples that the next time he drinks with them will be "in my Father's kingdom" (Mt. 26:29). Yet, in the scene of the eschatological judgment (Mt. 25:31-46; cf. also II Tim. 4:1) it is not the Father who is named as the king but the Son of man who sits on the glorious throne. In Luke's story of the talents a nobleman, Jesus presumably, goes away and receives a kingdom, returning to render judgment on his servants. The good thief asks to be remembered when Jesus comes into his kingdom (Lk. 23:42). The angel tells Mary that "of his kingdom there will be no end" (Lk. 1:33; cf. also Heb. 1:8). The passion stories of all four Gospels make it clear that in the perspective of the evangelists Jesus is himself a king, though not of this world (Jn. 18:33-37).

The relation between the Father's kingdom and Christ's is explicitly averted to in Lk. 22:29-30 — "I assign to you, as my Father assigned to me, a kingdom, that you may eat and drink at my table in my kingdom." Paul implies a like assignment by the Father in I Cor. 15:24-28 even as he writes of the

Son's kingdom being handed back to the Father. I Thess. 4:17, which speaks of the saints joining the Lord in the air, could well be an expression of a rule shared by Christ with the saints, air being the realm of demons over whom the glorious Jesus rules. Revelation seems to indicate a similar handing over of the Son's kingdom to the Father (1:5-6) and later indicates that the dead in Christ will also reign with Christ (20:4-6). Hebrews has God acknowledging the unending character of the Son's kingdom (1:8). Ephesians speaks of the single "kingdom of Christ and of God" (5:5) as does Revelation (11:15; 22:1).

This cascading assignment of kingly power is of considerable importance when assessing the role of the Spirit in this successive handing over that will be explored in more detail in the next section. Two preliminary points are worth making, however.

First, there are temporal distinctions in the human experience of the Spirit which parallel the distinction made vis-à-vis the kingdom[25]. The prophets of the Old Testament, up to and including John the Baptist, were inspired by the Spirit (Mt. 22:43; Mk. 12:36; Lk. 1:15, 17, 41; Lk. 2:25-27; Acts 1:16; 4:25). The disciples themselves presumably cast out demons and healed in the power of the Spirit before Jesus' death and resurrection. And yet that earlier period which characterized the disciples is sharply distinguished from their later experience of the Spirit (Lk. 24:48-48; Jn. 7:39; 14:1, 26; 15:26; 16:7, 13; Acts 1:8; 2:14-21; II Cor. 3:8; Eph. 3:5). This disjunction is already suggested in the testimony of John (Mt. 3:11; Mk. 1:8; Lk. 3:16; Jn. 1:33). John, the "greatest" of the Old Testament prophets, is less than the least in the kingdom of God (Mt. 11:11; Lk. 7:28). It seems unlikely that a comparison is being made between those reigning in heaven and the earthly John. Further, any view that John himself would not, upon his death, enter the same kingdom of God is equally unlikely. The comparison makes the most sense as one in the present temporal order. For instance, the baptism by John was only by water for repentance whereas the baptism by the disciples of Jesus is the baptism in the Holy Spir-

---

[25] Cf. DUNN, "Spirit and Kingdom" and *Jesus and the Spirit*, p. 89.

it itself (Acts 8:15, 17-19; 9:17; 19:6; Gal. 3:5). But this present experience of the Spirit, complete with the power to work the signs of the kingdom, is itself provisional. It is a promise or seal guaranteeing the future (II Cor. 1:22; 5:5; Gal 3:14; 5:5; Eph. 4:30; Heb. 9:8)[26]. One who has been baptized in the Spirit must walk in the Spirit, must perfect their holiness, if they are to enter into the kingdom at the end (Rom. 8:9-16, 23; II Cor. 3:18; 7:1; Gal. 3:3; 5:16-25). Indeed, it is possible to have been baptized in the Spirit but to fail to inherit the kingdom of God (Gal. 5:21; Eph. 4:30; I Tim. 4:1).

The second point in the comparison between the history of the kingdom and the Spirit is that, like the kingdom, there is a succession with regards the giving of the Spirit. The Spirit comes upon Jesus at his baptism by John (Mt. 3:16; Mk. 1:10; Lk. 3:22; Jn. 1:33). John later reinforces this dependence of Jesus on the Father for giving the Spirit when, in his Gospel, Jesus says he will send the Spirit from his Father (15:26; cf. 14:26). Then, as the disciples will be assigned a kingdom, they are also given the Spirit (Lk. 24:49; Jn. 20:22; Acts 1:4-5; 2:1-4; 4:31) and, indeed, are themselves empowered to impart that Spirit to others (Mt. 28:19; Acts 8:15, 17-19; 9:17; 19:6; Gal. 3:5)[27].

* * *

What is clear from this whole discussion of the relationship between the Spirit and the kingdom of God is that the history and reality of the kingdom is very closely tied to the gift of the Spirit that is the end term of the Son's mission from the Father. It is not that the kingdom is simply to be identified with the gift of the Spirit but rather that the two are inseparable; God and Christ concretely exercise their dominion through the Holy Spirit who is active within the believer. And this begins to suggest the substance of the relationship between the Church and the kingdom. If, as Irenaeus asserts, "where the Church is, there is the Spirit of

---

[26] DUNN, "Spirit and Kingdom", p. 36-37.

[27] Ibid., p. 39, speaks of "a two-fold dispensational divide" but pays too little attention to earlier bestowals of the Spirit — Jesus is "the unique bearer of the Spirit" in Luke and this in spite of Lk. 1:15, 41.

God; and where the Spirit of God is, there is the Church, and every kind of grace"[28], then it is also true that the Church and the kingdom of God are intimately connected. The usual way of connecting them is along the temporal axis: the kingdom is the eternal kingdom in heaven; the Church is the kingdom here on earth, a mixed reality and in pilgrimage to its true country. This, however, moves us toward Augustine and the next section.

II. Images of the Trinity and the Redeemed Community

Among the suggestions that Moltmann makes in his work on the Trinity and the kingdom one of the more interesting is his insistence on the need to develop a theological understanding of the kingdom of the Spirit. He takes inspiration from Joachim of Fiore but manages to purge the most problematic aspects of Abbot Joachim's thought. He was reacting to the orthodox Protestant doctrine of the kingdom which reduced the historical kingdom to two forms: the kingdom of the Father — of nature, and the kingdom of the Son — of grace[29].

Augustine, the Spirit, and the City of God

Augustine provides useful resources for such a project, as much in terms of the consistency of the imagery that he uses as in any explicit statements. A useful starting point is a classic expression of God's rule in the world found in the third book of the *De Trinitate*. The immediate context is a discussion of the theophanies of the Old Testament and whether God himself effected those visible manifestations or whether the agency of angels was used. This leads to a discussion of the mediation of the divine will in the natural order: "The order of nature, to be sure, declares itself in various ways; in all of them it serves the divine command. ... Not one of them occurs

---

[28] Adv. Haer. III.xxiv.1. Dunn, "Spirit and Kingdom", expresses the relation between the Spirit and the kingdom in similar terms: "Where he is the Kingdom is" (p. 37); "It is not so much a case of Where Jesus is there is the Kingdom, as Where the Spirit is there is the Kingdom" (p. 38).
[29] MOLTMANN, *The Trinity and the Kingdom*, pp. 203-9.

independently of God's will, though many people do not see this"[30]. His first example is the human body which "is governed by the soul breathed into it; this soul is rational, and so although it is subject to change, it is capable of sharing in that wisdom which is changeless"[31]. He explores this in the case of a single wise man and then notes that "we could extend the point to cover a whole community of such wise men, or to the state — even to the whole world — provided the government of its human affairs were in the hands of wise men"[32].

Augustine observes, however, that "this happy situation does not yet exist, for we first need to be trained to mortality in this exile of ours" and turns finally to the heavenly realm itself:

> There the will of God presides, as in his house or his temple, over the spirits who are joined together in the highest concord and friendship, fused indeed into one will by a kind of spiritual fire of charity (*quodam spiritali caritatis igne conflatis*) .... From that lofty throne, set apart in holiness, the divine will spreads itself through all things in marvelous patterns of created movement, first spiritual then corporeal; and it uses all things to carry out the unchanging judgment of the divine decree, whether they be corporeal or incorporeal things, whether they be non-rational or rational spirits, whether they be good by his grace, or bad by their own will[33].

What is of particular interest in this is the description of the union of spirits as the fusion by the fire of love into one will. It is a recurring image. A similar image inspires Augustine's description of the "heaven of heavens" in the *Confessiones*: "your own house ... a pure mind, most harmoniously one (*concordissime unam*) by the established peace of holy spirits, citizens of your city in heavenly places above these present heavens"[34].

---

[30] *De Trinitate* III.ii.7. The translations are from EDMUND HILL, O.P., *The Trinity*, The Works of Saint Augustine I.5 (Brooklyn, N.Y.: New City Press, 1990).
[31] *De Trinitate* III.ii.8.
[32] *De Trinitate* III.iii.9.
[33] *De Trinitate* III.iv.9.
[34] *Confessiones* XII.xi.12. The translation is from John K. Ryan, *The Confessions of St. Augustine* (New York: Doubleday/Image, 1960).

Augustine goes on to affirm in the *Confessiones* that souls in pilgrimage here on earth seek to dwell in this house[35]; indeed, that heavenly city is our true country[36]. This is thematized in the *De civitate Dei*: "I treat of it [the city of God] both as it exists in this world of time, a stranger among the ungodly, living by faith, and as it stands in the security of its everlasting seat"[37]. Speaking of the members of Christ's body, the Church, Augustine uses the same imagery used for the heavenly city:

> "so they are cleansed by the mediator that they may be one in him, not only by virtue of the same nature whereby all of them from the ranks of mortal men are made equal to the angels, but even more by virtue of one and the same wholly harmonious will reaching out in concert to the same ultimate happiness, and fused somehow into one spirit in the furnace of charity (*concordissimam uoluntatem in unum spiritum quodam modo caritatis igne conflatam*)."

He goes on to explain: "that just as Father and Son are one not only by equality of substance but also by identity of will, so these men, for whom the Son is mediator with God, might be one not only by being of the same nature, but also by being bound in the fellowship of the same love"[38]. But, of course, this unity of love between the Father and the Son is the Holy Spirit.

The bishop of Hippo makes this last point explicitly in his sermons on Pentecost:

> That gust (*Flatus ille*) was purging their hearts of worldly chaff; that fire (*ignis ille*) was consuming the straw of ancient lusts; those tongues they were speaking in, filled by the Holy Spirit, were prefiguring the Church of the future through the languages of all nations ... the devout humility of the faithful has brought to the unity of the

---

[35] *Confessiones* XII.xi.13.
[36] *Confessiones* VII.xx.26. Cf. also *De civitate Dei* XV.15.
[37] *De civitate Dei* I.Pref. The translations are those of Henry Bettenson, *Concerning the City of God against the Pagans* (Harmondsworth, Middlesex: Penguin Books, 1984 [1972]).
[38] *De Trinitate* IV.ix.12.

Church the variety of their different languages; so that what discord had dissipated charity (*caritas*) might gather together, and the scattered members of the human race, as of one body, might be attached to their one head, Christ, and so reunited, and fused together into the unity of the holy body by the fire of love (*in sancti corporis unitatem dilectionis igne conflarentur*)[39].

Augustine's intent is ultimately Eucharistic; the unity of the body of Christ is in view, not only on the level of the community itself, understood in terms of extrinsic relations, but also in terms of a unity that is effected at the interior depths of the individual. In the *De civitate Dei* he makes this dual focus clear

> To this God we owe our service — what in Greek is called *latreia* — whether in the various sacraments or in ourselves. For we are his temple, collectively, and as individuals. For he condescends to dwell in the union of all and in each person ... When we lift up our hearts to him, our heart is his altar. We propitiate him by our priest, his only-begotten Son. We sacrifice blood-stained victims to him when we fight for truth 'as far as shedding our blood'. We burn the sweetest incense for him, when we are in his sight on fire with devout and holy love[40].

He underscores this last point, uses it to shift the focus from the individual to the community, and then makes the Eucharistic allusion explicit:

> how much more does the soul itself become a sacrifice when it offers itself to God, so that it may be kindled by the fire of love ...
> So then the true sacrifices are acts of compassion, whether towards ourselves or towards our neighbours, when they are directed towards God ... it immediately follows that the whole redeemed community, that is to say, the congregation and fellowship of the saints, is of-

---

[39] *Sermones (184-229Z) on the Liturgical Seasons* 271. The translation is from EDMUND HILL, O.P., *Sermons*, The Works of Saint Augustine III.6 (New Rochelle, N.Y.: New City Press, 1993).

[40] *De civitate* Dei X.3.

fered to God as a universal sacrifice, through the great Priest who offered himself in his suffering for us — so that we might be the body of so great a head ... This is the sacrifice of Christians, who are 'many, making up one body in Christ'. This is the sacrifice which the Church continually celebrates in the sacrament of the altar, a sacrament well-known to the faithful where it is shown to the Church that she herself is offered in the offering which she presents to God[41].

It is no accident, then, that Augustine concludes his discussion of the divine will, with which this section began, by providing yet another, Eucharistic example of the way God's power, in the person of the Spirit, reaches down and orders all things, even corporal reality, to effect the consecration of the sacrament of the Body and Blood of the Lord[42].

Analogies of the Trinity

In line with his development of a social understanding of the Trinity Moltmann understands the image of God in terms of "fellowship with other people"[43] which corresponds to "the open, unifying at-oneness of the three divine Persons in their relationships to one another. This points to a political order where there is no supremacy or subjection of one person to the other[44]. It also points to a "presbyterial and synodal church order and leadership based on brotherly advice"; "authority and obedience are replaced by dialogue, consensus and harmony"[45]. It is certainly true that such a democratic or synodal view of political and ecclesial order coheres very well with the unifying power of the Spirit vis-à-vis the kingdom or city of God which has been developed above. Where the Spirit is, there is fellowship and love and mutual submission. Moltmann is not wrong to affirm these things. The problem is that it is an incomplete vision.

---

[41] *De civitate* Dei X.7.
[42] *De Trinitate* III.iv.10.
[43] MOLTMANN, *The Trinity and the Kingdom*, p. 155.
[44] Ibid., p. 192.
[45] Ibid., p. 202.

Symptomatic of this is the clash between this democratic, synodal view and the family analogy of Gregory of Nazianzus which he favorably cites in contrast to the Augustinian psychological analogy[46]. Families, however, are not synodal in structure; children are in submission to their parents who exercise authority over them. Likewise, Jesus Christ is not in a synodal relationship with his Church; he is a monarch. It is true that he seats the Church on his own throne but this assignation or handing over of power cannot be understood synodally; it is a grant of power from one to another which does not nullify the power and authority of the one making the grant; it is not true that "authority and obedience are replaced by dialogue, consensus and harmony." The Church is in harmony with Christ, to be sure, but the Church remains obedient to Christ as well, just as Christ remains obedient to the authority of the Father even in his harmony with his Source. All things are submitted to the Son except he who submits all things to him and when this is done Christ submits himself to the Father (I Cor. 15:24-28).

There are further problems with both the family analogy and with a broader social analogy. With regard to the former the order of processions are in effect reversed, with the son/Son proceeding from the mother/Spirit rather than viceversa. To be sure, this is not a grave problem for some Eastern theologians who profess agnosticism with regard to the order of processions in the Trinity; it should be more of a problem for Moltmann since the Spirit's procession from the Father "has as its premise the generation of the Son"[47]. With regard to Moltmann's social analogy, understood in terms of relations between individuals, it is not able to preserve the threeness of the Persons of the Trinity. Synods, for example, are typically composed of scores of persons; families rarely have only one child. For a social analogy to work one must

---

[46] That he is intent on this analogy seems clear from his singling out of the male-female relationship as exemplifying the image of God as fellowship. Ibid. p. 156. This idea is already found in Karl Barth's treatment of Gen. 1:26 in *Church Dogmatics*, III.1: *The Doctrine of Creation*, trans. J.W. EDWARDS, et al (Edinburgh: T. & T. Clark, 1958), pp. 181-206.

[47] MOLTMANN, *The Trinity and the Kingdom*, p. 183.

locate the imaging of the Trinity some place other than in the persons themselves constituting that society.

The construction of such an analogy was the point of my own work, *Trinity and Marriage in Paul*. There, I establish an extensive set of criteria, based on an analysis of Augustine's *De Trinitate*, governing the construction of a theologically useful social or communitarian trinitarian analogy. Using themes developed from an analysis of Paul's treatment of various communities I set out the social triad of commonality, institutionality, and valuative dynamics as providing in the social context what memory, understanding, and will provide for the individual understood as imaging God. The preeminent exemplar of such a social imaging of the Trinity is found in the Church which, on the one hand is marked by oneness, and on the other by catholicity, apostolicity, and holiness[48].

This analogy does not replace either the psychological or the interactional (or love or marital) analogies but rather complements them and brings to completion the various locations in human reality where a human imaging of the Triune God can be seen: the individual, the community, the individual in communitarian union[49]. The prime exemplar for this is Jesus Christ who images the Triune God in himself, in his union with His Church, and in the Church itself which, in being derived from Christ, is found to be like Christ in imaging God: "and we all, with unveiled face, beholding the glory of the Lord, are being changed into his likeness from one degree of glory to another" (II Cor. 3:18).

It is pointless, then, to oppose these different modes of imaging God as if they were mutually exclusive. The synodal character of the Church, understood either in terms of the union of bishops with each other or more generally of the union of all Christians with each other and grounded in the

---

[48] EARL C. MULLER, S.J., *Trinity and Marriage in Paul: The Establishment of a Communitarian Analogy of the Trinity Grounded in the Theological Shape of Pauline Thought*, American University Studies, VII.60 (New York: Peter Lang, 1990). The marital community rather than the ecclesial was focused on as providing a more manageable set of texts to work with. Marriage is also the prime exemplar of the interactional, or love analogy. A summary of the criteria is found on pp. 241-43. The terms of the triad are discussed from a sociological perspective on pp. 275-82, from a theological perspective, on pp. 283-301.

[49] Ibid., pp. 348-61.

action of the Spirit of God unifying the universal Church, should not be opposed to the apostolic and hierarchical character of the Church which is, in its turn, grounded in the handing over of the kingdom to the Son by the Father and the parallel handing over of either the kingdom by Christ to the Church which reigns with him (Lk. 22:29-30; II Tim. 2:12; Rev. 20:4-6; 22:5) or authority in that Church to the Twelve and, implicitly, to their successors (Mt. 16:19; 18:18; 19:28; Lk.22:30; Jn. 20:23; Rev. 4:4; 11:16; 20:4). A bishop or any other person with authority in the Church who exercises that authority in an domineering and oppressive fashion is not acting like Christ who came, not as one lording it over his disciples, but as one serving them, as one who empowered them, but that sinners occupy such positions does not nullify the action of Christ in putting power into human hands. It also follows that the chief service that such authorities in the Church should perform, then, is the empowerment of those over whom they have been placed.

In the end the unity to which Christians are called is effected by God in three inseparable ways. It is effected in the single individual, the bishop, who stands "in persona Christi" and as such stands proclaiming the good news of the kingdom of God as the visible sign about which Christians gather in that worship of the Church in which the kingdom, in which Christ himself, is rendered really present to his people. It is effected in the marital union which binds together, not only individual Christians, but the Church with Christ, of which the former is a sacramental sign. It is effected in every individual member through Baptism and Confirmation and in the community as a whole, in the gift of Christ to his Bride which empowers her, in the fire of the Spirit who is that love which fuses us together and joins us to Christ and who distributes gifts as he chooses for the upbuilding of the body.

III. A Brief Political Postscript

Moltmann at several points turns his attention to political theory and the political theology that can serve to inform such theory. He asks "which political options are in accord with the convictions of the Christian faith" and in line with his own rejection of monarchical monotheism concludes that "it is not the monarchy of a ruler that corresponds to the triune God; it is the community of men and women, without privileges and without subjugation"[50]. This, implies a rejection of monarchical forms of government and an embracing of democratic forms.

In point of fact a pure democracy has never been practiced in the history of the world. Ancient Greece excluded any number of individuals from effective voice in the affairs of the community and modern democratic governments are invariably republican in form. The impossibility of achieving consensus among millions of peoples, all of them fallen, preclude anything but a representative democracy. On the other hand, monarchy is itself not necessarily opposed to rule by the people. It was, after all, the people who insisted to Samuel that a king be appointed over them (I Sam. 8). And, as Moltmann's critics have pointed out, the monarchy in Israel was not only sanctioned by God but, in David, was established by an everlasting grant which has been fulfilled in the kingship of Christ. It is, accordingly, a mistake to contrast monarchical and democratic systems as if one were more in accord with Christian faith than the other.

Still, the question of whether some vestige of the Trinity can be discerned in political structures is of some interest. One cannot, however, dispense with the question of unity in such a consideration; indeed it must be the starting point for one's reflection since before any discussion of the government of a community can profitably be undertaken the community itself must be given some sort of definition. What is the unity of a comm-unity? A government, any government, will inevitably be some expression of that unity and in the practical order it serves to preserve that unity. When this ceases to be the case governments fall. This is true of the most benevolent as well as of the most malevolent of governments. That which unites a community may be noble sentiments of human dignity or it may be the point of a gun. The second and inseparable consideration will be how the com-

---

[50] MOLTMANN, *The Trinity and the Kingdom*, p. 198.

monality, institutionality, and valuative dynamics, characteristic of all communities, are concretized in the governing structures of a society.

Above I suggested three locations for the human imaging of the Triune God: the individual, the community, the individual in community. The tri-unity of a community can accordingly be manifested in a three-fold manner. If this is manifested in a single individual the form of government is monarchical, whether in the person of a hereditary monarch or in the person of a dictator or president-for-life. All expression of the commonality, institutionality, and valuative dynamics of the community are localized in the monarch, however much they may be delegated in the practical order. Where the tri-unity of a community is manifested in a "communitarian" or democratic fashion the commonality, institutionality, and valuative dynamics of the community will tend to become codified in distinct executive, legislative, and judicial branches of government with the first also providing the visible symbol for the unity of the community though that unity is, in point of fact, borne by all three of the branches insofar as they mutually interpenetrate each other. The governmental structure of the United States provides an example of this approach. The final approach will provide a mix between monarchical and communitarian structures. Government will still be divided into judicial, legislative, and executive branches but there will be a person-to-person delegation of power in the executive — the monarch or the president who hands over certain executive powers to a prime minister. Perhaps not by accident this sort of structure has often emerged in countries that have had a tradition of monarchy.

None of these systems of government have a natural or theological advantage over the others. Thomas, echoing the sorts of discussions found in Plato and Aristotle, notes that "one can more efficaciously bring about unity than several"[51], a point he subsequently grounds in the divine monarchy[52].

---

[51] *De regno, ad regem Cypri* I.ii.17. The translation is from GERALD B. PHELAN, *On Kingship to the King of Cyprus*, rev. by I. TH. ESCHMANN, O.P. (Toronto: The Pontifical Institute of Mediaeval Studies, 1949).

[52] Ibid., I.ii.19.

This observation, however, is true even in the modern democratic context where such a unitary function is exercised by an elected president rather than a hereditary monarch. More important is Thomas's conviction that "the way to govern may be learned from the divine government of the world"[53]. But this requires that those who govern exercise wisdom, that they themselves have been converted to the Lord. A democracy is not any the less wicked than a monarchy when the people individually and through their representatives sanction abortion, racism, corruption, and all manner of other social ills. And it is far more difficult to remedy the moral ills of an entire people. The only perfect society is the city of the Great King which has its seat in heaven. Other societies and governments are mere vestiges of this.

---

[53] Ibid., II.iii.102.

The Church and the Kingdom of God

WILLIAM HENN

The relation between the Church and the Kingdom of God has generated a vast body of literature, which treats not only the biblical research relevant to this theme, but also its evolution in patristic thought and in the history of theology right up until the present time[1]. The following short essay can only hope to savor a portion of this material, organizing it into reasonably limited topics which indicate some of the important issues concerning the Church-Kingdom relation. Because of apparent conflicts about whether the Church should be identified with the Kingdom, it is essential to begin by clarifying the terminology (Part I). Having done this, I will take up how the Church-Kingdom relation affects the foundation of the Church (Part II), her nature (Part III), the Church-World relationship (Part IV) and the Church's mission *ad gentes* (Part V).

I. A QUESTION OF TERMINOLOGY

In 1952, Henri De Lubac wrote that the tradition was unanimous in its interpretation of Mt 19,28[2], the text in which Jesus responds to Peter's question concerning the fate of those who have left everything to follow him with the promise: "Truly I say to you, in the new world, when the Son of man shall sit on his glorious throne, you who have

---

[1] A very select bibliography of works concerning the Kingdom of God divided into the categories Old Testament and Intertestamental Period, New Testament, Middle Ages and Modern, can be found in BENEDICT T. VIVIANO, *The Kingdom of God in History*, Wilmington 1988, 155-159. A more complete and current bibliography can be found in JOHN FUELLENBACH, *The Kingdom of God. The Message of Jesus Today*, Maryknoll 1995, 319-328.
[2] HENRI DE LUBAC, *Méditation sur l'Église*, Paris 1954[3], 61-62.

followed me will also sit on twelve thrones, judging the twelve tribes of Israel". According to De Lubac, this verse had never been understood as meaning that Jesus wished to project into eternity the ecclesiastical hierarchy which exists on earth or that there would be some power in heaven analogous to that exercised by the Church "here below". Rather, the promise to the Twelve was seen as the eminent example of the fulfillment of the promise made to all who would follow Christ, which appears in the very next verse: "And everyone who has left houses or brothers or sisters or father or mother or children or lands, for my name's sake, will receive a hundredfold, and inherit eternal life (Mt 19,29)"[3].

De Lubac's point, in this section of the second chapter of his *Meditation on the Church*, is to underscore the radical difference between the Church in history, on the one hand, and the ultimate destiny of human beings in God's plan of salvation, on the other. This destiny is spoken of in the book of Revelation as the "new Jerusalem coming down out of heaven from God" (Rev 21,2.10). The transformation between the current situation of humankind and that future state will be so complete that Augustine speaks of it as a holocaust[4] and Newman writes: "Holy Church in her sacraments and her hierarchical appointments, will remain, even to the end of the world, after all but a symbol of those heavenly facts which fill eternity"[5]. In this state of final glory, the use of sacraments will cease. All human mediations of salvation will lose their reason for being, when the voice of God is heard directly and

---

[3] As evidence of this common interpretation, de Lubac lists: Origen, *In Matt.*, XIV 22-23; Jerome, *In Matt.*, XIX 27-29; Augustine, *In Psalm.* 86, n. 4; *De Civitate Dei* l. XX, c. 5; Gregory the Great, *In Ezechielem*, l. I, hom. 2, n 18; *Moralia in Job*, l. VI, n. 23-24; l. X, no. 52; l. XX, n. 41; l. XXVI, n. 31 and 51; Bede, Homilia 17, *in die natali sancti Benedicti*; Alexander of Hales, *Summa*, l. III, p. I, tract. 8, m. 5, c. 1 ad 3m and c. 2; Bonaventure, *De sanctis Apostolis Petro et Paulo* sermo 3; Thomas Aquinas, *Summa*, suppl., 2, 89, a. 2.

[4] *In Psalmum 65*, n. 18: "Quid est holocaustum? Totum incensum, sed igne divino. Holocaustum enim dicitur sacrificium, cum totum accenditur. ... Holocausta ergo promittit; corpus Christi loquitur, unitas Christi loquitur: *Introibo in domum tuam in holocaustis*. Totum meum consumat ignis tuus; nihil mei remaneat mihi, totum sit tibi. Hoc autem erit in resurrectione iustorum *quando et corruptibile hoc induetur incorruptione, et mortale hoc induetur immortalitate....* ... totum ex mortali vita consumetur, ut in aeterna vita consummetur: erunt ergo illa holocausta". From Sant'Agostino, *Esposizioni sui salmi*, II, Roma 1970, 518-521.

[5] J.H. Newman, *Apologia pro vita sua*, London 1929, 27.

God is seen face to face. As the last pages of scripture note: "And I saw no temple in the city, for its temple is the Lord God the Almighty and the Lamb. And the city has no need of sun or moon to shine upon it, for the glory of God is its light, and its lamp is the Lamb" (Rev 21,22-23)[6].

These affirmations appear in a meditation about the Church. It was not De Lubac's intention to reflect precisely upon the Kingdom of God or its relation to the Church. Nevertheless, he seems to presuppose a certain identity between the two. He posits three successive stages in the life of the Church which are divided from each other by two transformations: the first occurring when "Israel according to the flesh" gave way to "Israel according to the spirit", and the second consisting of that glorious transfiguration "when the Church on earth, passing to its definitive state, becomes the Kingdom of heaven. Then she will become *that which she is*. Because from the beginning she is this Kingdom in seed"[7]. These words bear striking resemblance to Vatican II's statement: "Henceforward the Church ... receives the mission of proclaiming and establishing among all peoples the Kingdom of Christ and of God, and she is, on earth the seed and the beginning of that Kingdom" (LG 5). One wonders whether the drafters of LG 5 had De Lubac's meditation in mind when they wrote those words[8].

Here we see two affirmations which appear to be in tension: a) the final destiny of human beings is a state strikingly different from that which they now know, even those who currently make up the Church on its earthly pilgrimage and, nevertheless, b) the Church is already the Kingdom of God, at

---

[6] Cf. DE LUBAC, 64-65, who also applies to this transformation the words of the famous eucharistic hymn: "... et antiquum documentum novo cedat ritui"! The book of Revelation not only speaks of the "the new heaven, new earth and new Jerusalem" which will appear at the end of history, but consistently makes use of "kingdom" language (4,1-6; 5,10.13; 11,17-18; 12,10) as well.

[7] "Car dès toujours elle est ce royaume en germe". DE LUBAC, 54, who quotes Augustine, *De Civitate Dei* l. XX, c. 9, n. I and Gregory the Great, *In Evangelia*, l. I, hom. 12, n. 1.

[8] L.D. CHRUPCALA, "La chiesa e il regno di Dio. Il Rapporto definito nella *Lumen gentium*", Antonianum 69, 1994, 223, note 44, provides a list of later statements by Paul VI, the Secretariat for Non-Christians, the International Theological Commission, the Congregation for the Doctrine of the Faith, the Seventh Synod of Bishops and John Paul II, which repeat LG 5's expression "germen et initium".

least in seed. The possible confusion generated by such affirmations is compounded by the fact that, in De Lubac's essay, the word "church" does not mean simply a precise, identifiable reality such as the "Roman Catholic Church" or even all Christian communities, taken as a whole. Rather, he is thinking of a bigger reality, which includes what Sertillanges had called "the Church before the Church" and about which Origen said that it was founded not only upon the apostles but also upon the prophets, among whom was to be included even Adam, the first human being[9]. This is the group of the saved which has also been called the Church "a tempore iusti Abel usque ad ultimum electum, ab initio mundi usque ad finem"[10].

In this text from the early 1950's, then, the Church *is* the Kingdom, but with the important provisos that: 1) the Church's present state is radically inferior to what she will become in the glorious transfiguration at the end of time and 2) the word "church" must be understood as in some way including all those who will be saved. Such clarifications help to diminish what might otherwise seem as an irreconcilable opposition between De Lubac and some of the more recent authors who have written about the relation between Church and Kingdom. John Fuellenbach twice quotes Richard McBrien's statement that "the most serious pre-Vatican II ecclesiological misunderstanding" was the affirmation "that the Church is identical with the Kingdom of God here on earth. If it is, then it is beyond all need for institutional reform, and its mission is to bring everyone inside lest salvation elude them"[11]. Jacques Dupuis has analyzed the affirmations of *Lumen gentium* (1964), the International Theological Commission's *Themata selecta de ecclesiologia* (1985) and

---

[9] DE LUBAC, 47 and 51-52.

[10] See the frequently cited study by Y. CONGAR, "Ecclesia ab Abel", in: *Abhandlungen über Theologie und Kirche. Festschrift für Karl Adam*, Düsseldorf 1952, 79-108. Vatican II, in LG 2, also recalls the patristic theme of the Church "ab Abel", giving references to Gregory the Great, Augustine and John Damascene. This expression appeared already in the draft of the Constitution on the Church from 1963, to which was appended a note to the above cited article by Congar. See *Acta Synodalia Sacrosancti Concilii Oecumenici Vaticani II*, II/1, Città del Vaticano 1971, 222.

[11] JOHN FUELLENBACH, *The Kingdom of God: The Message of Jesus Today*, 16 and 265; citing RICHARD MCBRIEN, *Catholicism*, London 1981, 686.

John Paul II's *Redemptoris missio* (1990), showing that the earlier two maintain a substantial identity between the Church and the Kingdom, while the latter posits a clear distinction between them[12]. For Dupuis, this distinction is of fundamental importance in making theological sense of the salvation of those millions of "others" who do not belong to any Christian community as well as opening the possibility for affirming that the various non-Christian religions play some positive role in the salvation of their adherents. From the perspective of biblical exegesis, R. Schnackenburg writes:

> Let us ask ourselves here immediately about the relationship between the Church and the Kingdom or Lordship of God. Is the Church the Kingdom of God on the earth, admittedly in a provisional form, until the Kingdom is fulfilled eschatologically? This view, long held within Catholic theology even though with various nuances, but which leads to a dangerous image of the Church, to a triumphalistic understanding of the earthly Church, is definitely to be rejected. True, in the New Testament the Church is seen in strict relation with the Lordship of Christ, for example in Col 1,12f: "God has delivered us from the dominion of darkness and transferred us to the Kingdom of his beloved Son". But it is not that we *are* the Kingdom of the Son, we are only received into his Kingdom. Christ exercises his lordship of grace in the Church by means of the Holy Spirit; but the Church remains a community of human beings who are at the same time sinful and weak[13].

Comparing the affirmations of De Lubac, on the one hand, with the more recent statements by Fuellenbach, Dupuis and Schnackenburg, on the other, one is struck by the fact that the word "church" is used in very different ways by these authors. The more recent writings tend to understand the Church as a visible, institutionally identifiable reality, which, according to Vatican II, may be said to "sub-

---

[12] J. DUPUIS, "L'Église, le Règne de Dieu et les 'autres'", *Revue de l'Institut catholique de Paris* 46, 1993, 95-119.

[13] R. SCHNACKENBURG, "Signoria e regno di Dio nell'annuncio di Gesù e della Chiesa delle origini", *Communio* 86, 1986, 41-42.

sist in" the Catholic Church, although its elements are also present in other Christian communities, which are also used by the Holy Spirit as means of salvation[14]. Clearly the patristic and scholastic theological tradition, as it has been harvested by such writers as De Lubac, has not always restricted the word "church" to such an institutionally identifiable community. Vatican II itself includes passages which suggest either a more restricted use of the word "church" (LG 8, on the Church "one, holy, catholic and apostolic" "constituted and organized as a society in the present world") or a more all encompassing use (LG 2, the Church of all the just; see also LG 13: "All human beings are called to this catholic unity which prefigures and promotes universal peace. And in different ways to it belong or are related: the Catholic faithful, others who believe in Christ, and finally all mankind, called by God's grace to salvation").

This difference in the way the word "church" is used suggests that there may be greater agreement than one may at first expect between writers who affirm a certain identity between Church and Kingdom, on the one hand, and those who emphasize the distinction between the two, on the other. When the International Theological Commission affirmed that there can be no difference between the Church and the Kingdom in their final state of completion, it was precisely within the context of the more traditional theological view which considers the Church as including all of the just. This is clear from its statement that, if one is a "member of the Kingdom", he or she also at least implicitly belongs to the Church[15]. This allows the Commission to affirm both a unity and a difference between Church and Kingdom. There would be a substantial conflict between these positions only if "church" meant exclusively the institutional Church for De Lubac and the International Theological Commission, or if the "Kingdom" was in no way present within or related to

---

[14] See LG 8 and UR 3. A fine explanation of these texts from Vatican II can be found in FRANCIS A. SULLIVAN, *The Church We Believe In: One, Holy, Catholic and Apostolic*, New York 1988, 23-33.

[15] International Theological Commission, "Temi scelti d'ecclesiologia", in: *Civiltà Cattolica*, anno 136, 1985/IV, 446-482, thesis X ("L'Indole escatologica della chiesa: Regno di Dio e Chiesa"), section 2 ("La Chiesa e il Regno"), 480-481.

this visible Church for Fuellenbach, Dupuis and Schnackenburg. But in neither set of authors is this true. The difference between their positions seems to be more one of accent or emphasis than of direct contradiction, even though, from a merely verbal perspective, one side appears to affirm what the other side denies — i.e. that the Church and the Kingdom can be identified.

II. The Foundation of the Church in Light of the Kingdom

The most important paragraph of Vatican II about the Kingdom of God is probably LG 5[16], which relates it to the Church precisely within the context of the Church's *foundation*: "The mystery of the holy Church is already brought to light in the way it was founded. For the Lord Jesus inaugurated his Church by preaching the Good News, that is, the coming of the Kingdom of God...". It was not accidental that LG 5 used this context in introducing the theme of the Kingdom of God. Many publications about the relation between the Church and the Kingdom sooner or later recount the story of Loisy's attempt to defend the Catholic conviction of the need for the external, visible structures of the Church against Harnack's interiorized view of "the essence of Christianity", an attempt which led Loisy to coin the unhappy phrase: "Jesus foretold the Kingdom and what came to be was the Church"[17]. This slogan can suggest that, if Jesus had proclaimed the immanent arrival of the Kingdom of God, then the foundation of a Church would probably have been far from his thought or intention. Moreover, the slogan posits a rather sharp distinction between the Kingdom and the Church. Thus an appreciation of the eschatological dimension of Jesus' mission seemed to separate Church from King-

---

[16] Of the 36 times which the word "kingdom" appears in *Lumen gentium*, 10 are found in LG 5. See X. Ochoa, *Index Verborum Concilii Vaticani Secundi*, Roma 1967, 423.

[17] A. Loisy, *L'Évangile et l'Église*, Paris 1902, 111. For a well documented account of the birth of this phrase, see F. Schüssler Fiorenza, "The Birth of a Slogan", in his *Foundational Theology: Jesus and the Church*, New York 1984, 60-64. See also J. Haughey, "Church and Kingdom: Ecclesiology in the Light of Eschatology", *Theological Studies* 29, 1968, 75; Chrupcala, 215; Fuellenbach, 4.

dom and to call into question the previously held conviction that Jesus intended to and actually did found the Church[18].

Various attempts were made to overcome these difficulties. Authors argued that, far from replacing it, the Church was actually a necessary means for the continuation of Jesus' proclamation and inauguration of the Kingdom[19]. A common thread among these discussions was the emergence of a more nuanced understanding of what it means to say that Jesus "founded" the Church. The International Theological Commission provided a good summary of this new understanding of "foundation" when it described the various developments and stages in the *process* of the foundation of the Church. This process included many elements: the Old Testament promises concerning the People of God to which Jesus' preaching made references, the invitation to be converted and believe in him which Jesus addressed to his listeners, the call and institution of the Twelve as a sign of the future reestablishment of Israel, the giving of a special name and role to Peter among the disciples, the rejection of Jesus by Israel and the split between the Jewish people and the disciples of Jesus, the historical fact that Jesus continued to preach the universal reign of God (consisting of the gift of his life to all human beings) in the institution of the Last Supper and in his freely assumed passion and death, the reconstitution of the community around Jesus after the resurrection, the sending of the Holy Spirit to make the Church a new creature, the mission of the disciples to the gentiles, the constitution of the Church of the gentiles, and the definitive break between the "true Israel" and Judaism[20].

---

[18] Schlüssler-Fiorenza nicely sketches out how such a questioning of Jesus' intention to found the Church radically challenged the contemporary Catholic view of the task of fundamental theology, helping to explain why Loisy was so vigorously opposed by the Catholic hierarchy.

[19] Some good efforts to explain this, each having its own particular slant, can be found in H. KÜNG, "The Coming Reign of God", in: *The Church*, Garden City 1976, 69-144; A. ANTÓN, "El Evangelio del Reino (*'euaggelion tês basileias'*) y la *'Ekklêsia'* de Cristo", and "La preformación de la *'Ekklêsia'*", in: *La Iglesia de Cristo*, Madrid 1977, 364-420; and F. SCHLÜSSLER FIORENZA, "The Foundation of the Church", in: *Foundational Theology*, 57-192.

[20] "Temi scelti d'ecclesiologia", thesis I ("La fondazione della chiesa a opera di Gesú Cristo"), section 4, 450-451.

That this foundation included so many facets and unfolded over a considerable period of time helped to explain how one could see a fundamental continuity between Jesus' preaching of the Kingdom and the historical origins of the Church[21]. Jesus can be seen as gathering around himself a community to share his mission and of seeing its purpose precisely in service to the Kingdom[22]. This more comprehensive view of the "foundation" of the Church shows that a sharp separation between Jesus' mission and the origins of the Church, simply because the evangelists speak much about the Kingdom and rarely use the word "church", is too simplistic. In addition, it underscores the fact that the very nature of the Church needs to be understood in terms of the Kingdom of God.

III. The Nature of the Church in Light of the Kingdom

If, as Schnackenburg notes, the Kingdom of God "represents the final aim of all of the saving interventions of God"[23], then the Church must be seen as in some way subordinate to it. The way in which such subordination characterizes the nature of the Church is perhaps best understood in terms of eschatology and sacramentality.

From the point of eschatology, the Church is seen as not yet that complete realization of God's lordship which will come to pass only at the end of the ages. Recognition of this fact leads to a much more modest view of the Church, a point voiced by many of the interventions during Vatican II.

---

[21] Ecumenically, divided Christian communities seem to be in substantial agreement about the foundation of the Church by Jesus. In his summary, H. SCHÜTTE, "La Chiesa: voluta, fondata, realizzata da Dio Uno e Trino", in: *La Chiesa nella comprensione ecumenica*, Padova 1995, 30-36, presents material from ecumenical dialogues which affirm that the Church comes about because of the activity of the whole Trinity, her foundation being attributed in a special way to the Son. However, the further question of whether quite precise aspects of Church life, such as specific ministerial structures, are also established by God and thus *iure divino* is still a matter of disagreement among Christian communities.

[22] A. ANTÓN, *La Iglesia de Cristo*, 389-420, comes up with a particularly good expression when he writes of the "preformation" of the Church during the earthly ministry of Jesus.

[23] R. SCHNACKENBURG, *La Chiesa nel Nuovo Testamento*, Brescia 1975⁴, 199.

For example, Bishop Van der Burgt asked for the inclusion in the Constitution on the Church a clear statement "quod Ecclesia in hoc mundo tendens ad plenitudem et perfectionem regni Dei, bene conscia sibi sit conditionis suae adhuc imperfectae"[24]. As a pilgrim, the Church "in its sacraments and institutions, which belong to this present age, carries the mark of this world which will pass, and she herself takes her place among the creatures which groan and travail yet and await the revelation of the children of God (cf. Rom. 8,19-22)" (LG 48). The council fathers seemed to be pointing out what might be called a double "imperfection" on the part of the Church. On the one hand, the Church humbly acknowledges its need for ongoing reform and further growth in the living of those values of the Kingdom which Jesus preached in the parables and the sermon on the mount[25]. On the other hand, no matter how great may be the realization of these values during the Church's earthly pilgrimage, the final consummation will infinitely transcend that "figure of this world which is passing away" which marks the Church in the present age (cf. 1 Cor 7,31; 1 Jn 2,17). There is a quantum leap between this age and the next, about which Paul joyfully exalts: "no eye has seen, nor ear heard, nor the heart of man conceived, what God has prepared for those who love him" (1 Cor 2,9; citing Is 64,4; cfr. Is 65,17).

Secondly, the Church is subordinate to the Kingdom in so far as she is an instrument of its realization. She has not her reason for being in herself but rather serves the Kingdom and helps to bring it about by her proclamation and action. In this sense, to speak of the Church as a sacrament of unity with God and of union among all human beings, is to under-

---

[24] In: *Acta Synodalia* II/2, Città del Vaticano 1972, 59. Chrupcala, 216-220, indicates several interventions in which the bishops emphasized this characteristic of imperfection and the notion that the Church must continually grow. It is interesting that both Cardinal Döpfner (*Acta Synodalia* I/4, Città del Vaticano 1971, 184) and Bishop Volk (*Acta Synodalia* II/2, 46) emphasized the need to avoid an identification of the Church and the Kingdom. Notwithstanding this insistence, according to Dupuis, 101-102, the council did not succeed in avoiding such an identification.

[25] See Chrupcala, 216-220. For a brief statement relating the Kingdom of God to Jesus' parables and sermon on the mount, see J. FUELLENBACH, "The Language of the Kingdom: Parables in the Teaching of Jesus", and "The Sermon on the Mount and the Kingdom of God", in: *The Kingdom of God*, 70-78 and 117-121.

stand the Church as a sacrament of the Kingdom[26]. The International Theological Commission took up the question of the appropriateness of calling the Church a "sacrament of the Kingdom". After noting that this expression itself is not used by Vatican II, the Commission nevertheless concluded that it is an appropriate description of the Church for the following reasons[27]. First of all, LG 1 had already spoken of the Church as a "kind of sacrament"; the expression "sacrament of the Kingdom" rightly focuses attention upon the difference between the Kingdom in its state of fulfillment, on the one hand, and the limitations of the Church during her pilgrim journey, on the other. At the same time, the word "sacrament" conveys the fact that the reality of the Kingdom is truly already present in the pilgrim Church, as LG 3 states: *iam praesens in mysterio*. Thus the Church is not merely a sign (*sacramentum tantum*); rather, the reality signified, i.e. the Kingdom, is also truly present in her (*res et sacramentum*). Finally, to speak of the Church as a sacrament of the Kingdom has the double advantage 1) of not limiting the Church to her temporal and earthly dimension and 2) of not limiting the Kingdom to its state of fulfillment at the end of time. The Church's future is the Kingdom and the Kingdom is really present in mystery even now in the Church.

These two ways of expressing the nature of the Church as related and subordinate to the Kingdom, i.e. eschatologically and sacramentally, coalesce in a eucharistic vision of the Church[28]. Already Schnackenburg's *The Church of the New*

---

[26] G. GASSMANN, "The Church as Sacrament, Sign and Instrument. The Reception of this Ecclesiological Understanding in Ecumenical Debate", in: G. LIMOURIS, ed., *Church, Kingdom, World: The Church as Mystery and Prophetic Sign*, Geneva 1986, 1-17, notes that the language of Church as sacrament has been acceptable within an ecumenical context precisely because of its ability to convey that the Church is in service to a greater reality, the rule of God and "his universal plan of salvation for all humankind in Jesus Christ" (p. 14).

[27] The following comments paraphrase "Temi Scelti d'Ecclesiologia", 482.

[28] A fine presentation of the relation between the Church and the kingdom in light of the eucharist is J.M.R. TILLARD, "Chiesa di Dio e Regno di Dio", in his *Chiese di chiese. L'ecclesiologia di comunione*, Brescia 1989, 67-90. Here both kingdom and Church are understood within the framework of "communion", which nicely opens the way for seeing both in relation to the eucharist. John Paul II later also uses the language of communion to describe the Kingdom; see *Redemptoris missio*, 15.

Testament presents a biblical basis for seeing the Eucharist as the moment and place where the intimate link between the Church and the Kingdom is most sharply brought into focus[29]. Mark's account of the Last Supper closes with Jesus' words: "Truly, I say to you, I shall not drink again of the fruit of the vine until that day when I drink it new in the Kingdom of God" (Mk 14,25; cf. Mt 26,29 and Lk 22,16.18.30). Thus the Eucharist is situated within the context of the eschatological Kingdom. In his handing on of the story of the origins of the Lord's supper, Paul also clearly sees its celebration within an eschatological context: "For as often as you eat this bread and drink the cup, you proclaim the Lord's death until he comes" (1 Cor 11,26).

But the link between Church and Kingdom in the Eucharist is still more profound. It is with his blood that Jesus establishes the new covenant (Lk 22,20; 1 Cor 11,25), "the divine order of eschatological grace for the whole of humanity"[30]. Only in virtue of the universal efficacy of the blood of this covenant (Mk 14,24; Mt 26,28) is it possible for human beings to be saved. In the celebration of the Lord's Supper, the Church is clearly presented as belonging to this Kingdom; she celebrates this covenant, established by the blood which, according to the Lucan account, is poured out "for you" (22,20; cf. Lk 22,19 where Christ's body is given "for you"). The eschatological benefits of salvation are intended "for you" — which must be understood as including those believers in Christ who are actually celebrating the Eucharist.

The link between Church and Kingdom in the Eucharist finds a precious early expression in the ancient Eucharistic prayers which are found in the *Didache*:

> As this broken bread, once dispersed over the hills, was brought together and became one loaf, so may thy Church be brought together from the ends of the earth into thy Kingdom.

---

[29] Cf. SCHNACKENBURG, *La chiesa nel Nuovo Testamento*, 203-204.
[30] SCHNACKENBURG, *La chiesa nel Nuovo Testamento*, 203.

And:

> Be mindful of thy Church, O Lord; deliver it from all evil, perfect it in thy love, sanctify it, and gather it from the four winds into the Kingdom which thou hast prepared for it.

Finally, the celebrant proclaims:

> Let His Grace [Christ] draw near, and let this present world pass away. [To which the assembly responds:] Hosanna to the God of David. ... O Lord, come quickly. Amen[31].

These biblical and patristic testimonies about the Eucharist caution against forcing too sharp a contrast or division between the Church and the Kingdom, in a way which is not sufficiently sensitive to the delicate nature of the relation between the two. The international dialogue between Catholics and Orthodox cannot be accused of such insensitivity as it tries to capture in words the deep interrelation between Eucharist, eschatology and sacramentality:

> Christ, Son of God incarnate, dead and risen is the only one who has conquered sin and death. To speak, therefore, of the sacramental nature of the mystery of Christ is to bring to mind the possibility given to man, and through him, to the whole cosmos, to experience the "new creation", the Kingdom of God here and now through material and created realities. This is the mode (*tropos*) in which the unique person and the unique event of Christ exists and operates in history starting from Pentecost and reaching to the Parousia. However, the eternal life which God has given to the world in the event of Christ, his eternal Son, is contained in "earthen vessels". It is still only given as a foretaste, as a pledge.

> At the Last Supper, Christ stated that he "gave" his body to the disciples for the life of "the many", in the Eucharist. In it this gift is made by God to the world,

---

[31] This English version of the *Didache* is taken from *Early Christian Writings*, translated by Maxwell Staniforth, Middlesex 1968, 231-232.

but in sacramental form. From that moment the Eucharist exists as the sacrament of Christ himself. It becomes the foretaste of eternal life, the "medicine of immortality", the sign of the Kingdom to come[32].

In this sacramental vision, the dialogue partners recognize that eternal life is given to the world "in earthen vessels" and "as a foretaste, as a pledge". Thus the Eucharist is "the sign of the Kingdom to come". The presence is real. Nevertheless, the mode (*tropos*) in which the Christ event exists and operates "from Pentecost and reaching to the Parousia" is sacramental. As such, the Church is an intimate part of this operation. Whether Christ's activity in bestowing eternal life can in some way be said to occur outside the visible confines of the Church is not addressed here. A different context is needed to raise and respond to that question.

Part III of our essay has considered the relation between Church and Kingdom from an ecclesiological perspective — that of the nature of the Church. The same can be said for the previous section, Part II, which discussed the Church's foundation. The following two sections will shift the perspective rather substantially. Instead of beginning from an ecclesiological perspective, they will look instead from the angle of vision of the relation between the Kingdom and the World (Part IV), on the one hand, and between the Kingdom and the "others" who do not share in the Church's Eucharistic celebrations (Part V), on the other. The change in perspective will highlight other aspects of the Church-Kingdom relationship than those which we have considered thus far.

---

[32] Joint Commission for Theological Dialogue Between the Roman Catholic Church and the Orthodox Church, "The Mystery of the Church and of the Eucharist in the Light of the Mystery of the Holy Trinity", in *Information Service* N. 49, 1982 II/III, 107-112 at 107. Another fine ecumenical presentation of the relation between Church and Kingdom within the context of the Eucharist is Faith and Order Commission, "Baptism, Eucharist and Ministry: Eucharist", paragraphs 22-26 [entitled "The Eucharist as Meal of the Kingdom"], in: Harding Meyer and Lukas Vischer, ed., *Growth in Agreement*, New York 1984, 479-480.

IV. THE CHURCH-WORLD RELATIONSHIP IN LIGHT OF THE KINGDOM

As we have seen, when writing about the Church in the New Testament, Rudolf Schnackenburg provides some insights about the Eucharist which tend to highlight the profound link between Church and Kingdom. In an earlier study precisely about the Kingdom, however, the same author writes:

> The Kingdom of Christ is ... a more comprehensive term than "Church". In the Christian's present existence on earth his share in Christ's Kingdom and his claim to the eschatological Kingdom ... find their fulfillment in the Church, the domain in which the grace of the Heavenly Christ is operative. ... But Christ's rule extends beyond the Church ... and one day the Church will have completed her earthly task and will be absorbed in the eschatological Kingdom of Christ or of God"[33].

The moment the perspective shifts from an attempt to explain the foundation or nature of the Church to an attempt to understand the Kingdom as such and, in particular, its relation to the present world in which we live, the emphasis on the Church diminishes. Now the "church" is understood as that visible community which can be distinguished from "the world".

The New Testament is not unambiguous about the world. It presents the world both as a negative reality which is infected by sin and opposed to Christ (cf. Jn 12,31-32) and as the all-encompassing creation whose destiny is to be "recapitulated" in Christ (cf. Eph 1,10). On the one side, Paul tells his readers not to be conformed to this world (Rom 12,2), that God has made the wisdom of this world foolish (1 Cor 1,20) and they have received not the spirit of the world but the Spirit which is from God (1 Cor 2,12). In John, Jesus prays for his disciples, who are "not of the world" (Jn 17,14; see 1 Jn 2,15-17; 5,19) and tells them not to be afraid, for "I have overcome the world" (Jn 16,33). Yet, at the same time, the New Testa-

---

[33] R. SCHNACKENBURG, *God's Rule and Kingdom*, New York 1963, 11.

ment presents a more positive vision of the world. Paul insists that there is only one God the Father and one Lord Jesus Christ "through whom are all things" (1 Cor 8,6; cf. Rom 11,36 "from him and through him and for him all things are"). All things will be restored and made new (Acts 3,21; cf. Rev 21,5). All of creation waits with eager longing and groans to be set free from its bondage to decay and to obtain the glorious freedom of the children of God (Rom 8,19-23). In the end, all will be made subject to Christ who will himself be subjected to the Father, so that God may be all in all (1 Cor 15,28). The full expression of this idea, in which all is subjected to Christ (Eph 1,21-22) and in which Christ reconciles (Col 1,20) and fills all things (Eph 4,10), is the affirmation that all will be recapitulated or reheaded in Christ (Eph 1,10).

This broader context of seeing the Kingdom as the final destiny of the whole of creation and thus as much bigger than the Church seems to be precisely the perspective adopted in the paragraph most fully dedicated to the Kingdom by Vatican II's Constitution on the Church in the Modern World, GS 39.

> We know neither the moment of the consummation of the earth and of man nor the way the universe will be transformed. The form of this world, distorted by sin, is passing away and we are taught that God is preparing a new dwelling and a new earth in which righteousness dwells, whose happiness will fill and surpass all the desires of peace arising in the hearts of men. ... and all of creation, made for man, will be set free from its bondage to decay.

> When we have spread on earth the fruits of our nature and our enterprise — human dignity, brotherly communion, and freedom — according to the command of the Lord and in his Spirit, we will find them once again, cleansed this time from the stain of sin, illuminated and transfigured, when Christ presents to his Father an eternal and universal Kingdom "of truth and life, a Kingdom of holiness and grace, a Kingdom of justice, love and peace". Here on earth the Kingdom is mysteriously present; when the Lord comes it will enter into its perfection. (GS 39).

This paragraph appears at the end of Chapter Three of the first part of *Gaudium et spes*. This placement is quite important for interpreting the text, in light of the plan which governs the structure of GS. The four chapters which comprise its first part speak about the nature 1) of human beings (par. 12-22), 2) of human community (par. 23-32) and 3) of human activity (par. 33-39), before finally addressing, in the fourth chapter (par. 40-45), 4) the way in which the Church relates to these human realities. GS 39's statement that "Here on earth the Kingdom is mysteriously present" appears *before* the attempt to relate the Church to either the Kingdom or the world (GS 40-45). Earlier, LG 3 had stated that the Kingdom of Christ is "present in mystery" in the Church. The implication of this sentence from GS 39 is that one cannot simply limit the "mysterious presence" of the Kingdom in the world to the Church. The Kingdom is also already "mysteriously present" in the world as it groans toward full liberation in Christ.

The use of the word "mystery" in both LG 3 and GS 39 could suggest that one should not sharply contrast or oppose these presences of the Kingdom. Perhaps it would not be unfaithful to Vatican II to see in GS 39's statement about the Kingdom a development similar to that which the council had earlier made in LG 8 and 15 and in UR 3 concerning the relation between the Catholic Church and the other Christian communities. There the council recognized "elements of ecclesiality" in the other communities which allowed the Holy Spirit to make use of these other Christian communities as means for the salvation of their members. These elements (belief in Jesus Christ as Lord and Savior and in the Triune God, the celebration of baptism and other sacraments, the acceptance of the Bible as the Word of God, the living of the theological virtues in cooperation with grace and so forth) also allowed Vatican II to recognize a certain real, though imperfect communion among all Christian communities even now in their division. Ecumenism is nothing other than the effort to render this imperfect communion complete.

Might not a similar insight be discerned in the council's assessment of the relation between the Church and the world? The Church is presented as the community in which the Kingdom is present in seed, even in an indefectible ("most sure") way: "Hence that messianic people, although she does not include all men, and at times may appear as a small flock, is, however, a most sure seed of unity, hope and salvation for the whole human race" (LG 9). And yet elements of the Kingdom may also be understood as existing "outside" of this community. "Nor is God remote from those who in shadows and images seek the unknown God, since he gives to all men life and breath and all things (cf. Acts 17,25-28), and since the Savior wills all men to be saved (cf. 1 Tim 2,4)" (LG 16). Speaking of those who do not know God but who, under "the influence of grace", seek to lead a good life, the council adds: "Whatever good or truth is found amongst them is considered by the Church to be a preparation for the Gospel and given by him who enlightens all men that they may at length have life" (LG 16). These texts speak of grace, goodness and truth which are related to the Gospel and to the Kingdom of God but which clearly are presented as existing "outside" of the visible Church.

Just as the "ecclesial elements" present outside the Catholic Church establish a degree of real, though imperfect communion between that Church and the other Christian communities, so too might not the "eschatological or Kingdom elements" which exist outside of the Catholic Church and the other Christian communities establish a degree of real, though imperfect communion between the Church and the world? Just as the communion which exists between divided Christian communities provides the basis for ecumenical collaboration, so the communion which exists between Church and world provides the basic for collaboration to bring about the Kingdom of God. Christians have a right and a duty to cooperate, not only with other Christians, but also with any parties who share the values of the Kingdom, so as to bring to greater realization the lordship of God in the concrete cultural, political and economic structures which characterize human society.

Because the Kingdom is the ultimate destiny of all of creation, the mission of the Church cannot be understood as a flight from this world to another, better one (*fuga mundi*).

GS 39 gives a well balanced expression to this principle, when it affirms: "That is why, although we must be careful to distinguish earthly progress from the increase of the Kingdom of Christ, such progress is of vital concern to the Kingdom of God, insofar as it can contribute to the better ordering of human society". In fact, it is incompatible with the proclamation of the Gospel of Christ's Kingdom to be unconcerned about the betterment of human life in this world[34]. Jesus' paradigmatical Kingdom activities of preaching the good news to the poor and of healing those in suffering demonstrate the profound harmony between the Church's mission to continue Jesus' realization of the Kingdom, on the one hand, and the Church's action on behalf of justice, peace and the integrity of creation, on the other[35]. Within this context, important themes which merit a substantial discussion, but which cannot be treated here because of the limits assigned to the present paper, include the impact of the Church-Kingdom relation on the social doctrine of the Church[36], on the vision of the Church's mission according to

---

[34] Thus, the second ordinary Synod of Bishops in 1971, in its document entitled "Justice in the World", in: A. FLANNERY, ed., *Vatican Council II: More Post-Conciliar Documents*, Northport 1982, 695-710 at 696, taught: "Action on behalf of justice and participation in the transformation of the world fully appear to us as a constitutive dimension of the preaching of the Gospel, or, in other words, of the Church's mission for the redemption of the human race and its liberation from every oppressive situation".

[35] This insight has found acceptance within ecumenical dialogue. A particularly fine effort to express the relation of the Church and the World in light of the Kingdom of God is the Faith and Order Commission Study Document entitled *Church and World*, Faith and Order Paper No. 151, Geneva 1990, 92 pages. Chapters Two and Three of this text root the Church-World relationship in Jesus' own activity on behalf of the kingdom. Subsequent chapters then apply these principles to specific problems which call for a Christian response in today's world.

[36] John Paul II closes his *Centesimus annus*, about the Church's social doctrine in light of the hundredth anniversary of its first landmark papal encyclical *Rerum novarum*, with references to the kingdom: "In every age the true and perennial 'newness of things' comes from the infinite power of God, who says: 'Behold, I make all things new' (Rev 21,5). These words refer to the fulfilment of history, when Christ 'delivers the Kingdom to God the Father ... that God may be everything to everyone' (1 Cor 15,24.28). But the Christian well knows that the newness which we await in its fulness at the Lord's second coming has been present since the creation of the world, and in a special way since the time when God became man in Jesus Christ and brought about a 'new creation' with him and through him (2 Cor 5,17; Gal 6,15). In concluding this Encyclical I again give thanks to Almighty God, who has granted his Church the light and strength to ac-

the theology of liberation[37], and on the specific mission of the Christian lay person[38].

V. THE CHURCH'S MISSION *AD GENTES* IN LIGHT OF THE KINGDOM

Among the documents of Vatican II, the Decree on the Church's Missionary Activity has the third highest incidence of the word "Kingdom"[39]. This is hardly surprising inasmuch as the mission of the Church is to advance the Kingdom. Some passages of *Ad gentes* could be understood as suggesting an identification between the two (cf. the terminological issue which was discussed in part I of the present essay)[40]. In

---

company humanity on its earthly journey towards its eternal destiny". For material which can provide a basis for developing the relation between the kingdom and the Church's social doctrine, see: T. HERR, *La dottrina sociale della chiesa: Manuale di base*, Casale Monferrato 1988; W. KERBER, H. ERTL and M. HAINZ, ed., *Katholische Sozallehre im Überblick. 100 Jahre Sozialverkündigung der Kirche*, Frankfurt am Main 1991; T. LÓPEZ, "La doctrina social de la Iglesia: balance del postconcilio", *ScriptTh* 22, 1990, 809-842; J.A. COLEMAN, ed., *One Hundred Years of Catholic Social Thought: Celebration and Challenge*, Maryknoll 1991.

[37] Central to the theology of liberation is the relation between the Kingdom of God the situation in which people live today. This is well expressed in the foundational work of GUSTAVO GUTIERREZ, *A Theology of Liberation*, Maryknoll 1973, especially 153-188. For further materials, see A.T. HENNELLY, ed., *Liberation Theology: A Documentary History*, Maryknoll 1990, 547 pages; and J.J. ALEMANY and J.L. BARBERO, "Teología de la liberación. Bibliografía de revistas 1970-1988", *MiscCom* 46 (1988) 489-584. Relevant studies include: Ignacio Ellacuría, *Conversione della chiesa al regno di Dio*, Brescia 1992; and Rosino Gibellini, *Il dibattito sulla teologia della liberazione*, Brescia 1986.

[38] It is quite striking that 11 of *Lumen gentium*'s 36 references to the kingdom appear in its Chapter Four on the laity. *Apostolicam actuositatem* also includes 5 references to the kingdom. See: Ochoa, 423-424. The reason for this is that the specific mission of the lay person is identified in its "secular character", by which they "seek the kingdom of God by engaging in temporal affairs and directing them according to God's will" (LG 31). G. Magnani's insightful essay, "La cosidetta teologia del laicato ha uno statuto teologico"?, in: R. Latourelle, ed., *Vaticano II: Bilancio & Prospettive*, Assisi 1987, 493-543, challenges whether this division of labor, which specifies the secular as the proper sphere of lay activity, sufficiently reflects what he calls the "laicità" of the Church as a whole. *Christifideles laici* 15 reaffirms the "secular character" of the laity.

[39] According to Ochoa, 423-424, the word "regnum" appears 36 times in *Lumen gentium*, 14 times in *Gaudium et spes* and 8 times in *Ad gentes*.

[40] For example, AG 1 can give the impression that the apostles' activity of "preaching the word of truth" and of "begetting churches" is equivalent to the spreading of the kingdom of God. AG 9, 15, 40 and 42, while never actually stating that the Church is the kingdom, also are phrased in a way which suggests their fundamental identity.

so speaking of the Church's mission, does the council wish to suggest that those who are "outside of the Church" are also "outside of the Kingdom" or, to put it yet another way, "outside of salvation"?

The answer to this question, to be found in the council's statements about the salvation of those who are not Christians, is a clear "no". The basic soteriological-ecclesiological principle is enunciated in LG 16:

> Those who, through no fault of their own, do not know the Gospel of Christ or his Church, but who nevertheless seek God with a sincere heart, and, moved by grace, try in their actions to do his will as they know it through the dictates of their conscience — those too may achieve eternal salvation[41].

The references here to "no fault of their own" and "conscience" make it clear that this text focuses on the question of the salvation of the individual. On the other hand, paragraph 2 of *Nostra aetate*, the Declaration on the Relation of the Church to Non-Christian Religions, goes beyond this consideration of the individual and offers an estimation of other religions as such:

> The Catholic Church rejects nothing of what is true and holy in these religions. She has a high regard for the manner of life and conduct, the precepts and doctrines which, although differing in many ways from her own teaching, nevertheless often reflect a ray of that truth which enlightens all men. Yet she proclaims and is in duty bound to proclaim without fail, Christ who is the way, the truth and the life (Jn 14,6).

These positive assessments of the possibility for salvation of individuals who are not Christians and of the elements of truth and holiness in other religions can call into question the need for the missionary activity of the Church *ad gentes*. To some extent, John Paul II's encyclical letter about the per-

---

[41] See also GS 22: "For since Christ died for all, and since all men are in fact called to one and the same destiny, which is divine, we must hold that the Holy Spirit offers to all the possibility of being made partners, in a way known to God, in the paschal mystery".

manent validity of the missionary task of the Church, *Redemptoris missio*, was intended as a response to this challenge. Toward the beginning of this letter, he asks: "Is it not possible to attain salvation in any religion? Why then should there be missionary activity"? (RMi 4).

In addressing this apparent dilemma, John Paul first emphasizes the need to maintain two principles which may, at first sight, seem to be in tension:

> It is necessary to keep these two truths together, namely, the real possibility of salvation in Christ for all mankind and the necessity of the Church for salvation. Both these truths help us to understand the one mystery of salvation, so that we can come to know God's mercy and our own responsibility. Salvation, which always remains a gift of the Spirit, requires man's cooperation, both to save himself and to save others. This is God's will, and this is why he established the Church and made her a part of his plan of salvation[42].

The pope resolves the tension between the universal possibility of salvation and the necessary mediation of the Church by appealing to God's will. God wills that human beings cooperate with his saving action. As such, God wills to make the Church a "part of his plan of salvation".

How is the Church a part of this plan? This is unfolded especially in Chapter II of *Redemptoris missio*, which relates Christ, the Kingdom of God and the Church to each other. The Kingdom is made present by Christ (RMi 13) and is meant for all people; all are called to become "members" of it (RMi 14). The Kingdom is spoken of as "communion": "The

---

[42] RMi 9. J. DUPUIS, *Jesus Christ at the Encounter of World Religions*, Maryknoll 1991, 108-109, reports the insistence of GAVIN D'COSTA, *Theology and Religious Pluralism: The Challenge of Other Religions*, Oxford 1986, upon "two basic axioms of the Christian faith: the universal salvific will of God and the necessary mediation of Jesus Christ (and the role of the church) in every salvation mystery". The original french version of Dupuis' book is from 1989. Thus both his text and that of D'Costa precede John Paul II's *Redemptoris missio* in affirming these two basic axioms or principles. Perhaps one can see a difference between the papal encyclical and the earlier two texts in that the pope writes simply about the "necessity of the church for salvation", while Dupuis reports D'Costa as affirming the "necessary mediation of Jesus Christ (and the role of the church) in every salvation mystery". The pope's statement would seem to be a bit stronger ecclesiologically.

Kingdom's nature, therefore, is one of communion among all human beings — with one another and with God" (RMi 15)[43]. The Kingdom of God is "the manifestation and the realization of God's plan of salvation in all its fullness" (RMi 15). An important paragraph about anthropocentric, theocentric and ecclesiocentric misinterpretations[44] of the relation between Christ, Kingdom and Church (RMi 17), leads to the affirmation that "the Kingdom cannot be detached either from Christ or from the Church" (RMi 18). The pope explains:

> Likewise, one may not separate the Kingdom from the Church. It is true that the Church is not an end unto herself, since she is ordered toward the Kingdom of God of which she is the seed, sign and instrument. Yet while remaining distinct from Christ and the Kingdom, the Church is indissolubly united to both. Christ endowed the Church, his body, with the fullness of the benefits and means of salvation. The Holy Spirit dwells in her, enlivens her with his gifts and charisms, sanctifies and constantly renews her. The result is a unique and special relationship which, while not excluding the action of Christ and the Spirit outside the Church's visible boundaries, confers upon her a specific and necessary role; hence the Church's special connection with the Kingdom of God and of Christ, which she has "the mission of announcing and inaugurating among all peoples" (RMi 18).

To flesh out this "special and necessary role" Chapter II of *Redemptoris missio* concludes (par. 20) with a listing of several ways in which the Church is "at the service of the Kingdom": by proclaiming Christ, by establishing Christian communities, by promoting the values of the Kingdom and by intercession.

---

[43] Who could fail to hear in these words an echo of LG 1's description of the Church: "... the Church, in Christ, is in the nature of a sacrament — a sign and instrument, that is, of communion with God and of unity among all men ...".

[44] A good survey of various attempts to fashion a Christian theology of religions, which explains how the terminology "ecclesiocentric, Christocentric and theocentric" are used by contemporary authors, can be found in J. DUPUIS, *Jesus Christ at the Encounter of World Religions*, 91-110.

Redemptoris missio attempts to provide the rationale for the ongoing missionary activity of the Church, especially in light of the possibility of salvation within other religions. In doing so, it rejects both ecclesiocentrism ("the Church is not an end unto herself") as well as a simple identification between the Church and Christ or the Kingdom ("while remaining distinct from Christ and the Kingdom"). Still, a dominant interest is to show that one cannot separate the Kingdom from the Church. Thus the dominant interest governing the insights of *Redemptoris missio* remains ecclesiological; the focus is, after all, the mission of the Church.

A somewhat different perspective characterizes the document entitled *Dialogue and Proclamation*, produced jointly by the Pontifical Council for Interreligious Dialogue and the Congregation for the Evangelization of Peoples. Here one finds a passage which not only speaks of the relation between Christ, the Kingdom and the Church but which also is concerned to bring into light the place of world religions in God's plan of salvation. Because of this broader context, it may offer the most satisfying summary which has thus far appeared in an official document.

> To the Church, as the sacrament in which the Kingdom of God is present "in mystery", are related or oriented (*ordinantur*) (cf. *Lumen gentium*, 16) the members of other religious traditions who, inasmuch as they respond to God's calling as perceived by their conscience, are saved in Jesus Christ and thus already share in some way in the reality which is signified by the Kingdom. The Church's mission is to foster "the Kingdom of our Lord and his Christ" (Rev 11,15), at whose service she is placed. Part of her role consists in recognizing that the inchoate reality of this Kingdom can be found also beyond the confines of the Church, for example in the hearts of the followers of other religious traditions, insofar as they live evangelical values and are open to the action of the Spirit. It must be remembered nevertheless that this is indeed an inchoate reality, which needs to find completion through being related to the Kingdom

of Christ already present in the Church yet realized fully only in the world to come[45].

Here one sees a clear recognition of a sharing by those of other religious traditions of "the reality which is signified by the Kingdom". The Church's role includes both "recognizing that the inchoate reality of this Kingdom can be found also beyond the confines of the Church" and, at the same time, helping this inchoate reality "to find completion through being related to the Kingdom of Christ already present in the Church".

These reflections upon the mission of the Church *ad gentes* in light of her relation to the Kingdom have produced several clarifications. The Church is not an end in itself; she is distinct from the Kingdom. Nevertheless she is inseparable from it as its servant. This service includes many activities, among which are the explicit proclamation of Christ and the formation of new Christian communities. But this service also includes the fostering of evangelical values and the intercession for the coming of the Kingdom[46]. Perhaps the most delicate question emerging in this area of the Church-Kingdom relationship is what might be called the question of "instrumentality".

From the perspective of the Church, one needs to ask whether the fact that she is described as the "universal sacrament of salvation" (LG 48; AG 1; GS 42 and 45) implies some mediation on her part in the process of salvation of those who are not Christians. Pope John Paul asserts that "for such people, salvation in Christ is accessible by virtue of a grace which, while having a mysterious relationship to the Church, does not make them formally part of the Church, but enlightens them in a way which is accommodated to their spiritual and material situation. This grace comes from Christ...". (RMi 10). In what does this "mysterious relationship" consist? J. Dupuis seems to understand the rejection of "ecclesiocentrism" and the fact that people can be saved without being

---

[45] Paragraph 35 of *Dialogue and Proclamation*, in Pontifical Council for Interreligious Dialogue, *Bulletin*, No. 77, 1991, 225.

[46] Paragraphs 17-39 of *Evangelii nuntiandi* are dedicated to describing the "complex, rich and dynamic reality which is called evangelization" (17).

"formally a part of the Church" as implying that the "necessity" of the Church is not such that "access to the kingdom is only possible through her"; one can take part in the Kingdom of God "without being a member of the Church and without passing through her mediation"[47]. On the other hand, F. Sullivan maintains that, as universal sacrament of salvation, the Church's mediation needs also to be understood as, in some way, universal in extension. The Church clearly serves as an instrument of salvation for those who are Christians; but at least by means of intercession, especially during the celebration of the Eucharist, the Church prays and offers Christ's sacrifice for the salvation of all people[48]. Thus her intercessory mediation extends to all who are being saved.

Obviously this is a delicate point about which care for truth counsels caution. The official texts themselves emphasize that the salvific action of God outside of the visible confines of the Church takes place in "ways known to God" (AG 7; GS 22), which suggests that these ways may not be easily known by those who are not God. John Paul II states that the grace which saves those who do not explicitly believe in Christ has "a *mysterious relationship* to the Church" (RMi 10; emphasis mine). In light of this, great modesty is both justified and called for in making claims about this matter. While the position of Dupuis has the advantage of more clearly avoiding any vestige of a mistaken ecclesiocentrism, it seems to me that the clearer affirmation

---

[47] "La présence de l'Église-signe dans le monde témoigne donc que Dieu y a établi son Règne en Jésus-Christ. Par ailleurs, en tant que signe efficace, elle contient et produit la réalité qu'elle signifie, et donne accès au Règne de Dieu par sa parole et son action. Mais l'Église n'en appartient pas moins à la sphère sacramentelle et donc au domaine du relatif. Sa nécessité n'est pas telle que l'accès au Règne de Dieu ne soit possible qu'à travers elle; les 'autres' peuvent faire partie du Règne de Dieu et du Christ sans être membres de l'Église et sans passer par sa médiation". In: J. DUPUIS, "L'Église, le Règne de Dieu et les 'autres'", 114. In another place — *Jesus Christ at the Encounter of World Religions*, 106, Dupuis writes: "It seems difficult to conceive how the salvific mediation of the church beyond its own frontiers might be understood. As essentially sacramental, the salvific mediation of the church is exercised by the proclamation of the word and the sacraments. While reaching the church's members, and to some extent its future members, it does not reach the members of other religious traditions. Thus, although we have come by a different route, we are back at the viewpoint we have considered above. The ecclesiocentric outlook, even in its attenuated form, must be transcended".

[48] SULLIVAN, *The Church We Believe In*, 122-128.

of mediation in the position of Sullivan better harmonizes with the teaching that the Church is the universal sacrament of salvation. Moreover, Sullivan's view has the advantage of placing the entire question within the context of the Eucharist, which, as we have seen above, is a most congenial framework for understanding the relation between Church and Kingdom.

A second question along this line concerns the "instrumentality" of the other religions. Is the saving grace of Christ, by which persons from other religious traditions take part in the Kingdom, in some way mysteriously conveyed through the writings, rites and communal life of the religious communities to which these individuals belong? Here one would want to exercise care in distinguishing mediation by the Church, which stands in explicit reference to Christ's salvific activity, from the "mysterious way" in which the grace of Christ may work even outside the Church. But given such caution, it seems possible and even reasonable to affirm that a "non-Christian" who is saved is so saved not in spite of any influence from his or her religious tradition but rather, to some degree, because of it[49]. This is not to deny that, objectively speaking, there may be significant deficiencies in the doctrine or practice of that tradition.

Conclusion

This overview of the more important issues which cluster around the relation between the Church and the Kingdom has shown that one can not adequately understand the former without relating it to the latter. Given the actual economy of salvation as willed by God, this affirmation can also be reversed. Not only is it impossible to understand the

---

[49] J. Dupuis points out that, while Vatican II affirmed that the Spirit makes use of non-Catholic Christian communities as means of salvation in UR 3, "the council does not explicitly say this with regard to other religious traditions, and rightly so". Still, "while the council does not explicitly say that the religious traditions are means of salvation ... in dependence on the active presence of the Christic mystery in them, it nevertheless moves in that direction". In: *Jesus Christ at the Encounter of World Religions*, 138. The entire Chapter Six of this work, 125-151, constitutes a good argument in support of this view on the basis of anthropological, Christological and ecclesiological principles.

Church except in light of the Kingdom, but at the same time the Kingdom itself can be adequately understood only in light of the fact that the Church is its germ and beginning, the instrument chosen by Christ to be the special means for spreading his reign throughout the world.

We have seen that, in recent decades, there has been a shift away from the patristic and scholastic custom of giving the word "church" such a wide meaning that it included all who are being saved. The more restricted use of the term does not seek to deny the insights which the earlier usage conveyed, but rather to better serve the Church of today, with its keen awareness of the values inherent in other religions and in the world at large and its effort to work together with these others in order to realize more fully God's Kingdom. Aside from treating questions of terminology, however, our study has shown that the Kingdom is of tremendous significance for the way in which one understands the Church's foundation, nature, relation to the world and mission *ad gentes*. Attentiveness to the Kingdom prevents theologians from giving too triumphalistic an explanation of this foundation, nature, relation and mission. To that extent, the Church's relation to the Kingdom encourages ecclesiology to be worked out in a more modest key.

But such a vision of the Church as servant to the Kingdom ultimately allows her true glory to be seen. Ecclesial triumphalism is pale, when compared with that more humble ecclesiology, in which the face of the Church reflects the face of Isaiah's suffering servant (Is 42,1-4; 49,1-7; 50,4-11; and 52,13-53,12), who is Jesus Christ himself, the light of the nations (*lumen gentium*; Is. 49,6). The Church seeks no Kingdom of her own, but rather serves as instrument in bringing about that Kingdom which gathers all human beings, and indeed the whole cosmos, into one in Christ. This servant Church is the one who has learned by heart the words of Jesus her Lord: "Come to me all you who are weary and find life burdensome, and I will refresh you. Take my yoke upon your shoulders and learn from me, for I am meek and humble of heart" (Mt 11,28-29). To be thus united in heart with the Suffering Servant is most fitting for the Bride, whom Christ loved and for whom he "gave himself up ... that he might sanctify her ... that he might present the Church to himself in splendor, without spot or wrinkle or any such thing" (Eph 5,25-27). This Church is the one who prays each day, especially during the Eucharist: *Adveniat regnum tuum*! To serve as humble sign and instrument of this advent is her greatest glory.

The Eucharist and the Kingdom of God

PHILIP J. ROSATO

For Catholic theologians, used to basing their arguments on showing the perennial relevance of past salvific events, one of the unforeseeable yet intriguing results of the Second Vatican Council, which retrieved the teachings that the Church is on pilgrimage towards the Kingdom of God and that the Eucharist is the foretaste of the Messianic banquet to be enjoyed there, has been the task of formulating arguments capable of indicating the anticipatory effect of future salvific events. In order to meet this challenge, it has proven beneficial for Catholic theologians to dialogue with experts in the fields of religious sociology, cultural anthropology and political science. Apart from gaining further insight regarding the interrelationship of faith and culture, such dialogue has been motivated by the pastoral necessity to explain the eschatological dimension of Church teaching to Catholics themselves by employing categories of thought about the future which are connatural to them.

From sociologists of religion, Catholic scholars have understood the need to present Christian rituals as prophetic events rather than as sacred obligations, since human beings generally experience communitarian and future-oriented religious actions as conducive to fostering social harmony and advancement. From cultural anthropologists, they have learned to appreciate the inherent force of religious symbols with regard to openness to the radically new, whether this be comprehended as a return to the original wholeness of creation, or as an inbreaking of its much desired future fulfillment. And from political scientists, they have grasped the indispensable role of formulating moral values in the process of determining public policy, since a theory of civil improvement is best realized when its underlying ethical motivation is freely adopted by most members of the group. Thus, arriving at restatements of Catholic teaching on the Church and on the Eucharist in terms of prophecy, openness to the radically new and ethical values has necessitated examining Scripture and Tradition from quite different points of view than those preferred even in the first half of the twentieth century.

This essay is an attempt to explain how Catholic retrieval of the traditional teaching that the Eucharist as a *signum progno-sticum*, or as a sign which truly prefigures the Messianic banquet in the Kingdom of God, has been reinforced by reading the data of Scripture and Tradition in terms of prophecy, openness to the radically new and ethical values. Thus, the first sub-division of these reflections is entitled "The Central Theme of the Kingdom of God in the Prophetic Act Performed by Jesus at the Last Supper". This initial section, based on biblical theology, shows how consciousness of the importance of prophecy for contemporary Catholics has led to renewed understanding of the symbolic gestures employed by Jesus throughout his ministry, and especially towards its dramatic conclusion. By transfinalizing or transcreating the bread and wine which he then distributed to his disciples, Jesus acted in the Cenacle in a decidedly prophetic manner, and urged his disciples to do likewise.

The second sub-division, entitled "The Eschatological Dimension of the Eucharist as Presented in the Documents of Vatican II", is meant to demonstrate how the search of Catholics for the radically new induced theologians to situate dogmatic statements about the Eucharist against the wide horizon of human cultural evolution. Such an horizon makes it evident that human development must invariably include concern for the future of the inorganic and organic realities of the planet, on which the physical and social well-being of the human race depends. The eschatological approach to the Eucharist which the bishops at Vatican II articulated fulfills this need for such a broad horizon, since it views the consecrated elements as the real foreshadowing of the final consecration of the whole cosmos at the arrival of the Kingdom.

And the third sub-division is entitled "Eucharistic Grace and the Task of Transforming the World in Anticipation of the Arrival of the Kingdom". Here the ethical responsibility is described which results from participating in the Eucharist perceived as the pre-figurement of the Messianic banquet. This imperative is shown to be grounded both in the moral intention of Jesus in enacting the prophetic gestures in the Cenacle and in culminating them Calvary, and in the concern of his followers for the future liberation of all created realities, symbolized as they are by the broken bread and poured out wine which are the focal points of this ritual. Receiving the transfinalized or transcreated Eucharistic elements spurs Christians to engage in activities which foster the transformation of their environment as means of inaugurating the coming Kingdom of God.

In order to assure that a common vocabulary mark each sub-section of this essay, two linguistic liberties have been taken which call for some brief explanation at the start. The three divine Persons of the Trinity are referred to not only as the Father, the Son and the Holy Spirit, but also as the Creator, the Recreator and the Transcreator, respectively. Given the topic of this essay, it is helpful to make use of a common stem, by which to designate the one God of creation, and of two different prefixes, by which to designate how the original creation is ever more perfected by the distinctively redemptive mission of the second divine Person and the distinctly sanctifying mission of the third divine Person. Moreover, these distinctions facilitate the exposition of the Eucharistic elements as transfinalized or transcreated realities, which the Recreator introduced into history in the Upper Room for a group of his disciples, and which the Transcreator continues to produce in the liturgical assembly so that countless Christians may participate in the real anticipation of the heavenly banquet.

1. The Central Theme of the Kingdom of God in the Prophetic Act Performed by Jesus at the Last Supper

The sociologists of religion point out the positive function which the prophetic model of ritual exercises on whatever environment in which it is found. As opposed to the magician, who receives clients in search of divine favor but does not create community among them or encourage them to join their attainment of salvation to that of others, the prophet sits among the adherents to the numinous power present in their midst, fosters interaction among them, and teaches them the moral and social implications of being beneficiaries of divine grace[1]. The behavior of Jesus seated at table with his disciples on the eve of his death illustrates the prophetic model of religious leadership. As he employs bread and wine in performing his ritual acts at the Last Supper, the modern reader can understand that these elements are microcosms of the entire creation: of inorganic and organic matter shaped by human minds and hands into effective means to sustain well-being and life, and to stave off malnutrition and death. Thus, the goal or the end of these nutritional elements is to preserve the vitality of the corporeal and spiritual dimensions of human existence in the world[2]. Jesus shares these elements with his disciples, thereby forms communion with them, and explicitly urges them to do what he did, to break bread and to pass the cup to others.

In Judaism, God is understood as desiring to grant human beings a share in the divine life, so that they may communicate it to many others in his name. Thus, in *Psalm* 23: 5, God is presented as "preparing a banquet" for Israel and as confirming that its cup would be "overflowing". Jesus was well aware of these connections between the bread and wine which are corruptible and the banquet in the Kingdom of God which would have no end. He often sat at table with sinners, broke bread and shared wine with them as signs of the inbreaking of the Kingdom of God into their lives seemingly destroyed by religious impurity and social emarginalization[3]. In giving bread to the countless numbers of hungry people who followed him into the desert, he meant to foreshadow their final participation in the abundance of God, despite their apparently futile pilgrimage within history[4].

---

[1] Cf. E. DURKHEIM, *Le forme elementari della vita religiosa*, Milano 1963, 49-50.

[2] Cf. E. SCHILLEBEECKX, "Transubstantiation, Transfinalization, Transignification", in *Worship* 40 (1966) 324-338.

[3] Cf. H. SCHÜRMANN, "Jesus' Words in the Light of his Actions at the Last Supper", in *Concilium* 4 (1968) 61-67.

[4] Cf. D. BOROBIO, *Dimensión social de la liturgia y los sacramentos*, Bilbao 1990.

These texts explain why in the *Gospel of John*, Jesus is said to have identified himself as the new "manna", the bread come down from heaven, so that those who eat of his Word and of his Flesh, and drink of his Blood, already are sustained by everlasting life, and will be raised up on the last day of time (cf. Jn 6: 52-56). Thus, the Kingdom-oriented consciousness of Jesus placed the Last Supper against the vast panorama of human hope in immortality[5].

At table in the Cenacle, Jesus enacted a "prophetic sign", that is, one which was extraordinary in the eyes of his disciples, caused them to be united in pondering what he was doing, provoked them to moral conversion in the face of his generosity, and anticipated the Kingdom of God in their midst[6]. With regard to this last characteristic of a prophetic sign, it can be said that Jesus associated his self-giving through the bread and wine to the final generosity of God at table with renewed human beings in the eternal Kingdom. This is evident in those texts which have led some exegetes to question whether Jesus actually ate or drank at the Last Supper; he seems to have been so overwhelmed by the radicality of the gesture of identifying himself with the Paschal lamb of Exodus and with the Messianic lamb of the Kingdom that he began an eschatological fast, although he encouraged his table-companions to eat and drink[7]. This would mean that the following words concerning the Kingdom of God justify why Jesus refused to partake in food and drink on the eve of his death: "For, I tell you, I shall not eat of it until it is fulfilled in the Kingdom of God" (Lk 22: 16); "From this moment on, I will not drink of the fruit of the vine until the Kingdom of God comes" (Lk 22: 18).

Thus, it can be said that Jesus changed the goal of the bread and the wine on the table in the Cenacle. These elements no longer had the goal natural to them, that is, keeping his companions from starvation and death; they assumed a new goal, that of joining them, at that moment in history,

---

[5] Cf. A. NITROLA, *L'Eucarestia, forza dell'unità. La dimensione escatologica dell'Eucarestia nel dialogo tra cattolici e protestanti*, Casale Monferrato, 1992.
[6] Cf. J. ESPINEL, *La cena del Señor, acción profetica*, Salamanca 1976.
[7] Cf. J. JEREMIAS, *The Eucharistic Words of Jesus*, London 1966.

to the bread and wine to be enjoyed at the heavenly banquet in the presence of the Messiah[8]. Once Jesus had died and been raised to new life, his disciples would understand that in fact they had been granted an anticipated experience of the Messianic banquet while in the Upper Room Jesus was with them offering them the transfinalized bread and wine. This interpretation appears well suited to explain the forceful promise made by Jesus to his disciples at the end of the Last Supper: "You are those who have continued with me in my trials; as my Father appointed a Kingdom for me, so do I appoint for you, that you may eat and drink at my table in my Kingdom, and sit on thrones judging the twelve tribes of Israel" (Lk 22: 28-30)[9].

Furthermore, the words of Jesus "Do this in memory of me" (Lk: 22: 19) gain a more poignant and existential significance in the light of his prophetic act of having transfinalized or transcreated the bread and wine employed by him at table in the Cenacle. Because of the ambiguous grammatical meaning of the genitive "of me", it has been suggested that Jesus could have said "Do this, so that my Father may be mindful of my act". In this way, the accent falls not so much on a command to do exactly what Jesus had done, but on an invitation to pray to the Father, so that he would never reject the seemingly blasphemous act of Jesus who interpreted the most sacred ritual of Judaism in terms of his own Body and Blood to be offered for the redemption of all, and in terms of his desire to inaugurate the Messianic banquet once and for all within history[10].

In other words, Jesus was painfully aware that, if the Father should repute his audacious salvific act, then he and his disciples would indeed be blasphemers; but, if he should accept the actions of Jesus in the Cenacle on behalf of the definitive salvation of all people, then he would have indeed ushered into time the beginning of the unending meal of the

---

[8] Cf. M.D. HOOKER, *The Signs of a Prophet: the Prophetic Actions of Jesus*, Cambridge, 1996.
[9] Cf. N.A. BECK, "The Last Supper as an Efficacious Symbolic Act", in *Journal of Biblical Literature* 89 (1970) 192-198.
[10] Cf. P.J. ROSATO, *Introduzione alla teologia dei sacramenti*, Casale Monferrato 1992, 82-92.

Kingdom of God. This interpretation of the words of Jesus regarding the future task of the disciples explains why the Christian Eucharist is a prayer directed to the Father, so that he might accept once again, as he once did in raising Jesus from the dead, the sacramental re-presentation of his actions in the Cenacle and on Calvary, so that they might give new life to the people of every age who await in hope for definitive salvation[11].

This eschatological interpretation of the Last Supper, which provides the basis of the Kingdom-oriented understanding of the Eucharist, can be briefly summarized in the following way: *Jesus changes the inherent goal of the bread and the wine so that they become real symbols of his encouraging self-gift to his cynical or dejected followers, and effective signs of their mission to inaugurate his redemptive Kingdom in the world.* The phrases "changes the inherent goal" and "become real symbols" indicate that, both at the Last Supper and at the Eucharistic liturgy, the intention of Jesus, in transfinalizing the elements, is to conjoin a sacred meal taking place in history to the Messianic banquet transcending the realm of space and time; the transcreated elements no longer belong to the original creation, but are the real symbols of the Messiah awaiting humanity in the Kingdom[12]. This real entrance of the future into the present is achieved by Jesus through the act of rendering the bread and wine essentially transformed means of communicating to human beings his eschatological victory on the Cross over their sin, despair and death. Thus, in the brief statement the contrast between the adjectives "encouraging" and "cynical/dejected" emphasizes that Jesus desires to provide his scoffing accusers as well as his desolate disciples a completely unexpected foretaste of the heavenly banquet so that, in a united way, they could become in history living witnesses to his victorious existence in the Kingdom[13].

With the phrase "encouraging self-gift" the summary statement affirms that Jesus, acting through his Spirit in the

---

[11] Cf. G. MARTELET, *The Eucharist and the Cosmic Christ*, New York 1975.
[12] Cf. F.X. DURRWELL, *L'Eucaristia, sacramento del mistero pasquale*, Assisi 1983.
[13] Cf. G. WAINWRIGHT, *Eucharist and Eschatology*, New York 1981.

liturgy of the Church, ontically changes the inherent goal of the bread and wine so that they transcend their previous purpose of safeguarding human persons from physical death, and take on their new purpose of furnishing them real symbols of their immortal life in and through him. Those who receive the transfinalized sacramental species are therefore challenged to turn from cynicism or despair in the face the sufferings of the world, and to take up the demanding task of seeking the Kingdom of God and his justice (cf. Mt 6: 33), and of being ready, when necessary, to suffer for the sake of justice and to know that theirs is the Kingdom of heaven (cf. Mt 5: 10)[14]. In effect, this eschatological reading of the Last Supper and of the Eucharist brings out quite forcefully the prophetic model of religion, by which the sociologists claim that the worship of God is translated into social cohesion and moral unity which have great relevance for the betterment of human communal existence.

2. THE ESCHATOLOGICAL DIMENSION OF THE EUCHARIST AS PRESENTED IN THE DOCUMENTS OF THE SECOND VATICAN COUNCIL

In a most significant passage from the *Pastoral Constitution on the Church in the Modern World*, the bishops at Vatican II voiced the need to employ insights from the human sciences, so as to carry out pastoral work effectively at the present time: "In pastoral care, appropriate use must be made not only of theological principles, but also of the findings of the secular sciences, especially of psychology and sociology. Thus the faithful can be brought to live the faith in a more thorough and mature way"[15]. Another of the social sciences not mentioned here is cultural anthropology which studies, as an integral part of understanding all civilizations, the power of symbols in helping people to project and to realize their aspirations. One of the latter is the desire for the totally new, that is, for a future which would overcome all

---

[14] Cf. K. RAHNER, "The Presence of Christ in the Sacrament of the Lord's Supper", in *Theological Investigations* IV, 287-311.
[15] *Gaudium et Spes*, 62.

the obstacles which keep civilizations from intellectual and moral, social and political decadence[16].

Even if the bishops at Vatican II did not explicitly illumine the Eucharist in relation to the Kingdom of God by means of such anthropological insights, they did place this sacrament against a wide cultural backdrop: "The Holy Spirit frees all Christians so that, by putting aside love of self and bringing all earthly resources into the service of human life, they can devote themselves to that future when humanity itself will become an offering accepted by God. The Lord left behind a pledge of this hope and strength for life's journey in that sacrament of faith where natural elements refined by human beings are changed into his glorified Body and Blood"[17]. The future fulfillment of all earthly resources is the cultural aspiration, in terms of which the Eucharist can be explained as a sure pledge.

Further on in the same passage the bishops explicitly treat the eschatological aspect of the Eucharist: "In the sacrament of faith, the Lord provides a foretaste of the heavenly banquet"[18]. In making this and similar affirmations, the bishops do not officially sanction any term such as "transfinalization" by which the Eucharistic change is attributed to the entirely new goal which the bread and wine, understood as *creatures awaiting fulfillment*, are granted at the consecration. But they do indicate that neglect of this theme can keep Christians from appreciating the Eucharist as the sure focal point which guides their way as the pilgrim People of God[19]. There is no doubt that, in conformity with the general adherence of the bishops to a paschal and eschatological perspective in restating the entire theological tradition of the Church, a specifically future-oriented viewpoint marks their presentation of the Eucharist.

In the *Constitution on the Sacred Liturgy*, the sacrifice of the Mass is viewed both from the Pauline perspective that it is the sacramental perpetuation of the death and resurrec-

---

[16] Cf. V. TURNER, "Ritual Symbolism, Morality and Social Structure" in *African Systems of Thought*, ed. M. Fortes and G. Dieterlen, Oxford 1965.
[17] *Gaudium et Spes*, 38.
[18] *Ibid*.
[19] *Ibid*. The text refers to the Eucharist as the "itineris viaticum" of the Church.

tion of Christ "until he comes again" (1 Cor 11: 26), and of the Thomistic perspective that it is a "paschal banquet in which Christ is consumed, the mind filled with grace and a pledge of future glory is given to us"[20]. Thus, the bishops clearly do not intend to affirm that the Eucharistic species simply point to the future heavenly banquet to be offered by Christ at his second coming. Instead, they desire to assert that the consecrated elements truly contain as well as symbolize the eschatological Lord who will gather all his disciples at the banquet table in his Kingdom. The Lord's Supper is, therefore, just as much a privileged participation in the yet awaited consummation of salvation in the *Eschaton*, as it is the unique share in its historical foundation in the Cenacle and on Calvary[21]. Consequently, the Eucharistic change can be as adequately explained whether it is understood as an effective prolepsis, or in breaking, of the eschatological banquet at which Jesus the enthroned Messianic Lamb will preside in the Kingdom, or as an effective anamnesis of the paschal banquet at which Jesus, having identified himself with the slain Exodus Lamb, presided in the Cenacle[22].

The continuity between these two approaches is suggested in a passage from the *Dogmatic Constitution on the Church* in which the role of presbyters at the Eucharist is described as that of leading the assembled community towards the eschatological banquet which will have no end, while at the same time officiating at the paschal banquet which takes place in history: "Until the coming of the Lord (cf. 1 *Cor* 11:26), presbyters re-present and apply in the sacrifice of the Mass the one sacrifice of the New Testament, namely the sacrifice of Christ offering himself once and for all to his Father as a spotless victim (cf. *Heb* 9: 11-28)"[23]. This complementarity between a "past-actualizing" and a "future-anticipating" explanation of the Eucharistic ritual is also emphasized in a text which conjoins the anamnetic and the prognostic aspects of the sacrifice of the Mass by means of a reference to its fu-

---

[20] *Sacrosanctum Concilium*, 46.
[21] Cf. W. BEINERT-J. RATZINGER, *Il problema della transustanziazione e del significato dell'Eucaristia*, Roma 1969.
[22] Cr. J. KODELL, *The Eucharist in the New Testament*, Wilmington 1988.
[23] *Lumen Gentium*, 28.

ture cessation at the coming of the Lord: "Through the ministry of priests, the spiritual sacrifice of the faithful is made perfect in union with the sacrifice of Christ, the sole Mediator. Through the hands of priests and in the name of the whole Church, the Lord's sacrifice is offered in the Eucharist in an unbloody and sacramental manner until he himself returns"[24]. Thus, the re-actualizing and pre-figuring dimensions of the Eucharist are interrelated by the bishops at Vatican II in such a way that the ultimate goal of the first is found in the second, and the historical ground of the second in the first. The rediscovery of scriptural and liturgical insights which this affirmation of complementary ways of regarding the efficacy of the Eucharistic change entails is undoubtedly one of the most remarkable achievements of the Council[25]. For, it enriches Eucharistic spirituality by encouraging Christians to base their hope on the past, present and future dimensions of the eschatological victory of Christ. And it directs theologians to enter into ecumenical dialogue with their Protestant colleagues not simply to defend the Eucharist as the re-presentation of the paschal sacrifice of Calvary, but also to search for agreement on this sacrament as the pre-presentation of the Messianic banquet of the Kingdom.

Moreover, aware that modern persons are particularly concerned with assuming responsibility for the future of the earth, the bishops indirectly advocated an eschatological explanation of the Eucharistic change in a number of passages which attribute the inherent dynamism of the Church to this sacrament. In the *Decree on the Church's Missionary Activity*, for example, the celebration of the Eucharist is presented as an entrance into the forward-directed mission of Christ: "Therefore, let missionaries as God's co-workers (cf. 1 *Cor* 3: 9), raise up congregations of the faithful who will walk in a manner worthy of the vocation to which they have been called (cf. *Eph* 4: 1), and will exercise the priestly, prophetic and royal office which God has entrusted to them. In this way, the Christian community becomes a sign of God's presence in the

---

[24] *Presbyterorum Ordinis*, 2.
[25] Cf. W. KASPER, "Unità e molteplicità degli aspetti dell'Eucaristia" in *Communio* 18 (1985) 37-60.

world. For, by reason of the Eucharistic sacrifice, the community is ceaselessly on the way with Christ to the Father"[26]. By stressing the inextricable connection between the ecclesio-sacramental and the cosmico-eschatological activity of Christ, the bishops at Vatican II clearly situated the paschal banquet of the Church within an evolutionary world-view, and thus indirectly interpreted the consecrated bread and wine as "transfinalized" elements.

This technical term means that the bread and wine, as creatures ultimately destined to be transformed with humanity in the new heaven and the new earth, already attain this final goal through the Eucharistic consecration. As transfinalized or transcreated realities, they serve as channels of immortal life for the members of the Church because of their proleptic, or future-anticipating, identity with the Body and Blood of Christ awaiting his disciples at the heavenly banquet in his Kingdom[27]. That the bishops at Vatican II favored this view is confirmed by a text concerning the responsibility of Christians to "make ready the material of the celestial realm" and "to devote themselves to that future when humanity itself will become an offering accepted by God"[28]. Since the transformed natural elements are immediately mentioned after these phrases, it is clear that the bishops regarded the Eucharistic anamnesis and epiclesis as effecting an essential change of the bread and wine whose inherent goal is no longer that of keeping people from starvation and death. The invocation of the Holy Spirit and the recitation of the words of Christ allow these material goods of the earth to pass from their original creaturely end, that is, preserving human beings from physical deterioration, to their new end as transfinalized creatures, or as food and drink from heaven, that is, providing Christians within history the first fruits of immortal life[29].

---

[26] *Ad Gentes*, 15.
[27] Cf. P.J. ROSATO, "La transustanziazione nella luce della nuova creazione", in *Via, Verità e Vita* 32 (1983) 43-52.
[28] *Gaudium et Spes*, 38.
[29] Cf. J. MOLTMANN, *La Chiesa nella forza dello Spirito, un contributo per una ecclesiologia messianica*, Brescia 1976, 359-274.

If at present the transfinalized elements are received only by the Christian community gathered at Eucharistic worship, their very existence is meant to provide all humanity, and indeed the whole cosmos, with hope. For at the Mass the praise offered to the Creator-Father through the elements, whose goal has been essentially changed, is the real foreshadowing of that praise to be given him when, at the end of time, the entire human race and every other creature become a perfect offering. This can occur only through the completed mission of the Recreator-Son and that of the Transcreator-Spirit. This forward-pointing understanding the Eucharistic change, and the eschatological notion of sacrifice on which it is based, in no way degrade the traditional assertions that the Kingdom of God has already broken into history on Calvary and that the Christian community is presently a new creation because of the paschal victory of the crucified Jesus and the descent of his Holy Spirit[30].

Yet, after Easter and Pentecost the specifically sacerdotal ministry both of the baptized and of the ordained consists in collaborating with the Holy Spirit in directing the world, already redeemed by Christ, to its immediate and unending participation in the victory he has won. Thus, belief in the Eucharist as the anticipatory presence of the Lord of the new creation forcefully reminds the whole priestly community of Christians to look hopefully to the final goal of its temporal ministry whose continuing efficacy stems from the paschal mystery: "Since all these ministerial activities result from Christ's Passover, they will be crowned in the glorious return of the same Lord when he himself hands over the Kingdom to his God and Father"[31]. At the Eucharist, a real foretaste of this moment is sacramentally available to the baptized and the ordained in and through the new creatures on the altar, the bread and wine whose inherent goal has once and for all been transformed by the Christ, the first-born of all creation, and the first-born from the dead (cf. Col 1: 15, 18). This specifically Christian concept of the totally new, which for cultural anthropologists is an inherent aspect of human civi-

---

[30] Cf. J.-M. TILLARD, *L'Eucaristia, Pasqua della Chiesa*, Assisi 1965.
[31] *Presbyterorum Ordinis*, 2.

lization, can be associated either with the lustral symbolism of Baptism or with the convivial symbolism of the Eucharist. The eschatological approach to understanding and explaining the Eucharist proves to be the most forceful way of assuring that the new life first attained at the Baptismal font is continually nourished at the Supper of the Lord[32].

3. Eucharistic Grace and the Task of Transforming the World in Anticipation of the Arrival of the Kingdom

Political scientists stress the importance of moral values in the formulation of efficient and lasting public policy. Such an insight has led Christian theologians to view Christian orthodoxy, or correct belief, as insufficient if it is not manifested in Christian orthopraxy, or correct behavior[33]. It follows that the theological explanation of Eucharistic grace, as deriving from receiving the consecrated elements endowed with a totally new finality, accentuates the eschatological being and mission conferred on Christian communicants. Above, it was noted that the relationship between consuming the transfinalized Eucharistic elements and assuming the task of transforming the world can be derived from the unique nature of this sacrament in which the crucified and risen Jesus ceaselessly directs his followers ahead in history towards the Father.

This link between the Eucharist, as transcreated bread and wine, and the Kingdom, as the final goal of human history, enabled the bishops at Vatican II to conceive the grace of this sacrament as the moral impulse by which Christians are constantly to orient creation itself towards its full liberation (cf. Rom 8: 18-25). Mindful of the dynamic hope which the *Per Ipsum* at the close of the Eucharistic canons lends to Christian existence, the bishops describe the specific effect of this sacrament in terms of participation in the eschatological

---

[32] Cf. J. McKenna, "The Eucharist, the Resurrection and the Future", in *Anglican Theological Review* 60 (1978) 144-165.

[33] Cf. J. Haughey, "Eucharist at Corinth: You are the Christ", in *Above Every Name: The Lordship of Christ and Social Systems*, ed. T. Clarke, New York 1977, 107-133.

mission of the triune God. Thus, in treating the grace which is conferred by the transfinalized elements, they appeal to the revealed truth that the triune God continually actualizes the salvation of the world by first approaching humanity through the movement "Father → Son → Spirit", and then by aiding humanity to its transhistorical fulfillment through the movement "Spirit → Son → Father"[34].

In a passage from the *Decree on the Ministry and Life of Priests*, it is particularly evident that the bishops viewed these two movements of the triune God as converging at the Eucharist and thus as determining its effect on communicants; the passage in question comprises a transition from the final paragraph describing the cultic office of presbyters to the initial one delineating their pastoral function: "Let priests take care to cultivate an appropriate knowledge and facility in the liturgy, so that by their own liturgical ministry, the Christian communities entrusted to them may ever more adequately give praise to God, the Father and the Son and the Holy Spirit... To the degree of their authority and in the name of their bishop, priests exercise the office of Christ the Head and the Shepherd. Thus they gather God's family together as a brotherhood of living unity, and lead it through Christ and in the Spirit to God the Father"[35].

By referring in these passages both to the original and to the eschatological movements of the Trinity within history, the bishops clearly identify the Eucharist as the pivotal point at which the self-communication of the Father in the Spirit-filled Jesus meets humanity, so that humanity can return in the Spirit-filled Jesus to the Father. Thus, the praise offered to the Father, the Son and the Spirit at the *Gloria* culminates in the praise offered in the Spirit through the Son to the Father at the *Per ipsum*. Both forms of praise are rendered by human beings who stand in time between the resurrection of Jesus and the arrival of the new heaven and the new earth. Hence the transcreated bread and wine symbolize and contain the Lord of the whole cosmos who is liberating

---

[34] Cf. P. J. ROSATO, *Introduzione alla teologia dei sacramenti*, Casale Monferrato, 1992, 137-143.

[35] *Presbyterorum Ordinis*, 5-6.

it until it reaches its fulfillment, along with human beings, in the eschatological Kingdom. For this reason, the reception of the transfinalized elements intensifies the future-oriented existence and mission of Christians[36].

In the *Decree on the Apostolate of the Laity* the connection between such an existence and the secular task it entails is succinctly stated: "In the pilgrimage of this life, hidden with Christ in God and free from enslavement to wealth, Christians aspire to those riches which remain forever, and generously dedicate their entire selves to spreading the Kingdom of God and to fashioning and perfecting the sphere of earthly things according to the spirit of Christ"[37]. This synthetic description of Christian hope as a way of life dedicated to perfecting the world also serves to illumine the eschatological dimension of Eucharistic grace: the reception of the transfinalized elements on the altar grants Christians immortal nourishment for their journey in history towards the Kingdom. As pneumatic, or Spirit-filled, bread and wine (1 Cor 10: 3-4) which partake in the glorified existence of Christ with the Father, the elements no longer belong to this world. For, they contain in themselves and pre-present to Christians sojourners in history the Lord of the perfected state of created things who will come at the end of time. Partaking of such eschatologically transformed food and drink at the Eucharist enables Christians to exist not for themselves but for Christ, the Alpha and the Omega (Rev 21: 6). This entails refashioning the world in ways consonant with the hope which the bread from heaven and the cup of unending salvation provide them[38].

For these reasons, the bishops at Vatican II present the Eucharist as the ground of the hope of the pilgrim Church. At this sacrament Christians, repeatedly discouraged by the seeming victory of death over life, consume the transfinalized natural elements which truly signify for them and communicate to them the transfigured Body and Blood of Christ and his attainment of Messianic glory. Thus enjoying within

---

[36] Cf. J. ALFARO, "Eucaristia y empeño cristiano para la transformación de el mundo", in *Cristología y antroplogía*, Madrid 1973, 513-527.
[37] *Apostolicam Actuositatem*, 4.
[38] Cf. B. HARING, *Morale e sacramenti*, Roma 1976.

history the food and drink of immortality, they set out once again on the mission of orienting all things towards their transhistorical goal, and in this way render their lives and labors, carried out in the Spirit of the glorified Christ, a sacrifice most pleasing to the Father[39]. In other words, Eucharistic grace consists in caring for all created things, along with the Transcreator-Spirit and the Recreator-Son, and of directing them to their final goal in the Creator-Father. This understanding of Eucharistic grace seems adequately to reflect the principal theological insights which underlie Catholic teaching concerning this sacrament. It not only points to Christ Omega and to the Messianic banquet in his Kingdom which he is pre-paring for his followers, but also pre-presents symbolically and offers gratuitously to them the divine host himself and the end-time feast. The concepts transfinalization and transcreation help Christians to view the Eucharist, the Church and the Parousia as inseparably joined mysteries of divine salvation which will culminate in the final transformation of human existence and of all created things in Christ Alpha and Omega[40]. Thus, the Eucharist as eschatological food and drink is the divine answer to the human search for the totally new and for the proper means of bringing matter itself to an ever greater perfection. Eucharistic realism with regard to the elements transmuted into the sacramental Body and Blood of the New Being, Jesus Christ (cf, *Eph* 2: 15), furthers ecclesial realism. For the reception of the transfinalized elements consolidates the communion of Christians who are thereby granted an ever fuller participation in the immortal life of Jesus Christ into whom they were first incorporated through Baptism (*Jn* 3: 3-6)[41]. Since all these perspectives of biblical eschatology are fundamental to the Catholic understanding of the Eucharistic change, the bishops at Vatican II wanted both to reaffirm them, and to place them within an evolutionary world-view through what can

---

[39] Cf. M. Azevedo, "Eucharistie, responsibilité, partage au niveau de la culture, de l'economie e de la foi", in *Eucharistie, responsibilité, partage*, Symposium internationale du Congrès eucharistique, Toulouse 1981, 599-680.

[40] Cf. P. Lebeau, *Le vin nouveau du royaume. Etude exégetique et patristique sur la Presence Réele*, Paris 1966.

[41] Cf. E. Schillebeeckx, *I sacramenti, punti d'incontro con Dio*, Brescia 1966.

be called their implicit recognition of the validity of the concept transfinalization.

The theological method *fides quaerens intellectum eschatologicum* was already employed prior to Vatican II, especially in the writings of those theologians living in countries where the question of the future of humanity was, and in some cases still is, acute because of the insistence of rightist or leftist dictatorships that human beings are solely objects within an ideological and supposedly beneficial political system[42]. In presenting the Eucharist, the bishops at Vatican II were intent on supporting such theologians in their efforts to emphasize the bread from heaven as the self-gift of Jesus Christ, the Alpha and the Omega of history who, having won on the Cross a definitive victory over evil and death, already awaits in glory the entrance of humanity and of all created things into his Kingdom. Yet this future consummation of the cosmos is not purely an event postulated by the Church; the real sacramental pre-presentation of the Messianic banquet in the Eucharist is determinative of the eschatological existence of the Church within history. For in the Eucharistic change and in the grace it communicates, a sure pledge of the transformation of the natural world is given to Christians by the Holy Spirit, so that they can be filled with hope as they strive within history to steer all things towards their promised perfection in the Kingdom of God and of his Christ[43].

Thus, the logic characteristic of the method *fides quaerens spem* is proleptic in nature, since advocates of this method claim that what is humanly reasonable is enhanced rather than diminished by faith, which allows the endless future of humanity with God to be accessible within history in an anticipatory fashion. In particular, belief in the promise made by Jesus in the Upper Room that, should the Father vindicate his sacrificial death, he would prepare a place for his own at his table in his Kingdom (*Lk* 22: 29-30) does not lessen the concern of Christian communicants for the future

---

[42] Cf. E. DUSSEL, "Il pane della celebrazione liturgica: segno comunitario di giustizia", in *Concilium* 18 (1982) 102-116.

[43] Cf. V. CODINA, "Sacramentos", in *Mysterium Liberationis* II, Madrid 1990, 267-294.

of the earth, but lends this concern its deepest motivation and its social efficacy[44].

Furthermore, according to the *analogia spei*, which renders the claims made by advocates of the eschatological method of theology especially audacious, every act of human hope, made in the face of injustice and violence, is an implicit affirmation of the truth of the promises of God. All human beings who hope can find in the words concerning the Kingdom which were spoken by Jesus in the Cenacle both an answer to their questions about the ultimate future of human existence, and a stimulus to their immediate efforts to transform the world according to the principles of justice and fraternity. By believing that Jesus is now in his Kingdom and bestows through the Eucharist a solemn pledge of the future participation of all his disciples in his unending joy and peace, Christian communicants deepen and give fuller expression to their human hope and to their faith as *fides in qua spes exprimitur*; thus they experience through Eucharistic grace the need to take responsibility for creation, which in the consecrated species already has attained its fullness in advance, and which thus deserves to be cared for and furthered[45].

It thus seems most important today that theologians, pastors and catechetics underline the interpretation of the Eucharist as the sacrament of the new creation which comes to human beings from the future of the cosmos. This theological explanation in fact responds to a principal question of human beings at this time; for, amazed by the unforeseeable development of science, they ask not so much "Where does matter come from?", as "Where is matter going to?". The use of the terms transfinalization and transcreation as means of illuminating the meaning of transubstantiation rests on adherence to a metaphysics which is more dynamic, relational and ecological[46]. Dynamic, because it places the Eucharist in the movement "Spirit → Son → Father" by which the triune God leads all created realities into the glory of the Kingdom. Relational, because it unites the members of the pilgrim

---

[44] Cf. L. BOFF, "¿Como celebrar la Eucaristia en un mundo de injusticias?", in *Teología desde el lugar del pobre*, Santander 1986, 101-112.
[45] Cf. A. GERKEN, *Teologia dell'Eucaristia*, Roma 1977, 254.
[46] Cf. E. SCHILLEBEECKX, *The Eucharistic Presence*, London 1968.

Church on earth to the Messiah and Lord, Jesus Christ, their Head. Ecological, because it emphasizes that all creatures of the cosmos who enjoy life in the Holy Spirit are being directed to their definitive consummation, for wherever the divine *Pneuma* is acting, there the *Eschaton* is already present.

These dynamic, relational and ecological aspects of the metaphysics implied in the terms transfinalization and transcreation can be further delineated as follows. As the New Being, Jesus is the Alpha and the Omega, the beginning and the end of the history of the cosmos (cf. Rev 22: 13). He invites the inorganic and organic elements of the original creation, and the human community which dwells in it and is responsible for it, to the heavenly banquet in the glory of the Father. This invitation "from the future" is acted upon in and through the sacramental and apostolic life of the Church by means of the Holy Spirit who, breaking in from the fulfillment of creation, orients all things ahead towards this goal[47]. By transforming bread and wine, elements of the original creation, into the *loci* of the "new creation" in the Eucharist, the Spirit guides evolution towards its trans-historical goal in a most intense manner. The consecrated bread and wine already participate in the fullness of the new creation through the eschatological action of the Holy Spirit. Existing to the fullest degree in the movement "Spirit → Son → Father", the Eucharistic elements give hope to the macrocosm of which they are symbols, that is, of inorganic matter, of living wheat and grapes, and of creative human beings.

Explaining the transubstantiated bread and wine in terms of completed creatures also has the advantage of making Christians aware of the diverse political attempts to realize the renovation of society within history[48]. Since the responsibility for the renovation of society is an inherent aspect of Eucharistic grace, Christians who receive it should be attentive to the sincere desires of those who engage in political life and manifest values aimed at social and ecological betterment. Knowing that the absolute goal of the history of the

---

[47] Cf. B. FORTE, *La Chiesa nell'Eucaristia. Per un'ecclesiologia eucaristica*, Naples 1975.

[48] Cf. T. BALISURIYA, *The Eucharist and Human Liberation*, New York 1978.

cosmos is already present in the Eucharist, Christians can view all those human beings who in an explicit, or in implicit way, live according to the values of justice and love, and of respect and responsibility for creation, as inaugurating the Kingdom of God within history[49]. Since the behavior of those who eat and drink of the transfinalized bread and wine ought to be "for the better" of society and of creation, and not "for the worse" (1 Cor 11: 17), they should not only admire consistently and interpret theologically what others are doing on behalf of the preservation of the ecosystem, but should also foster their efforts and join in them. Because of their faith in the Eucharist as the pre-figurement of the Kingdom, Christians should practice social love by making their own the causes of all those who try to renew the face of the earth.

---

[49] Cf. J. PAGOLA, *La Eucaristia, experiencia de amor y de justicia*, Santander 1991.

Il regno di Dio e la vita consacrata

JACQUES SERVAIS

LA VITA CONSACRATA INTESA COME ATTESA OPERANTE
DEL REGNO DI DIO

Fra i principali documenti conciliari che trattano della vita consacrata, il decreto *Ad Gentes* sull'attività missionaria della Chiesa occupa un posto non irrilevante[1]. Non solo attribuisce alla promozione di questa forma di vita un ruolo essenziale nel più generale compito del missionario di formare la comunità cristiana, ma ribadisce con forza il dovere a tal riguardo degli istituti di perfezione, compresi quelli secolari che lavorano nelle missioni[2]. Detti istituti, specialmente quelli di vita attiva,

---

[1] Cf. N. HAUSMAN, *Vie religieuse apostolique et communion de l'Église. L'enseignement du Concile Vatican II*, Paris 1987, 29-37. — I testi magisteriali vengono citati secondo la versione italiana dell'*Enchiridion vaticanum* [= *EV*], Bologna 1976ss; si seguono in generale, per le fonti bibliografiche e i documenti del concilio Vaticano II e della Santa Sede, le abbreviazioni e sigle ivi riportate (cf. *EV* 13, XXIII-XXX). Per i Padri della Chiesa, citiamo la versione delle traduzioni italiane reperibili. Per gli autori moderni, rimandiamo alle traduzioni italiane, pur offrendo in generale una propria versione dall'originale.

[2] Una nota, all'inizio del cap. IV precisa: «"Institutorum" nomine veniunt Ordines, Congregationes, Instituta et Associationes quae in Missionibus laborant». Nel numero intitolato «Promuovere la vita religiosa», AG 18 sottolinea l'importanza, nell'insieme della Chiesa, della vita vissuta nella pratica dei consigli, poiché essa «attraverso una più intima consacrazione a Dio, fatta nella Chiesa, dimostra anche chiaramente ed esprime l'intima natura della vocazione cristiana» (*EV* 1, 1146). Il decreto adopera però ancora il termine «religioso» che non comprende ogni tipo di vita consacrata, come ad esempio quella degli istituti secolari, considerati, nel *Perfectae Caritatis* (PC 11: *EV* 1, 735) come nel Motu Proprio *Primo Feliciter* di Pio XII, quali istituti «non religiosi». Il *Codice di Diritto canonico* del 1983 utilizzerà l'espressione «vita consacrata per consiliorum evangelicorum professionem» che permette di includere gli istituti secolari. Cf. H. BÖHLER, *I consigli evangelici in prospettiva trinitaria. Sintesi dottrinale,* Cinisello Balsamo 1993, 84 e 176. — In questo articolo, intendiamo la vita consacrata in base alla nozione alla quale, nel CIC, si riferiscono le «norme comuni a tutti gli istituti» di questo tipo (cann. 573-606). Cerchiamo così di valutare, nel suo significato teologico, la posizione giuridicamente nuova che, con il presente Diritto canonico, gli istituti secolari hanno ricevuto nell'insieme della Chiesa.

si interroghino, esso dice, «se sono in grado di estendere la propria azione al fine di espandere il regno di Dio tra le genti»³. La Chiesa apostolica, alla quale spetta estendere sempre di più questo regno (Mc 13,10), e affrettare così il giudizio della terra e delle sue opere (2 Pt 3,12), conta su di essi perché si compia la condizione per la venuta del giorno del Signore: l'annunzio del vangelo al mondo intero. Infatti, «il periodo dell'attività missionaria si colloca tra la prima e la seconda venuta di Cristo, in cui la Chiesa, come la messe, sarà raccolta dai quattro venti nel regno di Dio. Prima appunto della venuta del Signore, il vangelo deve essere predicato fra tutte le genti»⁴.

La salvezza attualizzata da Gesù Cristo nella storia va resa nota a tutta la creazione. La missione cristiana ha fin dalle origini un orizzonte universale, corrispondente alla natura stessa della Chiesa cattolica, la quale, secondo l'espressione di Bossuet ripresa da H. de Lubac, è «Gesù Cristo diffuso e comunicato»⁵. Si svolge all'insegna dell'urgenza escatologica: «il tempo ha imbrogliato le vele» — dice Paolo, usando un termine nautico tecnico —, ormai si è fatto breve (1 Cor 7,29). Per la loro vocazione specifica, i membri degli istituti di vita consacrata, a imitazione dell'Apostolo (cf. Rm 15,19ss), sono chiamati a proseguire con rinnovato impegno la loro attività evangelizzatrice, perché, proclamata dappertutto la presenza del regno futuro, il Figlio dell'uomo possa «radunare tutti i suoi eletti dai quattro venti, da un estremo all'altro dei cieli» (Mt 24,31).

Ora, se da una parte, il regno appartiene all'ordine delle realtà ultime, e se, d'altra parte, secondo l'interpretazione corrente, la vita consacrata assume nella Chiesa il valore speciale di segno escatologico, sembra ovvia la conclusione del decreto conciliare che, più degli altri fedeli, le persone consacrate debbono per priorità farsi i messaggeri di questo regno

---

³ AG 40: *EV* 1, 1232. Cf. LG 44: *EV* 1, 405; PC 5: *EV* 1, 723.
⁴ AG 9: *EV* 1, 1108. Cf. Ap 14,6.
⁵ BOSSUET, *Allocution aux nouvelles catholiques* (Œuvres oratoires 5, Lebarcq, t. 6, 508; citato in H. DE LUBAC, *Catholicisme*, Paris, 1947⁴, 25 (trad. it. Milano 1992², 23); più avanti l'autore precisa: «La Chiesa non è cattolica perché attualmente è diffusa su tutta la faccia della terra e conta un gran numero di aderenti. Essa era già cattolica il mattino della Pentecoste [...]. Se è vero che deve dilatarsi necessariamente nello spazio e manifestarsi agli occhi di tutti, non è tuttavia di natura materiale, ma spirituale» (*Ibid.*, 26; trad. it. 24).

finale. Non è proprio questa la loro vocazione distintiva quale venne messa in risalto nell'esortazione apostolica post-sinodale *Christifideles laici* del 1988? Ivi spiega Giovanni Paolo II, in un discorso più ampio sugli stati di vita cristiana come modalità diverse e complementari: «Lo stato religioso testimonia l'indole escatologica della Chiesa, ossia la sua tensione verso il regno di Dio, che viene prefigurato e in qualche modo anticipato e pregustato dai voti di castità, povertà e obbedienza»[6]. Con questa affermazione, il Papa non fa altro che assumere l'insegnamento della *Lumen Gentium* e anzitutto della *Gaudium et Spes*. La Chiesa non ha qui città permanente, va in cerca della futura. Lo stato religioso manifesta l'eccellenza del regno di Dio, la sua «elevatezza sopra tutte le cose terrestri e le sue esigenze supreme»[7].

Presente senza particolari rilievi nel magistero precedente, l'idea di quell'attesa operante del regno è stata ripresa e ampiamente sviluppata nella recente esortazione apostolica post-sinodale *Vita consecrata*. Questo documento — abbandonando la terminologia più limitativa di «stato religioso» — mette di nuovo in risalto il ruolo di segno escatologico della vita consacrata, in quanto essa attesta che il regno futuro, il mondo definitivo, già inaugurato con il ministero, la morte e la risurrezione di Gesù, deve ancora realizzarsi totalmente. Fra i fondamentali stati di vita che esprimono, ognuno nel suo modo, l'unico mistero di Cristo, la vita secondo i consigli evangelici assume nella Chiesa un significato peculiare: «annuncia e in certo modo anticipa il tempo futuro, quando, raggiunta la pienezza di quel regno dei cieli che già è presente in germe e nel mistero, i figli della risurrezione non prenderanno né moglie né marito, ma saranno come angeli di Dio (cf. Mt 22,30)»[8]. Citando

---

[6] CfL 55: *EV* 11, 1850.

[7] LG 44: *EV* 1, 406; sul regno di Dio, cf. LG 5: *EV* 1, 289-290. In GS 38, il Concilio situa in questi termini la missione della vita religiosa rispetto a quella del laicato: lo Spirito «chiama alcuni a dare testimonianza manifesta della dimora celeste col desiderio di essa, contribuendo così a mantenerlo vivo nell'umanità; altri li chiama a consacrarsi al servizio degli uomini sulla terra, così da preparare attraverso tale loro ministero la materia per il regno dei cieli» (*EV* 1, 1437).

[8] VC 32 (= *Vita consecrata. Sulla vita consacrata e la sua missione nella Chiesa e nel mondo*. Testo integrale con introduzione e guida alla lettura dell'Abate G. Farnedi O.S.B., Casale Monferrato 1996; qui come negli altri documenti magisteriali si cita secondo la numerazione ufficiale dei paragrafi).

le parole di Gesù: «là dove è il tuo tesoro, sarà anche il tuo cuore» (Mt 6,21), il documento le interpreta in questo modo:

> Il tesoro unico del regno suscita il desiderio, l'attesa, l'impegno e la testimonianza [...]. Le persone che hanno dedicato la loro vita a Cristo non possono non vivere nel desiderio di incontrarLo per essere finalmente e per sempre con Lui. Di qui l'ardente attesa, di qui il desiderio di «immergersi nel Focolare d'amore che brucia in esse e che altri non è che lo Spirito Santo» (B. Elisabetta della Trinità)[9], attesa e desiderio sostenuti dai doni che il Signore liberamente concede a coloro che aspirano alle cose di lassù (cf. Col 3,1). Fissa nelle cose del Signore, la persona consacrata ricorda che «non abbiamo quaggiù una città stabile» (Eb 13,14), perché «la nostra patria è nei cieli» (Fil 3,20). Sola cosa necessaria è cercare «il Regno di Dio e la sua giustizia» (Mt 6,33), invocando incessantemente la venuta del Signore[10].

La vita consacrata è segnata, quindi, da una «tensione totalizzante che anticipa [...] la perfezione escatologica»,[11] attirando i fedeli «verso quel mistero del regno di Dio che [...] attende la sua piena attuazione nei cieli»[12]. Il richiamo all'attenzione della sua natura escatologica non è rimasto inosservato. In un articolo intitolato *Speranza ed escatologia. La testimonianza della vita consacrata*, B. Secondin saluta nell'esortazione post-sinodale il riemergere delle dimensioni essenziali, che rischiavano di cadere nell'oblio. Infatti, «la centralità dell'attesa del ritorno del Signore e la testimonianza della caducità, di conseguenza, di ogni altra realtà storica, hanno caratterizzato la vita consacrata dall'origine ai nostri giorni»[13]. Per secoli la «utopia» di cui vive la «memoria-vigilia» del monaco, «aveva avuto il ritorno al paradiso, la vita angelica e la fuga dal mondo come topografia specifica»[14]. Ora, però, secondo l'autore, si è verificato un considerevole

---

[9] *Le ciel dans la foi. Traité spirituel* I, 14: *Œuvres spirituelles*, Paris 1991, 106.
[10] VC 26.
[11] VC 16; cf. 27.
[12] VC 1.
[13] *RITC Communio* 148 (1996) 40.
[14] *Ibid.*, 41; cf. 45.

cambiamento di prospettiva. Ormai, «l'attesa del futuro è presentata come passione per il possibile nel tempo presente, come un processo maieutico di vaste proporzioni, per far germogliare dalla terra giustizia e fraternità, vicinanza e gratuità, trasfigurazione e fede»[15]. Con l'Incarnazione realizzata in Cristo salvatore, Dio si è fatto il futuro assoluto dell'uomo e la storia dell'uomo è diventata «promissio inquieta»: «memoria di una promessa che fermenta la storia e vigilanza, ossia attenzione ad ogni segno che annuncia l'irruzione dell'alba definitiva»[16]. La profezia del «nuovo mondo», cominciato in Gesù Cristo, rimanda al di là delle condizioni attuali di vita, verso un *eschaton* che si fa operante già dentro la storia, in virtù dell'agire cristiano. Assumendo le sue responsabilità nei confronti del regno di Dio, il religioso, a detta di P. Secondin, è chiamato a «esprimere ma anche [a] organizzare la speranza, che apra allo stesso tempo al futuro di Dio e al presente degli uomini, in mezzo ai quali Dio viene ad abitare»[17].

È giustificata questa interpretazione «utopistica» del regno di Dio e della vocazione del religioso? È pienamente consona non solo con la totalità della dottrina magisteriale, ma anche con la divina rivelazione[18]? Non è il nostro intento affrontare la problematica con tutta l'ampiezza che essa meriterebbe. Col proposito di interrogare tale interpretazione, che gode di non poche adesioni, tenteremo di precisare, da un lato, quale sia il significato teologico del regno di Dio, e dall'altro, quale sia la responsabilità specifica della vita consacrata. Si pongono infatti due domande. La prima è quella dell'indole escatologica della Chiesa intera, la quale, dichiara la *Lumen Gentium*, ha ricevuto dal suo Fondatore, «la missione di annunziare e instaurare in tutte le genti il regno di Cristo e di Dio, e di questo regno costituisce in terra il germe

---

[15] *Ibid.*, 47.
[16] *Ibid.*, 45.
[17] *Ibid.*, 47. Per una discussione del concetto di utopia applicato alla teologia, si veda I. MANCINI, *Teologia, ideologia, utopia*, Brescia 1974, specialmente l'«epilogo».
[18] La rivelazione, che viene tramandata dalla Chiesa, come dice il Concilio, tramite «la sacra tradizione e la sacra scrittura dell'uno e dell'altro testamento» (DV 7: *EV* 1, 881) costituisce il principio di discernimento per ogni sviluppo di dottrina teologica o spirituale, nonché per ogni orientamento pastorale e ricerca di rinnovamento dei nostri istituti.

e l'inizio»[19]. La seconda domanda, alla quale potremo poi rispondere succintamente, concerne più specificamente la missione particolare dello stato dei consigli evangelici nella compagine dei vari stati di vita di cui, secondo l'insegnamento del magistero, recentemente ribadito[20], è costituita la Chiesa.

Interpretazioni monastiche della venuta del regno

L'annunzio e l'instaurazione del regno escatologico non appartengono per privilegio a una categoria di fedeli senza competere prima di tutto alla totalità del Nuovo Popolo di Dio. Il «dovere di diffondere dappertutto il regno di Dio», che «sentono profondamente i Padri conciliari in unione con il romano Pontefice»[21], non spetta solo alle persone consacrate. È il dovere di tutta la Chiesa nella sua essenziale vocazione missionaria[22]. Infatti, come spiega bene il Decreto *Apostolicam Actuositatem* sull'apostolato dei laici,

> la Chiesa è nata con il fine di rendere, mediante la diffusione del regno di Cristo su tutta la terra a gloria di Dio Padre, partecipi tutti gli uomini della redenzione salvifica e per mezzo di essi ordinare effettivamente il mondo intero a Cristo. Tutta l'attività del Corpo mistico ordinata a questo fine si chiama apostolato, che la Chiesa esercita mediante tutti i suoi membri, naturalmente in modi diversi[23].

Per chiarire il legame fra il regno di Dio e la vita consacrata, occorre quindi puntualizzare il senso generale del messaggio evangelico su questo regno. Per poter rispondere alla prima domanda, si devono per prima cosa scartare alcune spiegazioni insufficienti.

Una spiegazione classica lega fortemente la venuta del regno con lo sforzo religioso-etico della vita cristiana intesa come ascesi spirituale. A tal riguardo, non c'è dubbio che nel loro modo di esprimersi i Dottori del monachesimo non

---

[19] LG 5: *EV* 1,290.
[20] CfL 55: *EV* 11, 1849-1851; VC 16; 31-32.
[21] AG 42: *EV* 1, 1241.
[22] AG 1-2: *EV* 1, 1087-1091. Cf. LG 17: *EV* 1, 327.
[23] AA 2: *EV* 1, 916.

hanno sempre mantenuto tutto l'equilibrio della verità evangelica. Molto presto si è capito l'annunzio di Gesù: ἡ βασιλεία τοῦ θεοῦ ἐντὸς ὑμῶν ἐστιν (Lc 17,21), facendo del regno una realtà interiore, mentre esso riguarda tutto il popolo al quale giunge tramite la sua azione di salvezza (cf. Lc 11,20). Invece di: «Il regno di Dio è in mezzo a voi», è alla vostra portata, si è capito e tradotto: «Il regno di Dio è dentro di voi». Tale interpretazione ha incontrato il favore degli ambienti monastici, a cominciare da sant'Antonio di cui il biografo, sant'Atanasio, riporta la prima grande catechesi:

> I Greci fanno viaggi e attraversano il mare per apprendere le lettere, noi non abbiamo bisogno di viaggiare a motivo del regno dei cieli, non dobbiamo attraversare il mare a motivo della virtù. Il Signore ci ha prevenuto e ci ha detto: «Il regno dei cieli è dentro di voi». La virtù, dunque, non ha bisogno che della nostra volontà, dal momento che si trova dentro di noi e si forma a partire da noi[24].

Questo insegnamento che ha talmente colpito Basilio tanto da indurlo a lasciare la sua carriera di retore per ritirarsi nel Ponto, in un luogo solitario, dove potesse «abbandonare se stesso», «purificare» la sua anima[25], eserciterà un influsso enorme sulla spiritualità posteriore. Massimo il Confessore, in cui confluiscono tutte le correnti della patristica greca, riporterà, tre secoli più tardi, la stessa interpretazione:

> L'espressione: *Si è avvicinato il regno dei cieli* (Mt 3,2) non implica, io credo, restrizione temporale. Infatti *non sopraggiunge visibilmente né diranno: — Eccolo qui, eccolo là* (Lc 17,20-21), ma presuppone lo stato di una predisposizione verso di esso da parte di coloro che ne sono degni. Dice infatti il Vangelo: *Il regno di Dio è dentro di voi* (Lc 17,21). Il regno di Dio e del Padre si trova in potenza in tutti i credenti, in atto in coloro che hanno deposto completamente ogni disposizione di vita naturale

---

[24] ATANASIO, *Vita di Antonio* 20,4-5: *SChr* [= *Sources Chrétiennes*] 400, 188; trad. it. a cura di L. Cremaschi, Roma 1984, 121. Cf. *Contro i pagani* 30: *SChr* 18bis, 150.

[25] BASILIO DI CESAREA, *Lettera* 2: *PG* 32, 224a e 228a. Cf. *Regole ampie*, qu. 6: *PG* 31, 925a-928b. Cf. J. GRIBOMONT, «Le renoncement au monde dans l'idéal ascétique de saint Basile», *Irénikon* 31 (1958) 282-307, 460-475.

dell'anima e del corpo, hanno raggiunto quella sola dello spirito e possono dire: *Vivo, ma non più io: vive in me Cristo* (Gal 2,20)[26].

Anche se non del tutto conforme al testo del Vangelo, l'interpretazione rimane giusta fintantoché non si capisce il regno nel senso della mistica intellettualistica di un Evagrio Pontico. Secondo questi, che fu discepolo di Basilio ma prese in seguito un'altra strada, si giunge al regno quando la mente umana arriva a conoscere Dio. Dato che la mente è, di sua natura, incorruttibile, destinata alla visione eterna di Dio, questo regno è, stando alla speculazione pseudo-origenista di Evagrio, «la conoscenza della Santa Trinità, una scienza che si estende e si applica alla costituzione della nostra mente e ne supera l'incorruttibilità»[27]. Tale singolare interpretazione, estranea al Vangelo, si deve capire in base alla concezione che i primi monaci hanno della virtù morale. Essi vedono nella πρακτική anzitutto la lotta interiore del cristiano alla ricerca della perfezione morale, come un cammino verso la purezza dell'anima, senza la quale non può esserci visione spirituale di Dio. Scrive ad esempio Cassiano, assumendo, per il brano

---

[26] Massimo il Confessore, *Il Dio-Uomo. Duecento pensieri sulla conoscenza di Dio e sull'incarnazione di Cristo* 91-92: trad. it. a cura di A. Ceresa-Gastaldo, Milano 1980, 107. Altrove, Massimo commenta la stessa idea dicendo che il regno di Dio si può raggiungere già con l'allontanamento dell'ira e della concupiscenza: «Conveniente dunque con l'allontanamento dell'ira e della concupiscenza secondo la preghiera sopraggiunge la potenza del regno di Dio e del Padre per coloro che, dopo la perdita di quelle, sono considerati degni di dire: *Venga il tuo regno* (Mt 6,10), cioè lo Spirito Santo, per coloro che grazie al principio e al modo della mitezza sono stati resi già tempio di Dio mediante lo Spirito (cf. Ef 2,21-22). Dice infatti: *Su chi mi poserò se non sul mite e sull'umile e su chi teme le mie parole?* (Is 66,2), cosicché risulta di qui chiaramente che il regno di Dio e del Padre è degli umili e dei miti. *Beati i miti*, dice infatti, *perché essi erediteranno la terra* (Mt 5,4)» (*Interpretazione del "Padre nostro". Umanità e divinità di Cristo:* trad. it. a cura di A. Ceresa-Gastaldo, Roma 1990², 74).

[27] Evagrio Pontico, *Trattato pratico sulla vita monastica* 3: SChr 171, 500; trad. it. a cura di L. Dattrino, Roma 1992, 65. La conoscenza della Trinità supera l'incorruttibilità della mente in quanto facoltà di contemplazione naturale; essa sola dà compimento alla mente, essendo coesiva alla sua sostanza. H.U. von Balthasar, che ha dimostrato l'origine evagriana dell'opera *Selecta in Psalmos* comunemente attribuita a Origene, ha messo più volte in guardia contro l'indole sistematica di questo pensiero. Non esita a scrivere: «È indubitabile che la mistica di Evagrio considerata nel suo sistema del tutto logico, si avvicina sostanzialmente più al buddismo che al cristianesimo» («Metaphysik und Mystik des Evagrius Ponticus», *ZAM* 14 [1939] 38-39).

di Lc 17,21 menzionato, il significato *intra vos* della traduzione latina: «Tutto sta nel santuario profondo dell'anima. Quando il diavolo ne è stato scacciato e i vizi non vi regnano più, conseguentemente si instaura in noi il regno di Dio»[28]. Più avanti, il monaco di Provenza chiarisce il suo pensiero: «Come, con la connivenza nel vizio, si apre il regno del diavolo, così si possiede quello di Dio con la pratica delle virtù, nella purezza del cuore e con la scienza spirituale»[29]. I meriti morali sono quindi il principio, o almeno il motivo, della venuta del regno nell'anima. Certo, egli non dubita che lo sforzo umano sia, come tale, incapace di raggiungere la perfezione. Ma a parer suo, Dio vi risponde normalmente col conferire, per mezzo della contemplazione, il suo regno interiore[30].

Nonostante la grazia sia ribadita, l'accento della vita cristiana si sposta così impercettibilmente sulla natura umana e le possibilità sempre attuali della sua libertà. Troppo fiduciosi nella loro pratica di vita, gli asceti mettono l'opera personale in primo piano, col rischio di sottovalutare di fatto il ruolo della grazia. Ponendosi dal punto di vista soggettivo di questi, i Cappadoci li incoraggiano in quel senso, invitandoli a sforzarsi perché lo Spirito possa agire in loro. Significativo di questa tendenza è il *De Instituto christiano*, nel quale Gregorio di Nissa rivolge alle comunità di monaci organizzate da suo fratello Basilio un insegnamento sull'ascensione, sulla vetta scoscesa della virtù, basato sul concetto di «sinergia» fra la nostra opera e l'opera dello Spirito che restaura in noi la libertà inefficace dopo la colpa originale[31].

---

[28] GIOVANNI CASSIANO, *Conferenze spirituali* I 13: *SChr* 42, 91.

[29] *Ibid.*, I 14: *SChr* 42, 93.

[30] Sul rapporto fra regno e contemplazione, cf. M. OLPHE-GALLIARD, art. «Cassien», in *DS* 2, col. 227.

[31] Alla prova di questo moralismo stoico dal quale il pelagianesimo prenderà il suo avvio, L. BOUYER (*La spiritualità dei Padri [III-VI secolo]. Monachesimo antico e Padri*, nuova ed., Bologna 1986, 86), rimanda al seguente testo del *De Instituto christiano* (ed. Jaeger, p. 46; cf. GREGORIO DI NISSA, *Fine, professione e perfezione del cristiano:* trad. it. a cura di S. Lilla, Roma 1990², 27): «La perfetta volontà di Dio è che la forma della pietà sia assunta dall'anima, quest'anima che la grazia dello Spirito fa fiorire fino alla suprema bellezza concorrendo agli sforzi di chi vi si conforma... Il corpo cresce senza di noi... ma la misura e la bellezza dell'anima, nel rinnovamento della sua concezione accordatale dalla grazia dello Spirito per lo zelo di colui che la riceve, dipendono dalla nostra disposizione: nella stessa misura in cui sviluppi le tue lotte per la pietà, si sviluppa anche la grandezza dell'anima per

Memore delle persecuzioni di Decio e Nerone, durante le quali i cristiani, infiammati dallo Spirito, rendevano la loro confessione a Cristo, Ilario di Poitiers mantiene meglio l'equilibrio della dottrina cattolica circa il regno. Commentando Mt 6,30, ribadisce la gratuità totale del dono divino:

> [Dio] esige che riponiamo tutta la nostra speranza nella fede delle sue promesse e nella potenza della sua virtù, affinché, rimossa la preoccupazione dei beni di cui abbiamo bisogno, noi aspettiamo piuttosto tutto da colui, dal quale riceviamo l'origine della nostra stessa vita, e cerchiamo il regno di Dio con il servizio della nostra vita (cf. Mt 6,33). E la ricompensa di coloro che vivono una vita retta e perfetta consiste nel passaggio dalla materia di questo corpo corruttibile alla sostanza nuova dei cieli e nella trasformazione della corruzione terrena nell'incorruttibilità celeste[32].

Qui non c'è ancora quell'etica delle opere che diventerà un pericolo latente quando al martirio delle prime generazioni cristiane si sostituirà stabilmente il monachesimo[33]. Qui regge soltanto l'etica del puro amore con il quale il cristiano si adopera per il regno di Dio. Più di un millennio e mezzo dopo, una carmelitana ritroverà la stessa intuizione. «Gesù [...] vuole regalarci gratuitamente il suo Cielo», scrive Teresa di Lisieux, alludendo probabilmente a Rm 3,24. «Più uno è debole, senza desideri né virtù, più è idoneo alle operazioni di

---

mezzo di queste lotte e di questi sforzi». Nello stesso tempo il p. Bouyer giustifica Gregorio dalle critiche, concludendo: «Tuttavia, per Gregorio, non bisogna mai dimenticare che lo sforzo umano dell'asceta è sempre visto come uno sforzo nella e sulla base della fede, e dunque per mezzo della forza di quello Spirito la cui manifestazione sarà il suo fine» (*Op. cit.*, 87). A conferma di questa osservazione, si può addurre il commento di Ct 1,12, tratto dalle *Omelie sul Cantico dei Cantici*: «Con tutte le buone azioni attuate in noi per mezzo della virtù, [l'odore profumato] imita colui che è la vera virtù, della quale il profeta Abacuc dice che essa comprende tutti i cieli (Ab 3,3)» (*Omelia* III: ed. Jaeger, p. 90; trad. it. a cura di C. Moreschini, Roma 1988, 95). — Non pretendiamo qui di dare una valutazione generale delle tendenze semipelagiane presenti negli ambienti monastici di allora, ma vogliamo attirare l'attenzione su una possibile deviazione, ancora oggi ricorrente, del senso del regno.

[32] ILARIO DI POITIERS, *Commentario a Matteo* 5, 12: *SChr* 254, 164; trad. it. a cura di L. Longobardo, Roma 1988, 85.

[33] Conformemente all'idea del monachesimo quale «cotidianum martyrium» (GIROLAMO, *Lettera* 3, 5: *PL* 108, 31), CASSIANO vede nei monaci dei «martiri viventi» (*Conferenze spirituali* XVIII 7: *SChr* 64, 21).

questo Amore consumante e trasformante...»[34]. Il solo appoggio sul quale contare è quello dell'amore divino, tanto misericordioso da ricompensare perfino la virtù — del resto non senza togliere perfino l'idea del progresso spirituale o dell'efficacia del sacrificio[35]. Non si tratta affatto di una dottrina nuova. È quanto ha sempre insegnato la Chiesa orante, come risulta dal Prefazio dei santi I, nel *Messale Romano*: «...eorum [Sanctorum] coronando merita tua dona coronas»[36].

Il regno di Dio e la sua venuta dipendono unicamente dall'azione di Dio e dalla sua misericordia. È un regalo che il Padre prepara per il «piccolo gregge» eletto (Lc 12,32; 22,29). Non è questione di buone opere umane, non è neanche qualcosa che uno costruisce e si procura con l'impegno sociale o la lotta politica. Contro la tentazione di chi concepisce erroneamente la venuta del Giorno del Signore, del regno messianico, come un trionfo politico, il profeta Isaia ammonisce di non accelerare la sua realizzazione (Is 5,19; cf. Am 5,18). «Colui che crede, non vorrà affrettare niente», Buber chiosa Is 28,16. L'uomo deve conformarsi al tempo di Dio «nell'abbandono confidente» (Is 30,15). La fede vigilante è quella che lascia avvenire i disegni di Dio nella pazienza di un cuore rinfrancato. Il Vangelo fa il paragone con l'agricoltore che lascia che il seme cresca da sé, «come, egli stesso non lo sa» (Mc 4,27). La *lettera di Giacomo* riprende il paragone per illustrare le caratteristiche dell'atteggiamento da assumere nel tempo della prova che precede la parusia — non solo la pazienza, ma

---

[34] Teresa di Lisieux, LT 197 (Lettera del 17.09.1896): *Correspondance générale*, t. II, Paris 1992², 895-896.

[35] Osserva H.U. von Balthasar riguardo alla piccola via: «[...] nel Nuovo Testamento la ricompensa di Dio è una cosa che riguarda la sua grazia, un momento della sua smisurata misericordia. Dio è così misericordioso che ricompensa *perfino* la virtù. Teresa raggiunge così la classica formulazione della dottrina cattolica sul merito elaborata da Tommaso d'Aquino, il quale da una parte fa risalire a una libera disposizione dell'amore divino ogni corrispondenza fra merito e ricompensa, e dall'altra spiega l'amore soprannaturale nell'uomo come il principio di ogni "merito" (*S. Th.* I-II 114, 4)» (*Schwestern im Geist*, Einsiedeln 1973, 253 [trad. it. *Sorelle nello Spirito*, Milano 1991³, 204]). Il sacrificio supremo è quello dell'amore che ignora se stesso: «Ah c'est là un grand amour d'aimer Jésus sans sentir la douceur de cet amour... c'est là un martyre... Eh bien *mourrons Martyres*. Oh! ma Céline... le doux écho de mon âme comprends-tu?... le martyre ignoré, connu de Dieu seul, que l'oeil de la créature ne peut découvrir, martyre sans honneur, sans triomphe...» (LT 94 [Lettera del 14.07.1889]: *Correspondance générale*, t. I, Paris 1992², 494).

[36] Cf. Agostino, *Esposizione sui salmi* 102, 7: *Opere* XXVII/1, 592ss.

anche la perseveranza e la fermezza d'animo: l'agricoltore non cerca di produrre per forza la pioggia: «aspetta pazientemente il prezioso frutto della terra finché abbia ricevuto le piogge d'autunno e le piogge di primavera» (Gc 5,7). Così anche Paolo ammonisce i cristiani bramosi che non possono aspettare con quiete la venuta del Signore: «l'operosità della fede» e «la fatica dell'amore» che è capace di soffrire nel servizio della Chiesa, non si avverano senza la costanza, «la pazienza della speranza» (1 Ts 1,3), che però «non è diretta a nulla di terreno ed ecclesiale, ma unicamente a "Cristo"»[37].

IL REGNO DI DIO INTESO IN CHIAVE POLITICA

Nel corso della storia, non sono mancati tentativi di elaborare una teologia politica che ponga le basi all'edificazione di un regno di Dio stabilito *hic et nunc*. Ripetutamente si è creduto di poter trovare in sant'Agostino una dottrina cristiana dello Stato, vale a dire una dottrina che fonderebbe la costituzione dello Stato sulla giustizia evangelica, il dono divino che Gesù ha lasciato in eredità alla sua Chiesa (cf. Mt 5,10. 20; 6,1)[38]. Non c'è da meravigliarsi che la tentazione sia stata sentita particolarmente dai religiosi, in cui facilmente si è prodotto lo spostamento dal piano soprannaturale dell'escatologia al desiderio inquieto di costruire una *sancta res publica christiana*, incarnando l'ideale cristiano nella storia. Fra i tanti nomi che andrebbero evocati, basta menzionare l'arcivescovo di Bourges, Gillo da Roma, detto anche *Aegidius Romanus*, dell'Ordine dei frati eremiti di sant'Agostino,

---

[37] H.U. VON BALTHASAR, *Thessalonicher- und Pastoralbriefe des heiligen Paulus*, Freiburg, 1992², 16 (trad. it. *Le Lettere ai Tessalonicesi di san Paolo*, Milano 1992, 18). CIPRIANO dà come un commento di questo insegnamento quando insegna: «Il fatto stesso di essere cristiani è questione di fede e di speranza; ma perché la speranza e la fede possano arrivare a portare frutto, è necessaria la pazienza. [...] L'attesa e la pazienza sono necessarie perché portiamo a compimento quello che abbiamo cominciato a essere e raggiungiamo quello che speriamo e crediamo perché Dio ce lo rivela. [...] [Anche la carità] può perseverare tenacemente per il fatto che sa sopportare tutto» (*Vantaggi della pazienza* 13 e 15: *SChr* 291, 214-218). Sul legame fra la pazienza e le tre virtù teologali, si veda anche GIOVANNI TAULERO, *Sermoni* 23 e 64: *Predigten*, Trier 1987², vol. 1, 156. e 498.

[38] Sul vero significato di queste parole nel discorso della montagna, si veda A. FEUILLET, «Le Sermon sur la Montagne. Les deux aspects de la justice», *RCI Communio* 3 (1978) 2, 5-12.

uno dei più illustri rappresentanti di questa corrente, autore di un *De ecclesiastica potestate*. P. de Lubac ha analizzato e criticato con acribia quest'opera, redatta nel 1301 per giustificare Bonifacio VIII[39]. Mostra che l'idea di giustizia e di pace con la quale il religioso ritiene di poter fondare la rivendicazione di un «regno [...] istituito dal sacerdozio»[40], procede da una grave confusione fra gli ordini naturale e soprannaturale, i quali, pur non essendo separati, debbono rimanere distinti. Da un altro punto di vista, il filosofo Claude Bruaire spiega, in riferimento al rapporto fra giustizia politica e misericordia divina: «Occorre tenere distinti e uniti degli *ordini* di giustizia, nel significato che Pascal dava a questo termine, ossia dei livelli di senso nell'esistenza, livelli nel contempo gerarchizzati e irriducibili»[41].

Non si debbono quindi né separare né confondere speranza escatologica e impegno per la liberazione temporale. Da un lato, la prima non si sostituisce alla seconda; anzi, ne lascia intatta la necessità nel suo ordine e ne ravviva l'esigenza. Avverte la *Gaudium et Spes:*

> L'attesa di una terra nuova non deve indebolire, bensì piuttosto stimolare la sollecitudine nel lavoro relativo alla terra presente, dove cresce quel corpo dell'umanità nuova che già riesce a offrire[42].

D'altra parte, nella sua sovrabbondanza di misericordia e di amore, la giustizia divina, che si fa presente in questo mondo con la venuta del regno, trascende infinitamente la razionalità distributiva che contrassegna la giustizia umana, naturale. È il punto che ha chiarito ulteriormente l'istruzione sulla libertà cristiana della Congregazione per la Dottrina della Fede:

---

[39] H. DE LUBAC, «Augustinisme politique?», in *Théologies d'occasion*, Paris 1984, 255-308, in particolare 289ss.

[40] AEGIDIUS ROMANUS, *De ecclesiastica potestate*, ed. R. Scholz, Weimar 1929, libro 1, cap. 5.

[41] C. BRUAIRE, «La justice et le droit», *RCI Communio* 3 (1978) 2, 3.

[42] GS 39: *EV* 1, 1440. Più avanti, la costituzione pastorale spiega che tutti i buoni frutti dell'attività umana, svolta sotto la dipendenza dello Spirito Santo, noi li ritroveremo «purificati da ogni macchia, illuminati e trasfigurati, allorquando il Cristo rimetterà al Padre il regno eterno e universale: "che è regno di verità e di vita, regno di santità e di grazia, regno di giustizia, di amore e di pace" (*Missale romanum*, Praefatio Festi Christi Regis)» (*Ibid.*: *EV* 1, 1440).

> La vigile ed operosa attesa della venuta del regno è pure quella di una giustizia finalmente perfetta per i vivi e per i morti, per gli uomini di tutti i tempi e di tutti i luoghi, che Gesù Cristo, costituito giudice supremo, instaurerà. Una tale promessa, che supera tutte le possibilità umane, riguarda direttamente la nostra vita in questo mondo. Infatti, una vera giustizia deve estendersi a tutti, portare la risposta all'immenso cumulo di sofferenze che gravano su tutte le generazioni. In realtà, senza la risurrezione dei morti e il giudizio del Signore non c'è giustizia nel senso pieno di questo termine. La promessa della risurrezione viene gratuitamente incontro al desiderio di vera giustizia, che abita nel cuore umano[43].

Il vangelo della salvezza non va ridotto a un vangelo terrestre; il rifiuto di ogni secolarizzazione nonché di ogni assorbimento della realtà umana in quella ecclesiale, preserva intatta la speranza nel regno. La giustizia alla quale aspiriamo è la giustizia integrale, la quale richiede da noi la promozione della giustizia sociale e politica tramite l'ordine dello spirito umano, ma ci mantiene nell'attesa orante del dono escatologico della misericordia di Dio, di ordine prettamente soprannaturale.

IL REGNO DI DIO SULLA SOGLIA DEL TEMPO TERRENO

Conviene ora interrogarsi sulla natura del regno di Dio, il quale — avverte il Vangelo — è essenzialmente un «mistero» (Mc 4,11). Le parole con le quali Gesù Cristo inaugura la sua predicazione in Galilea concernono esplicitamente questo regno, e non la sua persona. «Il tempo è compiuto e il regno di Dio è vicino; convertitevi e credete al vangelo» (Mc 1,15p). Il tempo fissato per l'adempimento delle promesse è venuto, egli annuncia. Con la presenza e l'attività di Gesù, il regno atteso è imminente, è sulla soglia del tempo terreno, anzi ha già avuto inizio segretamente e sta per manifestarsi a tutti.

---

[43] CONGREGAZIONE PER LA DOTTRINA DELLA FEDE, *Libertatis Conscientia* (22.03.1986), 60: *EV* 10, 275. Cf. ID., *Libertatis Nuntius* (06.08.1984): *EV* 9, 866-987.

Certo, nell'interpretare il messaggio dicendo che Gesù Cristo è la αὐτοβασιλεία, il regno in persona[44], Origene ne coglie un aspetto essenziale. Infatti, Gesù non rimanda soltanto, come gli antichi profeti, alla venuta futura del regno; con il suo comparire, è il regno che si avvicina in modo definitivo. Mettendo in contrasto l'economia provvisoria dell'antica Legge con la fede in Cristo, diventata stabile, san Giovanni della Croce pone bene in risalto il compimento della rivelazione quale lo espone l'inizio della *lettera agli Ebrei* (1,1-2).

> Dandoci il Figlio suo, che è la sua parola, l'unica che Egli pronunzi, in essa [Dio] ci ha detto tutto in una sola volta e non ha più niente da manifestare. [...] È rimasto quasi come muto non avendo altro da dire poiché, dandoci il Tutto, cioè suo Figlio, ha detto ormai in Lui tutto ciò che in parte aveva manifestato in antico ai profeti. [...] Prima parlav[a] ma unicamente per promettere Cristo e gli uomini [lo] consultavano solo per chiedere e aspettare Lui nel quale dovevano trovare ogni bene, come ora tutta la dottrina degli evangelisti e degli apostoli fa capire[45].

Il regno di Dio che Gesù è venuto ad annunciare, è intimamente legato alla sua stessa persona ed esistenza. Egli si capisce come il regno fattosi avvenimento per l'uomo. Chi lo incontra, è messo davanti alla scelta di cui Mosè era l'annunciatore per il popolo: «Vedi, io pongo oggi davanti a te la vita e il bene, la morte e il male [...]. Scegli dunque...» (Dt 30,15.19). Ma la scelta si svolge ora nel contatto stesso con lui.

In lui il tempo è compiuto[46], dopo di lui, non possono venire altri profeti comme quelli dell'Antica Alleanza, ma solo Dio stesso.

> Tutte le dimensioni del tempo si concentrano in Lui: l'intero passato si presenta di nuovo in Lui come nella promessa compiuta, e tutto ciò che può avvenire da parte di Dio, ci è rivolto in Lui quale presenza; dopo questo

---

[44] ORIGENE, *Commento al vangelo di Matteo* XIV 7 (ad Mt 18,23): *GCS* 40, 289.
[45] GIOVANNI DELLA CROCE, *Salita del Monte Carmelo* II 22, 3-5: *Obras*, Burgos 1987, 296-298; *Opere*, trad. it. a cura di F. di S. Maria, Roma 1991⁶, 173-175.
[46] Cf. Gal 4,4; Ef 1,10.

[Gesù] che viene, non viene più alcuno; a partire da Lui, non ci si può appellare ad alcuno[47].

La promessa divina del regno venturo è totalmente adempiuta nell'esistenza umana, temporale, di Gesù, perché egli non è soltanto un profeta, investito della parola e della forza di Dio, che annunzia la salvezza; come dice H.U. von Balthasar, «l'esserci [*Da-Sein*] di questo uomo è la venuta [*Kommen*], il sorgere [*Werden*] del regno»[48]. Esiste una fondamentale identità fra l'io di Gesù che inizia la sua attività in Galilea e l'inaugurazione del regno. Eppure, questo non significa che egli produca semplicemente da se stesso questo regno. Occorre evitare il cortocircuito al quale può portare la formula origeniana e lasciare piuttosto aperta l'affermazione, come fa il teologo di Basilea che ha coniato una formula un po' diversa: «mentre egli va, il regno viene»[49]. Infatti, Gesù Cristo proclama la venuta del regno in quanto uomo, e dunque, secondo l'espressione di M. Heidegger, un «essere-per-la-morte», un essere la cui vita è interiormente indirizzata alla morte. Ma la sua morte non è però come la nostra: con essa, egli raggiunge la situazione escatologica del mondo, con essa si compie «il giorno del Signore» (1 Cor 1,8), manifestazione gloriosa della fine dei tempi, che è insieme il giorno del giudizio e quello della redenzione per il mondo. Nell'andare alla morte, prendendo su di sé, come «Agnello immolato» (1 Cor 5,7; Ap 5,6.12), il peccato del mondo (Gv 1,29), Gesù porta agli uomini la salvezza definitiva, presente nel giudizio della Croce (Mt 24,30; Ap 1,7).

Questo regno è solamente opera di Dio: le attese, le resistenze, i calcoli, i piani, le costruzioni dell'uomo non possono né accelerarne né ritardarne la venuta. È «lasciato per testamento» (Lc 22,29), «dato» a chi si converte e crede, e lo può quindi «far fruttificare» (Mt 21,43). Nei Vangeli Gesù parla volentieri in parabole del regno di Dio. Lo annuncia in termini velati, non accessibili a tutti: «Chi ha orecchi intenda» (Mt 13,43), egli dice. Ma non tutti sembrano possedere le

---

[47] H.U. VON BALTHASAR, «Improvisation über Geist und Zukunft», in *Spiritus Creator*, Einsiedeln 1967, 146 (trad. it. Brescia 1983², 138).
[48] H.U. VON BALTHASAR, *Zuerst Gottes Reich*, Einsiedeln 1996, 10.
[49] *Ibid.*

orecchie per udire e ascoltare il messaggio recondito delle parabole. Queste rimangono un mistero per la maggioranza. Infatti, il regno che si fa presente con la venuta di Gesù si manifesta in maniera nascosta. Massimo il Confessore, commentando la parola di Es 15,18 che traduce «Il Signore regna sul secolo e nel secolo ed oltre», spiega che la conoscenza del regno, dataci dalla Scrittura, concerne cose superiori al secolo. «Il puro regno di Dio è qualcosa oltre i secoli: infatti non è permesso dire che il regno di Dio abbia avuto inizio o sia raggiunto dai secoli o dai tempi»[50].

Perciò, spesso Gesù dischiude il senso delle parabole circa il regno solo ai suoi discepoli, cioè a quelli che ha chiamato con una vocazione speciale. Non si tratta soltanto di una spiegazione estrinseca, verbale o puramente concettuale: è per opera dello Spirito Santo che gli apostoli comprendono, è lo Spirito che dona orecchi per capire non meramente la verità che Gesù ha, ma bensì quella che egli è (Gv 14,6). D'altra parte, uno si apre a questo regno solo con l'impegno di una vita totalmente donata. La verità, ad un tempo divina ed umana, dell'esistenza e della missione redentrice di Gesù non si afferra come un teorema matematico. Per conoscere la verità, occorre fare la verità (Gv 7,17), vivere nella verità. Non c'è accesso al regno che si avvicina con la venuta di Cristo, se non percorrendo la sua strada, seguendolo personalmente. In altre parole, perché «i misteri del regno» (Mt 13,11) portino frutto nei cuori, è necessario che gli ascoltatori possiedano almeno un inizio di comprensione delle cose di Dio (cf. v. 12). Laddove, per grazia di Dio, esso esiste, lo Spirito Santo «viene in aiuto alla nostra debolezza» (Rm 8,26) e, per mezzo dei credenti, il regno di Dio si fa strada in questo mondo.

Ora, il tempo della sequela possiede in se stesso il carattere di brevità caratteristico del tempo del maestro: «Ecco, io oggi scaccio i demoni e compio guarigioni; e il terzo giorno avrò finito. Però è necessario che oggi, domani e il giorno seguente io vada per la mia strada, perché non è possibile che un profeta muoia fuori di Gerusalemme» (Lc 13, 32-33)[51]. Il

---

[50] MASSIMO IL CONFESSORE, *Il Dio-Uomo*, op. cit., 86: trad. it. 104.
[51] L'idea della brevità del tempo è soprattutto ribadita nel IV vangelo: Gv 7,33; 12,35; 13,33; 14,19; 16,16-19.

tempo del regno che viene con la morte di Gesù è così impellente da non consentire ai cristiani di installarsi in esso con comodo; lo ribadisce con forza san Paolo in 1 Cor 7,29-31, indicando le conseguenze da tirare dal «pochissimo tempo» che ci rimane (Eb 10,37; cf. Is 26,20 gr.). A tutte le vicende della nostra vita è applicato un coefficiente negativo: piangere come se non si piangesse, aver moglie come se non la si avesse, comprare come se non si possedesse... Il commento di H.U. von Balthasar a questo brano evidenzia che l'attesa operante del regno di Dio non è tanto specifica della vita consacrata, come sembrava prima. Infatti, è a quelli che chiameremmo oggi i «laici» che l'Apostolo si rivolge quando invita i cristiani, impegnati nelle vicende del mondo, a non impantanarsi nelle preoccupazioni di questa terra:

> A causa del tempo che stringe e della scena del mondo che passa, tutti i beni che abbiamo e usiamo per forza nel mondo, devono essere posseduti e utilizzati in una indifferenza tale che vi si possa rinunciare ogni momento. Il tempo ci è prestato solo con la possibilità di essere ritirato ogni momento[52].

L'atteggiamento richiesto da tutti quanti sono stati chiamati alla conversione ed all'accoglienza del Vangelo mediante la fede[53], è quello espresso nella preghiera del Padre nostro: «Fa' che venga il tuo regno» (Mt 6,10; Lc 11,2). Con tutta la sua esistenza — attraverso i suoi comportamenti nonché le sue azioni —, il cristiano desidera che il regno iniziato con la vita, la morte e la risurrezione di Gesù Cristo venga presto rivelato e definitivamente riconosciuto sulla terra intera, perché l'approssimarsi di questo regno è divenuto, dopo la Pasqua, salvezza offerta a tutti gli uomini[54]. La salvezza non è una realtà di ordine «puramente soprannaturale», sospesa al di sopra della vita terrena, riferita esclusivamente a Dio e alle cose religiose, ma concerne il mondo e l'uomo tutto intero, è

---

[52] H.U. VON BALTHASAR, *Licht des Wortes*, Freiburg i. Br. 1992², 145 (trad. it. *Luce della Parola*, Casale Monferrato 1990, 161).

[53] Cf. 1 Ts 1,5-6.9; 2,13; Col 1,5-6.

[54] Si veda su questo tema: J. SERVAIS, «Comunione, universalità e apocatastasi: sperare per tutti?», *RITC Communio* 148 (1996) 24-39.

qualcosa di avvolgente: l'Incarnazione e la Redenzione sono l'elevazione e il compimento della realtà creaturale[55].

Certo, il vangelo mette prettamente in rilievo la chiamata dei discepoli che lasciano la famiglia, i parenti, la professione, per seguire Gesù ovunque vada[56]. Non vi è dubbio che la vocazione qualificata alla vita consacrata venga condizionata da un lasciare tutto (Lc 14,28.33), un tutto indivisibile, che include i viventi e i morti (Mt 8,21-22). Ma non è forse questa una esigenza che in fondo vale per tutta «la stirpe eletta» (1 Pt 2,9; cf. 1,1; 2 Pt 1,10), quindi anche quelli che rimangono all'interno della loro attività e professione nel mondo?

Il fedele è quello che appartiene a Dio, non al mondo. L'indifferenza, intimamente legata con il servizio del regno, trova il suo criterio nella preghiera di Gesù per i suoi: «Non chiedo che tu li tolga dal mondo, ma che li custodisca dal maligno. Essi non sono del mondo, come io non sono del mondo» (Gv 17,15-16; cf. vv. 11.14). Non si tratta di voler «uscire dal mondo» (1 Cor 5,10). È in mezzo al mondo che si svolge l'apostolato, come risulta dall'esperienza dei primi cristiani (cf. 2 Cor 2,15; At 5,41). La separazione dal mondo non significa necessariamente un lasciare il proprio ambiente: dopo essersi alzato per seguire, Matteo torna a sedersi a tavola — con Gesù e i suoi — nella propria casa (Mt 9,10). Il discepolo non è chiamato in vista di una perfezione spirituale privata, bensì per l'opera di redenzione del mondo (Gv 15,8.16) in Cristo, per Cristo e con Cristo. Ritorna nel mondo per operarvi efficacemente, come la lampada innalzata che risplende per tutti quanti sono nella casa (Mt 5,15p). Dal di dentro degli ordinamenti terrestri del mondo decaduto, deve, pur obbedendo alle loro leggi, mantenersi pronto a lasciare ogni momento questo mondo, sapendo che la sua patria è il regno di Dio. Invece di lasciarsi catturare da esso, il cristiano appartiene al Signore: deve comportarsi da «cittadino degno del vangelo» (Fil 1,27; cf. 3,20), «cercare ciò che sta in alto», consapevole che il suo fine è «lassù, non sulla terra» (Col 3,2-

---

[55] Cf F. WULF, «Theologische Phänomenologie des Ordenslebens», *MS* 4/2, 481-482, citando K. RAHNER, «Immanente und transzendente Vollendung der Welt», in *Schriften* VIII, 593-609.

[56] Si rileggano a questo proposito fra altri i segueni brani: Lc 5,11; Mt 4,20; 4,22; Mc 1,20; Mt 9,9; Lc 5,28.

3). Se, come dice Paolo, «chi è sposato» «si trova diviso» (1 Cor 7,34), non è a causa delle realtà terrestri in cui vive: non ha forse Cristo condotto una esistenza dentro il mondo, senza per questo allontanarsi minimamente dal Padre e dalla sua volontà? Se è diviso, è perché è tentato di preoccuparsi delle cose del mondo più delle cose del Signore, dimentico della sua missione di «collaboratore in Gesù Cristo» (Rom 16,3). Ma a considerare l'esempio lasciato da questi, non dovrebbe essere diviso: come «eletto di Dio, santo e amato» (Col 3,12), aspira continuamente a passare dalla divisione all'unità del suo stato cristiano nel mondo.

LA MISSIONE SPECIFICA DELLO STATO DEI CONSIGLI EVANGELICI

Con le nostre riflessioni ribadiamo quanto la *Lumen Gentium* afferma dell'indole escatologica della Chiesa intera, ma non imbocchiamo forse così una strada difficile, dato che, come ricordato, la stessa costituzione nonché molti altri documenti magisteriali vedono proprio in tale dimensione la specificità degli istituti religiosi? Con questo interrogativo si giunge alla seconda domanda, posta, all'inizio, in riferimento all'interpretazione «utopistica» della vocazione consacrata. A nostro parere, la visione escatologica, promossa nei nostri tempi da taluni teologi non fornisce una spiegazione sufficiente della vita secondo i consigli. Presentando brevemente le idee di uno dei suoi prominenti pensatori, vorremmo mostrare, per finire, che essa non rende tutto l'equilibrio della dottrina del Vaticano II. E questo ci consentirà di tirare alcune conclusioni circa la missione propria di questa forma di vita rispetto alle altre nella Chiesa.

K. Rahner, in un articolo del 1964[57], scorge il comune denominatore dei consigli evangelici innanzitutto nel loro carattere di rinuncia. Nell'abbandonare, ciascuno nel suo modo, dei valori terrestri, tutti e tre i consigli rappresentano delle possibilità di garantirsi la fede trascendentale. Egli ritie-

---

[57] K. RAHNER, «Über die evangelische Räte», *Schriften zur Theologie* VII, Einsiedeln 1966, 404-434 (trad. it. «Sui consigli evangelici», in: AA.VV., *I religiosi oggi e domani*, Roma 1968², 73-122).

ne di dare in questo modo ragione al X canone del decreto tridentino *Matrimonii perpetuum,* nel quale, in riferimento a Mt 19,11s e 1 Cor 7,25s.38.40, la verginità o il celibato viene presentato come «cosa migliore e più felice» (Denz 1810). Contrariamente a una opinione diffusa[58], il teologo tedesco vede giustamente nella vita consacrata una speciale vocazione da parte di Dio. Ma, come è stato rilevato[59], la sua spiegazione di questa quale segno escatologico è alquanto unilaterale.

Secondo Rahner, la pratica dei tre consigli è soggettivamente, per chi vi è chiamato, il mezzo — «relativamente» — migliore, in quanto essi comportano un elemento di rinuncia che contrasta con l'aspirazione normale alla ricchezza mondana, all'amore umano e all'autonomia personale. Se i consigli sono inoltre, conformemente all'affermazione magisteriale, il mezzo «oggettivamente» migliore, questo non significa che tale scelta implichi, «per se stessa» e «necessariamente», un amore più grande, una più grande realizzazione, neanche che chi li abbraccia sia più perfetto di chi resta nel mondo. La rinuncia imposta da questa pratica è una manifestazione della fede nella grazia di Dio in quanto superiore al mondo della peccaminosità infralapsale. I consigli non si possono dire un mezzo migliore «in sé», nella misura in cui il termine «mezzo» fa anche riferimento al soggetto che lo usa. Costituiscono in modo assoluto una scelta migliore in quanto la negazione di sé e l'esercitarsi nel vivere la passione di Cristo sono una oggettivazione dell'indole trascendentale della fede cristiana. In tale forma di vita, la fede amante e sperante nella grazia di Dio superiore al mondo trova una rappresentazione visibile. In essa, si scorge il segno escatologico della Chiesa, tutta intera protesa verso il suo fine soprannaturale.

I consigli possono e debbono essere concepiti come una testimonianza escatologica, nella misura in cui oggettivano e manifestano quella fede che, nella speranza, tende

---

[58] Rinviamo ad esempio a J.M. TILLARD, *Devant Dieu et pour le monde,* Paris 1974, 61-67, dove l'autore collega la vocazione a una propensione «iscritta nei pigmenti della persona». Altri autori, come F. WULF (*art. cit.,* 466-467) o J. DANIÉLOU («Il carattere specifico della vita religiosa», VitaCon 10 [1974] 525), mettono meglio in risalto il carattere soprannaturale della vocazione.

[59] Cf. L. GUTIÉRREZ VEGA, *Teología sistemática de la vida religiosa,* Madrid 1976, 314-328.

verso le realtà future, che sono l'adempimento della grazia accolta in quella fede. Nella misura in cui questa oggettivazione epifanica della grazia vittoriosa e della fede è l'oggettivazione di quella stessa grazia, che dà il suo consenso al mondo (sia pure, proprio, attraverso la Croce) e lo trasfigura, questo carattere di segno dei consigli concerne la Chiesa nella quale si realizza la consacrazione del mondo, la realtà mondana — è cristiana[60].

Nella vita dei consigli, in altre parole, il regno di Dio manifesta la sua venuta come la grazia accordata al mondo intero, con irrevocabilità escatologica, in Gesù Cristo e nella sua morte.

Il rimprovero serio che si deve fare a questa concezione puramente escatologica è che essa impedisce alla radice ogni collegamento fra la vita consacrata e la vita laicale. Difatti, se la pratica dei consigli è tipica della fede trascendentale, propria dei religiosi in quanto essa ha un carattere escatologico essenzialmente sopramondano, questo implica che l'esistenza cristiana del laico non può come tale, nella sua «materialità» intramondana, lasciare apparire la trascendenza della grazia[61]. Ora, su questo punto, il magistero ha fatto delle chiare dichiarazioni in senso opposto. Va citato fra altri il recente documento post-sinodale, il quale ribadisce, accanto a quella escatologica, la dimensione incarnatoria della vita consacrata. Essa rifulge con peculiare evidenza negli Istituti secolari:

> [...] *Vivere la consacrazione a Dio nel mondo* attraverso la professione dei consigli evangelici nel contesto delle strutture temporali, per essere così lievito di sapienza e testimoni di grazia all'interno della vita culturale, economica e politica. Attraverso la sintesi, che è loro specifica, di secolarità e consacrazione, essi intendono *immettere nella società le energie nuove del Regno di Cristo*, cercando di trasfigurare il mondo dal di dentro con la forza delle Beatitudini[62].

---

[60] K. RAHNER, *art. cit.*, 433 (trad. it. 121).

[61] *Ibid.*, 430 (trad. it. 116). Cf. ID., «Zur Theologie der Entsagung», *Schriften zur Theologie* III, Einsiedeln 1956, 62.68-69.

[62] VC 10. Cf. la lettera apostolica di GIOVANNI PAOLO II alle persone consacrate, *Litterae encyclicae* (22.05.1988), cap. IV: *EV* 11, 691.

La missione del laico, avevamo ribadito precedentemente, ha essa stessa un'indole escatologica. Dobbiamo affermare adesso, a conclusione della nostra indagine, che la vita consacrata non è, di per sé, incompatibile con l'impegno laicale nel mondo[63]. Anzi, essa consiste nel penetrare il mondo come il «sale della terra» (Mt 13,33p). «Il regno dei cieli», dice il Vangelo usando un'altra immagine, «si può paragonare al lievito, che una donna ha preso e impastato con tre misure di farina perché tutta si fermenti» (Mt 13,33p; cf. 1 Cor 5,6-7; Gal 5,9). La persona consacrata sta nel cuore della Chiesa, laddove il mondo decaduto è trasformato nel regno di Dio. È chiamata a realizzare in tutta radicalità, quanto il Decreto conciliare *Apostolicam Actuositatem* descrive come compito specifico dei laici:

> Nel pellegrinaggio di questa vita, nascosti con Cristo in Dio e liberi dalla schiavitù delle ricchezze, mentre tendono ai beni che durano in eterno, con animo generoso si dedicano totalmente ad estendere il regno di Dio e ad informare e perfezionare con spirito cristiano l'ordine delle realtà temporali[64].

Il *Codice di Diritto canonico* riassume bene l'essenziale di questa vocazione e missione: i consacrati sono dei cristiani che, «chiamati con speciale vocazione», «seguono Gesù più da vicino per l'azione dello Spirito Santo» nella sua «missione di salvezza»[65]. Alcuni di essi, volendo operare «dal di dentro del mondo», «si sforzano di permeare ogni realtà di spirito evangelico per consolidare e far crescere il Corpo di Cristo»[66]: sono i membri degli istituti secolari, con il loro carisma speciale di unità di vita escatologica e incarnatoria. Infatti, afferma Balthasar, «il regno di Dio che sta venendo (come Chiesa)

---

[63] Fra tante dichiarazioni, si ricordi questa, tratta dalla *Lumen Gentium:* «I religiosi pongano ogni cura, affinché per loro mezzo la Chiesa ogni giorno meglio presenti Cristo ai fedeli e agli infedeli, o mentre egli contempla sul monte, o annunzia il regno di Dio alle turbe, o risana i malati e i feriti e converte a miglior vita i peccatori, o benedice i fanciulli e fa del bene a tutti, sempre obbediente alla volontà del Padre che lo ha mandato» (LG 46: *EV* 1, 411).

[64] AA 4: *EV* 1, 926.
[65] CIC, cann. 573-574.
[66] CIC, can. 713. Cf. *Primo Feliciter, AAS* (1948), n. 2: «veluti ex saeculo».

non può venire se non *nel mondo*»[67]. Se si può dire che la vita consacrata va intesa come attesa operante di questo regno, è necessario aggiungere che, proprio nella misura in cui la pratica dei consigli evangelici consente al cristiano di seguire incondizionatamente il Signore, essa apre in modo esimio alla realizzazione della centupla fecondità apostolica da Lui promessa «già al presente… insieme a persecuzioni» (Mc 10,30).

In sintesi, è la Chiesa nel suo insieme ad essere il lievito operante nel mondo, il regno di Dio in divenire. D'altro lato, la parte veramente santa della Chiesa, il suo nucleo soprannaturale, per così dire, è formato da uomini spirituali che hanno messo la loro intera esistenza a disposizione del regno di Dio, in un atteggiamento d'amore fondamentalmente collegato ai consigli evangelici. Secondo il teologo svizzero, che offre, a nostro parere, la dottrina più equilibrata su questo argomento, lo stato dei consigli è quello che dà la forma agli altri stati di vita nella Chiesa. È un abbozzo dell'ideale ecclesiale per tutti, un tentativo di prolungamento dell'ideale della «vita apostolica», quale fu vissuta alle origini della Chiesa. E questo, non solo come un segno escatologico della Chiesa compiuta nell'al di là, ma bensì come un tentativo per incarnare, per quanto possibile, la santità della Chiesa nel qui ed oggi del mondo. Per mezzo dei consigli evangelici, che costituiscono l'elemento formale della realtà cristiana, il regno di Dio viene inserito nel mondo, il che non può non provocare la «divisione» di cui parla 1 Cor 7,34. La vita consacrata è infatti lo spirito del tutto; ciò che ha di speciale è, fin dal principio, posto a disposizione di questo tutto. In una formula concisa: la vita dei consigli è «il particolare dell'universale»[68]. Questa formula esclude che la natura dei consacrati venga interpretata in modo limitativo, mettendo fra parentesi tutto ciò che è esistenza laicale nel mondo. Il che presuppone però anche che «l'universale stesso è un particolare, di fronte a un ancora più universale»[69], quindi che la Chiesa tutta intera è lievito per il mondo, come il regno è *forma informans* dell'universo che Cristo è venuto a salvare.

---

[67] H.U. VON BALTHASAR, *Gottbereites Leben*, Freiburg 1993, 131; cf. 42.
[68] ID., *Sponsa Verbi*, Einsiedeln 1961, 447 (trad. it. 422).
[69] *Ibid.*

Kingdom of God and Salvation
(A Note on Rearranging the Great Tradition)

FRANZ JOSEF VAN BEECK

I

Vatican II is now more than thirty years behind us, and the number of its living participants has shrunk to only a handful, if for a moment we disregard the *periti* and the other former council officials who have since joined the ranks of the College of Bishops, some of whom (perhaps underestimating the fact that their participation included elements of bias and did not involve the "care of all the churches", concretized in the responsibility of actually voting on the decrees) are a little too willing to describe themselves as "participants". Most of us older Catholics have become accustomed to "the changes of Vatican II"; those of us who teach in universities know that the present generation of Catholic students is no longer aware of any such changes. The Council has become "history", in the bad sense of the word. Even those of us who were somewhat theologically aware when the Council was happening are now liable to forget or overlook the extent and the significance of the "rearrangement of the themes and emphases of the Catholic faith and identity experience" which Vatican II inaugurated[1]. In other words, Catholics are now liable to underestimate what still remains to be done and understood in the wake of the Council. A case of familiarity breeding contempt?

It is often said that the postconciliar generation, which by and large seems to feel at home in today's Catholic Church, has "accepted the Council"; yet it is important to

---

[1] Cf. F.J. VAN BEECK, *Catholic Identity After Vatican II: Three Types of Faith in the One Church* (Loyola University Press, Chicago: 1985), p. 4.

realize that this reflects the sensibility and the perception of a generation of Catholics that is aging fast. If Catholics under the age of, say, forty or fifty have "accepted" the Council, they have done so largely implicitly, *not by significant choice*. Their present concern, and the concern of their children if any, is liable to be not with the Council but with the Church today[2]. Conversely, those among the younger Catholics who feel unhappy with much in today's Church (often, it would appear, on largely political, socio-economic, and psychological grounds) and yearn for the alleged beauty of the preconciliar era do not truly *know* what they are yearning for; and in any case, the few survivors who might teach them fairly about things preconciliar either are either not interested or too young to do so. So the waves made by the Council — whether of enthusiasm or of consternation — are over. There are those, of course, both on the right and the left, who are calling for a Vatican III. They are unlikely to find a hearing any time soon.

Pope John Paul II, in many ways the voice of the many others who have a sounder sense of history and of the catholic tradition, keeps on insisting that we are still in the process of integrating the Council experience and incorporating its decrees into the life of the Catholic Church, and will be for some time to come. This is liable to be true. After all, Councils are *symbolic* events; they are not so much "held" (let alone "organized") as *celebrated* — something the Preparatory Commission for Vatican II had occasion to find out, with a vengeance[3]. That is to say, like any symbolic

---

[2] A recent, very informal survey conducted by two theology professors at a sizable Jesuit college in the United States has strongly suggested this. The survey, conducted between 1995 and 1997 by John P. McCarthy and Michael Schuck among 400 undergraduate students, revealed that 69% of the students denied that they preferred "to think of a 'higher power' rather than of 'God'", and that 83% affirmed that they "should know more about Christianity"; at the same time 77.5% denied that "churches best express religious values".

[3] Rumblings of conciliar thunders to come could be heard at the meetings of the Central Preparatory Commission in January, 1962, when the *schema* "On Inviolately Preserving the Deposit of Faith" (*De deposito fidei pure custodiendo*. in: *Acta et Documenta Concilio Oecumenico Vaticano II Apparando*. Series II [*Praeparatoria*]. [Rome: Typis Polyglottis Vaticanis, 1964-69]. Vol. III/I, pp. 15-23, 54-89) ran into heavy weather. After noting that "our faith has no foundation other than the Word of God", Cardinal Achille Liénart denounced the *schema*'s re-

event (and like any liturgy), Councils are possessed of a curious, concentrated intensity, amounting to a "contraction of history" that demands that it be worked out slowly and deliberately, in real, non-symbolic time. Like the nodal points on a vibrating string, Councils (and some Councils more than others)[4] set the conditions for movement on *both sides* — the future as well as the past. They usually have been a good long time in the making, and they owe a lot of their intensity to movements in the past, which they must come to terms with. And on the other hand, the movements they unleash must have their day before they can fully enter the Church's bloodstream[5]. Only if and to the extent this happens can any new Council be fruitful.

II

Years ago, in an essay that has become a classic, entitled "Tradition and the Individual Talent", T. S. Eliot touched on the issue of newness, tradition, and reception as it affected him, the self-conscious poet-as-a- cultural-force *par excellence*. For him, the question was the relationship between contemporary poetry and the great tradition of poetry, and the demands the latter makes on the contemporary poet. He wrote:

---

liance "on rational arguments from theology and even on mere philosophy"; he was supported by Cardinal Joseph Frings: *Ibid.* II/II, pp. 279-423; quotations pp. 284-85). Mercifully, this schema never reached the Council floor. The *schema* on the sources of revelation had been firmly criticized in the same Commission, on November 10, 1961, especially by Cardinals Augustine Bea and Bernard Alfrink, the former of whom found much support among the Commission's members *(Ibid.* II/I, pp. 523-63, esp. 541-49). Cardinals Liénart and Frings led the charge against it on the Council floor, in unmistakable terms, on November 14, 1962 *(Acta Synodalia Sacrosancti Concilii Oecumenici Vaticani II.* [Rome: Typis Polyglottis Vaticanis, 1970-80]. Vol. I/III, pp. 32-36). In the end it was completely reworked and adopted as the Dogmatic Constitution on Divine Revelation *Dei Verbum* (cf. Joseph Ratzinger's essay in *Commentary on the Decrees of Vatican II*, vol. 3, p. 155-66; cf. also GERALD P. FOGARTY, *American Catholic Biblical Scholarship*, pp. 334-50).

[4] Alois Grillmeier has argued this in regard to the first four ecumenical Councils: cf. *Jesus der Christus im Glauben der Kirche*, Bd. 2/1 (Freiburg-Basel-Wien: Herder, 1986), pp. 238-60, 376-78; *Christ in Christian Tradition*, Vol. II, Part I (Atlanta: John Knox Press, 1987), pp. 210-30, 333-35.

[5] It would seem to follow that those who began to complain, not long after the Council, that the Council's achievements were lacking in depth of spirituality did not appreciate this. Councils resist premature diagnoses.

The existing order is complete before the new work arrives; for order to persist after the supervention of novelty, the *whole* existing order must be, if ever so slightly, altered; and so the relations, proportions, values of each work... toward the whole are readjusted; and this is conformity between the old and the new. Whoever has approved this idea of order will not find it preposterous that the past should be altered by the present as much as the present is directed by the past. And the poet who is aware of this will be aware of great difficulties and responsibilities[6].

What Eliot wrote applies equally well to the situation of Catholics in positions of leadership in the Church in the wake of Vatican II. Specifically (after all, they have traditionally been presumed to have, at least corporately, a distinctive position of leadership in the Church), he could have been writing about *theologians*, and especially about those theologians who study and teach (though, unfortunately, the two do not always go together in practice) "dogmatic" or "systematic" or "constructive" theology. What, then, are their specific "difficulties and responsibilities"?

The sensible answer to this question is that there are too many of them to enumerate. This essay, therefore, will not even come close to painting a complete picture. But it *can* consider one of them that commands a very broad view. It is the following. Vatican II brought about an enormous as well as long-overdue broadening of the Catholic theological horizon. The broadening is doubtlessly matches the fact that the Catholic (*i.e.,* "universal") Church is now, for the first time in history, also *empirically* universal; statistically speaking, the missionary Churches were overrepresented at Vatican II, even if many of their representatives were missionaries[7]. It is wise to stop and think here. Karl Rahner did so, and went on to explain, in a prophetic article, the fundamental theological

---

[6] *Selected Essays 1917-1932* (New York: Harcourt, Brace and Company, 1932), pp. 3-11; quotation, p. 5.

[7] To mention just one fact, there were a total of 77 Dutch-born bishops at Vatican II, but only 8 of them represented dioceses in the Netherlands.

significance of the Catholic Church's factual universality[8]. At Vatican II, the late Cardinal Suenens' restless awareness of this fact inspired the drafting of the Pastoral Constitution *Gaudium et Spes* — the first document which a Council has ever addressed to "the world. "If *Lumen Gentium*, the Church's fuller self-definition (the Church "*ad intra*") was to be taken seriously, Suenens insisted, it simply had to define itself and its mission to the world at large (the Church "*ad extra*") as well.

The point just made, about the broadening of the Catholic theological horizon, has been made (too?) many times before. What is often less well realized is that the moves just recounted involve a reinterpretation and rearrangement of the *Tradition as a whole.*

Why? The catholic understanding of the Tradition as a whole is an integral element in the catholic understanding of the Church. A fresh understanding of the Church's position in the world today with a view to the renewal of both Church and world, therefore, has to involve a rereading of the whole tradition.

Let us put this rather more negatively. Not surprisingly, the mood of theology during and immediately following Vatican II was characterized by attempts at both authority and originality (or "creativity"). The problem is that neither authority nor originality can be consciously intended. They have to be earned. History could have taught us this. Looking to the present moment for cues as to what is going to be authoritative or original does not work. For in the long run, authority belongs solely to the Tradition, and originality is recognized only by hindsight. Besides, theological originality is a matter of obedience to the Spirit; all the present moment has to offer is the urgency of a world forever in travail; the Church's present vocation in that world can be theologically discovered only by dint of discerning, often prophetic, interpretation.

---

[8] "Towards a Fundamental Theological Interpretation of Vatican II". *Theological Studies* 40(1979): 716-27. Incidentally, Rahner might have added that relative to the other Christian Churches and ecclesial communities, the Roman Catholic Church typically draws it membership from across the whole range of socio-economic stratification.

Now if a theologian (or, more likely, a school of theology) should turn out to be fortunate enough to become the medium of a constructive encounter between the authority of the Great, neverto-be-domesticated Tradition and a genuine understanding of the intractable present, and if new theological understanding should emerge from this, then the Tradition as a whole would stir and be aroused, and advance by one short but intrinsically authoritative step. Just as at least some modern poetry succeeds in rearranging the great tradition of poetry, some forms of "new theology" will have the same effect on the Great Tradition. But what has to be remembered is this: modern poetry that respects the great tradition is more likely to have the power to rearrange it than the mere pursuit of novelty. To renew the Great Tradition, modern theology will have to respect and reclaim it. Remember the *nouvelle théologie* and its insistence on *ressourcement*?

III

An important passage from the first Council of the Vatican can help put this issue in high relief. The Council taught that in the construction and elucidation of doctrine, biblical arguments must adhere to the true sense of Scripture, which the Church has always held and still holds. It also insisted that Catholic dogmas must be interpreted as meaning what Holy Mother Church had once and for all declared them to mean[9].

The *tone* of these affirmations obviously labors under the defensiveness so characteristic of the nineteen-century Catholic Church, under siege yet determined not to compromise the Great Tradition. Still, on closer inspection these affirmations turn out to *commend* renewal of theology, not forbid it. Against rationalist efforts to offer radical reconstructions of the Tradition, the Council demanded loyalty and faithfulness. But in doing so, it did not call for mere *reiteration* of the teaching tradition; rather, it encouraged the unbiased *study* of it, that is, at least implicitly, its *(re) interpretation.* Cardinal Newman had anticipated this by more than thirty years. In

---

[9] DS 3007; CF 217; DS 3020 *coll.* 3043; CF 136 *coll.* 139.

his tract "On the Introduction of Rationalistic Principles into Revealed Religion" of 1835, he had written:

> Revelation, as a Manifestation, is a doctrine variously received by various minds, but nothing more to each than what each mind comprehends it to be. Considered as a Mystery, it is a doctrine enunciated by inspiration, in human language, as the only possible medium of it, and suitably, according to the capacity of language; a doctrine *lying hid* in language, to be received in that language from the first by every mind, whatever be its separate power of understanding it; entered into more or less by this or that mind, as it may be; and admitting of being apprehended more and more perfectly according to the diligence of this mind and that. It is one and the same, independent and real, of depth unfathomable, and illimitable in its extent[10].

In the same way, Vatican I sought to avoid the extremes of both rationalism and fideism in theology, and write:

> if reason, illumined by faith, inquires in an earnest, pious and sober manner [cf. Tit 2, 12], it acquires by God's grace a certain — and most fruitful — understanding of the mysteries, both *by analogies drawn from what it naturally knows*, and *from the connectedness among the mysteries themselves* and [their connectedness] *with humanity's ultimate end*[11].

While insisting on the authority of the Tradition, therefore, Vatican I somehow never lost the deeply Catholic, theological sense of history. It understood what empowers and inspires theologians to study the Tradition and to teach it is their participation in the Church's *present faith-experience.* But it also understood that such "teaching authority" as theologians have traditionally enjoyed in the Catholic Church rests on the quality of their knowledge. Vatican I was insisting, in different words, what Aquinas had also insisted on,

---

[10] JOHN HENRY NEWMAN, *Essays Critical and Historical*, Vol. I (London: Basil Montagu Pickering, 1877), pp. 40-42.
[11] DS 3016.

viz., that while the *exercise* of the theologian's license to teach is an office of *charity* (or, in modern ecclesial idiom, a charism shared with the community)[12], the specific requirement for the *cathedra magisterialis* is "sufficiency of knowledge"[13]. And if Aquinas himself is in any way an example of what he meant, we can presume that what he had in mind was the knowledge of the Great Tradition (which he had cultivated as *Sententiarius*) *and* any kind of knowledge that is relevant to Christian and human life here and now (which he drew mainly from Aristotle). For only a discerning interpretation of the Tradition, by dint of an appreciative hermeneutic across space and time animated by concern about the present as well as the present state of the pursuit of knowledge in all its forms can succeed in discerning how the authoritative Tradition is to be *understood, appreciated*, and *furthered* here and now, precisely as a *living* Tradition.

IV

Let us now attempt to offer a sketch of one particular element in the recent broadening of the catholic horizon, *viz.*, catholic theology's understanding of the "Kingdom of God", and specifically, the Kingdom of God inasmuch as it conveys a new, "postconciliar" approach to both the Catholic (and Christian) culture, and the cultures largely shaped by non-Christian philosophical and religious thought and practice.

The phrase "Kingdom of God" had been part of the Christian idiom since the New Testament was written and canonized, of course, but the expression goes back to the earliest layers of the Hebrew Scriptures. Needless to say, Catholic theology had been well aware of this. Curiously, though, for ages, especially in the West, it did not recognize the Kingdom of God *as a theological issue in its own right, and thus, one in need of reflection*[14]. It was treated as a know

---

[12] THOMAS AQUINAS, *Quodlib.* III, 4, 1.

[13] *Ibid.*

[14] It is interesting to see how a reliable modern dictionary of theology published in 1963 (*Handbuch theologischer Grundbegriffe*, edited by Heinrich Fries [München: Kösel, 1963]) can limit the entry *Reich Gottes* to an account of the *scriptural* meanings of the phrase.

quantity. This is confirmed by a careful comparison of the systematic index in Hunermann's recent edition of Denzinger[15] with the indices of its predecessor, Schonmetzer's edition. In the systematic index of the latter, the phrase simply does not occur, whereas in the former it does. This would seem to be a sure indication that the Kingdom (or Kingship) of God (or, with a reverent semitism, "of the Heavens") did not become common currency in the teaching of the *magisterium* (and hence, in theological reflection) until the Second Vatican Council. The theme is a new arrival in the history of Catholic theology; presumably, this means that it is meant to raise and resolve theological issues of central importance.

V

Had the phrase "Kingdom of God" been irrelevant, then? Of course not. The expression is too frequent in the Gospels and the other New Testament writings to have escaped the attention of Catholic theology. Many of the ancient creeds explicitly profess the future kingship of Christ and declare that it will have no end, echoing the Angel's words in the Lukan annunciation narrative. The tradition is full of interpretations, ranging all the way from God's Kingship as the essential attribute of God by virtue of Creation, to the relationship between the Kingdom of Christ to be subsumed into the Kingdom of God at the general Resurrection. Origen, with his usual sense of drama and his fondness for expressive christological titles, puts his finger on the truly new element in the New Testament view of God's Kingdom; he does so by calling Jesus the *autobasileia* — "the Kingdom [of God] in person". Israel had undoubtedly felt encouraged to view itself as "a kingdom of priests", but the prophet who completed the Book of Isaiah had retrieved this ancient self-designation only to put it in an eschatological perspective[16]. The Christian Church will continue to do this, too, but it re-

---

[15] *Enchiridion Symbolorum Definitionum Declarationum de Rebus Fidei et Morum. Kompendium der Glaubensbekenntnisse und kirchlichen Lehrentscheidungen.* Edited by Heinrich Denzinger; revised by Peter Hünermann and Helmut Hoping. 37th edition, in Latin and German. Freiburg: Herder, 1991.
[16] Cf. Ex 19, 6; Ps 114, 2; Is 61, 6.

mains compelled by the New Testament to understand that the Kingdom of God must somehow also be a *present* reality, and one inextricably linked to the person of Jesus. In other words, the Christian Tradition never hesitated to point out that the Hebrew and Jewish conceptions of the Kingdom, which were largely eschatological, had to be modified to do justice to what was regularly referred to, in the Latin West, as the *Lex Nova* — the New Law. How this was to be done was not so clear, given the tensions inherent in the field of theological forces operating between present reality and future judgment. In the West, Augustine took the momentous step. While claiming that God's Kingdom is a present reality in the Christian Church, he insisted that it remains largely invisible, pending the general Judgment, which would finally dispose of the Kingdom of the Devil. Yet at the same time Augustine was so taken by the holiness of the Church's Scriptures, its sacraments, its reliable hierarchical structures, and its unquestionable pull toward holiness that many of his medieval readers became convinced that what he had meant to say was this: that the Kingdom of God simply was a present reality in the form of the Church, even though it still had the shape of the Church Militant. Needless to say, the Matthaean text in which Jesus promises Peter "the keys of the Kingdom of Heaven"[17] tended to reinforce this understanding, especially at the hands of Roman Pontiffs like St. Gregory the Great, who regarded the Church as the Kingdom of God in its campaign against the power and the glory of the world. Eventually, this led to the tacit, yet almost complete identification of Kingdom of God and Church. A succession of belligerent emperors and equally combative popes was waiting in the wings of history to make this a political fact. Names like Charlemagne, Henry II, Boniface III, and Julius II come to mind.

What "saved" Catholic theology at this stage was the fact that it made a move that would have been unthinkable in Judaism and early Christianity: it dropped the notion that "entering the Kingdom" simply *is* Salvation. As it became increasingly obvious that membership in the Church was a po-

---

[17] Mt 16, 18.

litical fact that did not necessarily involve Christian virtue, it began to point out that being part of the Kingdom of God involved no assurance of Salvation. Aquinas, following Augustine at some distance, can teach that *the Kingdom of God consists principally in interior acts*, and in exterior acts only insofar as they are inseparable from the interior ones[18]. The question had become: what kind of activity accords with the Kingdom of God? In other words, while the Church institutionally represents the Kingdom of God, what matters in the practice of Christian living is *Salvation*.

This was to lead to what is arguably the greatest liability of Christian theology from the Middle Ages on: *Salvation becomes the central theme of the Christian faith-experience, at the expense of the sense of the God's Kingdom as a present reality*. This requires some explanation[19].

Most of all, the move implies that conversion from sin and the gift of grace become the be-all and the end-all of the Christian faith-experience. In the Reformation, the centrality of these themes will become obvious in the form of doctrine; in Roman Catholicism, it will lead to attempts to evangelize and act that are nothing short of "imperial" — that perpetual reproach thrown at Rome by the Orthodox world. But far worse, this understanding affects the interpretation of God's Trinity. It becomes so predominantly *economic* and *soteriological* that God's own glory and mystery comes to be placed at the margins of the privileged experience of faith, from where it can move into an infinite distance in such a way as to cease to function positively, as Christianity's central theme. Consequently, the practice of the Christian faith introduces the believer, not so much to God, as to God's work. Being a Christian community becomes a matter, in Melanchthon's classic phrase, of "knowing his [Christ's] benefits"[20], rather

---

[18] *S. Th.* I-II, q. 108, a. 1, *ad 1*.

[19] In what follows, I am picking up themes with which I have elaborately struggled, mainly in *Christ Proclaimed* (New York: Paulist Press, 1979), *Loving the Torah More Than God?* (Chicago: Loyola Press, 1989) and *God Encountered* (Collegeville, MN: The Liturgical Press, 1989).

[20] *Loci Communes Theologici* (1521), p. 21; cf. *Loci communes von 1521* (Gütersloh, C. Bertelsmann Verlag, 1952), p. 7: "...hoc est Christum cognoscere beneficia eius cognoscere...".

than of becoming, in Christ, "partakers of the divine nature"[21] and thus, a community of praise and thanksgiving, and of witness to the living God's mercy and faithful love.

This has profound consequences in the area of christology. It removes from the heart of Christian theology what is perhaps the most central theological theme of the patristic tradition—a theme that gave rise to endless variations: "Out of limitless love God's Word, who is God's Son, became what we are, so as to make us what he is"[22]. This broad and capacious theme, known as the "exchange principle", had warranted, since Irenaeus, the Christian conviction that all of humanity and the whole world are now called into participation in the divine life — which is, by definition, *Salvation*. And this salvation is not only accomplished once for all, but also in course of realization now, and in expectation of total fulfillment — and all of this is set in the awareness of God, loving, living, and faithful, present in Christ on the strength of the Spirit, forever to be worshiped and glorified[23].

In the new configuration, only *one* of the Christian Faith's constitutive elements, namely, that of redemption from sin by divine grace, is selected to stand in for the whole. No wonder that the worship of God and the love of the whole world are no longer the heart of the Christian faith-experience. Conversion is. Of oneself, and of all others. Sinners are to be saved. The hunt is up.

VI

In retrieving the idea of *the People of God*, the Second Vatican Council also made it possible to retrieve the mentality of the Psalms, and especially of the royal Psalms, where Israel's narratives of sin, death, and salvation are invariably

---

[21] 2 Pet 1, 4.

[22] Irenaeus, *Adv. Hær.*, V, *Præf.*, PG 7, 1120B (*SC* 153, p. 14f.); ET Ed. J. KEBLE (Oxford, 1872), p. 449.

[23] It is worth noting that the early and mid nineteenth-century Tubingen School represents the exception to this dismal rule: inspired by the idea of the Kingdom of God and Hegel's philosophy of history, it succeeded in overcoming the dreadful foreshortening of the Christian faith-experience. Cf. the fine monograph by Christian Schutz in *Mysterium Salutis*, Bd. V (Zürich-Einsiedeln-Köln: Benziger Verlag, 1976), pp. 611ff.

placed in the context of abundant praise and thanksgiving, set in a wide and generous view of the whole world. It also made it possible to rediscover a Christian theme that plays only a subordinate role in the eucharistic theology of the West, both Catholic and Reformed, *viz.* the immemorial doxological shape of the eucharistic liturgy.

Before Vatican II, it looked as if all of Western Christendom, once cut off from the great doxological tradition of Orthodoxy, lost sight of the crucial *doctrinal* significance of what Dom Gregory Dix, in a classic treatment, had called *The Shape of the Liturgy.* It is not irresponsible to suggest that the opening sessions of Vatican II were an unintended conversion-experience. When the *schemata* developed by the Preparatory Commission were swept off the table, the Council decided, apparently at the suggestion of Pope John XXIII, to tackle the draft decree on the renewal of the liturgy as its first task. Not only did this (arguably providential) move set the tone for the rest of the Council; the reform of the liturgy (however much it still leaves to be desired) has been, to date, the Council's most pervasive achievement, with the deepest impact on the faithful at large. Praise and thanksgiving were allowed to occupy their central position in the Catholic Church once again. And by the same token, the Catholic Church could profess its deep affinity with all other Christians, with the Jews and the Muslims, with the Great Religions, and with people of every color seeking God with sincere hearts. The Age of Debate, of Victory and Defeat, was over, thank God. Catholics and the other Christians, now restored to their rightful status as *fratres separati*, can encounter the world without a militant agenda once again. The Tradition has been rearranged — at least as a matter of principle; it will take generations to map it out in detail.

VII

Let us conclude this essay, which has favored the large canvas and the broad brush so far, with something quite particular: a book written by an American theologian who has recaptured in his own way the Church's love of God's

Whole World. Besides, since it deals with India, it deserves a place in a journal dedicated to missionary theology.

In *Seeing Through Texts: Doing Theology Among The Śrīvaiṣṇavas of South India*[24], Francis X. Clooney, S.J. has given us an example of what can happen when a responsible Catholic theologian learns how to encounter the world without a combative agenda.

Father Clooney is a student of the Śrīvaiṣṇava tradition within South-East Indian Hinduism. His book is an exercise in "comparative theology" — a theological subdiscipline Clooney has helped define as an encounter between cherished religious commitments: "seeing Christianity and Śrīvaiṣṇavism together"[25]. He first introduces the ninth-century song cycle *Tiruvāymoli* and its saintly author, Śaṭakōpan — one of a circle of sages so united with the Lord Viṣṇu that his writings created theological tradition. For six centuries, they elicited exegesis, interpretation, and commentary, offered by *Ācāyas* (teachers) inspired by the great twelfth-century thinker Rāmānuja. Their writings became canonical; the tradition continues to this day.

Clooney then goes on to move us (in more ways than one) to accompany him, first through *Tiruvāymoli*, then through five *Ācāyas'* interpretative "takes" on it; *Tiruvāymoli*, they show, is meditation, narrative, and drama. In a beautiful chapter, these three functions turn into an invitation to participative understanding, along with the Śrīvaiṣṇava tradition, of *Tiruvāymoli* as a guide on the road to union with God.

The book's final chapter, modestly subtitled *Some Marginal Insights, Presented in Reflections*, brings in the theological harvest of the exercise: *Tiruvāymoli* invites any theologian to become a *prapanna* — one so "surrendered" as to have deeply savored, deeply enough to admit intellectual defeat before mystery. "Mystery" here is not so much the Mystery of Mysteries "in itself" (so to speak), but Mystery as expressed in and mediated by texts that have shaped and fash-

---

[24] SUNY Series, Toward a Comparative Philosophy of Religions. Albany: State University of New York Press, 1996. Pp. xxii + 351.
[25] *Seeing Through Texts*, p. 39.

ioned generations of Indian saints and sages living by the unspeakable desire for abandon to the Unknown that remains Unknowable. They did so in thought and text and action, using *Tiruvāymoli* and the commentaries on it as guides to contemplation, to life, and to practical decision-making. The foundation of this method of doing theology as well as its fruit is "a carefully cultivated intellectual virtue which extends the scholar to the limit and which can profitably inform the whole comparative enterprise. It is the ability to suspend ... the quest for ... system, to plead a kind of helplessness, at least for now. It is the cultivation of an openness not only to questions, but also to events, encounters, inclusions, and without protection"[26].

Echoes of Socrates? Yes, and in two ways. What we hear is not just Socrates observing he was wise enough to acknowledge his ignorance, but also Justin Martyr's profession of faith in the divine *Logos* known in Jesus Christ and *for that reason* also recognizable in the culture at large, through the utterances of the likes of Socrates.

Simply from the literary point of view, what Clooney does is delightful: ever so carefully, he introduces us, presumed literates, to great souls who have ventured to write elegantly and wittily, at the risk of being misunderstood, to bear witness to the inner affinity — in themselves *and* in their readers — with the Unknowable, in quest of loving union. Unable, perhaps, to share their "take" on the Transcendent, we Christian readers *can* be educated by their deeply educated fascination with It. Thus, in Clooney's company, ignorance turns into blessing; by enlightening us about what has happened on the way to God and to a truer self in India he teaches us *Christian* theology; we become more deeply Christian for pursuing understanding and love at their speechless best. In reading texts in this fashion, Clooney explains, "one is thrust forward in a kind of ecstasy, always *from* one's home position, but not limited within its boundaries anymore"[27].

---

[26] *Seeing Through Texts*, p. 310.
[27] *Seeing Through Texts*, p. 309.

In the Great Tradition, this method of theologizing is not really new, thank God. Clement of Alexandria, the Cappadocians, Evagrius Ponticus, and Augustine drew the best out of the world of letters that had civilized them; contentedly, they incorporated these *spolia Ægyptiorum* into the Tradition's journey through the desert on the way to the Promised Land. Medieval Christians developed and orchestrated the *pagan* convention of courtly love to explore the human potential not only for inner civilization and mutual regard, but also for mysticism, as C. S. Lewis showed in *The Allegory of Love*[28]. Dante consistently mines both Scripture and the literature of Rome and Greece as he travels from the Pit of Hell toward the Presence of God. A fourteenth-century French poet discovers morality in (of all people) Ovid. Chaucer quotes Paul to explain that *everything written* is scripture for our instruction[29]. Why? Because it is integral to the Great Tradition to *bring the whole world* home to God.

Late medieval nominalism, post-Reformation confessionalization, and Enlightenment rationalism drove this desire into abeyance, as if the world were merely a stage on which the salvation of (a portion of) humankind is enacted. But at Vatican II, we witnessed the recovery of Jesus' phrase "Kingdom of God". After a centuries-long dry spell, filled with self-important argument over sin and salvation at the expense of the praise of God and the pursuit of a reverent, loving, discerning love of the world, it is wonderful to watch the Great Tradition recovered and its generous vision restored.

---

[28] London: Oxford University Press, Geoffrey Cumberlege, 1936.

[29] The teller of *The Nun's Priest's Tale* in Chaucer's *Canterbury Tales* quotes the Letter to the Romans ("Whatever is written is written for our training": Rom 15, 6) for the entirely secular (but intensely human and hence, moral) purpose of telling his listeners not to stop at the mere story — the *sensus historicus* — of the fable of Chauntecleer and Pertelote he has just told, but to draw the moral lesson from it (VII 3441-42). As a matter of fact, Chaucer himself, speaking in his own behalf, can turn the end of *The Parson's Tale* into a little homily to urge his readers, on the authority of the same Pauline text, to believe in his own good intentions and put a favorable construction on his writings, even where they find them hard to take (X [I] 1080-85). Cf. *The Works of Geoffrey Chaucer* (London: Oxford University Press, 1957), pp. 205, 265.

Good News of the Kingdom or Good News of Jesus Christ?

LUCIEN LEGRAND

"Jesus went about,... proclaiming the Good News of the Kingdom" (Mt 4:23). "What we proclaim is not ourselves, but Jesus Christ as Lord" (2 Cor 4:5). Those two statements show great similarity: they refer to the Christian "proclamation", the *kerygna*. They show as well a great difference. Paul announced Jesus-Christ but Jesus did not announce himself. He announced the Kingdom. Therein lies a thorny problem of exegesis which is also a major problem of missiology. Granting that the Good News should be proclaimed, should we preach what Jesus-Christ preached or should we preach Jesus-Christ himself? Does evangelizing consist in announcing Jesus-Christ or, as Jesus did, in proclaiming, in words and deeds, the advent of the Kingdom of God? Is the Christian message a person or a cause?

In the Indian context, the question stands in the midst of a cross fire. On the one hand, there is the attraction of India towards the person of Jesus. A "Jesus *bhakti*" in India which finds expression at all levels and in all the layers of society. At a popular level, it is not rare to find a picture of the Sacred Heart figuring amidst the pantheon of a pious Hindu home or among the tutelar deities which a truck driver displays in his cabin. On the other hand, at a higher level, the fascination of Gandhi for Christ is well known. But it applies rather to his teaching; it is not the image of the Sacred Heart or of the Good Shepherd but the Sermon on the Mount that attracts the Mahatma:

> I have regarded Jesus of Nazareth as one amongst the mighty teachers that the world has had, and I say this in all humility. I claim humility for this expression for the

simple reason that this is exactly what I feel... I can say that Jesus occupies in my heart the place of one of the great teachers who have made a considerable influence on my life... I shall say to the Hindus that your lives will be incomplete unless you study reverently the teachings of Jesus. There is one thing that occurs to me, which came to me in my early studies of the Bible. It seized me immediately I read the passage: "Make this world the Kingdom of God and His righteousness and everything will be added unto you". I tell you that if you will understand, appreciate and act up to the spirit of this passage, you won't even need to know what place Jesus or any other teacher occupies in your heart"[1].

While popular Hinduism is drawn towards the *figure* of Jesus, the Hindu Sage admires the *teachings* of Jesus. On the one hand we have a *bhakti*, a *dharma* on the other.

The same ambivalence finds its way into Indian Christian theology when it attempts to formulate a specific christology. On the one hand, it is frequently alleged that India can hardly find any relevance in a Jewish figure limited within the narrow boundaries of the Semitic culture of twenty centuries ago. What matters for India is the Risen Lord, freed from his limited temporality through death and Resurrection, the cosmic Christ whom unknowingly Hindu Sages met in the ages past in their quest for the *Sat-Cit-Ananda*. On the other side, those in India who lean towards the liberationist approach stress the importance of the concrete Jesus of Nazareth, of what he taught and did, of his concrete options, of the way in which he lived and died. They condemn the dehistoricizing of Jesus as ideologically loaded, implicitly meant to take the edge off Jesus' option for the poor[2]. So who is the Christ of the Indian way? The temporal Jesus or an intemporal Christ? What is the Gospel message for India? What Jesus said and did concretely or what Christ symbol-

---

[1] *Gandhi in Ceylon*, p. 143, quoted in R. ELLSBERG (ed.), *Gandhi on Christianity*, New York: Orbis Books, 1991, pp. 23f.

[2] Cf. G. SOARES PRABHU, "The Kingdom of God: Jesus' Vision of a New Society," in D.S. AMALORPAVADASS (ed.), *The Indian Church in the Struggle for a New Society*, Bangalore: NBCLC, 1981, pp. 579f.

izes as an icon of perfection? We are again brought back to the dilemma between the reference to Jesus' message of the Kingdom and the proposition of Christ as an object of faith and worship.

The question can be put in terms of the problem raised by the first verse of Mark's Gospel: "The beginning of the Gospel of Jesus Christ". What does "Gospel of Jesus-Christ" mean exactly? Is it the Good News brought by Jesus, the Good News of the advent of the Kingdom in God's most unexpected and paradoxical manner? Or is it the Good News concerning Jesus-Christ, the proclamation of Jesus-Christ as Lord? Does the "of" (Jesus-Christ) connote an objective genitive (concerning JC) or a subjective genitive (which Jesus communicated)? Behind this fine point of grammar there lurks a major missiological issue. Should the Christian mission preach Jesus-Christ, the "name above all names" or, like Jesus, should it announce the Kingdom, witness to it, work and fight for it, build it? Is it the name of Jesus or the cause of Jesus which matters? Without claiming to consider all the aspects of the problem, we would like to cast some Scriptural light on the issue.

I. The "Kingdom"

We just referred to the phrase: building the Kingdom of God. It is commonly used. Yet it calls for closer examination. Though the image of building (*oikodomein*) and of construction (*oikodomê*) is frequent in the New Testament, it is never connected with the "Kingdom". The closest it comes to it is in the parable of the builder in the conclusion of the Sermon on the Mount.

> Every one who hears these words of mine and does them will be like a wise man who built his house upon the rock; the rain fell, the floods came and the winds blew and beat upon that house but it did not fall because it had been founded on the rock (Mt 7:24f).

The Sermon on the Mount has been called the "charter of the Kingdom" and actually the Kingdom is mentioned seven times in those three chapters (Mt 5-7). It began with the promise of the Kingdom to the poor and those who suffer for righteousness (5:3.10). We could expect that the conclusion would again refer to the Kingdom and that the one who wisely builds on the rock is thus building the Kingdom. But such is not the meaning of the text. Building on the rock does not refer to the Kingdom but to the attitude of the listener. The text does not say that one builds the Kingdom: one builds his life once he has heard the Word. One's life can be the outcome of the advent of the Kingdom. It is not the Kingdom.

The implied presupposition behind the phrase "building the Kingdom" is that the Kingdom refers to a certain ideal condition, a new world order in which cosmic harmony prevails on earth, peace replaces war in politics, justice and love embrace each other in society, and individuals enjoy health and sanity. The Kingdom would describe a situation that responds to all the ecological, socio-economic, psychological and spiritual demands of a fulfilled humanity. Such was God's plan of Creation. He has associated humankind to this task. Working for the Kingdom expresses this participation in God's project. The developmental model likes to characterize this cooperation in terms of "building" the Kingdom while the liberationist trend would rather speak of a "struggle" for the Kingdom.

There is no denying that those ideas are quite scriptural and do correspond to the basic biblical insight of a human being called from the beginning to be the tiller of God's garden (Gen 2:4-8), partner in the divine enterprise. It is true also that the Kingdom of God is not "a concept that can be precisely defined, but a polyvalent symbol standing for all Israel's hopes of liberation"[3]. But it remains that, at the centre of the semantic area covered by this symbol, the focal idea is that of God caming in His rule.

It is well known, yet it is always to be recalled and kept in mind, that the primary meaning of *basileia* is not kingdom, the *realm* or domain subjected to the rule of the king, but the *exercise* of that royal rule. In terms of Chomsky's transformational analysis, *basileia* is not an "object" but an

---

[3] SOARES PRABHU, *art. cit.*, p. 598, with reference to N. PERRIN, *Jesus and the Language of the Kingdom.* London: SCM Press, 1976, p. 33.

"event." "Kingdom of God" does not mean a territory that belongs to God but the coming of God into His rule and the exercise of that rule or sovereignty. Actually, it is the abstract rendering of the frequent acclamation of the Psalms: "The Lord reigns" in the psalms of YHWH's Kingship (Ps 93; 96-99). Late Judaism shunned the anthropomorphism of a God sitting as a king and replaced the divine action by abstract equivalents[4]. The expressions

> "kingship of God, kingdom of heaven" denote not the place or extent of the kingdom of God (i.e. the ordinary implication of the word kingdom) but rather the *fact* that God is king... this 'advent' of the kingship of the eternal God disclosing His righteousness and mercy in power and glory... This expression (of Good News of the Kingdom) precisely indicates an *event*... Thus it is impossible to think of the kingdom of God as the sovereign good or as an ideal to be sought or attained by man... On the contrary, it is the Kingdom which comes to man and which by that very fact raises for him the question as to whether he belongs to it or not"[5].

The primary stress of the *basileia* is its givenness and gratuity. The *basileia* is announced or proclaimed (Mk 1:15.38; Lk 4:43; 9:2.60; 16:16; Mt 24:14). It is near at hand (Mk 1:15; Mt 10:7; Lk 10:11; 21:31); it comes or it has come (Mt 6:10; 12:28; Lk 17:20; 22:18; Mk 9:1); it appears (Lk 19:11). It is given (Lk 12:32), inherited (Mt 25:34). In so far as human participation is concerned, it consists in "expecting" or looking for it (Mk 15:43; cf. Lk 2:25.38), "seeing" (Mk 9:1; Lk 9:27), being accepted as the greatest or the smallest (Mt 5:19; 11:11; 18:1). One can be invited (1 Thess 2:12), "sit" (Mt 8:11; Lk 14:15) and "drink" (Mk 14:25) at the table of the *basileia*. It can also be "taken away" (Mt 8:12; 21:43)

---

[4] Thus Aramaic *memra'* (the Word) for "God speaks", *geburtha'* (power) for "God is our strength/fortress", *shekinah* for "God dwells", etc.

[5] H. ROUX, "Kingdom" in J.J. VON ALLMEN, *Vocabulary of the Bible*, London: Lutterworth Press, 1958, pp. 217f. Cf. U. LUZ in art. *"Basileia"*, in H. BALZ-G. SCHNEIDER (ed.), *Exegetical Dictionary of the New Testament*, Vol. 1, T. & T. Clark, 1990, p. 202: "Jesus proclaims the Kingdom of God as an event. This is evident from the many temporal references associated with the *basileia tou theou.*"

from those who are not fit (Lk 9:62; 20:35). It can be "sought" (Lk 12:21) and mostly it can be asked for in prayer: the entreaty: "Thy Kingdom come!"is the ultimate human participation in the coming of God's *basileia*. In short, the human share in the coming of the Kingdom may consist in preparing before it comes, experiencing the joy of its blessedness at its caming, striving to keep oneself within its ambit and continuing to uphold its "righteousness"[6]. But fundamentally, the coming of God in his rule is a pure matter of God's initiative. It is his action, his grace, his free gift.

It will be noted that if, in the parable of the pearls, the merchant is in search of the pearls, in the parallel parable of the treasure, there is not even a "seeking" (Mt 13:44-45). Treasure stories abound in world folklores and most of the plot will consist in the arduous and adventurous quest for the hidden trove. The quest for the Holy Grail has been a powerful religious symbol in the West. It has its Eastern equivalent in Siddharta's initiatory journey from the Lumbini palace to the Bodhi, the "awakening" under the Bo tree of Bodh Gaya. But the structure of Jesus' parable is totally different. Unlike in the traditional trove folk tales, in Jesus' story, there is no seeking and struggling: "Finding is the first Act"[7]. The first characteristic of the treasure in the parable is its givenness. Any human effort and struggling will be subsequent to the revelation of the Rule of God: "in his joy, he goes and sells all that he has." Similarly in the Markan summary of Jesus' proclamation in 1:14, the coming of the Reign comes first. Then only follows the call to human participation through repentance: "The rule of God is at hand; repent".

Those distinctions are important to avoid any Pelagian understanding of the theme of the Kingdom. The Kingdom is not primarily the expression of Jesus' dream of a new world, but the affirmation of his absolute trust in the Father's love and power. The Kingdom is not first meant to be

---

[6] In connection with this "righteousness", the "political, economic and social dimensions of ancient oriental kingship by way of analogy must not be forgotten". D.C. DULING, art. "Kingdom of God" in D.N. FREEDMAN ET AL. (ed.), *The Anchor Bible Dictionary*, vol. 4, New York: Doubleday, 1992, p. 50.

[7] Cf. J.D. CROSSAN, *Finding is the First Act. Trove Folktales and Jesus' Treasure Parable*, Philadelphia: Fortress Press, 1979.

a coded idiom for the Christian utopia; it affirms God's eschatological advent in the person of Jesus-Christ. It is not a blueprint for a better world

> for the vision of Jesus is theological, not sociological. It spells out the values of the new society (freedom, fellowship, justice), not the concrete social structures through which these values are realized and protected. To elaborate these is our never-to-be-ended task - for no "perfect" society is possible in history. One cannot fully actualize the vision of Jesus: one can merely approach it asymptotically! Ultimatley, then, the vision of Jesus indicates not the goal but the way. It does not present us with a pre-fabricated model to be imitated, but invites us to a continual refashioning of societal structures in an attempt to realize as completely as possible in our times the values of the Kingdom[8].

The proper focus on the "Kingdom" will help us better to situate our problem: proclaiming Jesus or, like Jesus, proclaiming the Kingdom. Once it is understood that the Kingdom is an "event" and not an "object", the question of Jesus Christ or Kingdom is no longer that of the opposition of two objects, of an object of worship versus a programme of action. The question boils down to the relationship of two stages of an "event", the two stages of God's coming in power, glory and love, first in the ministry of Jesus and ultimately in his death and Resurrection. Objectifying the Kingdom and Christ sends us back to the old Platonic dualism between body and soul, worship and life, action and contemplation. It would set a dichotomy between *bhakti* and *dharma* which does not actually exist in Hindu thinking. On the contrary the relationship between the two stages of the manifestation of the coming of God in Jesus, in his incarnation and in his glorification, is a genuine New Testament perspective that enables us to understand better the meaning of both Kingdom and Resurrection.

---

[8] G. SOARES PRABHU, *art. cit.*, p. 607.

II. The Resurrection

The resurrection of Jesus-Christ is the focal point of the New Testament: "If you confess with your lips that Jesus is the Lord and believe in your heart that God raised him from the dead, you will be saved" says Paul (Rom 10:9). Or again, "if Christ has not been raised our preaching is in vain and your faith is in vain" (1 Cor 15:14). The matter being so vital to Christian faith, it is all the more important to perceive its meaning accurately. Resurrection means victory of life over death (1 Cor 15:54-57). But this victory is not just a matter of survival, of finding a way to overcome the universal anguish of death.

"Life" in the Bible is no mere biological existence. It is the fundamental attribute of the "living God" which he shared with the world in Creation, with his people in salvation and, in a particular unique manner, with His Son so that He may in turn give it to those whom the Father has entrusted to Him (Jn 17:2; cf. 5:26f). Jn especially sees Life as the sum total of God's gift to humanity. He uses the verb zên 17 times and the noun zôê 36 times. In general, the noun zôê is qualified by *aiônios*, eternal. This adjective does not denote so much life after death as participation in the fundamental attribute of the Eternal God. In Jesus Christ "the way, the truth and the life" (Jn 14:6), the believer receives "life", i.e. the plenitude and dynamism of the God who is the living one and source of life (cf. Jn 1:4.16; 3:16.36; 5:21, etc.).

Death is the opposite. It connotes whatever defeats God's plan, effects human alienation and cosmic corruption. It is the negation of whatever the "living God" is and wants to communicate. It is a "power", almost personalized, that exercises its nefarious "reign" over the world (Rom 5:14.17.21; 6:12), an antithesis to God's "reign".

Therefore, as victory of life over death, the Resurrection of Christ is not just a resuscitation, the reanimation of a dead body. For the New Testament and for Christian faith, it is the decisive divine intervention bringing to fulfilment God's creative and saving purpose. The resurrection of Jesus is a reversal of the Cross. The Cross meant the victory of Death; the Resurrection is the triumph of Life. The Cross had been humiliation; the Resurrection is glory (Phil 2:6-11). The Cross was the outcome of hatred and rejection; the Resurrection is the triumph of God's love. By crucifying Jesus, the "powers of this world" had repudiated what Jesus stood for; by raising him from the dead, God put his seal of approval on what the world had condemned.

Therefore the Resurrection is indissolubly connected with the drama of Calvary. It is the Resurrection of the man who was anathematized on the gibbet of Golgotha. Thereby a link is posited between the Risen Lord and the historical Jesus. For the execution on Calvary is not an accident; it is the outcome of a train of events, of attitudes and options assumed by the man from Nazareth, of an understanding of God and of God's Kingdom proferred by the one who called God his Father.

Particularly, the Resurrection reverses the trial of Jesus. It "justifies" him, showing him to have been in the right. In it, the "Advocate", as Jesus says in his last discourse,

> will confute the world and show where wrong and right and judgment lie... He will convict them of wrong by their refusal to believe in me; he will convince them that right is on my side, by showing that I go to the Father when I pass from your sight; he will convince them of divine judgement, by showing that the Prince of this world stands condemned (Jn 16:8-11 NEB tr.).

As the eschatological intervention of God the Creator and the Saviour, the Resurrection gives also a universal value to what Jesus said and did. Jesus becomes "the first fruit" (1 Cor 15:20), "the first born among many brethren" (Rom 8:29) and "of all creation" (Col 1:15), the new Adam (Rom 5:12-19; 1 Cor 15:45-48).

> He is the beginning, the first born from the dead that in everything he might be preeminent. For in him all the fullness of God was pleased to dwell and through him to reconcile all things on earth and in heaven making peace by the blood of his cross (Col 1:18-20).

In the Resurrection of Jesus, the disciples perceived the fulfilment of all the expectations and promises of the Old Testament. The apparently crooked lines of God's dealings with His people now became the straight lines of God's design when viewed in the perspective of the life, death and Resurrection of the one they could at last recognize as the Messiah.

The Resurrection validates and universalizes the mission of the "Galilean". Peter puts it neatly in the terse statement of his first missionary discourse: "God made him Lord and Christ this Jesus whom you crucified" (Acts 2:36). The trial of Jesus, leading to his crucifixion, has been declared null and void. Now the one who had been cast away is made the universal Lord and appears as the fulfilment of the messianic hope.

Still more concise a statement is the title of "Jesus Christ" which Mk (1:1) and Paul (Rom 1:4) present as a summary of their Gospel. The two words of this title are not a tautology, an empty synonymous pleonasm, as present common usage has it. The phrase is a synthetic predicament, expressing the paradox of the essential Christian mystery. *Jesus* is the man from Nazareth, the Galilean prophet, the reprobate of Golgotha. *Christ* is the Messiah, Son of God, to whom has been committed universal authority in heaven and on earth (Mt 28:18). The name "Jesus" refers to the historical reality, limited in space and time, of the one who announced the advent of God's Reign. The title "Christ" refers to the eschatological and universal validity given to the mission of Jesus by the Resurrection.

III. Gospel of the Kingdom - Gospel of Jesus-Christ

We may now go back to the question raised initially. What is the "Gospel of Jesus-Christ"? Is it the Good News of the Kingdom proclaimed by Jesus or the Good News concerning Jesus-Christ preached by the apostle Paul?

1. No dilemma

The two meanings are possible. The first one refers to the pre-paschal period; the second one to the post-paschal times. In the Gospels, Jesus announces the Good News that the Reign of God is coming. After the Resurrection, the disciples announce Jesus-Christ. The reason for this difference consists precisely in the Resurrection which has revealed how the Good News proclaimed by Jesus and lived by him are the perfect expression of the plan God proffered to human kind and of the kind of God this plan reveals. Jesus is the Good News, the ultimate *logos* (Jn 1:1-14), the *eikôn*, the perfect "image of the invisible God" (Col 1:15). Proclaiming him is nothing but showing him as the disclosure "of the light of the gospel of the glory of Christ who is the likeness of God". This is why the apostles preach "Christ as Lord", "for it is the God who said 'let light shine out of darkness' who has shone in our hearts to give the light of the knowledge of God in the face of Christ" (2 Cor 4:4-6).

2. Theological Implications

Therefore Jesus and Christ cannot be dichotomized. There is no ground for a dissociation between the Christ of faith and the historical Jesus, between a hidden cosmic Christ valid for all the Nations and Jesus of Nazareth whose Semitic limitations would make him alien and irrelevant to, say, Asian cultures. The Resurrection shows the two to be indissolubly connected.

Jesus is Christ: he is no longer a purely "historical" event conditioned in time and space and therefore of limited value as a model. The Resurrection has shown him to be more than a model. He is the embodiment of the mystery of God, the "image", the "Word".

Christ is Jesus: This Christ, perfect image of God, has not shed his humanity through his death and resurrection. In Christ the Lord, we do not see an abstraction or a disincarnated deity but the divine vindication of all that Jesus lived, stood and died for. The life of poverty, the option for the marginalized, the strategy of weakness, love and service as an expression of the might of God, whatever the Gospels narrate and report concerning Jesus, finally and particularly the Cross, are constitutive elements of the "image" of God, of the ultimate theophany given in Jesus-Christ. As John shows in his Gospel, the life and acts of Jesus are "Word made flesh", the manifestation of the divine "Glory full of grace and truth" (Jn 1:14f).

This manifestation of God in Jesus-Christ is shown by the Resurrection to be eschatological: for the Christian believer, it is ultimate and decisive. But its rooting in the ground of history puts it in solidarity with the whole history of mankind. Israel did not descend from heaven; it issued from Ur of the Chaldees and Canaan and developed in continuous interaction with Egypt, Sheba and Africa, Mesopotamia, Persia and Asia, Greece, Rome and Europe. The Galilean humanity of Jesus of Nazareth casts deep genetic and historical roots in all the layers of the human family. The eschatological and decisive significance of the Resurrection of Jesus-Christ being rooted in an incarnation is not exclusive but inclusive. What Jesus was and did was not a foil but a *sêmeion*, a sign "that the thoughts of many hearts may be revealed" (Lk 2:35)[9].

3. Missiological Implications

The dichotomy between announcing the Kingdom and preaching Jesus-Christ must be overcome. What is called for is a wholistic missiological perspective.

The Kingdom is not an ideology among others, even if better than others. It is not just a human utopia of justice, peace, love. It includes all these values but it is fundamentally an "act of God" and, through the Resurrection of Jesus-Christ, God's eschatological act. In the course of history, Jesus is not one more hero, one more great thinker, another man of vision and revolutionary. He is Jesus *Christ*: "God made him Christ and Lord" (Acts 2:36).

Reciprocally, Jesus-Christ is not just a name to be added to or substituted for other names of other deities. Christ is *Jesus*, a concrete figure who stood for a certain understanding of God as a Father, of his mind and will, who taught it, enacted it in a style of life and action, finally died for it. Liberation theology insists on the texts in which Jesus associated with the poor and the marginalized. The Passion and the

---

[9] For the experiential and theological development of this biblical insight, see J. DUPUIS, *Jesus Christ at the Encounter of Religions*, Maryknoll, New York: Orbis, 1991, who speaks of "complementary uniqueness" (p. 205).

Resurrection do play a great role in this liberationist approach but as Passion and Resurrection of the one who shared in the struggles and the fate of the oppressed and as his ultimate victory over the forces of servitude and death. Liberationist exegesis rightly considers that a Passion and Resurrection disconnected from their concrete incarnation in the life, message and praxis of the Galilean carpenter would be mere docetism.

Conclusion

A tension persists in the mission perspectives and in the praxis of the Churches. On the one hand, an "evangelical" tendency lays the stress on the proclamation of the name of Jesus-Christ the Lord. It would willingly take as its motto the words of Peter: "There is no other name under heaven given among mortals by which we must be saved" (Acts 4:12). On the other hand, an "activist" tendency insists on doing what Jesus did, standing for justice and healing, development and liberation. Its motto is the text of Is 61 quoted in Jesus' discourse in Nazareth: "Good News to the poor,... liberation to the captives,... freedom to the oppressed" (Lk 4:18).

There is certainly place for a pluralism of mission models[10]. But those diverse paradigms should not function in isolation or opposition lest they become sectarian. By proclaiming "I believe in Jesus-Christ", the Christian confession has a twofold object: Jesus *and* Christ. The synthetic character of this statement is also an invitation to transcend dichotomy and adopt a wholistic mission perspective.

The Christian faith and witness address themselves to Jesus who announced the advent of God's Reign in power and glory but in quite a paradoxical form: the power of God's Sovereignty operated in the weakness of servanthood and its glory manifested itself in the kenosis of love unto death. This concrete image, embodied in the person of the

---

[10] Cf. L. LEGRAND, *Unity and Plurality. Mission in the Bible*, Maryknoll, NY: Orbis Books, 1990, pp. 74-84, 149-152 and D.J. Bosch's *magnum opus, Transforming Mission. Paradigms Shifts in Theology of Mission*, Maryknoll, NY: Orbis Books, 1991.

"Marginal Jew"[11] of Nazareth, is an intrinsic aspect of Christian faith and witness. Christian existence and mission cannot by-pass this *margha* of the Galilean prophet which is ultimately the way of the Cross and which also opens on all the dimensions, personal, familial, socio-economic, ecological, political, of human existence[12].

But Christian faith and witness do not stop with this concrete programme, however lofty and inspiring it might be. Christian faith sees in the Kingdom the advent *of God*, in Jesus the *son of God* and in his resurrection the ultimate creative and saving *act of God*. "Jesuo-logy" is empty without Christo-logy and indeed Theo-logy:

> From first to last this has been the work of God... What I mean is that God was in Christ reconciling the world to himself... It is as if God were appealing to you through us... Sharing in God's work, we urge this appeal to you: you have received the grace of God; do not let it go for nothing (2 Cor 5:18-6:1 *NEB* tr).

Advent of God, the Kingdom cannot be reduced to a human agenda. This "reductionism" would indeed empty it of its substance. It is not just a matter of safeguarding the primacy of the "spiritual" over the "material": this would still remain within the confines of human nature. It is rather a matter of perceiving "the power of God unto salvation" (Rom 1:16), the "power of the Spirit" (Rom 15:13), the power of his Resurrection" (Phil 3:10).

---

[11] According to the title of the latest survey of the evidence on the Jesus of history by J.P. MEIER, *A Marginal Jew. Rethinking the Historical Jesus* (AncB Reference Library), New York: Doubleday, 1991-1994.

[12] "This is why evangelization involves an explicit message... about the rights and duties of every human being, about family life..., about life in society, about international life, peace, justice and development - a message especially energetic today about liberation" (*Evangelii Nuntiandi*, 29; cf. §§ 30-33). "The Kingdom is the concern of everyone: individuals, society and the world. Working for the Kingdom means acknowledging and promoting God's activity, which is present in human history and transforms it. Building the Kingdom means working for liberation from evil in all its forms. In a word, the Kingdom of God is the manifestation and the realization of God's plan of salvation in all its fulness" (*Redemptoris Missio*, 15). "Commitment to peace, development and the liberation of peoples; the rights of individuals and peoples, especially those of the minorities; the advancement of women and children; safeguarding the created world" (*RM* 37).

Reciprocally a sense of the intemporal grace of God that would overlook its concrete expression in Jesus' words and deeds, life style and options, in his Passion and in the praxis of the disciples would ignore the physical and historic reality of the Incarnation.

The reign of God is historic and trans-historic as Jesus Christ is Galilean and Lord of heaven and earth, as God is immanent and transcendent. But God alone can live His immanence in the infinite measure of His transcendence. In their limited existence, human beings cannot perfectly integrate the givenness of the Kingdom with its concrete realization in history and human praxis. Luke, the evangelist of social concern, is not John, the mystic. Francis Xavier and Thérèse of Lisieux present different images of the Mission. There will always be a variety of *margha: bhakti, jnana, dharma* are to "join hands", like "justice and peace" in the Psalm (85:10), in the complex world in which we live. Charisms complement each other. Only a pluralism of mission models, accepting and complementing each other, can do justice to the infinite richness of the treasure and to the impact of God's advent in His reign.

The Kingdom of God and Religious Pluralism

MARIASUSAI DHAVAMONY

Introduction

In the Christian theology of religions the theme of the Kingdom of God is central because the way one understands the Kingdom of God determines the place of world religions in the salvific plan of God, their relation to Jesus Christ as the universal and unique Saviour of mankind and their relation to the Church and its absolute character, their salvific role to their own adherents outside the visible Church, and finally their importance in the inter-religious dialogue and co-operation. Is the Church to be considered co-extensive with the Kingdom of God or a proleptic realization of it or its herald? The position taken with regard to these questions affects profoundly the theology of the Christian mission. In addition to this, liberation theologies in Latin America, Asia and Africa, theologies of interreligious dialogue and theologies of inculturation and local theologies have based themselves on the theology of the Kingdom of God as a valid paradigm to understand the life-situation of the Church in various continents today. Over and above this, the particularity and historicity of God's intervention in Jesus Christ and in his Church in salvation history have raised problems which some think could be solved only in the perspective of the Kingdom of God in its universal dimension.

In this paper we try to expound the Biblical understanding of the Kingdom of God before we approach the problem of world religions in relation to the Kingdom. We understand by the Kingdom of God not any territorial dimension of God but God's reign over mankind in salvation history. We do not intend to deal with the theology of liberation or of interreligious dialogue or of inculturation and local theologies. we do not again deal with individual religions. We are concerned here only with the Christian understanding of the role of world religions in the Kingdom of God.

1. THE PREACHING OF JESUS[1]

Jesus began his public ministry with the words: "The time is fulfilled[2], and the Kingdom of God is at hand; repent and believe in the Gospel". (Mk 1.15) Jesus' message concerned the character and the coming of his Kingdom of God. He spoke of God's Kingdom to Nicodemus[3] by night as he started his ministry (Jn 3.1-15) and to Pontius Pilate[4] before his death (Jn 18.33-8). we can say that his dominant message was about the Kingdom of God: what it was, how to enter it and how to live worthily as its 'citizen'. "I must preach the

---

[1] There are many studies which deal scientifically with this problem; we select only some of the most significant ones. RUDOLF SCHNACKENBURG, *God's Rule and Kingdom*, Herder and Herder, New York, 1963; G.R. BEASLEY-MURRAY, *Jesus and the Kingdom of God*, William B. Eerdmans, Grand Rapids, 1986; NORMAN PERRIN, *The Kingdom of God in the Teaching of Jesus*, SCM Press, London, 1963; Id. *Rediscovering the Teaching of Jesus*, Harper & Row, New York, 1967; Id. *Jesus and the Language of the Kingdom*, Fortress Press, Philadelphia, 1967; GEORGE E. LADD, *Jesus and the Kingdom*, SPCK, Londo, 1966; BRUCE CHILTON (ed.), *The Kingdom of God*, Fortress Press, Philadelphia, 1984; WOLFHART PANNENBERG, *Theology and the Kingdom of God*, The Westminster Press, Philadelphia, 1969; JOHANNES WEISS, *Jesus' Proclamation of the Kingdom of God*, Fortress Press, Philadelphia, 1971; T.W. MANSON, *The Teaching of Jesus*, Cambridge University Press, 1959; C.H. DODD, *The Parables of the Kingdom*, Nisbet, London, 1936; OSCAR CULLMANN, *Christ and Time*, Westminster, Philadelphia, 1950; Id. *The early Church*, Westminster, Philadelphia, 1956; O.E. EVANS, *Kingdom of God*, Interpretor's Dictionary of the Bible, III, pp. 20-23; A.M. HUNTER, *Interpreting the Parables*, SCM Press, London, 1960.

[2] This note of fulfilment is truly the distinctive element in Jesus' message, different from Judaism. The theme of fulfilment occurs very often in the Gospels. "The Spirit of the Lord is upon me, because he has annointed me to preach good news to the poor. He has sent me to proclaim release to the captives and recovering of sight to the blind, to set at liberty those who are oppressed, to proclaim the acceptable year of the Lord... Today this scripture has been fulfilled in your hearing". (Lk 4.18-21)

[3] By means of Jesus' encounter with Nicodemus John depicts the inbreaking of the New Age and Jesus as the Messiah. The dialogue here begins with the idea of rebirth but leads into discourse about the whole work of Christ.

[4] Jesus said, "My Kingdom does not belong to this world... My kingly authority comes from elsewhere... My task is to bear witness to the truth". (Jn 28.35 f) He has come to reveal God whose Kingdom is the truth.

good news of the Kingdom of God to the other cities also; for I was sent for this purpose[5]. (Lk 4.43) The time of which the Old Testament sages prophesied had finally arrived. God is supreme in heaven (Ps 95.3); he is supreme in nature (Ps 29.10); he is also supreme in the kingdom of men (Dan. 4.17,25,32). He is the King of the nations (Jer. 10.7). But the Lord is above all kings of Israel. The Old Testament expectation of the coming Kingdom was that it would be just (Jer. 23.5-6); that it would usher in peace (Jer. 23.1-6); that it would give stability (2 Samuel 7.10-16); and finally that the messianic Kingdom would be universal, over all peoples of the earth (Zech. 9.10). This Old Testament expectation was fulfilled by the coming of the Kingdom of God, as announced by Jesus.

The messianic Kingdom preached by Jesus was different from the Jewish conception of it. The blessings of the Kingdom were to be spiritual rather than material. Its glory was only to be revealed by suffering[6]. (Mk 8.31 ff) It was through Jesus' sacrificial death on the cross that forgiveness of sins was available and the new Covenant established. (Mt 26.26-9) The teaching of the Kingdom was the messianic mystery[7]. (Mt 13.11) The sphere of the Kingdom is the world but its origin is divine and its character is the spead of the truth by which men are set free. (Jn 18.37; 8.32,36) It works like leaven, conquering not by force from without but by grace from within. (Mt 13.33) It is one and the same thing to be a subject of God's rule[8], to have eternal life[9] and to be saved[10].

---

[5] This means the fulfilment of the eschatological hope and the coming of the messianic age. The presence of the Kingdom is an event, the gracious action of God.

[6] The coming of the Kingdom is realted to the death of Jesus. See Luke 17.25. Thi is illustrated again by the fact that the sayings about his death refer to him as the Son of Man. (Mk 8.31; 9.31; 10.33 f)

[7] 'The mystery of the Kingdom' is the unique element in Jesus' teaching about the Kingdom. He affirmed that the Kingdom has actually come upon men. (Mt. 12.28) It was present in his word and action; it was present in his person as the messianic salvation. This could be understood only by revelation.

[8] God's Kingdom is the main message of the Synoptic Gospels; the preaching of the Kingdom of God by Jesus.

[9] The eternal life is the main theme of John's Gospel. It stands for salvation described in the Synoptics as entrance into the Kingdom of God. To follow Jesus is to inherit eternal life, is to enter the Kingdom of God and is to be saved. (Cfr Mk 10.17-31)

[10] The most comprehensive word to express the richness and range of Christianity according to Paul is salvation. The proclamation of the present Kingdom

Righteousness is a mark of the Kingdom of God. Moral repentance is the first condition of entering into the Kingdom of God (Mk 1.15), involving the obedience of one's life[11]. (Mt 7.21 ff) It involves God's gift of grace rather than an achievement of man's effort[12]. It is the Kingdom of peace and brotherly love. (Mt 6.25-34; 18.15-35; Lk. 12.22-31) The Kingdom of God is universal in its scope, including the Gentiles, not only the chosen race. (Mt 8.11-12; Lk 13.28-30) The risen Lord declared that all authority was given him on earth as in heaven, and that therefore his Church was to go and make disciples of all nations and be his witnesses unto the utmost parts of the earth. (Mt. 28.10-19; Acts 1.8)

The Kingdom had already come with the preaching and ministry of Jesus. Jesus' works of healing were the signs[13] of the Kingdom. (Mt 12.22-30; Lk 11.14-23) By the death and the resurrection of Jesus the Kingdom had entered on a new phase. "God has made him both Lord and Christ, this Jesus whom you crucified". (Acts 2.24-36) This is also the theme of Pauline epistles. (Phil. 2.7-11)

The Kingdom of God means God's rule on earth and implies that God acts in history and works out a great and gracious purpose in it to an appointed end. It is God's reign becoming manifestly effective in human history and redeeming mankind. The parables portray the Kingdom as a present reality. They imply an eschatology that is in the process of realization. The moral teaching of Jesus, as found in the Sermon on the Mount, is his design for life in the Kingdom of God. The Beatitudes are the spiritual portrait of those who

---

leads to the proclamation of salvation wrought by the ministry, death and resurrection of Jesus Christ because by his death and resurrection he became all that the Kingdom contained.

[11] Jesus reinterpreted the role of the law, saying that the observance of merely ceremonial rules of purity could not accomplish God's purpose in the law, for purity was a matter of the heart rather than that of the hands. (Mk 7.13)

[12] All the blessings of the Kingdom are a reward which is utterly of grace of God. The reward is accorded to all who are faithful, regardless of the outcome of their labour. (Mt 25.21,23) While men have to seek the Kingdom yet it is God's gift. (Lk, 12.31-2)

[13] The presence of the messianic salvation is seen in Jesus' miracles of healing. The miracles are the signs of the Kingdom of God; namely, evidences of the presence of the messianic salvation. (Mt 11.4-5) The Kingdom of God is concerned not only with men's souls but with the salvation of the whole man.

belong to the Kingdom. The moral ideal of the Beatitudes is one of grace. Founded on the grace of the Father who grants the Kingdom to the child-like, they promise blessedness to all who are content to trust him to provide all good things, far from claiming any right for the benefits.

The Kingdom of God is centred in the person and work of Christ. There is a striking equivalence between the Kingdom of God and Christ, as seen in the following parallel texts: "The Kingdom of God come with power" (Mk 9.1) and "The Son of man coming in his Kingdom" (Mt. 16.28); "for my sake and the Gospel's" (Mk 10.39) and "For the sake of the Kingdom of God" (Lk 18.29). Again, it is significant that the Kingdom is promised only to those who are attached to Jesus' person and that being his disciple is the same as being in the Kingdom of God. (Mk 10.17-31; Lk 9.57-62) Again, "If I by the finger of God cast out devils, then the reign of God has come upon you". (Lk 11.20) Here we see a close link between his work and the Kingdom of God. Jesus claimed to be the bearer of God's Kingdom to men; in his ministry we see that rule embodied and in action.

Jesus believed that the Kingdom of God was present in himself and his ministry in a 'mystery' (Mk 4.11), but indeed nonetheless, really and dynamically present[14]. The 'mystery' is that the meaning of the inaugurated eschatology and the meaning of the Messianic Ministry of Jesus are one and the same. In the ministry, death and resurrection of jesus the Kingdom of God has come (Lk 11.20; Mt 11.12; Lk 16.16; 17.21). Jesus' proclamation had been: the time is fulfilled; the Kingdom of God has come; therefore repent and believe. The Apostles' proclamation was: the prophecies are fulfilled; the New Age has come with the event of Christ; therefore repent and believe. This proclamation of the ministry, death and resurrection of Jesus the Messiah specifies the significance of the proclamation of the Kingdom of God. The Good News of the Gospel was therefore not only a programme for human development, for human

---

[14] See G.B. BEASLEY-MURRAY, *Jesus and the Kingdom of God*. Eerdmans, Grand Rapids, 1987.

liberation, for the realization of peace and justice, but the proclamation of an act of God in Jesus Christ as the universal Saviour of mankind.

The 'Ethics of Jesus'

The moral teaching of Jesus is part and parcel of his religion and is not separable from it. The understanding of any part of his moral teaching demands a grasp of the whole religious context in which it has place. We can point out three characteristics of the moral teaching of Jesus. 1) The moral precepts are the revelation of the character of God and of the character which he demands in man. "You shall be holy as I am holy". 2) They are revealed through God's servants. 3) They are laid on people as an obligation, as a distinctive mark by which they are separated from all other peoples. The moral teachings of Jesus are conceived as proceeding from God through himself to the community of his disciples. Though the moral teachings of Jesus are valid universally, their primary application is to the community of his disciples who accept the Kingdom of God. (Mk 12.28-34)[15]

Jesus' ethical teaching must be studied in the context of the Kingdom of God and can be best interpreted in terms of the dynamic character of God's rule which has already manifested itself in his person but will be consummated only in the eschatological hour.

The Kingdom and the Church

Is the Kingdom the same as the Church? The present dimension of the Kingdom resides in the person of Jesus. The Church is the community of the believers in Jesus and his preaching of the Kingdom. As the community of Jesus Christ the Church is the sign and symbol of the Kingdom; as such the Church is not the Kingdom. The relation between the Kingdom and the Church can be explained as follows: 1) God's eschatological reign, as present in the person and work

---

[15] See T.W. MANSON, *The Teaching of Jesus*, Cambridge University Press, 1959, ch. IX.

of Jesus is in a special way related to the earthly community of Jesus in as far as it has a share in the saving graces of the present and the promises for the future. The Church is the community of those believers who are orientated to the Kingdom. Jesus has communicated the power of the present reign of God to Peter and his disciples who have the authority to teach and forgive, and have received the word and spirit of God. (Mt 19.28; Mt 16.18 ff) The "essential presence" of God's reign in the Church is sufficiently safeguarded if the forces and graces of salvation are recognized in it, though not exclusively[16].

The saving character of God's reign

The reign of God in the first place is the realization of God's redeeming will. The purpose of both the word and work of Jesus is to announce and offer God's salvation to all men. The content of his preaching is a message of salvation, joy and peace. First of all comes God's goodness and mercy, unparalleled in generosity of forgiveness. The Kingdom of God is proclaimed by Jesus as a saving grace for all who receive it and respond to it. God's love for sinners is a mark of God's eschatological reign. Grace is bestowed on all who accept the salvific Gospel of Christ and are converted. God's reign fulfills man's religious aspirations, and particularly the aspirations of those who suffer, are poor and are persecuted in this world.

God's reign is directed to all mankind. There is no limit to God's universal salvific will, for it extends to all, sinners and the just, Jews and Gentiles, the poor and the rich. The apparent contradiction between Jesus' opening the door of God's Kingdom to all and the confinement of his preaching to Israel and his forbidding the disciples to go to the Samaritans and the Gentiles, is resolved in the full synthesis of his doctrine. His promise to the Gentiles is contained in the words: "Many shall come from the East and the West and shall sit down with Abraham and Isaac and Jacob in the

---

[16] See RUDOLF SCHNACKENBURG, *God's Rule and Kingdom*, Herder and Herder, New York, 1963, pp. 230 ff.

Kingdom of heaven. But the children of the Kingdom shall be cast out into the exterior darkness". (Mt 8.11 ff; Lk 13.28 ff)[17] The proclamation and offer of salvation to the Gentiles is evident from the commission of the risen Lord to his disciples. (Mt 28.18-20). To propose the uncompromising demands of the Beatitudes of the Sermon on the Mount solely as a programme of social renovation is basically to misunderstand them. Jesus is not concerned merely with a progressive advance towards some earthly realm of peace but with the transformation of man himself so that he may have a share in the blessing of the Kingdom of God[18]

The preaching of the early Church was centred on the person of Jesus and on his mission, death, and the resurrection as we have explained before (1 Cor. 15.3-5; 1 Peter 1.18-21; 3.18-22). This preaching speaks of God's eschatological actions. Jesus' message of the Kingdom of God is absorbed into the Christ-event. The post-paschal faith sees the death and resurrection as the salvific event of the reign of God, proclaimed by Jesus. In Pauline theology, the Kingship of God is realized fundamentally in the Lordship of Christ. (1 Cor. 15.24; Col. 1.13) It is present in the faithful (Col. 3.1-4), in the Church, Christ's body. (Col. 1.18-24) According to John, the message of Christ is characterized by an eschatology (of life, death, judgement, joy and peace) which has been made a present reality[19].

God's reign is God's own trinitarian movement toward men and creature (ad extra) by which the God who dwells in perfect fellowship inherently (ad intra) as Father, Son and the Holy Spirit acts in sovereign grace towards men. God's reign proceeds from God the Father, reveals and effects salvation in and through the incarnate Son and elicits the human response of obedience to God through the power of the Holy Spirit. The Church in so far as it manifests the reign of God in its life and mission, is an instrument of the Kingdom, demonstrating, as his body on earth, the love and power of God, however imperfectly.

---

[17] See G.R. BEASLEY-MURRAY, op. cit., pp. 169 ff.
[18] See BENEDICT T. VIVIANO, *The Kingdom of God in History*, Michael Glazier, Wilmington, 1988, ch. 1. This contains a critique of R. Schnackenburg.
[19] R. SCHNACKENBURG, op. cit., pp. 104 ff.

Some mistaken notions of the Kingdom of God

First of all, the Kingdom is understood to refer ultimately to the religious experience, understanding it as the rule of God in the hearts of men. But the Kingdom of God as taught by Jesus is never something subjective, purely inward or spiritual but is always the objective messianic Kingdom. Secondly, the Kingdom is not to be taken to mean the exercise of the moral life in society, as the so-called Social Gospel Movement understood it. For God's rule cannot be identified with the ethical ideal of a just society.

Many liberation theologians maintain that salvation is identical with liberation from social, economic and political oppression. Liberation is part of salvation understood as well-being in the comprehensive sense. Certainly salvation is total well-being, but its basis is the spiritual dimension of reconciliation with God and participation in the divine life. The economic, social and political dimension of salvation, which constitutes liberation from oppression demands the liberating task of the Church but receives its motivation from the spiritual dimension of salvation.

Thirdly, in Jesus' teaching and ministry salvation means essentially participation in the reign of God through repentance and forgiveness of sin, reconciliation with God and restoration to wholeness through healing. (Mk 2.1-12; Lk 7.48-50; 11.20-22) Salvation means participation in the death and resurrection of Christ and the gift of the Spirit. (Jn 1.14-18; 3.14-18; Rom. 5.1-11) This participation involves forgiveness of sin through the sacrifice of Christ, communion with God and eternal life in the power of the Holy Spirit. (Rom. 3.21-6; 2 Cor. 5.16-20; 1 Jn 1.7-2.2; 4.9-14)[20]

Fourthly, some think that the Kingdom means an ideal society, an earthly utopia, to be built by men, following the guide-lines of Jesus' teaching. On the contrary, the Kingdom is primarily God's work rather than man's deed. It is God ruling and redeeming. Fifthly, it is considered to be a kind of biblical equivalent for the evolutionary process. But the biblical notion of the fulfilment of history does not involve a process

---

[20] See OWEN C. THOMAS, *Theological Questions*, Morehouse-Barlow Co., Wilton, 1983, pp. 73 ff.

of evolution from within but a divine intervention from without. Sixthly, there is the tendency to identify the Kingdom of God with any kind of ecclesial organization. This is a confusion of the divine rule with the people who live under it[21]. Seventhly, we cannot equate the Kingdom with the Church, for the Church is at the service of the Kingdom, its seed and instrument in the world. Eighthly, some hold that in Jesus' eyes the Kingdom was already realized by his coming. They have proposed a "realized eschatology"; i.e., the Kingdom has already come and the age of fulfilment has been ushered in through the ministry, death and resurrection of Jesus Christ. But we hold that the rule of God has been inaugurated by Jesus' coming and ministry but not yet fully realized, if it is destined to grow, although it is present in Jesus. Ninethly, some hold that in the eyes of Jesus the Kingdom was not present, but imminent. They interpret eschatology in wholly 'futurist' terms. In this case we cannot explain the role of the moral precepts of Jesus and the Sermon on the Mount which belong to the way of life of the Kingdom. The Beatitudes are eschatological and messianic; they are the marks of the presence of the Kingdom of God. They are the spiritual portrait of those who belong to the Kingdom. Tenthly, some affirm Jesus' expectation of the imminent end and suppose that any such expectation can only be ascribed to the primitive community. We cannot sustain it on the basis of exegetical findings.

In conclusion, when we analyse the meaning of the Kingdom of God, we have to be critical of any interpretation which advocates: the equation of the Kingdom with a Church or a movement; use of the Kingdom to justify a particular social or political programme; setting up one's own authority above or alongside God's authority; too strong emphasis on either personal piety or social responsibility; ignoring the priority of repentance and faith in Jesus and his work of salvation; and finally, undervaluing the dynamic of the Holy Spirit. The reign of God is the reign of the Trinity in men's hearts and institutions, and above all in the Church which is the sacrament of the Kingdom.

---

[21] See A.M. HUNTER, *Introducing New Testament Theology*, SCM Press, London, 1953, pp. 25 ff.

2. God's Reign and World Religions

God reigns in a general way in creation and in universal human history which includes world religions. He reigns in a particular way in the special history of his Kingdom (Israel, Jesus Christ and the Church). According to the Christian faith, to encounter Jesus Christ in the special history is to encounter God. God's reign is centred in this one particular man who is the ultimate meaning of history. In this particular man who is God incarnate and in his work is revealed the gracious and universal salvific activity of God. The reign of God in general is given a particular content through its link with the reign of Christ. (Rev. 11.15) Jesus Christ is not one of the many instances of the universal salvific activity of God but the one and unique Saviour. (Acts 4.12) In Jesus Christ the mystery of God's reign in history is revealed. The identity of the God who reigns is now made known in Jesus Christ. In Jesus God was at work, reconciling the world. (2 Cor. 2.518-19)

The Paradigm of the Kingdom

Jesus' proclamation of the Kingdom appears to be the most comprehensive and inclusive paradigm in the whole Bible. It is multidimensional and all-embracing. It is a dynamic reality which includes history and meta-history, creation, redemption and its consummation, the personal and social, the spiritual and material, the interpersonal and the cosmic, the human and the divine. It contains many pradoxes. It is grace and freedom; the manifestation of God's mercy and judgement; it is precept and counsel; it is God's plan and can be resisted or promoted by man. A paradigm is an integrated frame of reference, a model through which we see and interpret reality and to which we relate our experience and our data from reality. When we select one dimension of the Kingdom of God paradigm, we clearly miss the other fundamental dimensions of the Christian Gospel or even the whole basis of the Gospel message. In this context it is useful to indicate three kinds of reductionism. An explicit reductionism consists in proposing the whole meaning of the Kingdom under only one dimension and interpreting other dimensions as an off-shoot of the main dimension. The implicit reductionism will be to speak about only one dimension, being silent with regard to others, implying that others do not matter to the essential core of the Kingdom. A partial reductionism would be to consider the distinct by mutually inclusive dimensions as separate without giving a comprehensive interpretation of the various aspects of the Kingdom. For example, Kingdom-centrism is inclusive of Theo-centrism and Christo-centrism; we cannot separate the Kingdom from God and Christ.

Paul Knitter, following Sobrino, a liberation theologian, states: "With the vision and praxis of the Kingdom of God as our hermeneutical lens we can 'interpret' both our own tradition and other religions differently than in the past. In Sobrino's simple statement, we will judge between true and false prophets (both within and outside Christianity) not according to a priori, ecclesial criteria, but according to whether or not they are building the Kingdom for the poor". We will judge the Eastern symbols of reincarnation and karma, the Buddhist notion of Sunyata, the Taoist ideal of wu-wei not primarily according to their congruence with doctrinal statements on after-life, God, grace, but by whether they can produce fruits of human welfare. If they do, then we are obliged, as it were, to take up their doctrinal challenge"[22]. The Kingdom of God with its demands of justice, love, equality, makes up the inclusive totality presented by the Gospels. This means that Jesus was not ecclesiocentric, or Christocentric, or even theocentric but Kingdom-centred[23]. The Kingdom of God was for Jesus first of all an earthly matter, a socio-economic reality. By involving oneself in this socio-economic task, by transforming the lot of those caught in poverty and suffering, one would experience the reality and clarify the notion of God[24]. Such a kind of Kingdom-centredness does not tally with the Biblical evidence nor with the interpretation of the Biblical texts by the Christian tradition. Knitter affirms that in such a Kingdom-centred vision, Jesus remains unique, but with a uniqueness that is re-

---

[22] PAUL KNITTER, *Dialogue and Liberation*, The Drew Gateway, 58 (1988), p. 36.
[23] Ibidem p. 34.
[24] Ibidem pp. 34-5.

lational and complementary to other unique figures[25]. This again is the pluralist interpretation of the relation between Christianity and other religions which hardly safeguards the Christian faith itself. We have already referred to the interpretation of salvation, understood as the Kingdom of God by the Liberation theology. Besides, the Kingdom serves as a hermeneutic key only if it is inclusive of the Cross in order to be able to understand the true meaning of suffering, poverty and the lot of the oppressed. This precisely is the Christian understanding of human suffering and misery, distinct from that of other religions. Once again, the Kingdom is justice, peace and joy *in the Holy Spirit* (Rom. 14.17). The Kingdom was inaugurated by Christ as sign, anticipation and foretaste; and this sign, anticipation and foretaste are continued by the Holy Spirit and the Church until Christ's second coming. Justice, peace and joy can be understood and realized only in the trinitarian perspective of the Kingdom. The Kingdom is a spiritual blessing, a link with God. It is *also* God's way of addressing our social, political, and earthly needs, of asserting his rights and his will for justice over his creation. If it is illegitimate to understand the Kingdom as a purely religious and spiritual blessing, it is also illegitimate to understand it as a purely material blessing. The Kingdom of God is a comprehensive term for the blessings of salvation.

The specific characteristics of the Christian paradigm of the Kingdom of God are to be set forth clearly in order to have a genuine theology of religions. For the theology of religions is not universal in the sense of taking a common element in all religions and trying to understand the relation between Christianity and other religions; it is the Christian understanding of other religions, starting from the Christian faith and tradition.

Religious Pluralism in the Salvific Plan of God

The Bible emphasizes history as the vehicle of revelation and the nations as the object of God's redeeming purpose in such a way that there is not to be found in any other sacred

---

[25] Ibidem p. 42.

literature of the world such a pre-occupation with history. After the first period of world prehistory as presented in the Bible, which ends with the Flood, mankind begins anew with Noah and differentiates into different families, languages and nations. (Gen. 10.5,20,31) From this arise the varieties of cultural and religious expressions which form the history of mankind. In the New Testament Jesus is described as a 'light for revelation to the nations'. (Lk 2.32) There appears a consciousness that the promise made to Abraham is now being fulfilled by Jesus and his Kingdom. Jesus gives his disciples the mission of the servant as the light and salt of the world. (Mt 5.13-14; Isa. 42.6; 49.6) The early Christians knew of the risen Christ's sending them on a mission to the nations (Mt 28.19-20; Mk 16.15; Lk 24.47; Acts 1.8) which is in line with the eschatological signs of the earthly ministry of Jesus, the Prophecies of the Deutero-Isaiah, and Sinai Covenant. The Jews rejected the light; in the providence of God the messianic blessings of salvation reaches the nations through Christ. There will be a gathering of all nations before the throne of the King (Mt 25.32) and the righteous among the nations will receive their inheritance in the Kingdom of God.

In the perspective of the Biblical protology, man is not only placed at the top of creation, radically related to God and laden with responsibilities with other men, but he is also already connected with Christ and the Spirit, and called to a communion with God. After the fall man is not left alone without the divine image and love; but is called and led to salvation by God. God draws man to himself "to seek God, and it may be, touch and find him, though indeed he is not far from each one of us, for in him we exist and move, as some of your own poets have said: We are also his offspring". (Acts 17.27-28)

The interpretative principles of the religious pluralism are to be found in man's creaturehood and his supernatural vocation to salvation. Creation illumines the origin and expressions of the religious man in all his variety and unity which are the fruit of the history of different peoples and nations. The universal salvific will of God or the Reign of God in the world in a general sense is expressed in the religion of good conscience and good will through the history of mankind.

Then comes the period of election and the Covenant in which God enacted his salvific intervention in history. God's kingly rule over the entire world that he has made is a present and abiding fact. But this rule is only effectively realized when men in word and deed accept God's sovereignty. This obligation was assumed by Israel in the covenant at Mount Sinai. Hence in the OT the doctrine of the Kingdom is closely linked with the whole ordering of the life of the Israelite nation as an expression of the people's obedience to the divine Law. The association of the Kingdom of God with a concern for moral, political, and social righteousness in the history of a particular community is fundamental to Biblical thought. But there is something more in the OT idea of the Kingdom. God's rule could only be complete when it was recognized over all the earth and fully accepted by all men. The Israelites did not see this in the world around them and their own history was full of suffering and trouble, disaster after disaster, wandering and exile, apostasy and failure. So the Kingdom came to be associated not only with an existing community but with a hope for the future. Ultimately God himself would act, and at the end of history establish his royal rule over the universe. This hope was held by Israel in many different ways; often there was the expectation of a prince visibly ruling the Kingdom of the world, of a Kingdom established in a visible way, with Israel in power and great glory; there was also a picture of the old testament of Israel as God's servant, chosen for mission and privilege with the task of proclaiming the coming Kingdom to all nations, and bearing in hope the suffering and evil of the world until the Kingdom should come.

In the NT the hope of the OT is fulfilled. Christ came and announced that the Kingdom in its full sense was at hand. He brings the Kingdom with him. Where Christ is, there is the Kingdom; and he reigns in God's name. The Kingdom he brought was very different from the earthly power that many of his contemporaries expected, for it was achieved in the very crucifixion of Jesus on the cross. By his death all the forces hostile to God's rule were deprived of any real power once and for all: his resurrection showed that death itself was no longer the final and negative answer to human existence.

The Kingdom and eternal life are one in the NT and this is the realm into which men can enter in Christ.

How does Christ's redemptive work affect human existence in history? The redemptive incarnation means an ontological view of the renewing reality in man through his transformation and deification. But this takes place by faith in Jesus Christ as Redeemer. What has happened in Jesus Christ is the beginning of the transformation and transfiguration of the whole mankind. All things, including man's socio-cultural realities, have been redeemed by Christ (Ephesians and Colossians). The work of the Holy Spirit in this salvific work can be called ontological but its action is also psychological, social and external. In other words, the Spirit who touches the soul and enlightens the mind also renews the body and in a mysterious way affects the socio-political and cultural realities. Christ exercises his redeeming work on earth through the Holy Spirit[26]. As regards man, Christ's redemptive work has ontologically affected him in as far as he is orientated towards salvation. God's call for salvation and communion with him is real and ontological so that we can place this call in the universal history of God's Kingdom. Thus the other believers are ordained to the special history of the Kingdom of God, though they are already within the general history of the Kingdom. This universal salvific work of Christ through the Holy Spirit includes victory over sin and evil powers in the world. If man responds in faith to this call of God's Kingdom he will be saved.

God is revealed in his works in creation. Man can recognize the Creator through his creation, if only he consent to recognize him. (Rom. 1.19 f) God is recognizable by man because God himself desires it. "God himself makes it plain to them". (Rom. 1.19) Paul gives a salvation history interpretation to the knowability of God. This is not a theoretical knowledge of God because it involves an obligation. Failure to realize this possibility is culpable. This is the status of other religions in the general history of the Kingdom. Again, God's voice is recognizable in the conscience of man. God

---

[26] GUSTAV THILS, *Théologie des réalités terrestres*, Desclée de Brower, Paris, 1947-9, Vol. 1, pp. 86, 159; Vol. 2, 63 ff.; 67.

reveals himself in the conscience of every man as legislator of morality. (Rom. 2.14-15) God himself did not leave himself unwitnessed as the bestower of good things (Acts 14.15-17). Men are supposed to seek God; and yet he is not far from any one of them. (Acts 17.19-33) God is patient with the Gentiles, (Rom. 3.25) John's Gospel also speaks of God bearing witness to himself in the world. "All that came to be was alive with his life, and that life was the light of men". (Jn 1.4) Life means quickening power and light is moral and spiritual illumination. In this light man sees not only the world around him; but he understands himself and his life in the world. Without this illumination, life becomes anxiety and gloom. Light is the salvific remedy to this anxiety and gloom. Life and light are not simply human possibilites but with the Logos they are the gifts of God. God's being revealed and illumined is something effected by God. "The real light which enlightens every man was even then coming into the world". (Jn 1.9)

It is in the light of this Biblical teaching that we have to understand the place of other religions in the general history of God's Kingdom. These are the salvific values of other religions that are summed up in the expressions: seeds of the Word and rays of Light; the values of truth, goodness and holiness that are found in other religious traditions. These are the values inherent in other religions by reason of creation and of the universal economy of salvation. The universal history of the Kingdom finds its point of convergence in the person of Jesus Christ, universal mediator and the centre of the eschatological recapitulation of the whole of creation. (Eph. 1.13-14; Col. 1.15-21) The whole of mankind with its spiritual and cultural and socio-economic values is ordained eschatologically to Christ so as to become in him 'new creature'. It is true that salvation and recapitulation have already happened radically; but their historical existential dimensions have not yet been realized[27].

---

[27] See PIETRO ROSSANO, *Riflessi ecumenici di Cristo secondo Col. 1.15-20*, in: *La Cristologia in San Paolo*, Atti della XXIII Settimana Biblica, Brescia, 1976, pp. 282-284.

3. The Church, Sacrament of the Kingdom

The eschatological tension, 'already but not yet' towards the full realization at the end of times is the essential characteristic of the Kingdom and becomes the inexhaustible source for the Church. The Kingdom here on earth grows not by human efforts but by itself. (Mk 4.26-9) (LG 5) The best proof that the Kingdom exists already is that it grows; but if it grows it is a sign that it does not still exist in a certain sense; i.e., not yet in its perfection[28]. The miracles are the signs that the Kingdom is already present in some way; they are veiled manifestation of the glory of Christ. The Church on earth is the germ and beginning of the Kingdom; it receives the mission of announcing and inaugurating among all the nations the Kingdom of Christ and of God. (LG 5) The Church is not the perfect Kingdom but longs for it. Neither identity nor separation but the eschatological tension between 'the already and the not yet' defines the exact relation between the Church and the Kingdom. The Church is the beginning of the Kingdom and exists at the service of it as its instrument. The People of God have as goal the Kingdom of God. (LG 9) The human cultural progress is different from the development of the Kingdom of God. (GS 39) There is a syntony between the two: such a progress is of great importance to the Kingdom of God. (GS 39) in as far as it contributes to the better ordering of human society. The specific duty of the laity is to animate with the Christian spirit the temporal order according to the will of God. Looking at the Kingdom, the ecclesial community lives in hope which overcomes the world and walks on earth but its heart, attracted by glory, already foretastes its future. The community of faith is the eschatological community. Thus the Kingdom manifests the visible and invisible character of the Church, both its historical and its eschatological dimension. (LG ch. 7) The evocation of the Church as "seed" and "beginning" of the Kingdom expresses their simultaneous unity and difference[29]. The Kingdom mysteriously present (*in mystero*) is

---

[28] See G. PHILIPS, *L'Eglise et son mystère au Vatican II*, Paris 1967, p. 97.
[29] *International Theological Commission*, 1984, Select Themes of Eschatology, Documents, Ignatius Press, San Francisco, p. 303.

hidden in the world and history, and so not yet purified of elements that are a stranger to it. As a divine-human mystery, the Church transcends the sociological configuration of the Catholic Church. Belonging to the Kingdom cannot *not be* belonging — at least implicitly — to the Church[30]. One can make use of the expression: The Church, Sacrament of the Kingdom, because the term 'sacrament' is used analogically; because the purpose of the phrase is to express the relation between the Kingdom as fully realized and the Church as pilgrim. The 'sacrament' is understood in the sense of being present already in mystery, where the reality present in the sacrament, the pilgrim Church, is the Kingdom. Finally, the Church is a sign in which the reality signified is present as the reality of the Kingdom[31].

We can understand the Church as sacrament of the Kingdom in two aspects: the Church is the sacrament of unity and hope for the human race; the Church is the universal sacrament of salvation. Both these dimensions have been outlined by the Vatian II. First, "Since the Church is in Christ like a sacrament or sign and instrument of a very intimate union with God and of the unity of the whole human race, it desires now to unfold more fully to the faithful of the Church and to the whole world its own inner nature and universal mission". (LG 1) The goal of the Church is the Kingdom of God. The messianic people, the Church, is the seed of unity, hope and salvation for the whole human race. "Established by Christ as a communion of life, charity and truth, it is also used by him as an instrument for the redemption of all and is sent forth into the whole world as the light of the world and the salt of the earth". (LG 9) We have to note that there are here two different unities: the unity of the whole human race and the unity of the people of God, which in consequence of the double mission of the Son and of the Holy Spirit is both body of Christ and temple of the Holy Spirit. There is a bond between the two in the sense that the unity of the people of God can contribute very much to the human search for peace and unity. The ontological unity of

---

[30] Ibidem.
[31] Ibidem pp. 303-4.

the human nature (*genus humanum*) is the common basis both for the quest for unity among all men and nations and for salvation of all mankind. The eschatological message of the Church is the promise of the Kingdom of God, of the restoration of all creation, of the reign of justice and peace. The Church is the messianic people because it is the community called by God to bring to the world a promise of salvation which nourishes a hope for a common human destiny[32].

Secondly, the People of God is like a sacrament of salvation offered to the World. That is to say, God wishing with antecedent will the salvation of all men, has placed in the world a cause, sufficient by itself to carry out effectively this will. In the midst of the world and for the world the Church is the sign and the sacrament of salvation offered for all men. The Church is both visible and invisible, a spiritual community of grace and a society or a visible organism. In this respect the Church resembles the incarnate Word itself whose humanity was the living instrument of salvation. In a similar way the social organism of the Church serves the Spirit of Christ which vivifies it by way of building up the body. (LG 8 and 48) The Church is the visible form which receives God's grace according to the universal salvific plan of God, as it is realized through Christ, since the sacraments are the continuation of the presence of the incarnate Word. The Church is the effective sign of God's grace in Jesus Christ.

It is in this context that we face the problem of the salvation of other believers. Y. Congar speaks about "the sacrament of the neighbour". "I was hungry and you gave me food, etc." (Mt 25.35) Every man is in a sense an encounter with Christ. In every man there is something beyond what is seen where God works and makes himself accessible. This is profoundly linked to the mystery of the incarnation[33]. Again, the gifts of light and grace outside the visible Church are admitted, but they are received in view of the Church; the other believers that are saved are ordained to the Church. But the unity of mankind, as God wants it, cannot be achieved

---

[32] See Y. CONGAR, *La Iglesia, germen de unidad e de esperanza para todo el genero umano*, Misiones Extranjeras, VIII (1966), pp. 1-14.

[33] See Y. CONGAR, *Vaste monde, ma paroisse*, Paris, 1957, pp. 38-49.

outside the Church which is its sacrament. The recognition that goodness and truth are found in other religions means that they contain partial or incomplete values of salvation. As such they can mediate not as ways of salvation but as imperfect signs of salvation by means of which their adherents in good faith and honest conscience attain salvation in Christ. In this sense they belong to the general history of the Kingdom of God; though they do not belong to the visible Church, they are saved by the grace of Christ in view of the Church which is his body. If the specific difference between the Church and other religions is eliminated, the idea of the Church as the sacrament of salvation is lost and the idea of the particular sacraments develops *intra muros*[34]. This is why we have to say that the other religions belong to the Kingdom of God inchoatively. (R.M. 20) The difference between the Church and other religions is not of degrees; i.e., more complete and less complete; they are just incomplete; there is a specific difference, not merely of degree, between the general history of salvation and the special history of salvation, though the former is orientated to the latter and finds its realization. Sometimes other religions are called cosmic sacraments or sacraments of nature. This is say that they are not signs of grace but signs of good dispositions which can evoke and desire God's mercy and love to bestow grace.

The world religions are oriented to the Kingdom of God in their partial realization of the salvific message of the Gospel and hence are ordained also to the Church which is the sacrament of the Kingdom of God. (RM 12-19) Because the risen Lord sent the Holy Spirit to the Church, the spiritual and salvific forces of the Kingdom are present in the Church and through the Church then they are bringing about divine salvation in the world. The Church is the effective sign of divine salvation; i.e., the sacrament of the Kingdom of God. The Church as the universal sacrament of salvation has a divine mission in human history. Jesus Christ is the universal and unique mediator of salvation. This mediation is exercised through the Holy Spirit. The Church as the visible social body of Christ becomes the sign of his salvific

---

[34] J.J. VON ALLMEN, *Prophétisme sacramentel*, Neuchâtel-Paris, 1964, pp. 12-35.

work in the world, since the Spirit of Christ is invisible. The Church is a sign of the invisible and effective presence of the Kingdom of God. To have a divine mission in history means that the Church is constituted as sign or sacred instrument or simply a sacrament of divine salvation[35]. The Kingdom of God is Christ himself, and Christ is the head of the Church on earth and she is his body. In the outward, visible signs of the Church the reign of Christ is actually present here and now. The sacramentality of the Church is analogous to the redemptive incarnation. We really and actually encounter God in the man Jesus. Similarly we encounter Christ in the visible Church. Thus the Kingdom of God comes to us through the sign of the Church, for in it the manifestation of the Kingdom has already begun.

The followers of other religions, so long as it is their intention to do the will of God, then they too participate in salvation. The absoluteness of Christianity does not mean the possession of all truths nor 'the totalitarian levelling and inexorable imposition' (Paul VI) nor the negation of the values inherent in other religions by reason of the creation and of the universal economy of salvation. Positively it means that God intervened in history and manifested and realized his salvific will in the special history of salvation through Christ and his Church.

Conclusion

God made himself present in Christ in order to establish his Kingdom on earth. Christ not only preached but also established the Kingdom of God by his ministry, death and resurrection. The Kingdom of God is a state of things in the world in which God who is personalized Truth and Love, Holiness and Justice, rules and humanity as a result is transformed and saved, when it responds in faith and love to his reign. The Church is not identical with the Kingdom but is the instrument, instituted by Christ for the construction of the Kingdom through its preaching and administration of

---

[35] GERARD J. BEKES, *The Church: Sacrament of the Kingdom of God, The Dunwoodie Review*, 16 (1992-3), pp. 61-68.

sacraments. The reign of God is grace and glory, the whole epic of salvation, God uniting with humanity in mutual love and with eternal love. World religions in as far as they belong to the general history of the Kingdom of God which is the universal history of salvation, they contain salvific values which are objectively partial and incomplete in relation to the special salvation history by the mediation of Christ and his Church. These imperfect and partial salvific values can mediate for their followers of good faith and sincere heart to obtain God's grace and salvation. Not all values of the Kingdom are found in world religions. What they do possess tend to their fulfilment in Jesus Christ who is the truth, the life and the way to salvation.

In this context we can cite a passage from the FABC Theological Consultation Conclusions: "The Kingdom of God is universally present and at work. Wherever men and women open themselves to the transcendent divine mystery which impinges upon them and go out of themselves in love and service of fellow humans, there the reign of God is at work... In all such cases people respond to God's offer of grace through Christ in the Spirit and enter into the Kingdom through an act of faith... Thus they become sharers of the Kingdom of God unknowingly... A 'regno-centric' approach to mission theology does not in any way threaten the Christo-centric perspective of our faith; on the contrary 'regno-centrism' calls for 'Christo-centrism' and vice versa, for it is in Jesus Christ and through the Christ-event that God has established his Kingdom upon the earth and in human history. (Cfr RM 17-18)"[36]

---

[36] *Evangelization in Asia, Catholic International*, Vol. 3, n. 5.

The Kingdom of God in Monastic Interreligious Dialogue

JAMES A. WISEMAN

INTRODUCTION

The Kingdom

It is obvious that the two realities referred to in the title of this article could each be the subject of lengthy monographs, as indeed they have been[1]. All that is possible at the beginning of this short paper is a relatively brief definition of terms. Even the word *definition* is hardly appropriate in reference to the Kingdom of God, for the Kingdom is primarily a metaphor and, as such, resists all attempts at hard-and-fast definitions[2]. Frequent in the synoptic Gospels but quite rare in the Fourth Gospel, for our present purposes the Kingdom may best be described by a verse from St. Paul. Writing to the Romans, the Apostle affirms that "the Kingdom of God does not mean food and drink but righteousness and peace and joy in the Holy Spirit" (Rom 14:17). *Wherever* these and similar realities are found, *there* is the inbreaking of the Kingdom. But since these realities are by no means as prevalent in human society as one could wish, it must at once be added that there is a tension between the historical and eschatological aspects of the King-

---

[1] See, e.g., BRUCE CHILTON, *The Kingdom of God in the Teaching of Jesus* (Philadelphia: Fortress, 1984); GILBERT HARDY, *Monastic Quest and Interreligious Dialogue* (New York: Peter Lang, 1990).

[2] In fact, many contemporary scholars prefer the terminology "Reign of God" to that of "Kingdom," since the latter term can imply something more static than the dynamic reality referred to in the Bible by the Hebrew *malkut* or the Greek *basileia*. In this article, however, the more traditional English term will be used.

dom, between the "now" and the "not yet": the Kingdom is indeed already breaking in[3], but it is so far from being fully present that we constantly pray for its fullness every time we utter the second petition of the Lord's Prayer: "Thy Kingdom come".

Moreover, since the realities referred to by St. Paul in Romans are not confined within the boundaries of the Church as such, we should refrain from simply identifying Church and Kingdom, though this has at times been done in the past[4]. When such an identification has prevailed, there has followed an almost inevitable tendency to label members of other religious traditions simply as "pagans, idolaters, and unbelievers", whose prospects for salvation are minimal if not non-existent. This conviction inspired many of our most courageous and saintly missionaries to leave their native lands, as was notably the case with Blessed Marie of the Incarnation as she described her arrival in New France (Canada) in the mid-seventeenth century:

> We met numbers of savages along the shore, which gave us great joy. These poor people who had never seen anyone like us were filled with awe. And when they were told that we were the daughters of a chief who, out of love for them, had left our own country, our relatives, and all our comforts, and still more that we had come to teach their daughters so that they would not burn in [eternal] fire but would be instructed in what they must do to be happy forever — at this their astonishment knew no bounds[5].

Similarly, the nineteenth-century Swiss missionary Anastasius Hartmann, who later became bishop of Bombay,

---

[3] See, e.g., Lk 11:20: "If it is by the finger of God that I cast out demons, then the kingdom of God has come upon you." (Cf. Mt 12:28).

[4] See , e.g., ST. AUGUSTINE, *The City of God* 20.9: "...where both classes exist [i.e., those who keep God's commandments and those who do not], it [i.e., the Kingdom] is the Church as it now is, but where only the one [class] shall exist, it is the Church as it is destined to be when no wicked person shall be in her. Therefore the Church even now is the kingdom of Christ, and the kingdom of heaven" ("Ergo Ecclesia et nunc est regnum Christi, regnumque coelorum").

[5] *The Relation of 1654* 11.48, in *Marie of the Incarnation: Selected Writings*, ed. IRENE MAHONEY, O.S.U. (New York: Paulist, 1989), 135.

explained his departure for India in his leave-taking sermon with the words: "God is calling me from the fatherland to a land beyond the sea, ...among savage peoples who sit in darkness and in the shadow of death... If I leave you, it is for this reason alone: to snatch them from eternal destruction... and thus to save their souls"[6]. The heroism of missionaries like Marie of the Incarnation and Bishop Hartmann is beyond question and remains an inspiration for their successors today, but their particular motivation of saving non-Christians from almost certain damnation is nowadays scarcely to be found. Rather, in the well-known language of Vatican II's *Declaration on the Relation of the Church to Non-Christian Religions*, the Church "rejects nothing of what is true and holy" in other world religions and urges its members to "preserve and encourage the spiritual and moral truths found among non-Christians"[7].

At least part of the background for this more positive understanding of other religions is likely due to exegetical research by scholars like Rudolf Schnackenburg, whose study *God's Rule and Kingdom*[8] broke definitively with the earlier, common identification of the Church with the Kingdom on earth. In the same line, Pope John Paul II's encyclical *Redemptoris Missio* (1991), while explicitly keeping Church and Kingdom closely related to each other, may be regarded as the first document of the Roman magisterium to distinguish clearly between the two[9]. This opens up the way to affirm that something of the Kingdom's reality is to be found among persons adhering to other religious traditions, as Pope John Paul himself proceeded to do in the same encyclical when he wrote that "the inchoate reality of the kingdom can also be found beyond the confines of the church

---

[6] Quoted by WALBERT BÜHLMANN, *The Chosen Peoples* (London, 1982), 106.

[7] *Nostra Aetate*, n. 2.

[8] *Gottes Herrschaft und Reich* (Freiburg: Herder, 1959); English trans. by JOHN MURRAY: *God's Rule and Kingdom* (New York: Herder and Herder, 1963).

[9] See especially n. 18: "It is true that the church is not an end unto herself, since she is ordered toward the kingdom of God of which she is the seed, sign and instrument. Yet while remaining distinct from Christ and the kingdom, the church is indissolubly united to both". See, too, the comments on this encyclical in Jacques Dupuis, "The Church, the Reign of God, and the 'Others'", *Pro Dialogo* 84-85 (1994): 120.

among peoples everywhere to the extent that they live 'Gospel values' and are open to the working of the Spirit, who breathes when and where he wills (cf. Jn 3:8)"[10]. In large measure it is the conviction that these "Gospel values" and the working of the Holy Spirit may be found among all peoples — and found among them not simply in spite of their religions but as nurtured by positive elements within these religions themselves — that interreligious dialogue has been taking an increasingly prominent role in the Church since the Second Vatican Council. This is so much the case that Pope John Paul II has even said that engagement in such dialogue in one form or another is incumbent upon *every* member of the Church[11].

Monastic Interreligious Dialoque

Among the groups in the Church that have been singled out for a particularly intense involvement in such dialogue are the monastic orders. The charter statement of their involvement is regularly taken to be a 1974 letter from Sergio Cardinal Pignedoli, then president of the Vatican's Secretariat for Non-Christians, to Dom Rembert Weakland, who was at that time Abbot Primate of the Benedictine Confederation. The cardinal affirmed that

> the experience of our Secretariat in the dialogue with non-Christian religions... reminds us of the primary role that monasticism plays in the meeting with non-Christian religions, particularly those of Asia. Historically, the monk has always been the most typical example of the 'homo religiosus,' and as such he represents a point of

---

[10] *Redemptoris Missio*, 20. A very similar affirmation may be found in "Dialogue and Proclamation", jointly published in 1991 by the Pontifical Council for Interreligious Dialogue (PCID) and the Congregation for the Evangelization of Peoples. The text may be found in the PCID *Bulletin* 77 (1991): 210-50; see esp. n. 35.

[11] See, for example, his radio message to the peoples of Asia (Feb. 21, 1981), printed in *l'Osservatore Romano* (March 2, 1981): "All Christians must therefore be committed to dialogue with the believers of all religions, so that mutual understanding and collaboration may grow; so that moral values may be strengthened; so that God may be praised in all creation. Ways must be developed to make this dialogue become a reality everywhere, but especially in Asia, the continent that is the cradle of ancient cultures and religions" (n. 5).

contact and mutual understanding between Christians and non-Christians... If we were to present ourselves to Buddhism or to Hinduism, not to mention other religions, without the monastic religious experience, we should scarcely be credible as religious men[12].

Cardinal Pignedoli went on to note various ways in which monastics had already been involved in dialogue and expressed his "hope and encouragement that this work will be continued and developed still further". In response to that request, special divisions or boards were set up within the organization Aide Inter-Monastères (A.I.M.) in order to promote interreligious dialogue. At first these boards existed only in Europe and North America, but others have more recently been formed in Australia and India, with all four groups (and any future ones) now coming under a secretariat of their own rather than under the auspices of A.I.M. (which had been founded for the quite different purpose of supporting and nurturing monastic foundations in the young Churches). The North American board, which is known as Monastic Interreligous Dialogue and with whose work I am most familiar, has as its main purpose the fostering of involvement by North American Benedictine and Cistercian monastics, both men and women, in the encounter between Christianity and other world religions. Among the ways M.I.D. pursues this purpose are the publication of a thrice-yearly bulletin, the holding of national or regional conferences for the purpose of educating representatives ("contact persons") from individual monasteries in the practice of interreligious dialogue, the extending of hospitality and educational opportunities to monastics of other religions, and the organizing of actual dialogues with members of other religious traditions. For various and even somewhat coincidental reasons, the encounters promoted by M.I.D. in the past fifteen years have been mainly with Tibetan Buddhists, whereas those sponsored by the parallel group in Europe, Dialogue Interre-

---

[12] Quoted by ABBOT VIKTOR DAMMERTZ, O.S.B., "Opening Address by the Abbot Primate of the Benedictine Confederation [to the Asian Benedictine Conference at Sri Lanka]", *A.I.M. Bulletin* 29 (1980): 25.

ligieux Monastique, have been mostly with Zen Buddhists. However, overtures to Hindus, Muslims, and others have not been neglected and may well assume a more prominent position in the future.

The Gethsemani Encounter

In order to give a particular focus to the rest of this article and to permit a modicum of detailed commentary, the topic of "the Kingdom of God in monastic interreligious dialogue" will now be developed with special reference to a remarkable week-long encounter that took place in the summer of 1996 at the Abbey of Gethsemani in rural Nelson County, Kentucky. This meeting was orginally suggested by His Holiness the Dalai Lama at the Parliament of the World's Religions, held in Chicago in the late summer of 1993. The immediate occasion for his suggestion was a dialogue between Christians and Buddhists held in a large hall one morning near the end of the parliament, at which the Dalai Lama made a brief presentation. He felt that a similar dialogue, but lasting over a period of many days, would be most worthwhile; he further expressed the hope that it might take place at the Abbey of Gethsemani, where his friend Thomas Merton had been a monk for twenty-seven years before his death in 1968.

After all the detailed negotating and planning that lie behind any major conference had been carried out, the so-called Gethsemani Encounter opened on the evening of Monday, July 22, 1996, with approximately fifty active participants: twenty-five Buddhists, many of them being monks or nuns from Asian countries but with others representing Buddhist centers in the United States, and twenty-five Christians, most of them monastics in either the Benedictine or the Cistercian order. In addition, there were approximately sixty observers in attendance, many of them "contact persons" from American monasteries, together with some monks from the Gethsemani community and a few journalists. The complete text of all the talks that were given and extensive excerpts from the dialogue that followed each talk will soon be available in a book to be published by the Continuum Publishing Company of New York[13]. Rather than attempt to summarize the content of the papers and dialogue, I will instead show how certain traditional aspects of the Kingdom were present and fostered during this historic meeting.

Peace as a Sign of the Kingdom

Peace is one of the marks of the Kingdom that is noted by St. Paul in the fourteenth chapter of Romans and is surely associated with the Kingdom in the minds of many people today. There is no need to dwell upon the fact that relations between various religions have at times been anything but peaceful, so-called "wars of religion" being among the most vicious in recorded history. The Gethsemani Encounter, on the other hand, was a powerful reminder that persons of very different religious persuasions can live together most peacefully — and not at all at the price of watering down their respective beliefs. One reason for this is that a fundamental principle for fruitful interreligious dialogue was understood and adhered to by all: that we were together for the purpose of trying to present our own understandings of such realities as meditation, spiritual growth, discipleship, and personal and societal transformation as clearly and honestly as possible (and on the basis of our own *experience* of these realities), without in any way being in competition with other viewpoints or approaches. The participants worked intently at trying to understand one another, asked deep and probing questions in the trustful expectation that they would get honest responses, and were not embarrassed about admitting at times that they did not immediately have an adequate response to a particular question. All of this promoted a genuine spirit of peace and friendship that perdured throughout the week.

Seeing a spirit of peace strikingly modeled in the behavior of some of the participants was as important as the words they spoke. At one point a Buddhist speaker expressed a

---

[13] The book, co-edited by Professor Donald Mitchell of Purdue University and myself, will be entitled *The Gethsemani Encounter* and is scheduled for publication in September 1997.

clear and somewhat forceful disagreement with an interpretation of Buddhist doctrine that the Dalai Lama had himself brought up in an earlier presentation. This could have led to some sharp and acrimonious exchanges, for it was clear that one of the Dalai Lama's disciples was ready to get up and defend his master's interpretation. A few of us noticed, however, that the Dalai Lama unobtrusively gestured to him to "hold his peace" — the point at issue was not that important and could well have diverted attention from the topic at hand. Such behavior, noticed by only a very few of those in attendance, said as much about this man of peace as his many public addresses on the subject.

Similarly, the encounter was fortunate to have in attendance Maha Ghosananda, the patriarch of the Cambodian Buddhists and a man who has done much to help his devastated country return to a more humane way of life. Maha Ghosananda is a man of few words, but more than one observer remarked that simply seeing his peaceful, unforgettably radiant countenance was a lesson in itself. When he did speak, his talk concluded with words that significantly (and no doubt unintentionally) paralleled St. Paul's teaching about ourselves being "the temple of the living God" (2 Cor 6:16). Commenting on the fact that many of his fellow Cambodians feel that Maha Ghosananda and his disciples should not take an active role in working for peace and justice in their country but should instead remain permanently in their monasteries and temples, the patriarch concluded: "It is difficult for them to adjust to this new role, but we monks must answer the increasingly loud cries of suffering. We only need to remember that our temple is with us always. We *are* our temple"[14].

Some minutes later, in response to a request from a participant who was aware that walking meditation is a central practice in Ghosananda's tradition of Theravada Buddhism, the monk led everyone present in a slow, meditative walk from the abbey's chapter room out to the monastic cemetery, where he finally stopped in silent prayer before Thomas Merton's grave. It was evident from the faces of the partici-

---

[14] MAHA GHOSANANDA, "The Human Family", *Bulletin of Monastic Interreligious Dialogue* #56 (Fall 1996): 13.

pants that this was one of the most moving events of the entire week, unquestionably for many a sign that what Pope John Paul called "the inchoate reality of the Kingdom" will indeed be manifested beyond the confines of the Church to the extent that a person is "open to the working of the Spirit, who breathes when and where he wills".

Prayer as Fostering the Coming of the Kingdom

At the conclusion of his insightful article on the relationship of the reign of God to those who are not Christians, Jacques Dupuis, S.J., observes that one of the ways in which all peoples on earth can foster this reign is "by promoting religious and spiritual values"[15]. In one sense, this was done through every aspect of the Gethsemani Encounter, but it was especially evident in the fact that the meeting did not consist simply in listening to papers being read and engaging in dialogue about such material in the chapter room. The first scheduled event each morning, held in a quiet chapel located near the main entrance to the abbey church, was a period of silent prayer and meditation. A number of participants remarked on the final day that these early morning sessions were the most important part of the week for them, for these periods manifested more clearly than anything else that the participants were relying not on themselves but on Someone/Something more ultimate than themselves for nurturance, guidance, and support. As Pope John Paul said in his opening address at the historic World Day of Peace that was held at Assisi on October 27, 1986, "Religions are many and varied, and they reflect the desire of men and women down through the ages to enter into a relationship with the Absolute Being. Prayer entails conversion of heart on our part. It means deepening our sense of the ultimate Reality. This is the very reason for our coming together in this place"[16]. The pope's words are equally apt for expressing a major reason why many persons came together at Gethsemani and why

---

[15] "The Church, the Reign of God, and the 'Others'", 130.
[16] "Pope's Opening Address in the Basilica of Santa Maria degli Angeli", *Bulletin. Secretariatus pro Non-Christianis* 64 (1987): 30.

the first series of papers after the introductory talks on the opening night were on the subject of "The Practice of Prayer and Meditation in the Spiritual Life". Later in the course of each day there were further opportunities for sharing in prayer, an exercise which is sometimes called "the dialogue of spiritual experience" or "dialogue of the heart". Excessive wordiness was avoided by having some of the most common religious symbols figure prominently in the rituals: water, fire, flowers, incense, processions.

Without anyone having to verbalize the fact, all of this inculcated in the participants an awareness that in our respective spiritual traditions we are as much acted upon as acting, and that our very acting will in the long run be fruitless and counterproductive unless it proceeds from an awareness of a far greater Reality sustaining us. One of the speakers, Sr. Mary Margaret Funk, O.S.B., concluded her talk on *lectio divina* by referring to a brief conversation she once had with an elderly sister at her convent: "Once I was walking behind Sister Mary Robert going to Communion. She was 84. I told her that I hoped that when I was 84, I could walk with such poise and grace. She told me, 'You will, when you know that you are walking in the presence of God".' This kind of awareness, understood by Christians as awareness of God and by (some) Buddhists as awareness of their original Buddha nature, deepened each time the group came together for the practice of common meditation and was, in part, reflected in the respect and even reverence shown for one another throughout the encounter. One Christian participant said that he did not fully understand what Buddhists mean by Nirvana but that during one of the evening sessions he sensed that it must be akin to the state of the entire assembly at that point. More certainly, he might have said that it savored of the Kingdom for which Jesus taught his followers to pray and for which the Christians present were surely praying during the entire encounter.

Concern for the World as Building Up the Kingdom

A common criticism of some earlier understandings of the Kingdom is that they were too individualistic, with little or no attention being given to the communal dimension[17]. Similarly, a stereotypical view of monasticism sees it as severely cut off from the concerns of the world outside the monastery. These latter concerns, however, were very much on the minds of those who took part in the Gethsemani Encounter. Maha Ghosananda has already been quoted as saying that in his country the monks now generally understand that they may not simply remain inside their religious edifices, since "we *are* our temple". His sense of being called to promote the values of peace and justice in the larger world was shared by the others present at Gethsemani. Thus, the Dalai Lama remarked that he has learned much from observing the way Christians have worked for the good of those suffering from hunger, disease, lack of education, and other factors that keep people from living fully human lives. He added, as he has often done in other addresses, that he wants his own followers to learn from this example and to work with Christians to promote equality, justice, and social harmony in all parts of the world.

From the Christian side, the most direct call for such cooperation, among monastics in particular, was made by Professor Ewert Cousins of Fordham University. His paper "Building the Reign of God", called for

> a vision and a prophetic voice, ...a vision of an organically interrelated global community that is spiritual at its core and at the same time grounded in the natural world and the cosmos. This is what Benedictine and Cistercian monasticism has provided for centuries through its cultivation of contemplation and literally through its cultivation of the land, and through the cosmic symbols of its liturgy, which harmonize the community with the cycles of nature[18].

---

[17] See, e.g., BENEDICT VIVIANO, O.P., *The Kingdom of God in History* (Wilmington, DE: Michael Glazier, 1988). At one point Viviano criticizes Adolf Harnack's description of the Kingdom as being a "purely religious blessing, the inner link with the living God". Viviano admits that the Kingdom is, of course, a religious blessing, but he goes on to insist that "it is also God's way of addressing our social, political, earthly needs, of asserting his rights and his will for justice over his creation. A purely private, withdrawn spirituality is not a kingdom spirituality" (27).

[18] EWERT COUSINS, "Building the Reign of God", *Bulletin of Monastic Interreligious Dialogue* #56 (Fall 1996): 17.

Cousins concluded with the comment that the ongoing monastic interreligious dialogue between Christians and Buddhists that has developed in recent decades "may be the best example of the emerging global spiritual community with its accompanying dialogic consciousness"[19].

One of the great challenges confronting those who want to promote this "emerging global spiritual community" is that of how to deal with violence. The Dalai Lama's refusal to respond with hatred or violence to the Chinese persecution of Tibetan Buddhism is well-known, especially since his being honored with the Nobel Peace Prize in 1989. Somewhat less well-known is the way that Maha Ghosananda, over the objections of some of his own followers, helped build a temple for the Khmer Rouge at the Thai-Cambodian border in 1981. In responding to those who confronted him over his decision to help, he reminded them "that love embraces all beings, whether they are noble-minded or low-minded, good or evil... The unwholesome-minded must be included because they are the ones who need loving-kindness the most. In many of them, the seed of goodness may have died because warmth was lacking for its growth. It perished from coldness in a world without compassion"[20].

From the Christian side, a similar attitude toward persecutors was evident in remarks made about the seven Trappist monks of Our Lady of Atlas monastery in Algeria who had been murdered by the Armed Islamic Group (G.I.A.) several months earlier. Fr. Armand de Veilleux read moving excerpts from the testament of the superior of that community, Dom Christian de Chergé, written on the day that threats were first made against the monks but not opened and made public until after his violent death. The spirit of gratitude and forgiveness which permeated the testament appeared most powerfully in Dom Christian's final lines, addressed to his still-unknown murderer: "And you too, my last-minute friend, who will not know what you are doing, yes, for you too I say this THANK YOU AND THIS 'A-DIEU' - to commend you to this God

---

[19] Ibid.
[20] MAHA GHOSANANDA, "The Human Family", 12.

in whose face I see yours"[21]. This spirit of forgiveness was echoed at the Gethsemani Encounter by the extemporaneous remarks of Dom Bernardo Olivera, the Trappist Abbot General, who said that a desire to forgive welled up in his heart from the moment he first learned of the fate of the monks of Atlas. It was clear that his sentiments reflected not only Jesus' command to "love your enemies and pray for those who persecute you" (Mt 5:44) but also the teaching of the opening chapter of the Buddhist *Dhammapada*, whose "twin verses" include the line: "Hatred does not cease by hatred at any time; hatred ceases by love — this is an old rule". Those who came to the Gethsemani Encounter already committed to this way of life surely left with their commitment strengthened by the witness to the power of forgiveness, love, and compassion given by these and other speakers. In Christian terminology, the things said again and again in the chapter room unquestionably contributed to the building up of what some have called "God's peaceable Kingdom".

Conclusion:
Dialogue and the Proclamation of the Kingdom

An unprejudiced reading of the Gospels reveals the closest of ties between the Kingdom itself and the proclamation of it, whether by Jesus himself ("I must preach the good news of the kingdom of God to the other cities also, for I was sent for this purpose" [Lk 4:42]) or by those who wished to follow him ("Leave the dead to bury their own dead, but as for you, go and proclaim the kingdom of God" [Lk 9:60]). This clear dominical mandate has led some Christians to be suspicious of dialogue as being a way of avoiding the supposedly more demanding and Gospel-centered call to proclamation, or at least to wonder how dialogue relates to proclamation. It was with a view to resolving such problems or queries that the earlier-mentioned document "Dialogue and Proclamation"[22] was jointly issued by two units of the Roman Curia in

---

[21] "Testament of Dom Christian de Chergé, O.C.S.O.", *Bulletin of Monastic Interreligious Dialogue* #55 (Spring 1996): 22.
[22] See note 10.

1991. In concluding the present article, I wish to highlight certain key points from that document and then comment on them in the light of the Gethsemani Encounter.

"Dialogue and Proclamation" begins with an expansive understanding of "evangelization". Although the latter term does indeed have a narrow meaning, "namely, the clear and unambiguous proclamation of the Lord Jesus", the document points out that evangelization may also properly be understood in a broader sense to signify the mission of the Church in its entirety, which is "to bring the Good News into all areas of humanity, and through its impact to transform that humanity from within, making it new" (n. 8, quoting Pope Paul VI's *Evangelii Nuntiandi*). Dialogue is then described as belonging to this total ecclesial mission, for it includes "all positive and constructive interreligious relations with individuals and communities of other faiths which are directed at mutual understanding and enrichment" (n. 9). Proclamation, on the other hand, is defined as "the communication of the Gospel message... [and] an invitation to a commitment of faith in Jesus Christ and to entry through baptism into the community of believers which is the church" (n. 10). The concluding part of the document states that while all Christians are called to be involved in both of these ways of carrying out the one mission of the Church, they must bear in mind that dialogue can never simply replace proclamation but remains oriented toward it, for it is in proclamation that the Church's evangelizing mission reaches "its climax and its fullness" (n. 82).

This distinction between dialogue and proclamation was certainly understood and observed by all participants at the Gethsemani Encounter, where "the mutual understanding and enrichment" that come about through dialogue were what was sought by everyone present. Nevertheless, it should be noted that distinctions that seem quite precise in official documents often cannot be found quite so neatly in real life. Without in any way intending "proclamation", many of the Christian speakers expressed their personal love for Jesus Christ in so natural and spontaneous a way that one of the Buddhists remarked that if he had such love for Jesus, he would definitely become a Christian. From that reaction, one might well conclude that the Christian participants were often following the Gospel charge to "go into the whole world and proclaim the gospel to every creature" (Mk 16:15) without consciously intending to do so. In the circumstances, such proclamation was perhaps all the more impressive because of its unintentional nature. I do not expect that any Buddhist will become a Christian as a result of the Gethsemani Encounter, nor any Christian a Buddhist. There are, however, many reasons to conclude that this meeting was genuinely historic, bringing dialogue between these two great religious traditions to a new level or depth heretofore unrealized. The growth in understanding, friendship, and commitment to work for a more peaceful and just world that occurred during that week were certainly what Christians may properly call "working on behalf of the Kingdom". If other groups and organizations learn from the model of dialogue that was practiced at Gethsemani, then the long-term good resulting from the encounter could be very significant indeed.

The Kingdom of God in Latin American Liberation Theology

JOHN FUELLENBACH

"Nowhere is the pathos of liberation so trenchant as in the discourse on the Kingdom of God", wrote Claus Bussman". And in order to prove his findings he lists 20 quotes referring to the Kingdom of God taken from eleven liberation theologians. This shows how much the theme Kingdom of God is referred to in Liberation Theology[1]. The discovery of the Kingdom of God as Jesus' central concern is relatively recent. It can be dated within the last hundred years. Three different approaches to the Kingdom of God can be outlined which have been taken by scholars. These approaches are: Kingdom as *concept, symbol* and *liberation*.

The first one, the *Kingdom as concept* can be described as *author-centered*. Its question is: What did the authors of the Bible mean by this concept? To treat the Kingdom as concept means to assume that it leads to one clear and consistent idea. For example, the Kingdom of God is the final, eschatological and decisive intervention of God in the history of Israel in order to fulfill the promises made to the prophets. The concern was to find out what the phrase meant in the teaching of Jesus, although Jesus himself never defined the Kingdom with specific concepts.

The second approach insists on treating the phrase "Kingdom of God" as a *symbol* rather than a concept. Kingdom as a concept is regarded as too narrow and misleading. The idea of seeing the Kingdom as a symbol evokes a whole series of ideas since a symbol, by its definition, presents or

---

[1] C. BUSSMAN, *Who Do You Say*, pp. 130; 130-141.

elicits a whole range of concepts[2]. This second approach can be described as *text-centered*. Its question is: What does the text itself mean and what does it say today?

The third approach is undertaken in Latin America. The Liberation Theologians treat the phrase "Kingdom of God" neither as concept nor as symbol, but as a referent for historical liberation. In such a context the term yields a different understanding. At issue is the world-transforming dimension of the Kingdom. This approach can be described as *reader-centered*. Its question is: What does the phrase "Kingdom of God" have to say to the concrete situation of utter oppression and exploitation in which we now find ourselves? The intention of this theology is to recover the historical dimension of God's message and to move that message away from all abstract universalism so that the biblical message may be more responsive to the world of oppression and its social structures[3].

It might be worth noting how these three approaches are even linked to geographical areas. The discussion in terms of the first focus, the Kingdom as concept, was carried out largely in Europe (especially Germany and Britain); the second, the Kingdom as symbol, in North America; and the third, the Kingdom as liberation, emerged from Latin America The first approach tries to get *behind the text*, the second stays *with the text*, and the third stands *before the text* asking particular questions that arise out of the situation of oppression and dependence.

THE HERMENEUTICAL KEY TO THE KINGDOM ACCORDING TO LIBERATION THEOLOGY

Liberation Theology claims that the most adequate understanding of the Kingdom of God can be reached by focusing on liberation. In order to understand this claim it is necessary to grasp the frame of reference in which Liberation theologians theologize. This context, according to Liberation theologians, has grown due to the developments of

---

[2] N. PERRIN, *Jesus and the Language of the Kingdom*, 1975.
[3] A. PERNIA, *God's Kingdom and Human Liberation*, pp. 21-28.

the last 200 years regarding humankind's self-understanding and its role in history. A new historical situation and a new human self-understanding call for a re-thinking, they would say, of how the Bible should be read. This new historical situation has been brought about by two simultaneous and mutually dependent historical events that coincide with a new intellectual consciousness known as the Enlightenment. The first is the industrial revolution, which reveals humanity's capability of transforming nature. The second is the French revolution which in its turn demonstrated humankind's potential for transforming the social order. What, therefore, characterizes this new self-understanding is the human person's awareness of his capacity to transform both nature and the social order, and thus his active role in the transformation of history.

This self-understanding entails, above all, a new way of being a human person in history; whereby, men and women are more in command of themselves and their destiny in history. But this also implies a new way of being a Christian in the world and of living the faith in society. It demands that the Christian lives the faith in the context of the contemporary consciousness of the person being an active subject in the transformation of history. Persons will be fulfilled only in the measure that they actively participate in forging their own destinies.

From here a very different view of human history emerges. The Christian understanding of history is seen as an alliance between God and humanity. It is history between two partners, God and human beings. God is the master of history but humankind is another actor in the historical drama[4].

The hermeneutical approach proper

Liberation Theology joins the general disenchantment of contemporary theology with a purely historical-critical approach to interpreting the Bible, a disenchantment expressed in the search for alternative models of interpretation.

---

[4] R. COSTE, *Marxist Analysis and Christian Faith*, p. 72.

Historical criticism is concerned only with the "AUTHOR meaning" of the text, that is, with what the original author intended to say. This is understood as an objective entity existing independently of the concerns of the interpreter. The content is culturally neutral, universally valid and permanently relevant.

However the real question is: How do we discover the meaning of the text today? How does the text disclose itself to us in our time? The question is not so much what the text MEANT in the past, but what it MEANS now. In terms of Liberation Theology the question may be posed as follows: How can we discover the historical dimension of God's message and move that message away from all abstract universalism so that the biblical message may be "more responsive to the geography of hunger, the culture of violence, the language of the voiceless masses, the world of oppression, and the structure of an unjust social order"[5].

The proposed solution

Severio Croatto situates hermeneutics in the context of semeiotics, the science of signs, of which language, in the narrow sense, is the most comprehensive expression. Language, and therefore any text, contains a richness of meanings that cannot be reduced to only one. There is what could be called a surplus of meaning. A closure of meanings occurs through a particular linguistic performance when one meaning is selected from the many potential meanings by the original author and his addressees. Once that author dies and his addressees disappear the closure of meaning comes to an end and is converted into an openness of meanings available to any reader in another context. Therefore, to read a text leads not just to a rediscovery of the original meaning, but also to the production of meaning out of the reservoir of meaning implied in the text. As Croatto sees it, the text has not only a context-backward sense in the original historical context of the first closure meaning, but also a context-forward sense from which the text can be read so as to produce new mean-

---

[5] R. VIDALES, "Methodological Issues in Liberation Theology", p. 49.

ings. This does not mean the imposition of an alien meaning on the text because the meaning that is produced is potentially contained in the text's reservoir of meaning. The text itself remains normative[6]. Sandra Schneiders suggests an analogy. The reading of a text from a given context-forward is like a contemporary artist's creative rendition of a classical musical score which, while producing a new interpretation that goes beyond the intentions of the composer, nevertheless must remain faithful to the score itself[7].

By remaining faithful to the score, Liberation Theology regards its context-forward perspective as privileged because the Bible's own origin is marked by a profound liberation experience. Liberation hermeneutics appears to be more faithful to the biblical text and exhibits a closer harmony with the kerygmatic nucleus of the Bible. Liberation theologians are aware that this is a biased reading of the Bible but all seem to agree that no one can read the Bible in a purely neutral and impartial way. Every reader approaches the Bible from a definite context-forward perspective which expresses a particular way in which he or she conceives of reality and correspondingly acts. It can, therefore, be said that understanding the Bible is no longer a matter of seeking a bias-free reading but of opting for the bias appropriate for the right reading of the Bible.

The hermeneutics of Liberation Theology is quite simply the reading of the Bible from the perspective of the poor and oppressed, from the perspective of those who are persecuted in the cause of right, from the perspective of the condemned of the earth — for theirs is the Kingdom of Heaven[8]. Liberation Theology, however, does not regard its hermeneutics as one alongside other possible ways of reading the Bible. It claims, that it is the only way the Bible ought to be read, if it is to be read correctly at all. It is the hermeneutical key that unlocks the real meaning of the Bible.

---

[6] J.S. CROATTO, "Biblical Hermeneutics in the Theology of Liberation", pp. 140-167.

[7] S. SCHNEIDERS, "Faith, Hermeneutics and the Literal Sense of Scripture", p. 734.

[8] G. GUTIERREZ, *The Power of the Poor in History*, p. 4.

It is from this perspective that the appeal of Liberation theologians to the biblical theme of the Kingdom of God must be understood. Leonardo Boff, for example, suggests that "the Kingdom of God implies a revolution of the human world". Segundo insists that events of liberation in history stand in causal relationship to the Kingdom of God. In conclusion, we can say that the focus on the Kingdom of God as Liberation raises different questions than the other two ways of considering the Kingdom. For Liberation Theology the nucleus of attention is the world-transforming dimension of the Kingdom of God[9].

If we look at the content of the Kingdom of God which is definitely biblical in its origin, we have to admit that the interpretation of this phrase always operates from a pre-understanding that is not directly deduced from the Bible itself. Gutierrez defines the Kingdom of God as the fulfillment of the human beings' vocation to become God's children and one another's brothers and sisters. Boff conceives the Kingdom as the realization of humanity's fundamental utopian longing for a new world freed from all evil and fully tamed with love. Segundo sees the Kingdom as the "humanizing God" and the "full humanization of human beings". These pre-understandings cannot be claimed to be taken directly from the Bible itself.

THE PRE-PASCHAL JESUS AND THE RISEN CHRIST IN RELATION TO THE KINGDOM OF GOD IN LIBERATION THEOLOGY

Liberation theologians like to point out that "Jesus was not the absolute for himself". The absolute for Jesus was the Kingdom of God[10]. The appeal to the Kingdom of God centers on two biblical data: the historical or pre-paschal Jesus and the resurrection of Christ. This opens the question of how liberation theologians look at Jesus in relation to his Kingdom message.

---

[9] A. PERNIA, *God's Kingdom and Human Liberation*, p. 27.
[10] JON SOBRINO, *Jesus the Liberator*, p. 66.

The Historical Jesus and the Kingdom of God in Liberation Theology

The central Christian mystery which appeals to Liberation Theology most is the mystery of the incarnation seen as "the humanization of God" and the "divinization of human beings". For the Liberation theologians the incarnation demonstrates the profound historical character of salvation or the salvific dimension of human history. As Gutierrez puts it, "In Jesus God not only reveals himself, he becomes history"[11]. In the search for the "basic humanization of human beings" such emphasis on the humanity of Jesus in quite natural.

A second reason for putting the stress on the historical Jesus is the message of Jesus himself, the Kingdom of God. This Kingdom is seen as constituting the eschatological goal of history which transforms history itself. This theme can encompass realities that are not directly theological, such as the struggle for the basic humanization of human beings. The search for a new discourse about God that sheds light on the praxis of liberation cannot, therefore, disregard the historical Jesus' preaching of the Kingdom of God.

A third reason is the praxis of Jesus himself who in his actions and behavior demonstrated what the Kingdom concretely entails by showing its liberating force in his exorcisms and healings. This he did in particular in his confrontation with the groups in power and his solidarity with the poor and marginalized. The liberative praxis of Jesus is regarded as the model for the praxis of all Christians and of the Church in a situation of poverty and oppression.

The question often raised is what does "historical Jesus" mean? Is it the historical personage of Jesus of Nazareth uninterpreted by faith, the Jesus who walked this earth? The answer is No. Liberation theologians know only too well that it is impossible to 'reconstruct' the historical Jesus totally free of any prejudice and in a totally objective way. What they mean by "historical Jesus" is mostly the history of Jesus that is his life, ministry and death before the event of the res-

---

[11] "God's Proclamation and Revelation in History" p. 13.

urrection whether interpreted by faith or not[12]. The historical Jesus, therefore, really means the *pre-paschal* Jesus.

In the ministry of this Jesus, as the Gospels present him, the stress in Liberation Theology is put on the "liberative aspect" because only if it can be shown that the pre-paschal Jesus was truly concerned with liberating praxis can any claim be made that a liberation praxis is imperative for Christians and the Church today. The perspective from which this pre-paschal Jesus is seen or the "key" used to reach him is the praxis of liberation which then functions as the pre-understanding in all Liberation theologians' appeal to the pre-paschal Jesus. Concretely, this means that a special emphasis is given to Jesus' confrontation with the groups in power in society and to his solidarity with the poor and the marginalized in his time. This is what Segundo termed the "political key" to understand the pre-paschal Jesus.

All Liberation theologians do, however, in one way or other stress that while approaching the Gospel with that "key" they do not want to reduce all praxis of the pre-paschal Jesus to those features which they stress. They like to talk about "priorities" or aspects consciously or unconsciously suppressed in the discourse about the pre-paschal Jesus up to now.

The resurrection of Jesus and the Kingdom of God

The resurrection of Jesus constitutes an important datum for Liberation Theology. Two reasons are normally mentioned:

First, the resurrection of Jesus is seen as the "implosion" of the eschatological Kingdom into the present. The Kingdom is present in history now. The resurrection confirms Jesus' message of the Kingdom in a way that the risen Christ marks the anticipation (Gutierrez) or the personal realization (Boff), or the arrival in power (Segundo) of the Kingdom in history. The resurrection is the ultimate guarantee of the definite and complete realization of the Kingdom at the end of history. It grounds the hope that, contrary to appearances, the values of the historical Jesus will dominate all of reality

---

[12] SEGUNDO, *The Humanist Christology of Paul*, p. 169.

in the end. Or in the words of Boff, despite the existence of historical absurdities, creation as a whole is not derailed in its movement towards its goal which is the Kingdom of God.

The second reason for the importance of the resurrection is that it clearly shows the universality which characterizes the significance of the risen Christ. In Gutierrez' words, the resurrection "uproots" the risen Christ, "rips him out of a particular date and space", forcing upon us an understanding of the universality of the status of the children of God and the community of brothers and sisters that he announced[13]. The risen Christ takes on cosmic dimensions and is seen to be present anywhere in all persons, cultures, religions and the whole of creation.

It can be observed that Liberation theologians put the stress heavily on the anthropological significance of the resurrection and not as in traditional theology on the theological and Christological meaning of it. However, it is not as if the Liberation theologians would forget these latter aspects; they take them mostly for granted and when they refer to them they only repeat common views. All in all, it can be said that reference to the resurrection is rather scant especially when compared with the treatment of the pre-paschal Jesus. When Liberation Theology refers to the risen Lord it is always made in the light of the pre-paschal Jesus preaching the Kingdom of God. Therefore the resurrection is primarily interpreted as a confirmation of Jesus' message of the Kingdom and as a guarantee of its definite and complete realization of the end of history.

For Sobrino in particular the resurrection is not just the revelation of God's power over death but it is the triumph of justice over injustice. Only so can the resurrection unleash hope into history. Otherwise we may end up with a transcendence without history and a God without a Kingdom[14].

In traditional theology the resurrection is normally seen as interpreting the pre-paschal Jesus, while in the Liberation Theology the pre-paschal Jesus' preaching of the Kingdom seems to interpret the resurrection. The praxis of the pre-

---

[13] "God's Revelation and Proclamation in History, p. 15.
[14] *Jesus, the Liberator*, p. 124-125.

paschal Jesus is often presented as if the resurrection had already happened or in other words the epilogue often comes as the prologue. The center piece remains the praxis of the pre-paschal Jesus. And it is this center piece which gives meaning to the prologue or the epilogue[15].

The Characteristics of the Kingdom of God in Liberation Theology

Jon Sobrino has outlined some characteristics of the Kingdom of God which are basic and occur with different stress in the writings of almost all liberation theologians[16]. The main ones are:

The historical dimension of the Kingdom

Liberation Theology takes the essential historical dimension of the Kingdom of God most seriously. It leaves its appearance not to the end of history but insists on its actual realization in the present historical moment. The Kingdom of God can never be fully realized in history, since it is utopia, but this does not remove it from history. It obliges us to make it present through historical mediations and to bring it about at all levels of historical reality. This aspect has been brought out in various ways by different authors.

According to Gutierrez the heart of Liberation Theology is the notion of salvation, which he considers as the central theme of the Christian mystery. In summary form, these are the main points: The notion of salvation must be considered as historical. That means that it embraces all of human history, transforming it and leading it to its fullness in Christ. As the opposite to the Kingdom, sin is to be seen as a radically intra-historical reality, something the historical Jesus indicated clearly in his exorcisms and healing miracles[17].

---

[15] A. Pernia, *The Kingdom in Liberation Theology*, pp. 63-79.
[16] J. Sobrino, *Jesus the Liberator*, pp. 125-130.
[17] "Liberation Praxis", p. 62.

History itself is the location of God's self-communication and of Christ's liberating action, a view which Gutierrez shares with K. Rahner and others. Because of the presence of evil, however, history is a deeply conflictual reality.

The Kingdom of God is understood as the "global sense and meaning of history, both in the present and in its ultimate end". As the goal of all history, the Kingdom has to have deep consequences and strong implications for social and political praxis in the present. Underlying this is the insistence that there are not two histories, one sacred and the other profane, but that there is only one history, which he calls "Christo-finalized" history[18].

Boff sees the Kingdom in two ways, namely, the Kingdom of God as an eschatological reality at the end of history and the Kingdom of God as partially but concretely anticipated within history. First the Kingdom represents God's ultimate will for the world and the trans-historical goal of his work of creation. It proclaims that creation is not derailed — in spite of the existence of intra-historical absurdities and the historical possibilities of denial and rejection — because God will conquer and reign in the end[19]. But as such, the Kingdom is at the same time the fulfillment of humankind's deepest longing for a new world completely freed from all evil and fully tamed by love.

But Jesus did not just proclaim the Kingdom as coming only in the future but as here and now, breaking into the present. The Kingdom is a "process that begins in this world and reaches its culmination in the eschatological future". As Boff explains it: The liberation of Jesus has a twofold aspect.

> On the one hand he proclaims the total liberation of all history, not just part of it. On the other hand, he anticipates this total liberation in a process embodying partial liberation that remains open to complete fulfillment. If Jesus were to proclaim the utopia of a happy ending for the world without any anticipations of it in history, then he would be nurturing human fantasies that had no

---

[18] "Liberation Praxis", p. 64.
[19] *The Lord's Prayer*, pp. 60-61.

credibility. If he were to introduce partial liberation without offering a vision of future completeness, then he would be frustrating people's hopes and falling into an incoherent immediatism. Jesus does not do either. Instead both dimensions are found operating in dialectical tension in Jesus' work[20].

Jesus proclaimed that humankind's deepest longing is no longer purely "utopia" (nowhere), but already "topia" (somewhere). The Kingdom is therefore partially but concretely anticipated within history. Boff mentions three such anticipations of the Kingdom in history which can be discerned, although not to the same degree.

1. Jesus Christ as the Kingdom's personal realization in definite and eschatological form

Jesus is the Kingdom in person. In his action and behavior Jesus "historified" the Kingdom of God. His miracles demonstrate that the Kingdom is a present reality; his solidarity with the marginalized of society is to be viewed as incarnating the Kingdom and giving concrete shape in history to the attitude of God towards the lowly and the sinful. In doing so Jesus demonstrates who God really is.

Only in Jesus has the Kingdom been so fully demonstrated in a way that has never been repeated again. Jesus' life-style inside history demonstrated in a sacramental way, i.e., in an anticipatory way, the fullness of the Kingdom. Since he came, the Kingdom is partially possible for all human beings starting from their faith in Jesus Christ. The commitment to Jesus makes it possible to make the Kingdom present in the way he did through his activity and behavior. Only that commitment to act and to behave as he did will make it also clear to us who He was and who God is who acted in Him. Boff expresses here the general concern of all Liberation theologians with discipleship as an identity-instilling paradigm for the individual as well as for the Church as a whole.

---

[20] "A Christological View from the Periphery", p. 282.

2. THE CHURCH AS THE SACRAMENTAL ANTICIPATION OF THE KINGDOM

Because the Kingdom of God did not find a universal realization but only a personal one in the risen Christ, the Church arose as the community which continues to preach the message of the Kingdom to all peoples. What constitutes the Church is the faith in the risen Lord as the personal realization of the Kingdom of God. Therefore, the Church is the presence of the Kingdom in history, insofar as the risen Christ is present in this community of believers. But she is not the Kingdom insofar as the Kingdom is still to be realized eschatologically in its universal dimension. The Church must see itself totally in the service of the Kingdom. She is the sacrament of the Kingdom in the sense that she is a sign and instrument of the Kingdom's appearance and realization in history[21].

The Church is the sacramental anticipation of the Kingdom of God insofar as it is the "Body of Christ" in whom the Kingdom is realized. One has to be careful, however, with the expression "Body of Christ" since it does not refer to the physical body of the earthly Jesus but to that body in its risen state. Through the resurrection the physical body of Jesus has become a "spiritual body" (1Cor 14:44ff), an expression which points to the new reality of the risen Christ, one who is free from the limitations of earthy existence and is in global relationship to all reality. The Church refers to the pneumatic and risen body of Christ and is therefore to be defined as the sacrament of the risen Lord, who is the personal realization of the Kingdom of God in its definitive form. Insofar as the risen Christ is present in these communities through faith which calls believers together, we can say these communities are the place where the Kingdom becomes present in the world. These communities therefore seek to consciously practice and live out those features which characterize the shape of the Kingdom of God — equality, participation, fellowship and communion[22].

---

[21] BOFF, *Ecclesiogenesis*, p. 55.
[22] *Church: Charism & Power*, p. 145f.

3. Liberation Events as an Historical Anticipation of the Kingdom

The Church is truly a particular and a very significant mediation of the presence of the activity of the risen Christ in the world, but his presence and activity cannot be limited to the community of believers. Although the Church is the official and distinctive bearer of the Kingdom of God, she is not the exclusive bearer of the Kingdom.

The Kingdom is certainly the Christian utopia that lies at the culmination of history. But it must be repeated that this Kingdom is found in the process of history wherever the poor are respected and recognized as shapers of their own destiny. All individuals, institutions, and activities directed towards those ideals favored by the historical Jesus are bearers of that Kingdom. The Church is an official and distinctive bearer, but not an exclusive one[23].

Concrete instances of liberation make the Kingdom of God present in history. Where we find real growth in justice, where oppression is defeated and freedom is granted, there the Kingdom is present. Any partial and limited instances of historical liberation on the socio-economic-political level are to be seen as "real mediations" and "anticipatory concretizations" of the eschatological Kingdom. Whenever bonds of fellowship, of harmony, of participation and of respect for the inviolable dignity of every person are created, then the Kingdom of God has begun to dawn. Whenever social structures have been established in society that hinder persons from exploiting others, that do away with the relationship of master and slave, that favor fair dealing, then the Kingdom of God is beginning to burst forth like the dawn[24].

4. The Relationship between the Eschatological Kingdom and its Historical Anticipation

If historical liberations are real mediations and anticipatory concretizations of the Kingdom of God, the question has to be asked: What is the relationship between the King-

---

[23] *Church: Charism & Power*, p. 10.
[24] *The Lord's Prayer*, pp. 61-62.

dom as an eschatological reality and its historical anticipations? This is to be faced particularly in cases where historical anticipations of the eschatological Kingdom are events which are not directly or explicitly theological or religious. This is the question concerning the relationship between eschatological salvation and historical liberation or between integral liberation and partial liberations or between salvation in Jesus Christ and socio-political liberations.

Boff's basic position is that of "identification without total identity". There is only one history of reality. The Kingdom of God takes flesh here on earth in justice. This presupposes the ultimate truth of reality that all aspirations of people come down to a single one - a hunger and thirst for justice. In this world, however, one can never identify the Kingdom of God with a just society, but they do overlap. Boff likes to speak of an identification of the one in the other, though not of an identity of the one with the other. He views this relationship as one of "identification without total identity". In this sense he speaks often of "historical concretization" or "anticipation" or "mediation" of eschatological salvation[25]. Gutierrez agrees on this point fully with Boff when he writes:

> The growth of the kingdom is a process which occurs historically in liberation (insofar as liberation means a greater fulfillment of humanity) which is the condition for a new society, but the kingdom is not exhausted in it. While it is realized in liberating historical events, it denounces the limitations and ambiguities of historical liberation, announces its complete fulfillment and impels it effectively towards total communion[26].

Sobrino holds the same reservation. For him the Kingdom of God not only relativizes all social orders, it also serves to "hierarchize" them and judges them against the ideal of the Kingdom to come. He, as most liberation theologians, is firm in insisting against their critics that the King-

---

[25] *Integral Liberation*, pp. 20-24; 30-43.
[26] *Liberation Theology*, p. 104.

dom of God can never be fully realized before God's intervention in history[27].

Boff presents four models to clarify what he means by "identification without total identity". the *chalcedonian model*, the *sacramental model*, the *agape model*, and the *anthropological model*. The aim of these models are all the same. Boff wants to explain how the human and the divine, the spiritual and the material are two different entities but constitute a unity in duality. They are "without confusion and change but also distinct without division and separation". Like the two natures in Christ (Chalcedonian model), the sign and the signified (Sacramental model); the love of God and love of neighbor (agapic model); body and soul (anthropological model) are different yet form a unity so we should understand the relationship of God's eschatological Kingdom and the historical realization of it.

The liberation events as historical anticipations of the Kingdom constitute the specific concern of Liberation Theology. The ideals which the historical Jesus favored, constitute for Boff the key in discerning whether socio-political events genuinely anticipate the Kingdom of God in history. Insofar as socio-political events realize, no matter how partially, the ideals of the historical Jesus, these events are genuine instances of liberation and real anticipations of the Kingdom. The ideals favored by the historical Jesus are implied in the imagery of the parables which Jesus used in order to convey his message of the Kingdom. Basically they are expressed by the values of equality, participation, fellowship and communion — features which characterize the Kingdom of God.

THE KINGDOM OF GOD IN THE PRESENCE OF AND AGAINST THE ANTI-KINGDOM

The Kingdom of God as Jesus preached it is a statement about God and about human existence. It means the definitive manifestation of the sovereignty and lordship of God over a world in which satanic forces struggle for domination

---

[27] *Jesus the Liberator*.

with the forces of goodness. It implies the restoration of the whole of creation and the coming about of the "new heaven and the new earth"[28].

But it is most important to realize into what kind of world the Kingdom of God enters. Liberation Theologians are in no way naive not to recognize the real state of inner-earthly affairs. This world is under the power of the anti-kingdom. Therefore, according to Sobrino we must first establish the reality of the anti-Kingdom and we have to do it methodically and systematically. The anti-Kingdom is conceived not just as the absence or the not-yet of the Kingdom but its formal contradiction. Building the Kingdom means to undo the powers of the anti-Kingdom. How strong liberation theologians feel about this aspect may be seen in the following text by Sobrino:

> The coming Kingdom stands in *combative relation* to the anti-Kingdom. They are not merely mutually exclusive, but they fight against each other. The Kingdom is not being built from a *tabula rasa*, but in opposition to the anti-kingdom, and the persecution of those who are mediating the coming of the Kingdom is effective proof of this. This persecution, in its turn, becomes the criterion for the answer to the question whether the Kingdom is actually being built. Those who carry out purely beneficial activities are not persecuted, which means that they have not struggled against the anti-kingdom, and this, in turn, means that their activities are not, strictly speaking, signs of the Kingdom, since they are not activities like those of Jesus. Liberation theology finds it absolutely necessary to take the anti-Kingdom into account[29].

However, this should not lead us to despair because the outcome of this battle is assured: justice will triumph over all forms of evil. The Kingdom represents God's ultimate will for the world and the trans-historical goal of his work of creation. It proclaims that creation is not derailed — in spite of the exis-

---

[28] BOFF, *Jesus Christ*, p. 52.
[29] SOBRINO, *Jesus the Liberator*, p. 126.

tence of intra-historical absurdities and the historical possibilities of denial and rejection — because God will conquer and reign in the end[30].

THE KINGDOM BELONGS TO THE POOR

What Liberation Theology has become known for most is its "Preferential Option for the Poor". All liberation theologians would stress that the first addressees of the Kingdom are the poor. Who the poor are whom Jesus addressed is an open question and depends on who talks about it. But all seem to agree on the following points. The poor are the ones on the bottom of the heap in history and those who are oppressed by society and cast out from it. They are divided into two classes: First the *economically poor*. These are those who are hungry, and thirsty, who are weighed down by a burden, who are sick or in prison. These are those for whom life and survival are a hard task. Secondly, there are the *sociologically poor*. These are those who are despised by the ruling classes in society, those who are considered sinners, the publicans and the prostitutes, the simple minded, the least, those who carry out despised tasks. They are the marginalized those "whose religious ignorance and moral behavior closed, in the conviction of the time, the gate leading to salvation for them".

For them the Kingdom message of Jesus is destined, it belongs to them. The poor seem to be the ones who have a better grasp on the Good News of the Kingdom, since their situation is the best background for understanding it. If the Kingdom of God is Good News, its recipients will help in fundamentally clarifying its content, since Good News is something essentially relational, though not all Good News is equally so for everyone. Jesus proclaimed God's love to all but not in the same way. Segundo is concerned to stress that Jesus took no antagonistic stance nor did he show any sectarian behavior offering salvation to a specific group alone. He preached the Good News for all and presented the Kingdom as within the reach of all. "Jesus' praxis and activity never had an ant-, but always a pro character. But this did

---

[30] BOFF, *The Lord's Prayer*, pp. 60-61.

not prevent him from having a specific addressee in mind when proclaiming the Kingdom of God.

The Kingdom is for the poor because they are materially poor, the Kingdom is for the non- poor to the extent that they 'lower' themselves to these poor, defending them and allowing themselves to be imbued with the spirit of the poor. It is not admissible to ignore the material nature of poverty and to suppose that there can be a poverty of the spirit in and for itself with no relation to material poverty.

The poor are not morally better than the rich, they are human beings, which means, they are as sinful as the rest of humanity. We should prefer them not because they are good but because first of all God is good. He prefers the forgotten, the oppressed, the poor and the forsaken. It is following Jesus who had this preference that compels us to do the same. This option we all have to make whether we are poor or rich. The poor as well have to opt in favor of their brothers and sisters irrespective of race, social class and culture. The option for the poor is a decision incumbent upon every Christian[31].

Segundo's concern is the social background over against which Jesus' central message of the Kingdom has to be understood. This message revolves around three key words: "Kingdom", "poor" and "Good News". It is properly expressed in the phrase: The Kingdom of God is Good News for the poor! This message, as Segundo sees it, is simultaneously religious and political. Jesus shows a clear preference for the poor over the rich, because of the inhuman nature of their situation as poor people. As such, Jesus' proclamation of the Kingdom aroused "profound interest and passionate enthusiasm among his contemporaries"[32]. It became a divisive message since it touched on the socio-political reality of his native land.

Jesus' message of the Kingdom is directed against such an interpretation of Israel's faith which had marginalized more than half of the population. It was not an attack on the "politics of the Roman occupation" because that had hardly any influence on the simple people and their socio-political situation. Jesus struck at a much deeper level; he attacked the

---

[31] GUTIÈRREZ, "Option for the poor", pp 5-10.
[32] SEGUNDO, *Historical Jesus of the Synoptics*, p. 71.

whole theocratic structure of Jewish society as it had been interpreted by the religious and political elite. He undermined this structure by revealing a new image of God as "humane and humanizing", who cannot tolerate a situation which turns human beings into subhumans, nor can he allow the justification of such a situation by an appeal to God's will. For the God of Jesus, the human being constitutes a primary value. God's joy consists precisely in rescuing human beings from their misery and restoring their humanity to them. Therefore, by undermining the religious authority, Jesus exercised a much more subversive political activity than any direct political attack on the social structure of Israel at his time. His religious discrediting of the Pharisees undermined the very basis of the power of the real authorities who dominated the social system. That also accounts for the fact that they all, Pharisees, priests, elders and scribes had a common interest in getting rid of him because their status in society was at stake.

The demand of the Kingdom: Conversion to a liberating practice

The Kingdom message of Jesus carries with it certain demands. The first one is conversion which is first of all a call to personal conversion, and secondly, postulates a restructuring of the human world. Conversion, the basic imperative of the Kingdom, is not to be understood in general terms as being the same for everyone. Generally speaking it does not mean the performance of some pious exercises, but a change in the person's mode of thinking and acting before God in the light of the Good News of the Kingdom. It calls for a rupture with the established order and a decision in favor of the new order entailed in the Kingdom of God already present in the person of Jesus. The in-breaking Kingdom is not an idea but a mobilization for action. In short, the message of Jesus is action oriented. Conversion for Boff is ultimately adherence to the person of Jesus Christ and a readiness to comply with the exigencies of the message of the Kingdom[33]. The most outstanding

---

[33] *Jesus Christ Liberator*, pp. 55-65.

characteristic of the one who undergoes conversion is "a love that knows no discrimination". This fundamental equality of all before God, Jesus expressed most radically in the Sermon on the Mount. Therefore, the Kingdom of God is the reign of equality and freedom for all. Conversion is the altering of relationships and the implementation of these new relationships at every level of personal and social reality. Only in such relationships does the Kingdom become actively present concretely and tangibly[34].

For Segundo conversion means one thing for the rich, something different for the disciple and another thing for the poor. For the rich and powerful, it asks for a conversion to an appreciation of the value of the human being and his/her most urgent needs as the key for interpreting God's will. For the disciple of Jesus, it asks for the qualities of clear-sightedness, heroism and commitment to the task of dismantling the ideological mechanisms of religious-political oppression. For the poor and sinners, it asks for 'conscientization' by which they come to recognize their situation of oppression and realize they are the conscious subjects of their own development and humanization.

This presupposes that the Kingdom is somehow the object of human efforts and seeks its realization in history. To humanize human beings now means to build the Kingdom already in history. Here Segundo and Boff affirm in their own way what Gutierrez and Sobrino have to say about the Kingdom as gift and task

First: a call to divine filiation by which human persons become God's children. This is the vocation to complete union with God; our vertical vocation, the deepest aspiration of all human persons. Secondly: a call to human fellowship by which human persons become one another's sisters and brothers; the vocation to complete union among themselves.

These two aspects form the basic notion which governs Gutierrez' understanding of the Kingdom of God. Jon Sobrino also presents a similar notion in his Christology[35]. These two aspects make it possible for Gutierrez to speak of

---

[34] "A Christological View from the Periphery", p. 279.
[35] *Christology*, pp. 41-74.

the Kingdom as a GIFT as well as a TASK. In the call to divine filiation, the Kingdom of God is fundamentally God's true gift. But it is a gift that entails by necessity the task of creating an authentic community of brothers and sisters.

It is the gift aspect of the Kingdom that demands of us the task as a response. The achievement of true human fellowship in history constitutes an historical realization of the promise of total communion with God. But as an historical verification of such a promise, it immediately reveals the partial and incomplete character of the Kingdom now and opens up history towards the complete and total communion of human persons with God[36]. God's Kingdom is identical with God's will. They are inseparable. Gutierrez shares this view with Pannenberg who strongly advocates it. God's will is his reign of love in the world. It is a love that calls all human persons to total communion with him and with one another. Where God's will is done, i.e., where his Kingdom is put into practice, one encounters him as the true God of the Kingdom. Any worship, therefore, that is disassociated from building communion with our fellow human beings is idolatry.

Practice becomes the decisive criterion for understanding the Kingdom. As the gift of divine filiation, the Kingdom is accepted by carrying out the task of creating profound human fellowship in history. As the final goal of history, the Kingdom undertakes and transforms the whole of history. As with the will of God, the Kingdom is to be "done on earth as it is in heaven". But the will of God is precisely negated by situations of massive poverty, perceived both as unjust oppression and repression. To do the will of God in such a situation means to struggle for liberation. Doing so would bring about true human fellowship and thus put the Kingdom of God into practice. It would mean accepting the gift of God's Kingdom and realizing it in history by carrying out the task necessarily entailed[37].

The Kingdom of God, therefore, is the background against which, on the one hand, the situation of oppression

---

[36] *We Drink From our Own Wells*, p. 104; "Liberation praxis", p. 38.
[37] GUTIERREZ, "The Irruption of the Poor", p. 122.

and domination is denounced as sinful and incompatible with its coming, and in the light of which, on the other hand, every achievement of brotherhood or sisterhood and justice among persons is announced as a step towards total communion with God. Seen in the light of the Kingdom of God, the struggle for liberation is no longer solely a response to the economic, social and political situation of poverty and oppression. Neither is it simply an expression of the contemporary awareness of the human person's capacity to transform history. Rather it is fidelity to God's will and fidelity to the practice of Jesus whose proclamation of the Kingdom reveals God as Father and human persons as one another's brothers and sisters[38].

Conclusion

The Kingdom of God in Latin American Liberation Theology is viewed as the eschatological goal of history which transforms history itself. They seek to maintain the duality between the eschatological and the historical dimension of the Kingdom. This lead them to put a heavy stress on the notion of praxis or the world transforming dimension of the Kingdom and the role human beings have in such a transformation.

Accordingly, such a notion of the Kingdom may be expressed

> through the image of an eschatological banquet in the Father's house (Boff), at which fully humanized human beings (Segundo) equally participate (Boff) as children of the Father and as one's brothers and sisters (Gutierrez). It implies the full humanization of human beings (Segundo) and their total communion with God and with one another (Gutierrez), constituting thereby the realization of humankind's fundamental utopia (Boff). The Kingdom of God, however, is not just an eschatological reality at the end of history. Nor is it simply an object of passive hope. The Kingdom is also an object of

---

[38] GUTIERREZ, "Finding Our Way", p. 232.

human effort in history, entailing the task of creating a profound fellowship among human beings (Gutierrez), where human beings-turned-sub- humans have their humanity restored to them (Segundo) and where the ideals of the historical Jesus — expressed through values of equality, participation, fellowship and communion — are realized, albeit partially (Boff). To the extent that praxis of liberation performs such a task, it partially realizes (Gutierrez), concretely anticipates (Boff), and begins to build (Segundo) the Kingdom of God in history[39].

Selected Bibliography

Boff, Leonardo, *The Lord's Prayer: The Prayer of Integral Liberation*, Orbis Books, New York, 1983.
——, "Integral Liberation and Partial Liberations" in Leonardo and Clodovis Boff, *Salvation and Liberation. In search of a Balance Between Faith and Politics*, Orbis Books, New York, 1984.
——, *Jesus Christ Liberator*, Orbis Books, New York, 1978.
——, "A Christological view from the Periphery", in *Jesus Christ Liberator*, pp. 264-292.
——, *Ecclesiogenesis*, Orbis Books, New York, 1986.
——, *Church: Charism & Power*, SCM, London, 1985.
Bussman, Claus, *Who Do You Say? Jesus Christ in Latin American Theology*, Orbis Books, New York, 1985.
Coste, Rene, *Marxist Analysis and Christian Faith*, Orbis Books, New York, 1985.
Croatto, J.S., "Biblical Hermeneutics in the Theology of Liberation", *The Bible and Liberation*, ed. by N. K. Gottwald, Orbis Books, New York, 1983.
Fuellenbach, J. *Hermeneutics, Marxism and Liberation Theologgy*, Logos Publication, Manila 1989.
Gutierrez, G., *We Drink From our Own Wells*, Orbis Books, New York, 1985.
——, "Liberation and Salvation" in *A Theology of Liberation*, Orbis Books, New York, 1973, pp. 149-187.
——, *The Power of the Poor in History*, Orbis Books, New York, 1983.
——, "Liberation Praxis and Christian Faith" in *The Power of the Poor in History*, pp.36-74.
——, "Option for the poor", in *Mysterium Liberationis. Fundamental Concepts of Liberation Theology*, ed. by Ignacio Ellacuria and Jon Sobrino, Orbis Books New York, 1993, pp.235-250.
——, "God's Revelation and Proclamation in History", in *The Power of the Poor in History*, pp. 3-22.
——, "Finding our Way to talk about God", in *Interruption of the Third World*, ed. by F. Fabella & S. Torres, Orbis Books, New York, 1981, pp 222-234.

---

[39] Pernia, God's Kingdom, p. 194.

PERNIA, ANTONIO, *God's Kingdom and Human Liberation*, Divine Word Publication, Manila, 1989.
PERRIN, NORMAN, *Jesus and the Language of the Kingdom*, Fortress Press, Philadelphia, 1976.
SCHNEIDERS, S., "Faith, Hermeneutics and the Literal Sense of Scripture", *Theological Studies* 39 (1978): 719-736.
SEGUNDO, J.L., *The Humanist Christology of Paul*, Orbis Books, New York, 1986.
——, *Historical Jesus of the Synoptics*, Orbis Books, New York, 1985.
——, *The Liberation of Theology*, Gill and McMillan; Dublin and Orbis Book: New York, 1977.
SOBRINO, JON, *Jesus the Liberator*, Orbis Books, New York, 1978.
——, *Christology at the Crossroads*, Orbis Books, New York, 1978.
——, "The central position of the Reign of God in the Liberation Theology" in *Mysterium Liberationis. Fundamental Concepts of Liberation Theology*, ed. by Ignacio Ellacuria and Jon Sobrino, Orbis Books New York, 1993, pp. 350-387.
VIDALES, R., "Methodological Issues in Liberation Theology", in *Frontiers of Theology in Latin America*, ed. by R. Gibellini, Orbis Books, New York, 1979.

The Kingdom of God and Evangelization in Asia

PAPERS OF THE FABC THEOLOGICAL
ADVISORY COMMISSION

1) A JOINT CONSULTATION ON INTERRELIGIOUS DIALOGUE
Singapore, July 5-10, 1987
(FABC Papers n. 49)

THE JOINT STATEMENT

So the work to draft a joint declaration was taken up in different groups, which referred their work back to the plenary. The main task of writing was entrusted to a mixed drafting committee. Since there was not much time, it was decided to make a brief statement on the necessity and nature of interreligious dialogue and conclude this statement with some pastoral recommendations. The statement should be addressed in the first place to the Christian Churches in Asia, but the possible partners for dialogue from the other religions should be considered too. The statement starts with recalling the context of Asia with its many economic, political and religious problems. There is an obvious necessity, given the importance of the religions in Asia, that all religions in Asia should cooperate in building a more human society.

The theme of the consultation, "Living and Working Together with Sisters and Brothers of Other Faiths", indicates already that dialogue in the statement is not understood to be the discussion among specialists but as "dialogue of life in all its variety". It was stressed that dialogue includes the full witness of one's own religious conviction. Taking this into account, dialogue always deals with proclamation, witness and evangelization, but cannot be identified with them. It was explicitly mentioned that God's salvific work transcends the boundaries of the Church, because it is related to the bringing about of the Kingdom of God, which transcends the Church too. Christians see themselves as pilgrims who are on their pilgrimage together with the members of other religions. The church is called to render an effective witness and become a symbol of the Kingdom of God. The pastoral recommendations deal with practical implications resulting from the theological statement on religious dialogue. There is need to deal with interreligious dialogue in theological formation and in other areas of the Churches' life. Special mention is made of the problem of interreligious marriages. A further point is stressed when the phenomena of fundamentalism and fanaticism in various religions, which pose special problems for the development of a fruitful interreligious dialogue, are dealt with.

Mission and Dialogue

The problem of the relationship between dialogue and mission played an important role for the study groups, as well as during the common work in plenary session. There was a general agreement that the direct intention of causing a member of a certain religion to change his religious belief is incompatible with a genuine interreligious dialogue. At the same time, it was agreed that it is an essential part of interreligious dialogue to give each other a full witness of one's own religious conviction. The question of how the mandate to proclaim the Good News to every one and the witness to one's own religious conviction in an interreligious dialogue can be related could not be solved during this consultation. There were different opinions, on the one hand, according to one's confessional belonging, but there were nuances, too, among members of the same Church. The final statement avoided commiting itself and simply stated that mission and dialogue are related to one another but remain different. The Catholic participants argued more from the mission of the Church which they see as one, and which can be differentiated by making the distinction between mission and proclamation, which are then to be seen as integral, dialectical and complementary dimensions of this one mission of the Church.

Dialogue and Conversion

Taking as a starting point the view of the partner of the other religions, the Protestant theologians called for a clear distinction between mission and dialogue in order to avoid unnecessary misunderstandings and anxieties among the members of other religions. At the same time it would be easier to explain to the more fundamentalist groups in their own Churches that the great commandment to preach the Gospel is not necessarily impaired when entering into dialogue. The problem of conversion in interreligious dialogue proved the major theological issue at the consultation. In the first place there was general agreement that all partners in dialogue are called to convert "individually", that is to say, that they should progress in religious and spiritual development within their own religious tradition. The theological problems started with the question whether it is conceivable that in interreligious dialogue conversions from one religion to another can happen. Even agreed that such conversions should not be aimed at, there remains the possibility that they occur. In the eyes of Christian theologians conversions from Buddhism, Hinduism, Islam and other non-Christian religions do not constitute a great problem. There is no difficulty to speak in such cases about the work of the Holy Spirit.

2) THE URGENCY OF CHRISTIAN MISSION
The All-Asian Conference on Evangelization
Suwon, Korea, August 24-31, 1988
(FABC Papers n. 50)

THE STATEMENT OF THE CONFERENCE
EVANGELIZATION IN ASIA TODAY

1. The All-Asian Conference on Evangelization, held in Suwon, South Korea, August 24-31, 1988, and organized by the Office of Evangelization of the Federation of Asian Bishops' Conferences (FABC), brought together sixty of us: bishops, priests, Religious and laity. We came from fourteen Asian countires for eight days of prayer, reflection, listening and discussion on the word of God and the Christian message today.

2. We strove to understand the signs of the times, and to search for fresh ways to announce and share the Good News of God's Kingdom in Jesus Christ with all our Asian brothers and sisters. We listened to what each Church has to share about itself and what the Spirit has to say to the Churches of Asia.

3. As we are at the threshold of the third Christian millenium, we became more deeply aware than ever of the Asian peoples' providential hunger for a more profound human dignity, liberation from all oppressive structures, peace, reconciliation, and the fullness of salvation, which find their fulfilment in Christ, the Savior of humanity.

4. While some are open to the Gospel message, many are unable to see the true countenance of Jesus Christ in the Church. We see an increasing commitment to evangelization by all Christian Churches, and the new missionary movements among traditional Asian religions. We are also faced with the pervasiveness of the mass media which create a challenging new language and mentality in our culture, calling for the inculturation of Christ's message in contemporary society. In these situations, we need to look more deeply into the meaning and method of evangelization today.

5. The ultimate goal of all evangelization is the ushering in and establishment of God's Kingdom, namely, God's rule in the hearts and minds of our people. While we are aware and sensitive of the fact that evangelization is a complex reality and has many essential aspects — such as witnessing to the Gospel, working for the values of the Kingdom, struggling along with those who strive for justice and peace, dialogue, sharing, inculturation, mutual enrichment with other Christians and the followers of all religions — we affirm that there can never be true evangelization without the proclamation of Jesus Christ.

6. The proclamation of Jesus Christ is the center and the primary element of evangelization without which all other elements will lose their cohesion and validity. In the same way, evangelization will gather together the believing community, the Church, through faith and baptism. In the Church all men and women can find grace, reconciliation and new life, and through the Church we share these with others.

7. We are glad that the Second Vatican Council affirmed the presence of salvific values in other religions. We are grateful for the timely insights and the individual as well as community action of those calling for liberation from human misery and oppression. We also affirm that the primary task of the Church is the proclamation of the Gospel of Jesus Christ, calling to personal faith in him, inviting to membership in the Church those whom God has chosen, and celebrating salvation through Christ in our belonging to his Church. Every other task of the Church flows from and is related to this proclamation and its acceptance in faith. The Gospel fulfills all hopes, a Gospel which Asia and the whole world direly need.

8. In the context of the above, we asked ourselves: What is the Spirit calling us to do now as a response to the signs of the times? In prayer and discussion it once again became evident that, before all else, we need to be evangelized ourselves; we need to become more fully identified with Christ and the Gospel we proclaim. It also became evident that out message should be embodied in committed witness and authentic dialogue, shared with a knowledge and understanding of Asian religious experience and deep aspirations for salvation, on the one hand, and an adequate comprehension of the Asian realities of poverty and injustice, on the other.

9. The reports from the fourteen countries, talks by experts, prayer, and dialogue increased our awareness of the presence and saving power of God in all our Asian faith communities. He calls us to witness to Christ. He encourages us to enter into dialogue with the peoples of other religions of Asia. He asks us to face the poverty and growing pluralism of Asian societies, to respect and even enrich our traditional cultures, to contribute towards a more humanized Asian man and woman, to grow more deeply into Asian spiritualities, including the process of self-purification, and to present our local Churches as places of contemplation and grace. We concluded that all this cannot be achieved without serious prayerful reflection and action based on discernment of the word of God. With this, we will be in a good position to collaborate among ourselves and with all peoples in building the Kingdom of God.

10. Our prayer, reflection, and reports, moreover, left us with the strong conviction that evangelization belongs to the whole People of God. The laity should be encouraged to assume their role and responsability in the evangelization of Asia. Empowered by baptism and confirmation, nourished by the Eucharist, and given adequate formation, the laity are a vital, irreplaceable force to carry forward the task of evangelization.

11. The generosity and potential for leadership among women, as well as the dynamism and enthusiasm of youth, are indespensible resources for the growth of the Church.

3) EVANGELIZATION IN ASIA
FABC Theological Conclusions, Hua Hin (Thailand)
3-10, Nov. 1991

SOME THEOLOGICAL REFLECTIONS ON THE ASIAN CONTEXT OF EVANGELIZATION

26 In the first part of these conclusions we reviewed the Asian scene and asked what image our Asian Churches are projecting; in the second part we indicated some lines along which the Churches need to undergo a conversion in order to respond more adequately to the situation in Asia. This third part is a short attempt to reflect theologically on the questions which arise when the Church's evangelizing mission is confronted with the Asian context.

27 The main questions are the following: how do we understand the centrality and decisiveness of Jesus Christ in the context of religious pluralism? What is the role of the Church if the Kingdom of God is present ant operative beyond her boundaries? What does the mission of the Church consist in, if salvation in Jesus Christ is available to members of other religious traditions in the concrete circumstances of their lives? If interreligious dialogue is by itself an expression of the Church's evangelizing mission, why does announcing Jesus Christ and inviting people to become his disciples in the Church remain urgent? If people can be saved through Jesus Christ outside the Church, what motivation remains for proclaiming the Good News? Why, in the last analysis, must the Asian local churches be poor and inculturated?

Jesus Christ at the Center of Our Faith

28 Jesus Christ, the Son of God made man, is at the center of our Christian faith. In Him, God's age-long self-manifestation through human history has come to a climax. In Jesus, God has personally entered human history and has become a member of the human race. This total identification with us of the Son of God is ordained to sharing with us his Sonship of the Father. Jesus accomplished this mission throughout his earthly life, and singularly through the paschal mystery of his death and resurrection and the outpouring of the Holy Spirit at Pentecost. The paschal mystery in which the Christ-event culminates thus ushers in the renewal of creation and marks the decisive step in the establishment by God of his Kingdom on earth. It has cosmic implications and universal significance.

The Kingdom of God

29 The Kingdom of God is therefore universally present and at work. Wherever men and women open themselves to the transcendent divine mystery which impinges upon them and go out of themselves in love and service of fellow humans, there the reign of God is at work. As BIRA IV/2 puts it, "where God is accepted, where Gospel values are lived, where man is respected... there is the Kingdom". (II/1; FAPA II, 423). In all such cases people respond to God's offer of grace through Christ in the spirit and enter into the Kingdom through an act of faith. The document, *Dialogue and Proclamation* (DP) explains that, "concretely, it will be in the sincere practice of what is good in their own religious traditions and by following the dictates of their conscience that the members of other religions respond positively to God's invitation and receive salvation in Jesus Christ, even while they do not recognize or acknowledge him as their saviour". (cf AG 3, 9, 11; DP 29). Thus they become sharers of the Kingdom of God in Jesus Christ unknowingly.

30 This goes to show that the Reign of God is a universal reality, extending far beyond the boundaries of the Church. It is the reality of salvation in Jesus Christ, in

which Christians and others share together. It is the fundamental "mystery of unity" which unites us more deeply than differences in religious allegiance are able to keep us apart. Seen in this manner, a "regnocentric" approach to mission theology does not in any way threaten the Christocentric perspective of our faith. On the contrary, "regnocentrism" calls for "Christo-centrism", and vice versa, for it is in Jesus Christ and through the Christ-event that God has established his Kingdom upon the earth and in human history (cf RM 17-18).

The Role of the Church

31 In this universal reality of the Reign of God, the Church has an unique and irreplaceable role to play. This has been well indicated by the Theological Advisory Commission (TAC) of FABC in its "Theses on Interreligious Dialogue" (1987) when it said: "the focus of the Church's mission of evangelization is building up the Kingdom of God and building up the Church to be at the service of the Kingdom. The Kingdom is therefore wider than the Church. The Church is the sacrament of the Kingdom, making it visible, ordained to it, promoting it, but not equating itself with it" (6.3, FABC Paper No. 48, p. 16; cf also BIRA IV/2, II 1; FAPA II, 423).

32 The encyclical *Redemptoris Missio* (RM) explains the reason for this unique and irreplaceable role of the Church in relation to the Reign of God at whose service she is placed: "It is true that the Church is not an end unto herself, since she is ordered towards the Kingdom of God of which she is the seed, sign and instrument. Yet, while remaining distinct from Christ and the Kingdom, the Church is indissolubly united to both. Christ endowed the Church, his Body, with the fullness of the benefits and means of salvation. The Holy Spirit dwells in her with his gifts and charisms, sanctifies, guides and constantly renews her (LG 4). The result is a unique and special relationship which, while not excluding the action of Christ and the Spirit outside of the Church's visible boundaries, confers upon her a specific and necessary role". (RM 18).

33 Thus it is seen that if the Church is the sacrament of the Kingdom, the reason is that she is the sacrament of Jesus Christ himself who is the mystery of salvation, to whom she is called to bear witness and whom she is called to announce. To be at the service of the Kingdom means for the Church to announce Jesus Christ. For this task she is endowed with special gifts and charisms and guided by the Spirit. Due to such endowments the Reign of God is sacramentally present in the Church in a special manner; "she is the seed, sign and instrument" of the Reign of God to which she is ordained (RM 18).

Servant Churches

34 Nevertheless, the Church as a pilgrim in history belongs to the order of signs and as such, needs to be conformed to Jesus and his Reign, lest the quality of her witness be impaired and her signifying power obscured. This is why the Church must reproduce in herself the model of her master who became poor that we might become rich. The "self-emptying" of the Son of God in Jesus Christ is the decisive theological reason why the Church must be a poor Church; his identification with the figure of the "Servant of God" is the reason why she, in turn, must be a servant. The preferential option for the poor, which the Asian context demands from all local Churches, is in deep harmony with the nature of the Church herself as the sacrament of Jesus Christ, who, for us, became poor and made himself a servant. In order to be an effective sign and to bear a convincing witness, the pilgrim Church, not only in her members but "in so far as she is an institution of men on earth", is constantly in need of renewal and reform (cf UR 6; DP 36).

Inculturated Churches

35 The same conformity of the Church to her master is the decisive theological foundation for the inculturation of local Churches. The Son of God became man in Jesus in a particular place at a particular time of history, two thousand years ago in Palestine. Jesus was a Jew, deeply inserted in the culture of his people. The revelation he conveyed of the

mystery of God as well as the way in which he accomplished his messianic and saving mission are steeped in the religious tradition of Israel, even while they fulfill it in an unforseen manner. The mystery of the incarnation and the paschal mystery are at once the foundation and the model for the deep insertion of local Churches in the surrounding cultures, in all aspects of their life, celebration, witness and mission.

The Evangelizing Mission of the Local Churches

36 Local Churches, servant and inculturated, are the subject of the evangelizing mission. This mission, as the Secretariat for Non-Christians explained in a document of 1984, "is a single but complex and articulated reality", of which, while not claiming to be exhaustive, are mentioned the principle elements" as follows: 1) simple presence and living witness; 2) "concrete commitment to the service of humankind and all forms of activity for social development and for the struggle against poverty and the structures which produce it"; 3) liturgical life and that of prayer and contemplation; 4) "dialogue in which Christians meet the followers of other religious traditions in order to walk together towards truth and to work together in projects of common concern"; 5) "finally", there is proclamation and catechesis in which Jesus Christ is announced as saviour and people are invited to become his disciples in the Church. "The totality of the Christian mission embraces all these elements" (Dialogue and Mission, 13).

37 Speaking of the relationship between dialogue and proclamation, DP wrote: "dialogue... does not constitute the whole mission of the Church... it cannot simply replace proclamation but remains oriented towards proclamation in so far as the dynamic process of the Church's evangelizing mission reaches in it its climax and fullness" (DP 82; cf RM 55).

38 In response to the questions raised by the Asian context, it seems important to expand further on dialogue and proclamation, and to indicate the relationship which obtains between those two forms of expressions of the one evangelizing mission of our Churches.

Dialogue

39 In the pluralistic socio-political, cultural and religious context of Asia as delineated in the first part of these conclusions, the Church is called upon to be committed to dialogue in a special way. The Church, being committed to the Gospel of the Kingdom of God should acknowledge the same Kingdom at work in socio-political situations and in cultural and religious traditions and enter into dialogue with them.

40 The foundation of such a commitment to dialogue is not merely anthropological but primarily theological. In Christ, God has entered into a dialogue with human beings, offering them salvation. It is in faithfulness to this divine initiative that the Church should be committed to a dialogue of salvation with all women and men (DP 38). Moreover this dialogue is founded on the fact that Christ, the new Adam, is at work through his Spirit in all human persons to bring about a new humanity (DP 15).

41 The local Churches of Asia have to be committed to dialogue with socio-political movements and forces working towards integral development, social justice and peace. Possessing the same cultural heritage, we commit ourselves to dialogue with the various cultural traditions of Asia, for the construction of a more humane society. We engage in dialogue with the different religious traditions of Asia and collaborate with them in promoting human and spiritual values. We extend our commitment to dialogue to all those involved in preserving the integrity of creation.

42 The prophetic role of the local Churches in Asia urges them to act also as catalysts in facilitating dialogue between different socio-political forces, religions and cultures, so that they work together in building up a better society based on the values of the Kingdom.

43 Interreligious dialogue is of special importance in Asia where the great religious traditions continue to inspire and influence the lives of millions of people. The religious traditions of Asia command our respect because of the spiritual and human values enshrined in them. These are expressions of the presence of God's Word and of the universal action of his Spirit in them. For the Churches in Asia, to estab-

lish positive and constructive interreligious relations with individuals and communities of these religious traditions is an integral part of their evangelizing mission. Such a dialogue with other religions will also prepare the ground for interreligious and common actions for justice and peace, which will enable the local Churches of Asia to fulfil their prophetic role more effectively.

44 In order to have an authentic dialogue between the Church and other religious traditions, there should be a real dialogue between the different local Churches and other Christian communities in Asia. A divided Christianity can never enter into a real dialogue with people of other faiths. Hence, it is of utmost importance that the different local Churches of Asia foster dialogue and communion among themselves. In this context practical ecumenism, common witness and concerted action become vital.

45 Dialogue leads the partners to inner purification and total conversion if pursued with docility to the Spirit (RM 56). An authentic dialogue on the socio-political, cultural, religious and cosmic levels will help the Churches of Asia to be purified of their sin and to grow in their commitment to the Spirit of the Risen Lord who is universally present and active. In the same way such a dialogue will also make a demand on the other partners for a deeper commitment to the values of the Kingdom.

46 This on-going process of dialogue, effecting a deeper conversion to the Kingdom of God and commitment to the Spirit of the Risen Lord, will purify the local Churches more and more from sin and enable them to fulfil more effectively their evangelizing mission in Asia. At the same time, the multifaceted dialogue among all human groups, in whom the power of the Kingdom of God is at work, will eventually lead the Asian peoples to a fuller communion with God and among themselves, which is the ultimate goal of all evangelization.

Proclamation

47 Having recognised the universal reality of the Kingdom of God in which Christians and others belong and which they are called to promote together through in-

terreligious dialogue, we are faced with a double question: Why then does the proclamation of Jesus Christ remain necessary and urgent? Which motivation will spur the Asian local Churches to invite others to become Jesus' disciples in his Church?

48 The Church has received from the Risen Lord the commission to proclaim his Good News and to make disciples from among all nations (cf Mt 28:18-20; Mk 16:15-16; Lk 24:46-48; Jn 20:21; Acts 1:8). This commission takes on various shades of meaning in different texts: "announcing the Good News", "witnessing", "making disciples", "baptizing" and "teaching". Meanwhile the apostle Paul on his part stressed the urgency of such proclamation when he writes, "Everyone who calls on the name of the Lord shall be saved, but how are they to call... without someone to proclaim him?" (Rom 10:13-15). The same urgency of proclamation has been expressed by recent Popes, especially in the apostolic exhortation EN (22) and the encyclical RM (1-3). How are we to understand and implement the Lord's commission to his Church in the light of the Asian situation?

49 The Holy Spirit, in ways known to God, gives to all human persons the opportunity of coming into contact with the paschal mystery of Jesus Christ, and thus to obtain salvation (cf GS 22). The Church, as the visible sign and sacrament of the mystery of salvation, is in a unique position to offer them the opportunity of sharing in this mystery in a fully human way. She alone can convey to them the explicit knowledge of Jesus Christ, their savior and Lord, and invite them to celebrate in joy and thanksgiving the mystery of his passover at her eucharistic table. Only in the life of the Church is found the full visibility of the mystery of salvation. Only there do the children of God come to the full realization of what it means to share in the Sonship of the Son. Thereby, the Church's proclamation meets the deepest longings and aspirations of the human heart for liberation and wholeness of life. There, the seeds of the Word contained in the religious traditions of the world grow to maturity and come to fulfilment. In this manner the Church shares with others, "the fulness of the benefits and means of salvation" (RM 18) which she has received from her Lord and Master.

50 Motivation behind the Church's proclamation of Jesus Christ flows indeed from obedience to the mandate received from the Risen Lord. However a clearer perception of the Church's mission in the context of the Asian reality helps us discover even deeper motivations. Members of other religious traditions already in some way share with us in the mystery of salvation. If the Church is in love with her Lord she will feel the urge of sharing with them what she alone can offer: the Good News that the human face of God and his gift of salvation is found in Jesus of Nazareth. "here we are at the heart of the mystery of love" (DP 83).

51 The local Churches of Asia will proclaim Jesus Christ to their fellow humans in a dialogical manner (DP 70e; cf 77). The proclaiming Church encounters people among whom the rays of that Truth, which enlighten everybody coming into the world, are already present. This hidden presence is the starting point for the Church's proclamation. Thus, in announcing the Good News, both the proclaimers and the hearers will grow into the fulness of the mystery of salvation in Jesus Christ.

4) Theses on Interreligious Dialogue
An Essay in Pastoral Theological Reflection
(FABC Papers n. 48)

Thesis 2

Dialogue with other religions, which are significant and positive elements in the economy of God's design of salvation, is an integral dimension of the mission of the Church, which is the sacrament of the Kingdom of God proclaimed by Jesus. In Asia today, Christians, though they are a "little flock" in many places, animated by the Spirit who is leading all things to unity, are called to play a serving and catalyzing role which facilitates interreligious collaboration. This call challenges all the Churches to common witness as they grow together towards fuller ecumenical communion.

2. Commentary

2.1 The Second Vatican Council not only reaffirms the traditional doctrine that "the Holy Spirit in a manner known only to God offers to every man the possibility of being associated with his paschal mystery" [GS22; cf. *Lumen Gentium* (LG) 16; *Redemptor Hominis* (RH) 14], but has a positive view of these religions because they are ways through which the quest for God is expressed, given especially man's social nature [*Ad Gentes* (AG) 3; DH 3]. The common vocation of all peoples, who have God as their origin and goal is stressed [*Nostra Aetate* (NA) 2]. The Asian bishops "accept them as significant" and "acknowledge that God has drawn our peoples to himself through them" (FABC I, 14-15; cf. RH 6 and 12).

2.2 Its experience of the other religions has led the Church in Asia to this positive appreciation of their role in the divine economy of salvation. This appreciation is based on the fruits of the Spirit perceived in the lives of the other religions' believers: a sense of the sacred, a commitment to the pursuit of fullness, a thirst for self-realization, a taste for prayer and commitment, a desire for renunciation, a struggle for justice, an urge to basic human goodness, an involvement in service, a total surrender of the self to God, and an attachment to the transcendent in their symbols, rituals and life itself, though human weakness and sin are not absent.

2.3 This positive appreciation is further rooted in the conviction of faith that God's plan of salvation for humanity is one and reaches out to all peoples: it is the Kingdom of God through which he seeks to reconcile all things with himself in jesus Christ. The Church is a sacrament of this mystery — a symbolic realization that is on mission towards its fulfillment (LG 1:5; cf. BIRA IV/2). It is an integral part of this mission to discern the action of God in peoples in order to lead them to fulfillment. Dialogue is the only way in which this can be done, respectful both of God's presence and action and of the freedom of conscience of the believers of other religions [cf. LG 10-12; *Ecclesiae Sanctae* (ES) 41-42; RH 11-12].

2.4 Pope John Paul II has emphasized the unity of God's plan for humanity and the Church's mission with reference to it: "If it is the order of unity that goes back to creation and redemption and is therefore, in this sense, "divine", such differences — and even religious divergences — go back rather to a "human fact", and must be overcome in progress towards the realization of the mighty plan of unity which dominates the creation. There are undeniably differences that reflect the genius and the spiritual 'riches' which God has given to the peoples (cf. AG II). I am not referring to these divergences; I intend here to speak of the differences in which are revealed the limitations, the evolutions and the falls of the human spirit which is undermined by the spirit of evil in history (LG 16)... The Church is called to work with all her energies (evangelization, prayer, dialogue) so that the wounds and divisions of men — which separate them from their Origin and Goal, and make them hostile to one another — may be healed; it means also that the entire human race, in the infinite complexity of its history, with its different cultures, is "called to form the new People of God" (LG 13) in which the blessed union of God with man and the unity of the human family are healed, consolidated, and raised up" (Talk to the Roman Curia, Dec. 22, 1986, No. 6).

2.5 In Asia today the Christians are a "little flock". This could lead them to be self-defensive. Only an experience of the mystery in their own lives, in sacrament and community, a living contact with other believers in an atmosphere of openness and trust, an awareness of the universal dimensions of God's plan and the realization of one's very life as mission can help them to discover their obligation to dialogue. This obligation is in no way reduced because the other religious believers do not show an equal interest in dialogue, because dialogue is not simply an attempt at coexistence among religions, but a demand on the Church of its very life as mission. The interest and strength that come from such an awareness enable the Church not only to dialogue individually with each religion, but to render the service of unity by facilitating the encounter and collaboration among religions. Such a service of unity would certainly raise the question of the existing divisions among the Churches themselves in Asia and challenge them to move towards an ecumenical communion.

But this journey towards communion need not prevent, but rather encourage, the Churches in giving a common witness to their faith in Jesus and the Kingdom.

THESIS 3

Interreligious dialogue is a demand of our Christian faith in the Trinity, which is a mystery of communion in interpersonal dialogue. The unique and definitive action of the Father to save all peoples who have him as their origin and goal is leading all of us to a unity. Christ in whom God is reconciling all things to himself is urging the Church to be the servant of this communion. The universal presence and action fo the Spirit is calling everyone to the realization of the oneness of the Kingdom. As a response to this mystery, dialogue is a process of growing into the fullness of divine life. It is a participation in the quest of all peoples for the full realization of the Truth. It is LOVE for people which seeks communion in the Trinity.

3. *Commentary*

3.1 The basis of interreligious dialogue for us is our faith in the universal salvific will of God which is somehow leading all peoples to a unity, and our efforts to draw out the implications of that faith affirmation in our understanding of history and of our own role in it. It is more than the practical necessity of coexistence in one society of believers of different religions. Neither is it a consequence of the phenomenological notion that all religions are the same, at least, functionally.

3.2 One traditional view of salvation history conceived it as a narrowing of the plan and action of God progressivly from the nations to the Jews and then to Jesus, to open out again to the world through the Church and its mission. The appreciation of other religions as significant and positive elements in the economy of God's design of salvation has introduced a new paradigm that is Kingdom-centered, oriented to the future, and trinitarian. God's plan for the salvation of all peoples is one and unique. The Father, the Word and the Spirit never cease to be active in this world. God the Father has set his plan of universal salvation before the foundation of the world (Eph 1:3-6); and he made known to us this mystery of his will that in the dispensation of the fullness of times he might gather together in one all things in Christ (Eph 1:9-10). Christ, the Word by whom were all things created, became flesh and incarnated the saving mystery of God in his passion and resurrection (Col 1:14-16). It pleased the Father that in Christ all fullness should dwell; and having made peace through the blood of his cross, God is reconciling all things to himself (Col, 1:19-20). This reconciliation and peace is for all and reaches out to all peoples who are far and near through the presence and action of the one Spirit (Eph, 2:17-18) in ways unknown to us. Though all religions have a role in this mystery of God's plan, the Church is aware of being the continuation of the mystery of Jesus in the world and the sacrament of the Kingdom. The Kingdom of God will reach final fulfillment only on the last day. In the meantime, through various mediations, God is constantly challenging the freedom of peoples to obedience to his will, and people are responding in faith and good works. We should be careful not to separate the faith commitment from the creeds, symbols, rituals and actions through which this faith is mediated, expressed, celebrated and lived. There is no religionless faith in the incarnational economy that is ours, not only because the Word became flesh, but also because we are spirits-in-bodies.

3.3 The basis of dialogue then is divine and trinitarian: the creative and salvific will of the Father, the cosmic outreach of the redemptive action of Jesus who is the Christ, and the recreative and fulfilling mystery of the Spirit. Dialogue is historical: it is the progressive unification of all things, that is at once the action of God in history and the free cooperation of peoples in building their own future. Dialogue is human: it is the expression in community of the common pilgrimage of peoples towards fulfillment. Dialogue is ecclesial: it is the very being and life of the Church as mission.

3.4 Truth and love are universal and absolute values which urge us on in the way of dialogue, because their partial realization always cries out for fullness. Jesus, in whom the mystery of God's salvific plan is revealed and moves towards full realization, is the One who was born to bear witness to the Truth (Jn 18:37) and is himself the "Truth" (Jn 14:6). In Jesus, the incarnate Word of God, the Apostles and the early Church beheld the glory of the only Begotten Son of God, full of grace and truth. Our faith in Christ is engendered, nourished and fortified by the Holy Spirit who is the Spirit of Truth, who will guide us into all Truth (Jn 16:13). Hence, our faith in Jesus Christ urges us to enter into dialogue with other religions and through a common search to reach out to the fullness of Truth. Pope Paul VI has said. "Before speaking, it is necessary to listen, not only to a man's voice but to his heart... The Spirit of dialogue is friendship and, even more, is service" (ES 87). Dialogue proceeds from the "internal drive of charity" (ES 64). Pope John Paul II speaks of dialogue as a quest for truth: "Dialogue is a means of seeking after truth and of sharing it with others. For truth is light, newness and strength" (Talk to Other Religious Leaders in Madras, February 5, 1986, No. 4).

THESIS 4

Interreligious dialogue is a communication and sharing of life, experience, vision and reflection by believers of different religions searching together to discover the work of the Spirit among them. Removing prejudices, it grows towards mutual understanding and enrichment, towards a discerning and common witness and towards commitment to promote and defend human and spiritual values leading to deeper levels of spiritual experience. It is a journeying together in a communion of minds and hearts towards the Kingdom to which God calls all peoples.

4. *Commentary*

4.1 Interreligious dialogue is not primarily a relationship between two religions as social institutions, nor a comparison of two creeds or theologies, nor a tactical alliance for political action. It is a relationship between believers, who are committed to and rooted in their own faith, but open to the other believer and the Spirit in the context of the common origin and end of all human beings. Hence, sharing of convictions and experiences are more important than discussion of ideas.

4.2 Such dialogue is not only for the experts but for every one, the "simple" faithful, the theologians, the monks. It can take place at all levels: common life in its economic, social and political expressions as animated and challenged by religion; sharing of religious experience, sometimes even leading to actions like common prayer; elaborating a common vision for a new society in art, symbol and celebration; shared theological reflection in the light of faith on experiences and challenges undergone both by each one and by the community.

4.3 The goals of dialogue can be placed in an ascending order: mutual understanding, that dispels prejudices and promotes mutual knowledge and appreciation; mutual enrichment, that seeks to integrate into oneself values and experiences that are characteristic of and better developed by other believers for cultural, historical or providential reasons; common commitment to witness to and to promote human and spiritual values, like peace, respect for human life, human dignity, equality and freedom, justice, community and religious liberty, through awareness raising, prayer and action programs; shared religious experience, that constantly reaches out, in a deeper way, to the ultimate.

4.4 Religious belonging in a multireligious situation is a complex one. The primary religious community is, of course, the community of those who share the same faith. For the Christians it will obviously be the eucharistic community, but at the same time, the human community to which a person belongs in a multireligious situation, is not limited to the economic, cultural, social and political levels. There is also a community at a religious level underlying differences, which is to be explored and experienced in dialogue. Hence, the normal living and viable unit in a multireligious situation would seem to be a basic human community in which religions are not sources of differentiation and division, but help through dialogue, a common human pursuit of liberation and wholeness. In a multireligious situation, for a Christian who is aware of being in mission, belonging to such a human community would seem obvious. Such a community would be in its own way a symbol of the Kingdom.

5) Theses on the Local Church
A Theological Reflection in the Asian Context
(FABC Papers n. 60

Thesis 4

The Church is the assembly of believers whom God has called by the Gospel and who are baptized into Christ Jesus and live according to the Spirit. Christ is the head of this people of God in the new covenant. Gathered under the leadership of the successors of the apostles, the Church becomes the universal sacrament of the Kingdom of God, realizing in itself the mystery of God's will to unite in Christ all humanity and the whole universe.

4.1 The word *ekklesia* is the Greek term of the Hebrew *Qahal*, a term used to designate the community of Israel, who were liberated from slavery and conveyed by Yahweh in the desert to worship him. In the New Testament it designates the Church as the community of the believers whom God has called by the Gospel of Jesus Christ to reveal and realize his plan of salvation in the world (cf. Eph 1:19; Rom 16:25f; Eph 5:32).

4.2 Reacting against an overemphasis on the institutional aspects of the Church, the Second Vatican Council restored to their central place in ecclesiology the transcendent elements which distinguish the Church among all other human societies. This assembly of men and women owes its existence to the call of God, the Word of Christ, and the grace of the Holy Spirit. Men and women enter this community by being baptized into Christ's death and resurrection (Rom 6:3-4), becoming "whether Jews or Greeks, slaves or free persons", the Body into which they are baptized (1 Cor 12:13). It is the community which lives by the memory of Jesus of Nazareth handed down in the apostolic tradition, which proclaims and celebrates him as Lord and Savior in a fellowship presided over by the successors to the apostles, and awaits in hope his return in glory. Its eucharistic assembly is the pradigmatic realization of its inner life as participation in the mystery of Christ, the people of God, and the fellowship of the Holy Spirit: the Church from the Trinity (*Ecclesia de Trinitate*).

4.3 Christ and the Church belong together. The work of Christ for reconciliation and peace is brought about and completed through the Church (Col 1:15-23). The Church is a growing reality, growing into Christ who is the head and whose body is the Church (Eph 4:15-16). St. Paul used the image of the Body whose head is Christ (1 Cor 12; Rom 12:4-5). All the believers are "those sanctified in Christ Jesus, called to be saints together with all those who in every place call on the name of our Lord Jesus Christ" (1 Cor 1:2). They are also described as "God's chosen ones, holy and beloved" (1 Cor 3:12). The Church is described, further as "the temple of God" (1 Cor 3:16-17), where the Holy Spirit dwells (1 Cor 3:16). The Church is also the household of God "built upon the foundation of the apostles and prophets, Christ Jesus being the cornerstone" (Eph 2:20).

4.4 Gathered under the leadership of the successors of the apostles, the Church becomes the universal sacrament, sign and instrument of the Kingdom of God. The Kingdom of God is a mystery which is at once eschatological and a present reality. It is eschatological insofar as it foreshadows God's definitive reign which begins at the end of time. The different parables of the Kingdom allude to this (Mt 13:1-23). On the other hand, the Kingdom of God has appeared with the coming of Jesus (Lk 17:20-21; Mt 11:4ff.). It is identified with Jesus Christ (Jn 3:3-5; Mt 19:29; Lk 18:29).

4.5 It is the baptism that initiates one into faith in Jesus Christ and the Kingdom of God. Hence, there is a kind of identification between the Church and the Kingdom. The mystery of the Kingdom of God is, however, greater than the Church in extension. The Church is the sacrament of the Kingdom; its purpose is to make God's Kingdom sacramentally present as a salvific sign and instrument adapted to the time between Christ's resurrection and his return.

4.6 The Kingdom of God embodied in the Church is spiritual in nature, devoid of all earthly and political pretensions (Jn 18:36-37). Jesus is a spiritual leader and the charter of the Kingdom. The Sermon on the Mount is primarily a call to perfection in love characteristic of God's children, in imitation of their Heavenly Father (Mt 5:43-48). The condition for entering the Kingdom of God is spiritual: "to be converted and to become like children" (Mt 18:3), "to be born of the Spirit" (Jn 3:5). For this reason the Kingdom of God belongs to the poor in spirit (Mt 5:3).

4.7 But the spiritual nature of the Kingdom of God does not mean that the Church is invisible. Nor does it mean that the Church has nothing to do with the human realities of this world. Rather, the power of the Kingdom of God that is operative in the Church is revolutionary, affecting all the areas of human existence on earth. The metaphors of the city on a mountain and the light of the world (Mt 5:14-16) clearly imply that the Church is visible and that it exists for the world.

4.8 Christ who is the head of the Church is also the image of the invisble God, the first born of all creation, through whom and for whom all things were created (Col 1:15-18). The mystery of Christ is the mystery of God's will and his plan made known to us in all wisdom and insight (Eph 1:9). It is a plan for the fullness of time to unite all things in him, things in heaven and things on earth (Eph 1:10).

4.9 The salvific plan of God realizes itself in the history of all the peoples on the earth and moves towards the fullness of time, the *eschaton*. This is beautifully described by Paul when he says that "the creation waits with eager longing for the revealing of the sons of God" (Rom 8:19) and that "the creation itself will be set free from its bondage to decay and obtain the glorious liberty of the children of God" (Rom 8:21). Therefore, the historical reality of the Church as the realization of the mystery of Christ can never be properly understood except in the horizon of the anthropological and cosmic dimensions of this mystery.

6) Asian Theological Perspectives on Church and Politics
Theological Advisory Commission of FABC
(FABC Papers n. 63)

2.2 Motivation for Response: Christian

Apart from our human solidarity, the specific Christian vocation of the members of the Church in Asia calls for a definite stance and committed involvement in politics. The following are some of the biblical and theological baselines for this involvement.

2.2.1 Biblical Baselines

2.2.1.1 The Dignity and Social Nature of Human Beings

The Bible provides a strong basis for the Church's response to the socio-political realities. The dignity of the human person arises from the very fact of creation. "God created humankind in his image, in the image of God he created them; male and female he created them" (Gen 1:27). It is God's breath that makes man a living being (Gen 2.7). The whole earth and all that is in it were created for humankind (Gen 1:26-31). In Christ humankind was elevated to the destiny of the children of God which transcends the life of the present world (Eph 1:3-10). From their dignity as the children of God arise all their rights and duties, whether spiritual or political. From the very moment of creation the social nature of man is emphasized and man is called upon to live in communion with God and with one another and in harmony with the created world (Gen 1-2).

Human beings need to love and serve each other in order to grow into the fullness of life and attain their final destiny (Rom 13:8-10). This love and service, however, are not done in a vacuum but within the context of socio-political realities. Thus, the dignity and the social nature of the human person demand a positive response to the socio-political realities on the part of the Church.

2.2.1.2 Jesus and his Gospel to the Poor

The Gospel of Jesus Christ is the Good News of the Kingdom of God (Mk 1:14-15), or of liberation from sin and from everything that prevents man from enjoying the fullness of life according to his human dignity (Lk 4:18-19). In his teaching and ministry, Jesus himself showed a concern for persons and groups of all social levels and backgrounds, especially for the poor and the sick, for women and children, for Jews and gentiles (Lk 4:18-19; 6:20-21, 24-25; 7:22-23;

12:15-21; 16:19-31; 18:24-25). Jesus manifested a consistent concern for the poor. He frequently called upon those with possessions to use them to benefit the poor (Lk 16:19-31; 19:8-10). He asked the disciples to find ways and means to enable the poor to participate fully in the life of the community (Lk 14:12-14).

Jesus was sensitive to the contemporary social and political situation of oppression and injustice. His criticism of those who devour widows' houses (Lk 20:47), and his protest against those who profaned the Temple with religious as well as economic oppression (Lk 20:45-46) are all eloquent examples of this.

Hence, the Church, as the community of those who believe in the Good News of the Kingdom and have the mission to proclaim it (Mk 16:15), cannot be indifferent to the socio-political conditions of human beings. On the contrary, the Church has to be actively involved with socio-political issues since these touch on the Gospel itself. This is especially true in the Asian situation where the great majority of the people live in social conditions not befitting their human dignity.

2.2.1.3 *Jesus and the Socio-Political Order*

Jesus was not indifferent to the socio-political order of his time. He often taught and acted in such a way as to explicitly or implicitly call for radical modifications in the social and political patterns of the day. His insistence that social relationships be governed by service and humility (Lk 9:47-48; 14:7-11; 17:7-10) constituted a challenge to the existing social order. The existing social order presupposed domination, and violence was central to its effective operation (Mt 20:25-28). Jesus, in contrast, refused the use of violence and criticized the gentile kings for their practice of dominating their subjects. He never used his power to perform miracles solely for his own benefit.

In order to describe the power exercised by the rulers of his time, Jesus used two expressions, namely "lord it over" (*katakurieo*) and "exercise authority over" (*katexousiazo*), which mean lack of respect for the freedom of the subjects and using power for one's selfish interests respectively. On the other hand, he demanded that the exercise of authority should have the character of service. Such an exercise of authority called for a radical change in the existing socio-political structures.

The example of Jesus Christ should inspire the local Churches of Asia to be aware of their political responsibility in their countries. The Church should be actively committed to evangelizing the political life of Asia. Christians should themselves be imbued with the spirit of the Gospel and should see to it that the spirit of the Gospel penetrates every sphere and structure of political life in the varying situations of Asia.

2.2.1.4 *Jesus and the Political Authority*

Jesus himself asserts the duty of paying one's dues to the State, but without in any way reducing the claims of God: "Render to Caesar the things that are Caesar's, and to God the things that are God's" (Mt 22:17-21). If the State exercises authority by virtue of the divine commission, for the very same reason the exercise of this authority should not be absolute, but should respect God's sovereign power and authority in its various expressions in the society. The statement of Jesus regarding the problem of giving tribute to Caesar could be understood as a statement about the approach one should take towards the political and social structures. Caesar's realm or the social and political order of the Roman empire was in Jesus' view part of the larger order of creation whose only author is God. Therefore, the Roman social patterns were to be evaluated against the social patterns desired by God, and supported or not on that basis.

2.2.1.5 *Jesus: Critical towards the Political Authorities*

Jesus himself maintained a critical stance with respect to the political authorities and evaluated the social and political patterns under their rule on the basis of how closely they corresponded to the patterns desired by God. In fact, Jesus presented himself in the lineage of the ancient prophets who clearly participated in the political sphere and often took a stand against the politics of the kings of their times. Thus, people saw in Jesus the features of Elijah who came into politico-religious conflict with Ahab and Ahaziah, the kings of Israel (1Kgs 17-2Kgs 1; Mk 8:28; Lk 9:19). Jesus also showed features of Jeremiah (Mt 16:14), who linked the political future of the kingdom of Judah to a liberating change specifically in socio-political structures (Jer 22:3-5). Jesus' confrontation with Herod Antipas (Lk 9:9; 13:31-33) and the chief priests (Lk 19:47) is a clear proof of his prophetic and critical stance towards the political authorities.

2.2.1.6 *Confrontation between Jesus and the Political Authorities*

Jesus occasionally confronted the authorities of his time. For example, he violently expressed his protest against the corruption of the authorities in the religious and economic establishments associated with the Temple (Mt 21:10-17; Jn 2:13-22). He retorted with scorn to the threat of herod to kill him, and he did not allow his course of action to be determined by the wishes and policies of the political rulers of his times (Lk 13:31-33). Jesus questioned the legitimacy of the violence used against him during the trial in the house of Annas (Jn 18:22-23). These instances show that Jesus acted against social corruption, and that he did not passively accept the unjust violence exerted on him by the political authorities.

The early Church also had to confront the violent reaction of the political authorities. When Peter and John were arrested and warned by the members of the Sanhedrin against preaching in the name of Jesus, they boldly retorted: "You must judge whether in God's eyes it is right to listen to you and not to God" (Acts 4:18-21). Paul defended his legitimate rights as a Roman citizen when he confronted the Roman tribune (Acts 22:21-29). Hence, the early Church also gives testimony of having taken a bold stand against the unjust and violent use of political authority.

2.2.1.7 *The Church and the Political Authority*

All authority comes from God. This principle is accepted and held as true throughout the whole of biblical revelation. This is reflected in the various expressions of authority found in the biblical traditions, such as the authority of parents over their children (Lev 19:3), of the government over the people (1Kgs 19:15; 2Kgs 8:13), etc. Hence, the Church should respect the holders of political authority. The New Testament writers were concerned with the position of Christianity within the Roman empire. They spoke about the attitude that Christians should take regarding the political authority of their times.

Paul explicitly states, while exhorting the faithful to be subject to the governing authorities: "There is no authority except from God, and those that exist have been instituted by God" (Rom 13:1). The State exists for the sake of the good order (Rom 13:4). Paul does not hesitate to call the political ruler "God's servant" (Rom 13:4) and the government officials "ministers of God" (Rom 13:6). Those who resist the governing authorities resist what God has appointed. Therefore, Christians are subject to the State for the sake of conscience. For the same reason, they pay respect and legitimate taxes to the State (Rom 13:5-7). Prayers and supplications are to be offered for the political rulers (1Tim 2:1-7).

However, in imitation of Jesus, the Church has to take a critical and prophetic stance towards the political authorities, since they are especially responsible for the particular sociopolitical order on which depends the social welfare of the people. The Church, being the sacrament of the Kingdom of God which is concerned with the integral liberation and development of man, cannot be indifferent in the matter of taking such a political stance. Hence, the local Churches of Asia cannot endorse the social and political practices and patterns of the State unconditionally. They have to be evaluated against the standard of the social patterns demanded by the values of the Kingdom of God and must be supported or not on that basis.

2.2.1.8 *Confrontation between the Church and State*

The political authority can become a tool of the powers of evil. This is illustrated in the fact that the rulers of this world crucified the Lord of glory (1Cor 2:6-8). In fact, a tension between the political and spiritual powers and the consequent conflict are inevitable. The political authority could become sometimes the expression of the "world" which rejected Jesus and whose prince is the devil (Jn 12:31; 16:11). In this case, there can take place in the relationship between the State and the Church a confrontation between "the world" that rejected Christ and the Kingdom of God. Despite its attempt at justice, "the world" is incapable of perceiving the truth (Jn 18:37f) and of resisting corruption of the heart (Jn 19:12-15). Thereby, it becomes the devil's servant. Though the power of the devil has been basically destroyed by the glorification of Jesus (Jn 12:31), the struggle between these two powers will continue until the parousia. Therefore, the confrontation between these two powers can be realized in the confrontation between the Church and the State if the State does not respect the values of the Kingdom of God.

The experience of the Church towards the end of the first century, as described in the Book of Revelation, is a clear illustration of this possible confrontation. In fact, Jesus himself had foretold that his disciples would have the same fate as that of the prophets and of himself (Lk 6:22-23; Mt 5:11-12). If the Church is really prophetic, it will necessarily come into conflict with the State if the latter does not do justice to its God-given mission. In many Asian countries where Christians are a minority, it is quite possible for the Church to assume an attitude of neutrality at the cost of its prophetic mission. The Church has a definite and prophetic role to play in the socio-political life of the Asian people, not as an outsider or onlooker but as a community of people actively involved in it, and joining forces with the sisters and brothers of other faiths and cultures.

2.2.2 Theological Baselines

2.2.2.1 Christ's Intention for the Church

A great concern of the New Testament was to warn the Church, which was only a tiny minority, against being preoccupied with itself alone. Should that happen, the Church would remain a sect, a closed group, which would have no concern for the welfare of the world.

But this was not Christ's intention for the Church. He wanted his disciples to be "the light of the world" (Mt 5:14), and "the salt of the earth" (Mt 5:13). He commanded them to go forth and "make disciples of all the nations" (Mt 28:19), to preach the Gospel to every creature (Mk 16:15).

The mission of the Church has often been misinterpreted as though it concerned only the souls of persons and their salvation in the afterlife. Today, while insisting on the importance and primacy of the spiritual dimension of human life and on eternal salvation, the Church has repeatedly declared that its mission includes the salvation of the total human person even in his/her temporal dimensions.

> ... evangelization involves an explict message, adapted to the different situations constantly being realized, about the rights and duties of every human being, about family life, without which personal growth and development is hardly possible, about life in society, about international life, peace, justice and development — a message especially energetic today about liberation (*Evangelii Nuntiandi*, 29).

2.2.2.2 *Concern for the Human Being in All Dimensions*

Pope John Paul II, in his first encyclical *Redemptor Hominis*, has pointed out that the concrete human being, living in history, is "the way for the Church, the primary and indispensable way the Church must take, the way which is in a sense the basis of all the other ways" (no. 17). The clear implication of this is that the Church which does not pay attention to the human person in his/her historical concreteness is a Church that has lost its way.

That is why the 1971 Synod of Bishops does not hesitate to declare in the oft-quoted lapidary statement: "Action on behalf of justice and participation in the trasnformation of the world fully appear to us as a constitutive dimension of the preaching of the Gospel, or, in other words, of the Church's mission for the redemption of the human race and its liberation from every oppressive situation".

If the Church must be involved with the human being in his or her concrete historical reality and temporal dimensions, it cannot avoid involvement in political concerns and questions which pervade, influence and sometimes dominate the temporal life of people and affect deeply their salvation. Politics is an inescapable concern of the Church.

There is thus a necessity for the Church to involve itself with political concerns. This necessity is underlined by Pope Paul VI when explaining the links between evangelization and human promotion:

> ... how in fact can one proclaim the new commandment without promoting in justice and in peace the true, authentic advancement of man? We ourselves have taken care to point this out by recalling that it is impossible to accept "that in evangelization one could or should ignore the importance of the problems so much discussed today, concerning justice, liberation, development and peace in the world. This would be to forget the lesson which comes to us from the Gospel concerning love of our neighbor who is suffering and in need (EN 31)".

Note that the Pope says it is impossible to accept that evangelization could or should ignore problems concerning justice, liberation, development and peace — all of which are political problems. The Church cannot ignore these if it is to be true to the commandment of love which is the characteristic mark of Christ's disciple.

2.2.2.3 *Preferential Love of the Poor*

But this evangelical love today demands a love of preference for the poor, deprived and oppressed. This is a demand of the Gospel — not only a love for all but a preferential, though not exclusive, love for the poor. This preferential love calls for more than dole-outs, or even for development efforts with and on behalf of the poor. To be truly effective, this preferential love must seek the transformation of sinful structures or structures of injustice that prevent the poor from achieving their authentic human development. Once the Church, however, exerts efforts to bring about a transformation of social structures, it must enter the field of politics.

For example, in many places in Asia today the Church needs to speak for genuine agrarian reform, for a better distribution of wealth, for more just tax structures. It is called upon to lend its voice for just wages, for social security, speedy justice and genuine guarantees for human rights. Such an advocacy does not make the Church a competitor in the political arena, but makes it a prophetic voice of the voiceless, and an advocate of humanity. The Church must be ready to support such measures even at the risk of incurring the displeasure of vested interests.

In this regard, the mission of the Church implies five concrete tasks: *announcing* the Gospel values upon which every human community needs to be built; *denouncing* all situations of injustice, oppression, exploitation, manipulation and domination; *promoting* whatever helps the person and society to grow, after discerning the action of the Holy Spirit in the socio-political realities; *giving witness* as a community of people who, led by the Holy Spirit, serve their fellow citizens; and *educating* for justice by awakening consciences to a knowledge of the concrete situation, and by forming people to take political action.

2.2.2.4 *The Church - Sign and Instrument of God's Kingdom*

The Church's involvement in political concerns is rooted in its very being. For the Church is the universal sacrament of salvation both manifesting and exercising God's love for human beings (cf. GS 45).

The Church is the group of believers whom God has called by the Gospel and baptism into Christ to form a community dedicated to the salvation and transformation of the world. It is both the visible community in which the Kingdom of God is already experienced, though imperfectly, and the community which is called to reveal, announce and promote the full realization of the Kingdom. The Church is not an end in itself, but is a community which realizes itself in the measure that it puts itself concretely at the service of the Kingdom in different historical situations.

It is the vocation of the Church to be the sign of the Kingdom which is already operative in the world. This Kingdom is a Kingdom of holiness and grace, yes, — but also a Kingdom of justice and peace. When the Church embodies these values, it stands out as a challenge to the injustices of our Asian world in the midst of which it lives and which it loves. Its very existence will be a question posed to the injustice, the greed for money and power, and the self-centeredness that characterize so much of our Asian societies.

The Church is also the instrument of the Kingdom. It is not the only instrument of the Kingdom, but it serves and promotes the Kingdom together with all the other children of the Kingdom. To promote the Kingdom is to work for the realization of the values of the Kingdom, so that these values may be inscribed deeply in the fabric of Asian society. This is the work of the whole Church, for the values of the Kingdom and of the Gospel cannot be inscribed in Asian society without the active presence and participation of the lay faithful (cf. AG 21).

That is why Vatican II, in speaking of the Church as sacrament of salvation, speaks of it as the People of God. "For every benefit which the People of God during its earthly pilgrimage can offer to the human family stems from the fact that the Church is the universal sacrament of salvation", simultaneously manifesting and exercising the mystery of God's love for man" (GS 45).

Though the whole Church as People of God is called to be the sacrament of salvation, and consequently is charged with the mission of transfroming the world, the laity by reason of their specific vocation have a unique role to play in this mission. Their vocation to be Christians in the heart of secularity, and their expertise in secular affairs, capacitate them to be at the service of this transformation. Thus, it is they who must be in the forefront of the Church's involvement in politics.

2.2.2.5 *In Christ and Like Christ*

The Church is the sacrament of salvation. It is, however, in Christ, and only in Christ, that it is a sign and instrument of salvation (cf. LG 1,48). When the Church asks itself the reason for its involvement in the political life of the people, it must go back to Jesus Christ, the source of its life, the inspiration for its actions. This Christ "went about doing good works and healing all who were in the grip of the devil" (Acts 10:38). He preached the Kingdom and made it real to people by liberating them from sin, illness and death, and by uniting them in love for each other. He bestowed a salvation which renewed the whole human being and brought justice and love. The Church, in working for the temporal well-being of people and for the transformation of human relationships, thus makes present Christ's work and grace. It projects the face and heart of Christ.

2.2.2.6 *A Program*

While "Church as sacrament of salvation" expresses the being of the Church, it is also a programmatic title for the life of the Church itself. The Church must really embody and visibly manifest in itself the values of the Kingdom. It is the Lord's primary exhibit or sample of what he wants done in humanity. That is why the Synod on *Justice in the World*, ch. 3 (1971), warns that those who preach justice must first of all be just themselves. The Church's being and mission make demands on the Church itself. We shall look further into these demands in a later section.

We have just seen the human and Christian reasons that should motivate the Church and its members to respond to the socio-political situation in Asia. But the Church encounters obstacles which hinder it from responding as it should. We shall now look into these hindrances.

The Idea of the Kingdom of God in African Theology

A. Emmanuel Orobator

Introduction

As a cursory browse through the Synoptic Gospels confirms, exegetes and theologians are unanimous in pointing out that the kingdom of God is the central symbol or theme of Jesus' proclamation, mission and praxis[1]. The fine thread of this paradigmatic notion is intricately woven into the gospel both as its leitmotiv and ultimate consummation. Simply stated, the idea of the kingdom of God succinctly encapsulates the message that Christians are confronted with when they make the radical option for faith in Jesus who is the Christ.

The invitation to contribute this essay to this present volume outlined in precise terms the editor's expectation: *The idea of the Kingdom of God in African Christian Theology*. One unspoken presupposition of this title is that there exists in African Christian theology attempts to elaborate the idea of the kingdom of God. Unfortunately, the dearth of imagination that bedevils theological reflection in Africa does not spare this important tenet of Jesus' proclamation and praxis.

---

[1] The reader can consult with immense profit John Meier's excellent study of 'the kingdom of God' in *A Marginal Jew: Rethinking the Historical Jesus*, Vol. II (New York: Doubleday, The Anchor Bible Reference Library, 1994), 237-506. I shall rely on his study for the initial clarification of the biblical idea of the kingdom of God. Equally useful for this study is NORMAN PERRIN, *Jesus and the Language of the Kingdom*, in *The Kingdom of God*, ed. BRUCE CHILTON (Philadelphia/London: Fortress Press/SPCK, Issues in Religion and Theology 5, 1984), 92-106; RICHARD H. HIERS, *The Kingdom of God in the Synoptic Tradition* (Gainesville: University of Florida Press, 1970); RAYMOND E. BROWN, *An Introduction to New Testament Christology* (New York/Mahwah: Paulist Press, 1994), 60-70; JOHN FUELLENBACH, *The Kingdom of God: The Message of Jesus Today* (New York: Orbis Books, 1995); BRUCE CHILTON, *Pure Kingdom: Jesus' Vision of God* (Grand Rapids, Michigan: Eerdmans, 1996).

My initial research yielded meager results. This is an indication that unless one considers as significant Ghanaian Pan-Africanist Kwame Nkrumah's ideological twist: "Seek first the political kingdom", there is no serious attempt yet to relate this symbol, the kingdom of God, systematically to the African reality. Consequently, my attempt to explore the idea of the kingdom of God in African theology can hardly amount to a synthesis of preexisting or current approaches in the different schools of African theology[2]. Accordingly, any treatment of the subject must at this present stage bear visible traits of originality. Theological imagination and innovation will be given a full and free reign, in the hope that one is setting in motion a precedent on a subject deemed particularly useful to contemporary African Christianity. The idea of the kingdom of God, as it appears in the Synoptic Gospels, allows room for such deployment of the theological imagination; it is a dynamic and a functional symbol whose multifaceted application is never exhausted by a single level of interpretation.

The thesis that I advance in this essay is that the reality of life on the African continent permits a unique interpretation of this pivotal symbol of Jesus' proclamation and mission. This interpretation should contribute to the hermeneutics of the kingdom of God, a hermeneutics previously dominated by the positions of Western theologians and exegetes. Albert Schweitzer, Adolf von Harnack and Rudolph Bultmann come to mind, but their tendency to confine the idea of the kingdom of God to the innocuous domain of the personal and private must be judged as woefully inadequate, at least in what concerns the African situation.

Restricting the debate to the question of whether the kingdom of God coincides with the church or vice versa is

---

[2] There is, for example, Simon Maimela's attempt to relate Luther's idea of the twofold kingdom (kingdom of God ['children of Adam']) and (kingdom of the world ['all mankind']) to the South African situation of apartheid and white supremacist's regime. On this basis of this correlation he argues the case of the social role of the church, especially in the South African context. However, Maimela's article is not a direct study of Jesus' idea of the kingdom of God as it appears in the Synoptic Gospels. SIMON S. MAIMELA, "The Twofold Kingdom: An African Perspective", in *Theology and the Black Experience: The Lutheran Heritage Interpreted by African and African-American Theologians*, ed. ALBERT PERO and AMBROSE MOYO (Minneapolis: Augsburg Publishing House, 1988), 97-109.

another characteristically Western approach. The resolution of the resulting theological quandary has roots deep in the theological tradition of Roman North African doctor of the church, Augustine of Hippo. Fortunately, several years of theological research and debate have enlarged the ambit of our understanding of the idea of the kingdom of God. The significance of this symbol in the experience and expression of the Christian message has emerged with renewed vigor in contemporary theology. For this reason too, it is timely to consider what this symbol means in the context of the African reality.

The first section of this essay briefly explores and restates the Synoptic Gospels' idea of the kingdom of God. In the second part I propose a three-tier hermeneutical grid for understanding of the kingdom of God in African Christian theology. Far from rehashing the familiar interpretation of this central symbol, I will identify the contours or elements of a uniquely African interpretation without circumscribing it in watertight theological or exegetical categories. Finally, based on this hermeneutical grid, I will proffer an example of the idea of the kingdom of God in African Christian theology as it relates to the mission of the churches in Africa.

The Kingdom of God in the Synoptic Gospels

Whichever terminology is preferred, the kingdom of God (the kingdom of heaven, or the reign of God) is a symbol that ceaselessly overtakes its immediate referents in the Synoptic Gospels. Norman Perrin's preference for the term "tensive symbol" in describing its nature is apt here. One could say that from the moment of its appearance in the Synoptic Gospels, the rest of each evangelist's work is a labored commentary attempting to explore, explain and apply the highly 'elusive' resonances of the kingdom of God. This commentary also attempts to enlarge the Jewish understanding of the kingdom of God. Thus, the paradigmatic inauguration in Mark 1:15 of Jesus' public proclamation presupposes a link with a previous but still unfolding history of salvation as known to the Jews, which history attains a *kairos* moment at the time of Jesus' proclamation.

This idea of a link or continuity implies that the background of the kingdom proclamation of Jesus is deeply embedded in the teaching of the Old Testament. It is correct to say that, although the regular usage of the kingdom of God is limited to Jesus and the Synoptic redactors, the message it conveys, namely, God's universal sovereignty, finds immediate resonances in the collective (national) consciousness of the Jews. The basic idea is that God's reign or kingly rule, which marked the creation of the earth, stretches through all the moments of history and attains its consummation in an eschatological establishment of God's kingdom. This 'establishment' is not to be conceived as a geographically delineated territory or sphere. Rather, it is an effective and dynamic shorthand that signals the unsurpassable, universal presence of God as the overriding principle of all creation[3]. This notion recalls the Pauline idea of eschatological consummation when God will be "all in all" (1 Cor. 15:28).

It is necessary to recall at this point Jesus' characteristic phrase, "The kingdom of God *may be compared to...*" This phrase prefaces his attempts to elucidate the meaning of the kingdom of God. Jesus' approximative symbols and imageries of the kingdom are 'plastic' enough on the question of its nature. Precisely they excite theological imagination beyond the Synoptic Gospels' orbit for understanding the idea of the kingdom of God. This approximation of the idea of the kingdom precludes any univocal conception or application of its meaning. One fascinating indication of the analogical use of this symbol can be detected in the fact that the Jews both knew and did not know what Jesus meant by the kingdom of God. What the Jews understood (Zealots, Pharisees, Scribes, Sadducees, etc.) was in function of their immediate socio-political milieu, and their ideological agenda for reversing the oppressive elements of this milieu[4]. Nevertheless, whatever the Jews understood, it is conceivable that is

---

[3] In explicating the symbol Jesus sometimes employs spatio-temporal imageries. See, for example, Mark 14:25 parr, which suggests a *day* when Jesus shall drink *in* the kingdom.

[4] See, for example, the excellent 'reexamination' of the Zealots' agenda by WILLA BOESAK, *God's Wrathful Children: Political Oppression and Christian Ethics* (Grand Rapids, Michigan: Eerdmans, 1995), 69-107.

was related to the OT expectation that Yahweh will establish his kingdom on earth as a tangible reality. It is this expectation that perhaps grounds the belief of the Jews who "lived in the hope of seeing the kingdom of God" (Mark 15:43 parr. See Mark 9:1, Matt. 16:28, Luke 9:27).

One immediate conclusion that could be drawn from the foregoing is that the idea of the kingdom of God has a familiar ring in African history just as it did in Jewish national history. Africa is home to ancient and modern kingdoms. As geopolitical entities, these kingdoms embodied at various times in history the hopes of particular African peoples for security and collective well-being under the rule of a king. Examples of these kingdoms abound on the continent. In Africa south of the Sahara there flourished (and declined) in succession the kingdoms of Ghana, Mali, and Songhai from the 11th through the 18th centuries. The latter part of this period also witnessed the emergence of several others: Benin, Dahomey, Yoruba, Kongo, Ashanti, Swazi, Ganda, Zulu, etc.[5].

The point of citing these examples is to show that Africans do have an experience of kingdoms as a territorial sphere, realm or domain subject to the effective rule of a king. While this understanding lacks any eschatological or apocalyptic component comparable to some strands of Jewish understanding of the kingdom of God, one could contend that the African understanding (of the kingdom of God) has been influenced by its historical experience of kingdoms. This assertion is aptly illustrated by the dominant interpretation of the kingdom of God in popular African religiosity. The common understanding that underlies its interpretation in this religiosity is the conviction that God will offer access to the kingdom as a reward to the 'saved' in the dramatic event of the 'rapture' (cf. 1 Thess. 4:16-17). This entrance into God's eschatological domain is what is understood as 'the kingdom of heaven' in popular African religiosity.

In the throes of present socioeconomic and political crises, it is a common occurrence for religious leaders in

---

[5] See BASIL DAVIDSON, *African Kingdoms* (New York: Time-Life Books, 1966); KEVIN SHILLINGTON, *History of Africa* (New York: St. Martin's Press, Rev. ed. 1995); ELOCHUKWU UZUKWU, *A Listening Church: Autonomy and Communion in African Churches* (Maryknoll, New York: Orbis Books, 1996), 12-26.

Africa to offer their followers the understanding of the kingdom of God as an eschatological gathering of the pious: "The solution for most missionaries is to claim that the Gospel is concerned exclusively with spiritual matters, and that its goal is the preparation for the 'kingdom of heaven' not for the 'Kingdom of God' here on earth. Others justify themselves by suggesting that transformation of the social order is a matter of the future, but for the present the *status quo* must remain"[6]. Effectively this idea of the kingdom of God serves as a panacea for contemporary social crises. The result is too often a social escapism that denies the structural roots of the crises and freezes Christian social action or responsibility in the innocuous rhetoric of an otherworldly kingdom of God. In this context the radically subversive nature of the kingdom of God as proclaimed by Jesus pales into social passivity.

A second conclusion at this point relates to the fact that the message of the kingdom of God is heard in context. Jesus' audience heard and interpreted the message of the kingdom in the immediate context of economic and political oppression by the occupying Roman government. Understandably, the reaction of Jesus' apostles after the Easter event is couched in an expectation of the restoration of the Davidic rule as an embodiment of the promised messianic kingdom: "Lord, has the time come for you to restore the kingdom of Israel?" (Acts 1:6). That Jesus constantly attempts to adjust the dominant interpretation of the kingdom of God as a sociopolitical sphere in order to avoid any 'reductionism' is a fact. Yet, the question will need to be asked: What is the dominant context of the African continent in which the message of the kingdom of God is heard? This consideration allows us to explore and suggest what the idea of the kingdom of God implies in the African context.

---

[6] J.N.K. MUGAMBI, *From Liberation to Reconstruction: African Christian Theology after the Cold War* (Nairobi, Kenya: East African Educational Publishers Ltd., 1995), 229.

An African Reading of the Kingdom of God

Before proceeding any further it is important to restate the basic position of this essay. The kingdom of God is a multifaceted notion whose content and intent cannot be exhausted by any single hermeneutical paradigm. An African proverb says: *I pointed out to you the stars but all you saw was the tip of my finger.* Each hermeneutics of the kingdom of God yields at best no more than a 'tip' of its finger. I suggest, as paradigm for interpreting the idea of the kingdom of God in the African context, a three-tier hermeneutical grid: annunciation (good news), denunciation (prophetic action), transformation (praxis). From this triple-sided approach emerges a model of the kingdom of God that bears an African imprint. It is important to note at the outset of this analysis that the three elements of this grid closely overlap and, therefore, are to be taken together.

The Kingdom of God as Annunciation

Mark 1:15 offers the clearest indication of the urgency and imminence of the kingdom of God: "The time is fulfilled, and the kingdom of God is close at hand (has drawn near)...!" (cf. Matt. 4:17). Perhaps of greater significance is the oft-ignored connection between this paradigmatic proclamation and the idea of 'gospel' (good news). Many exegetes and theologians consecrate a great deal of energy to the task of determining the precise meaning of the material *terms* (time, fulfillment, kingdom, arrival, proximity) of this declaration to the detriment of the meaning it conveys. In Mark's unique evangelical agenda this proclamation is in fact *the* good news: The markan Jesus "proclaimed *the gospel* from God saying, '*The time is fulfilled, and the kingdom of God is close at hand*'". Matthew and Luke both make the same connection: "He went round the whole of Galilee teaching in their synagogues, proclaiming the *good news of the kingdom*..." (Matt. 4:23; 9:35). "Now it happened that after this he made his way through the towns and villages preaching and proclaiming *the good news of the kingdom of God*" (Luke 8:1; cf. 9:11). The implication of this connection is that the kingdom of God is *the* gospel. Accordingly, Ghanian theologian Kwame Bediako notes that: "[T]he Gospel as the 'good news to the poor' is the good news of God's kingdom and God's justice. It follows therefore that the Gospels's content is defined by what it means to the poor, namely, justice, just relationships, with God, among humans and with the environment..."[7]. This assertion relates the idea of the kingdom in African Christianity to a series of challenges and, at the same, reveals its precise meaning in an African context.

If the kingdom of God is the good news of Jesus, which — as indicated above — is heard in context, it must, therefore, speak to the situation of the African continent where it is proclaimed. There is a glaring paradox in the idea of the kingdom of God as good news in an African setting. Cardinal Hyacinthe Thiandoum of Dakar (Senegal) poignantly depicted this paradox at the African Synod in 1994. How, he queried, in a continent so full of bad news, can the gospel be 'good' news'? Stated differently, how can the idea of the kingdom of God portend good news at a time "when our [African] identity is being crushed in a mortar of merciless chain of events"[8]? Another bitter remark by an African Christian painfully expresses the frustration inherent in this paradox: "The Gospel may be good news indeed; but it has ceased to be good news to many of our people"[9].

The above point can be further illustrated. If the statistics of the 1996 *United Nations Human Development Report* are to be believed, one third of Africa's total population lives in a situation of real starvation. This precarious situation is aggravated by violent armed conflicts, which in turn have produced on the continent the world's largest population of refugees. Furthermore, of the forty-three poorest countries of the world, thirty-two are in Africa south of the Sahara. In addition, the continent holds the record for the highest rates

---

[7] KWAME BEDIAKO, *Christianity in Africa: The Renewal of a Non-Western Religion* (Maryknoll, New York: Orbis Books, 1995), 146.

[8] *Message of the Synod* (Nairobi, Kenya: Pauline Publications Africa, 1994), no. 15.

[9] Quoted in ELIZABETH ISICHEI, *A History of Christianity in Africa: From Antiquity to the Present* (Grand Rapids, Michigan: Eerdmans, 1995), 170.

of infant mortality. These statistics paint a gory panorama of a continent living in perpetual 'state of a holocaust'[10]. In Africa, therefore, the poor and the marginalized are not just a mere negligible class or agglomeration of classes. The poor in Africa are whole nations, whole peoples.

This gruesome panorama is not without implications for the idea of the kingdom of God. Precisely that is the point of this argument, that the idea of the kingdom of God in African Christianity must mean good news: food for the hungry, health for the sick, home for the refugee, peace for the troubled, and justice for the oppressed. This is the meaning of the idea of God's kingdom in Africa when it is considered — as I propose it should — *the* good news. As Kenyan theologian J. N. K. Mugambi contends:

> The Good News which Jesus proclaims to the world is not theoretical. It is practical. It is news which in real life rehabilitates individuals and groups that are marginalized by various natural and social circumstances. In contemporary Africa, the Good News understood in this way ought to rehabilitate the afflicted individuals in every region, country and locality. The Gospel ought to help Africans regain their confidence and hope...[11].

This assertion finds its ultimate foundation in the preaching and teaching of Jesus in the Synoptic Gospels. The examples could be multiplied but two will suffice to illustrate the point of this assertion.

First, one imagery or parable of the kingdom that is common in the Synoptic Gospels is the imagery of the wedding feast or banquet: "The kingdom of heaven may be compared to a king who gave a feast for his son's wedding...". (Matt. 22:2; cf. Luke 14:16-24). This imagery of the kingdom is particularly relevant to Africa, where the idea of a feast conveys a

---

[10] Cf. EFOE-JULIEN PENOUKOU, *Eglises d'afriques: propositions pour l'avenir* (Paris: Karthala, 1984), 92.

[11] MUGAMBI, *From Liberation to Reconstruction*, 176. My position in this essay is that it is not enough to 'rehabilitate' the marginalized and oppressed African people. The situation in Africa calls for a massive transformation of socioeconomic and political structures.

meaning that subsumes not just the immediate action of eating, but also the experience of inclusive fellowship in community, and the healing of rifts in social and personal relationships. An African proverb on the social value of feasting says: *Those who eat together do not eat one another*. One can equally recall here the apt reminder of the essence of feasting and eating in Africa by one of the character's in Chinua Achebe's classic novel *Things Fall Apart*: "A man who calls his kinsmen to a feast does not do so to save them from starving. They all have food in their own homes. When we gather together in the moonlit village ground it is not because of the moon. Every man can see it in his own compound. We come together because it is good for kinsmen to do so"[12]. Luke, the evangelist, interjects: "Blessed is the one who will share the meal in the kingdom of God!" (Luke 14:15; cf. Rom. 14:17). This is not to suggest that for Africans the "meal of the kingdom" dissolves into a mere eschatological utopia. Hardly. On the contrary, it must satisfy the contemporary deafening yearnings of Africans for bread that sates their hunger, and a meal that forges the bond of communion between African peoples torn apart by strife and violence.

The second example concerns the composition of Jesus's audience. The 'auditors' of Jesus' proclamation of the good news of the kingdom are the sick, who are afflicted by different kinds of illnesses. Matthew establishes a striking connection between Jesus' mission of proclaiming the good news of the kingdom and his action of "curing all kinds of diseases and illnesses among the people" (Matt. 4:23, 9:35; cf. Mark 1:39, 3:7-12; Luke 6:17-19). The reason for highlighting this aspect of the idea of God's kingdom is that it has a particular appeal in the African continent stricken by diseases of phenomenal proportions. The devastating scourge of AIDS has attained an epic proportion in the continent where one African out of every forty is HIV+. The situation is further compounded by the lack of adequate health facilities and infrastructures. A great deal of bitter truth is contained in the

---

[12] CHINUA ACHEBE, *Things Fall Apart* (New York: Anchor Books, Doubleday, First published in 1959), 166-167. See also JOSEPH HEALEY and DONALD SYBERTZ, *Towards an African Narrative Theology* (Nairobi, Kenya: Pauline Publications Africa), 254-290.

statement that "Africa is, quite literally, a sick continent"[13]. Besides, "even if AIDS [or the other ravaging diseases] could be stopped by a single glass of clean water ...most Africans would still have no access to the cure"[14]. The idea of the kingdom of God in Africa means health, freedom from the oppression of sickness and diseases.

Considered therefore at the first level of the three-tier hermeneutical grid, the idea of the kingdom of God is the annunciation of *the* good news in the context of bad news. Theological reflection on this "continent of misery" cannot make abstraction of this context — in which this good news of the kingdom is proclaimed — without losing its claim to credibility and relevance: "The objective poverty of the African people stares the African church and its theology in the face as both claim to bring these same people the liberating message of Christ's gospel. To do theology in Africa today and wink at the dehumanizing conditions of Africa's socioeconomic reality involves what John Calvin called 'nefarious perfidy', because this not only constitutes a betrayal of the gospel itself, but also the freedom of God's own people"[15]. Yet, if the idea of the kingdom of God in Africa is the annunciation of something radically new, it is also a denunciation of the status quo.

THE KINGDOM OF GOD AS DENUNCIATION

The idea of the kingdom of God, as it is presented in the Synoptic Gospels, sets itself in judgement, here and now, against other opposing *kingdoms*. These 'kingdoms' possess their own dynamics and act in view of carefully defined ends. One example of this opposition between the kingdom of God and other 'kingdoms' is found in the Beelzebub controversy, which pitted Jesus' proclamation against the obstinacy of the Jewish authorities. In this controversy Jesus alludes to the kingdom of Satan (cf. Mark. 3:22-27). The con-

---

[13] Quoted in JEFFREY GOLDBERG, "Our Africa Problem", *New York Times Magazine*, March 2, 1997, 35.
[14] Ibid., 62.
[15] EMMANUEL MARTEY, *African Theology: Inculturation and Liberation* (Maryknoll, New York: Orbis Books, 1993), 50.

clusion to this controversy is rendered with a note of urgency in Luke 11:20: "But if it is through the finger of God that I drive devils out, then the kingdom of God has indeed caught you unawares" (cf. Matt. 12:28). There is an unmistakable suggestion here of the irruption of the kingdom of God in the midst of opposition to Jesus' proclamation. Furthermore, in this controversy the drama of vicious opposition and tension between Jesus and the constituted religious and political authorities unfolds with increasing intensity. The denunciatory tone of Jesus' proclamation becomes equally pungent. One can recall, for example, the sevenfold indictment of the scribes and Pharisees (Matt. 23:13-32 par.). What is the relevance of this observation?

It was pointed out above that Africa has been and still is home to constituted kingdoms. With alarming intensity these kingdoms have become the private domains of despotic rulers, who plunder with impunity the vast resources of their political domain and 'bind' — as do 'unclean spirits' — most of the African people in poverty, ignorance and misery. A very appropriate analogy can be made here between the terminology of 'strong man', a pointed reference to Satan in the Synoptic Gospels (Matt. 12:29, Mark 3:27, Luke 11:21-22), and the growing number of African political leaders, civilian and military, who characteristically wear the title 'strong man'. The example is too obvious to warrant mentioning names. A close look at the method of operation of these African strong men reveals a scenario of tyranny, despotism, myriad forms of abuse of power and violation of human rights. If the idea of the kingdom of God in the context of Africa means good news, one cannot deny the fact that it is to such situations that this good news must be addressed. In other words, the good news of the kingdom of God assumes the character of a prophetic denunciation of oppressive socioeconomic and political structures. It also confronts these structures with alternative praxis based on the idea of the kingdom of God.

In sum, the thesis proposed in this section is that, in Africa, the idea of the kingdom of God calls for the prophetic denunciation of these 'strong men' (despots) and their 'kingdoms' (oppressive structures). Jesus' denunciation and 'plunder' of the kingdom of the 'strong man' sets the example. This idea of effective denunciation of the 'kingdoms' of African despotic rulers is not a mere rhetorical trifle. It carries with it a concrete risk, as can be seen, for example, in the following realistic response by the Ndebele (Zimbabwe) to the missionary enterprise: "We like to learn and hear about God and His Word but if we say openly that we belong to King Jesus, then we shall be accused of disloyalty to [King] Lobengula and of Witchcraft and killed"[16]. Allegiance to the kingdom of God is a risky subversion of the structures and 'kingdoms' of oppression.

The upshot of the foregoing is the basic presupposition that we must extend the meaning of the Beelzebub controversy beyond the ambit of exorcism and speak of it in terms of structures which set themselves against the reign of God. Through such extension, the idea of the kingdom of God emerges as a potent symbol for confronting and denouncing institutionalized dictatorship and abuse of power in Africa. For Africans, the idea of the kingdom of God includes the notion that: "To the kingdoms of the world there is an alternative and overarching kingdom, the Kingdom of God, to which the kingdoms of the world must bow and submit.... Undoubtedly Jesus' message about the Kingdom of God was not perceived as other worldly or as politically neutral by the authorities of his day"[17].

There exists yet another sense in which the idea of the kingdom of God can be conceived as a symbol of denouncing oppressive 'kingdoms' that resist the effective and universal establishment of the reign of God. Besides political oppression, there are other 'kingdoms' that afflict the African continent. These are often founded on carefully constructed models of injustice. The Cold War is an example of a type of

---

[16] Quoted in ISICHEI, *A History of Christianity in Africa*, 115.

[17] BEDIAKO, *Christianity in Africa*, 243; cf. UZUKWU, *A Listening Church*, 72-78. See also Monrovia's Archbishop Michael Kpakala Francis' excellent analysis of the factors that lead to dictatorship and make "the temporary tenure of office (in Africa) not fully comprehensible, not necessarily required by the population, and not at all acceptable to the office holder". MICHAEL K. FRANCIS, "The Church in Africa Today: Sacrament of Justice, Peace, and Unity", in *The African Synod: Documents, Reflections, Perspectives*, Africa Faith and Justice Network (Maryknoll, New York: Orbis Books, 1996), 119-130.

structural injustice which unleashed a wave of bloody conflicts across the continent. The enduring effects of this era linger, although the Western nations who fought their proxy wars on the turf of the continent have withdrawn into their characteristic shell of indifference. As Cameroonian theologian Jean-Marc Ela succinctly puts it: "For them, Africa has ceased to matter"[18]. Another example of such structures or kingdoms of injustice is the Economic Structural Adjustment Program (ESAP), which purposes to extricate the entire continent from the external 'debt trap' but lacks the needed innovation to stimulate effective economic growth and development. The point of this argument is that in this situation *also* the denunciatory character of the idea of the kingdom of God from the perspective of African theology finds material for prophetic action. Bediako expresses well the essence of this argument: "In other words, it is from the standpoint of the liberation of the Kingdom of God that theological activity can confront the 'other kingdom' which 'breeds poverty, destitution, injustice, tears, hard-heartedness, iniquity, discord and war, intolerance and persecution'"[19].

Prophetic denunciation, however, does not exhaust the meaning of the kingdom of God in the African context. Without a doubt, Jesus' denunciation of the unjust structures of his day was in clear anticipation of the inauguration of a new era, the era of God's universal reign: The time is fulfilled, the kingdom of God is close at hand! Although the contours of its eschatological consummation remained imponderable, the transforming effects of God's reign were already discernible in the mighty works and words of Jesus and in his call to repentance and faith: Repent, and believe in the gospel! The trajectory of the kingdom's message stretches from annunciation through denunciation to transformation; what is announced is truly realized in the praxis of Jesus of Nazareth. What does this third level of our hermeneutical grid entail?

---

[18] JEAN-MARC ELA, "The Church-Sacrament of Liberation", in *The African Synod: Documents, Reflections, Perspectives*, 132.
[19] BEDIAKO, *Christianity in Africa*, 161.

The Kingdom of God as Transformation

I suggested, in the preceding section, the need to effect a radical departure from the dominant idea of the kingdom of God in popular African Christianity; that is, the idea that it is a reward whose conferment is withheld until the hereafter, and whose beneficiaries are Christians who have lived a pious life devoid of social action in this present age. In other words,

> African Christians have been taught to seek the transformation of the religious sector, to save their souls. How this movement is related to the transformation of the whole society and the total person has often been left unsatisfactorily answered. There have been places and times when a good Christian would be one who kept aloof from politics which ...[is] dirty, from economics which endanger one's salvation of the soul, from culture which can taint pure Christian faith, from development which erodes the good virtues of Christianity[20].

In the face of widespread misery and hardships this oversimplified idea of the kingdom of God loses all its justification: "For Africans, a God who saves tomorrow is not a saving God"[21]. In Africa, the idea of the kingdom of God is inseparable from the radical transformation of structures that condition or determine the context of life. Only a flawed understanding of the content of Jesus' proclamation polarizes evangelism (saving souls) and socio-political involvement: both are parts of the Christian duty[22].

The argument can be taken further by asserting that the idea of the kingdom of God as touching life integrally, that is, all the conditioning factors of life in community, jibes well with the integral and holistic nature of the African's religious imagination or world view. This imagination or world view

---

[20] JOHN MARY WALIGGO, "Christianity and Liberation in Africa: Some Obstacles", in *Towards African Christian Liberation*, L. NAMWERA, A. SHORTER, et al, (Nairobi, Kenya: St. Paul Publications Africa, 1990), 32.

[21] HEALEY and SYBERTZ, *Towards an African Narrative Theology*, 176.

[22] BEDIAKO, *Christianity in Africa*, 141; cf. EUGENE HILLMAN, *Toward an African Christianity* (New York/Mahwah, New Jersey: Paulist Press, 1993), 12-25.

touches and embraces all aspects of nature[23]. The parables of the seed (Mark 4:26-29), the darnel (Matt. 13:24-30), the mustard seed (Mark 4: 30-32 parr.), and the yeast (Matt. 13:33, Luke 13:20-21) preclude any interpretation that separates the eschatological 'action' of the kingdom of God from the concrete history of the world. If anything, these parables suggest the inter-penetration of the eschatological kingdom of God and unfolding human history. This incursion of the kingdom of God into human history is less a violent eruption than a silent, but potent, irruption which transforms from within the whole of human history. "For look, the kingdom of God is in your midst!" (Luke 17:21).

The prayer of African Christians is: "Father God, let your Kingdom come in this land [here and now]!"[24]. It is the prayer of all Africans who believe that the kingdom of God bears a transforming impact on their conditions of life. God's kingdom becomes manifest in the radical transformation of those structures that oppress, dominate, enslave and marginalize human beings.

Jean-Marc Ela has suggested that: "Because of our situation, Africa must be perceived at its heart to be one of the privileged poles of liberation"[25]. This declamation is not to be adorned as a flattering epithet; it is a haunting reminder of the challenges that Africa poses to any idea of the kingdom of God that dares to be optimistic. The following argument seeks to make two points. First, the idea of the kingdom of God in African theology means the effective transformation of currently unjust and oppressive structures. Secondly, the church in Africa should not eschew the challenge to be at the vanguard of this project of transformation. To illustrate the first point I will draw from the resources of the 1994 African Synod. For the second point, the writings of South African theologian and anti-apartheid crusader Dr. Allan Boesak will be used to point out concrete vistas for the engagement of

---

[23] See AYLWARD SHORTER, *Christianity and the African Imagination: After the Synod Resources for Inculturation* (Nairobi, Kenya: Pauline Publications Africa, 1996), 21-25.
[24] ISICHEI, *A History of Christianity in Africa*, 141.
[25] ELA, "Church—Sacrament of Liberation", 133.

the churches in Africa in the proclamation of the good news of the kingdom of God.

The African Synod

The sixth chapter of John Paul II's Final Exhortation, *Ecclesia in Africa*, is aptly titled: 'Building the Kingdom' (nos. 105-126). At first glance, the idea of the kingdom of God is epitomized by two closely interrelated notions: justice and peace. The kingdom of God means justice and peace. These two notions define the content of the church's mission: "The Church as the Family of God in Africa must bear witness to Christ also by promoting justice and peace on the Continent and throughout the world" (no. 106). Besides this mandate, the proclamation of the good news of the kingdom obligates all Africans, Christians and non-Christians alike, to engage in the "promotion of integral human development" (no. 109). The specific elements of this integral human development include the entrenchment of "the rule of law" in all the spheres of life on the continent, the eradication of corruption in the interrelated areas of politics and the economy, the alleviation of crushing foreign debts, an end to the fratricidal wars, arms trade, and those customs and practices which deprive women of their rights and the respect due them.

The Synod's vision of promoting justice and peace, and integral human development, squares well with the idea of the kingdom of God presented in the Synoptic Gospels. Furthermore, it places the task of effecting this promotion at the doorsteps of the church in Africa: "The African church has understood that to establish the kingdom of God as preached by Jesus Christ, it must carry on the task of transforming unjust structures in society and within itself"[26]. This affirmation sets the stage for the examination of the second component of this section: the mission of the churches in Africa and the idea of the kingdom of God.

---

[26] Juan G. Monroy, "A Church Committed to Justice and Peace", in *What Happened at the African Synod?*, ed. Cecil McGarry (Nairobi, Kenya: Pauline Publications Africa, 1995), 117.

The Kingdom of God and the Mission of the Churches in Africa: An Example

If the idea of the kingdom of God in African theology culminates in the transformation of the unjust structures and conditions of life, the mission of the churches cannot be defined without taking the theme of liberation into consideration. Alan Boesak has developed a theological reflection that focuses on the mission of the churches in Africa in actualizing the tranformative meaning of the kingdom of God. Other lines of approach exist in African theology of liberation. The merit of Boesak's approach lies in the fact that it has effectively contributed to the transformation of the socioeconomic and political landscape of South Africa. Thus, the overriding interest in my choice of approach is its effectiveness.

How can the churches in Africa recommit themselves to the mission to transform society according to the paradigm of the kingdom of God? What is the mission of the churches in Africa, especially in a situation of injustice and oppression such as exists on the African continent? Boesak offers a new paradigm for rethinking the notion of mission based on the idea of the kingdom of God. His insights originated from a real rather than an ideal situation of the continent.

A Church in Situation

One insight that emerges clearly in Boesak's writings is the idea that the church in Africa needs to be a church-in-situation[27]. The church ought to 'pitch its tent' in the midst of the real life situation of the continent. It is here that the church is called to embrace — and imbue with Christian meaning — the joy and the hope, the grief and anguish of the men and women of this continent, especially those who are poor and afflicted in myriad ways, as its own joy and hope, grief and anguish[28]. In this situation of grief and anguish the

---

[27] I adopt the singular 'church' in this analysis with the understanding that whatever is said here concerns all the churches and ecclesial bodies in Africa.

[28] This is an adaptation of the much quoted opening lines of Vatican Council II's *Pastoral Constitution on the Church in the Modern World, Gaudium et Spes*, 7 December, 1965.

church in Africa receives and actualizes its mission to proclaim the good news of the reign of God. The historical situation in which the church in Africa finds itself is one which

> In too many places too many children die of hunger, and too many persons just disappear because they dare to stand up for justice and human rights. Too many are swept away by the tides of war, and too many are tortured in dungeons of death. In too many eyes the years of war have extinguished the fires of hope and joy, and too many bodies are bowed down by the weight of that particularly repugnant death called despair. Too many young persons believe that their youth and their future are already powdered to dust...[29].

This list of humanly contrived (and natural) woes can be extended indefinitely, but the central point here is that it describes the situation that exists in all parts of the continent with minimal exception.

To admit that the church in Africa is a church-in-situation is not merely to proffer an empty theological statement. It is a commitment to *see* and *embrace* the people of God to whom is addressed the liberating message of the kingdom. Undeniably, these people of God cannot be perceived as anyone other than the men and women, believing and unbelieving, who suffer the wounds inflicted on them by structures of injustice and oppression. Consequently, the church in Africa cannot absolve itself from its mission to be a church in a wounded continent: "For Africa is a wounded continent, and the wounds have not yet healed"[30].

Quite undeniably, therefore, the mission of the church becomes inseparably linked to the fate of the continent. In a continent afflicted by innumerable ills, the mission of the church is indiscernible apart from that situation of evil which oppresses the people of God[31]. The challenge here is for the

---

[29] ALLAN BOESAK, *If This is Treason, I am Guilty* (Grand Rapids, Michigan: Eerdmans, 1987), 28-29.

[30] ALLAN BOESAK, *Black and Reformed* (Maryknoll, New York: Orbis Books, 1984), 70.

[31] Cf. ALLAN BOESAK, *Comfort and Protest* (Philadelphia: The Westminster Press, 1987), 66-67.

church, in whatever community it finds itself on the continent, "[T]o identify with the past, the present and the future of the community that it serves.... [B]ecome a part of that community, so that it may understand the joys, sorrows, and aspirations of that community"[32]. Becoming a part of the struggle of the community amounts to imbuing that struggle with a distinctively liberating "Christian presence", and "taking responsibility for the historical reality into which the kingdom of God has entered"[33]. In the light of the foregoing, the mission of the church has nothing to do with engaging in a power tussle with political leaders. History teaches that such struggle to assert the so-called religious power of spiritual leaders over the secular power of temporal rulers has hindered rather than advanced the mission of the church in the world[34].

In the light of the foregoing, the church's realization of its mission of proclaiming the good news of the kingdom must be characterized by the virtue of compassion. The first decisive step in the experience of compassion is to embrace the actual, not virtual or ideal, situation of suffering. Yet, 'to embrace the situation' does not imply a masochistic complacency nurtured by a vain hope in God's reward outside the realm of human history. Mission informed by compassion implies active solidarity. It seeks to heal, not placate:

> First of all, healing presupposes brokenness and hurt. To recognize the hurt and brokenness in African churches and nations means to identify the causes of that brokenness. It means understanding that brokenness in terms of political, economic, and social realities as well as in terms of human alienation and suffering.
> Secondly, healing asks for the kind of solidarity with victims that does not come through formal acceptance of a creed, but through the sharing of the pain, by taking upon oneself the hurt of others. This at once opens a third perspective: it is the brokenhearted God, the suffering Servant of the Lord, who heals. In other words,

---

[32] BOESAK, *Black and Reformed*, 23.
[33] Ibid., 24, 74.
[34] See, for example, LEONARDO BOFF, *The Church: Charism and Power* (New York: Crossroad, 1985), 51ff.

true healing comes through the willingness to suffer, to take upon oneself the brokenness of the other[35].

The conclusion that can be drawn at this point is that to be a church-in-situation — a church immersed in the concrete realities of human life — is to face an inexorable challenge that subjects the credibility and relevance of the church's mission, as well as its identity as an agent of transformation, to scrutiny in any given situation or context. Thus the church finds itself challenged to bear witness to the good news of the kingdom not merely as vehicle for transmitting the message of salvation and liberation, but more importantly as an agent and community of compassion, solidarity and justice.

If the church in Africa is the church in the world, where the kingdom of God is already present and active, it is confronted, then, with the challenge to dare to be church: "The quest is for a church that dares to be *church*, that dares ...as did its Lord, to side with the poor and the downtrodden and to liberate the oppressed"[36]. One might ask, therefore, as does Boesak: "Will the churches of Africa be able to do all this?"[37]. This question helps to focus the discussion on the issue of neutrality.

The False Path of Neutrality

There is evidence to suggest that in many instances the church in Africa has become neutral. In other words, the clergy or church leaders have become indifferent to the situation of the children of God, the Family of God. A church that is neutral or indifferent to the situation of injustice in which it claims to be church loses credibility and relevance. It betrays its mission of proclaiming the good news of the

---

[35] BOESAK, *Black and Reformed*, 75-76; see also ALLAN BOESAK, "Reconciliation and Liberation in Black Theology" (Toronto: Ecumenical Forum of Canada, 1979), 4-5; ALLAN BOESAK and CHARLES VILLA-VICENCIO eds., *A Call for an End to Unjust Rule* (Edinburgh: The Saint Andrew Press, 1986), 155.
[36] ALLAN BOESAK, *Farewell to Innocence* (Maryknoll, New York: Orbis Books, 1976), 148.
[37] Ibid., 76.

kingdom of God. It ceases to be a true *ekklesia*, that is, the eschatological gathering of God's chosen people.

The advantage of placing the church in situation, as Boesak does, is that it reveals the hypocrisy and the impossibility of claiming innocence, neutrality or indifference. For "when the situation is as clear and unmistakable as it is with us, and when the cry of the poor and the wretched rises day and night to God, and injustice is there for everyone to see, then it is unforgivable for Christians to try to be neutral..."[38]. The people of God are the same men and women who labor under the yoke of blatant injustice and oppression. Any separation of Christian life and the socioeconomic and political conditions that affect this life creates a false dichotomy. Futhermore, to claim neutrality regarding these conditions amounts to a certain kind of 'heathenism'[39]. The point cannot be overemphasized that the situation of Africa is also the situation of the church in Africa. Whatever mark of injustice afflicts the men and women of our times also afflicts the body of Christ, because "we are the church": "We are the body of Christ. And as long as these things happen, we know that the body of Christ is being broken every single day. As long as these things happen, Christ is again persecuted, denied, and crucified"[40].

The grave effects of neutrality become more evident when considered as a form of partiality. In sum, in the context of the continent, a church that is neutral takes sides with the oppressor: "Neutrality is the most reprehensible partiality there is. It means choosing for those in power, choosing for injustice, without taking responsibility for it. It is the worst sort of politics, and the most detestable sort of 'Christianity' there is"[41].

If the church in Africa cannot maintain neutrality in a situation of social conflict, it therefore means that it must make clear choices. Boesak asserts: "The church must

---

[38] ALLAN BOESAK, *The Finger of God* (Maryknoll, New York: Orbis Books, 1982), 29; see also Boesak, *Farewell to Innocence*, 1-7.
[39] BOESAK, *The Finger of God*, 12.
[40] BOESAK, *If This is Treason*, 128.
[41] BOESAK, *The Finger of God*, 29; see also, *Black and Reformed*, 75. Evidently the same critique applies to an African theology that is silent and indifferent, which collaborates with any structure of social injustice. See BOESAK, *Farewell to Innocence*, 34; *Walking on Thorns*, (Geneva: WCC, 1984), 24.

choose. Either we are on our way to the new Jerusalem [the kingdom of God] or we perish with Babylon"[42]. The importance of making clear choices for justice precludes what Boesak aptly terms the "Reuben option". This latter describes that calculated lack of courage to opt for justice and embrace the risk of being church in a situation of social conflict. It is the uncomfortable state of mind of a church that has substituted the radical witness to the good news of the kingdom of God for the transient goal of survival and self-preservation[43]. The task facing the church in Africa is to become a "confessing church" or a "resurrection-church"; a church that is intolerant of injustice. The option to become a "confessing church" inevitably places it on the path of confrontation with the forces of injustice and oppression:

> A confessing church is not simply a church with a confession. It is a church which stands by the demands of the gospel no matter what the demands of the 'times', the 'situation', or the 'powers that are'. It is a church which challenges the world, not on the basis of power or arrogance but on the basis of our understanding and sharing of the suffering of God's children in the world. It is a church which learns to hear the voice of God in the cries of the suffering, the poor, and the oppressed[44].

An echo of this notion of a confessing church reverberates in the African Synod's Final Exhortation: "The Church as the Family of God in Africa must bear witness to Christ also by promoting justice and peace on the Continent and throughout the world... The Church's witness must be accompanied by a firm commitment to justice and solidarity by each member of God's people"[45].

---

[42] BOESAK, *Comfort and Protest*, 38; Boesak, *Walking on Thorns*, 17.

[43] Here it is important to recall the poignant observation by Danish martyr Kaj Munk regarding church symbolism: "The signs of the church have always been the dove, the lamb, the lion, and the fish, but never the chameleon". Quoted in BOESAK, *If this is Treason*, 47.

[44] BOESAK and VILLA-VICENCIO, *A Call for an End to Unjust Rule*, 154.

[45] JOHN PAUL II, *The Church in Africa: Post-Synodal Apostolic Exhortation* (Nairobi, Pauline Publications Africa, 1995), no. 105.

Proclamation and Liberation

The mission of the church is to proclaim the good news of the kingdom of God in words and deeds, just as Jesus did. The specific goal of this mission is liberation, God's gratuitous offer of salvation which transforms human life and structures. This implies that it does not suffice for the church to be in situation. It must make concrete choices based on the demands of the kingdom of God. Fidelity to this latter is a yardstick for measuring the church's accountability. The demand and promise of the kingdom of God find fulfillment in the effective liberation of the people of God from the yoke of oppression (cf. Luke 4:18-19). The church's radical option for this demand constitutes the touchstone of its authenticity and credibility in Africa. It is the mark of a true church. For if the message of Christ is the message of liberation,

> His message of liberation is [also] the message of the church in the world. This is the message the church in Africa must proclaim if it is to be authentic. It is the message of the God of the Bible: what God did for the people of Israel, God can do again today. It is the message that he who came to proclaim the acceptable year of the Lord is still the head of the church today[46].

The Scripture abounds with references to liberation as the central theme of God's relationship with the world. In fact, Boesak notes, "Nothing is more central to the Old Testament proclamation than the message of liberation. God's history with Israel is a history of liberation. Yahweh's great act of liberation forms the content of the life and faith, the history and confession of Israel..."[47]. Similarly: "The message of liberation forms the *cantus firmus* of the proclamation of the New Testament. Jesus did not alienate himself from the prophetic proclamation of liberation.... Jesus purposely places himself in the prophetic tradition of preaching the liberation message, offering himself as the fulfillment of the messianic prophecies"[48].

---

[46] BOESAK, *Black and Reformed*, 74; see also *Farewell to Innocence*, 147.
[47] Ibid., 17ff.
[48] Ibid., 20.

A quick glance at the African continent cannot but reveal the faces of millions of Africans who yearn to hear the word of the kingdom that liberates them from oppression and slavery. As Boesak rightly contends, they seek

> A word that shows the way out of the darkness of oppression, poverty, and misery. A word that is an inspiration to active participation in God's struggle for justice and liberation, yet at the same time is not itself an expression of demagogy. A word that holds on to the truth that God is on the side of the oppressed...[49].

That word is the good news of the kingdom of God.

It is in the midst of this deep yearning that the church discovers the nature and meaning of its mission. No amount of ingeniously contrived theological disquisitions can absolve the church in Africa from proclaiming the word of liberation in a situation of conflict. Liberation is integral, just as the idea of the kingdom of God implies God's universal reign over all the spheres of creation. It permeates all facets of human existence. To proclaim the word of liberation and opt for the least of God's people is what it means for the church to be a prophetic church. Prophecy is "much less predicting the future than contradicting the present"[50]. A prophetic church takes a critical distance vis-a-vis the ideology of the structures and perpetrators of injustice. It refuses to be seduced by the trappings of power and domination, "because its loyalty is not to any party or grouping, but ultimately to the Lord and his kingdom"[51]. In effect, the ultimate source of the liberating praxis of the prophetic church is found in Jesus Christ, whose praxis it proclaims and lives by: "It is the Word of God which is the critique of all human actions and which holds before us the norms of the kingdom of God"[52].

The central point of this argument relates to the nature and content of the proclamation of the kingdom of God in a

---

[49] BOESAK, *The Finger of God*, 2.
[50] BOESAK, *Walking on Thorns*, 29.
[51] BOESAK, *If This is Treason*, 17.
[52] Ibid., 14.

situation of social tension and conflict. Briefly stated: proclamation is praxis-oriented. According to Boesak, it is a "holy rage" for freedom and justice[53]. It means active commitment to the liberation of the children of God from the shackles that bind them to inhuman conditions of living. Such a praxis-oriented proclamation will not permit the church to shrink from confronting the forces and structures of injustice in society. It is not an exercise in futility to recall several instances in Africa where fervent prayer for the end of unjust rule, and disobedience to civil authority become not just a Christian responsibility but the honorable way out for the Christian[54]; "where words and statements will no longer suffice.... [Where] the church must initiate and support meaningful pressure on the entrenched system, as a nonviolent way of bringing about change"[55]; and, finally, "where the church has to offer a prophetic witness to the state"[56].

Generally, in the Catholic Church in Africa, when it comes to offering a prophetic witness to the state, the faithful, the church as the totality of its members, rely on the reluctant hierarchy. The net result is often a passive resignation that condones the status quo rather than challenge and transform it. Leonardo Boff's observation is particularly relevant to the situation of the Catholic Church in Africa: "This institutional sclerosis has kept the Church from responding properly to the challenges of the modern world. It has become conservative and has created a deep chasm between the Church-as-people of God and the Church-hierarchy in terms of ecclesial practice, between the Church that thinks, speaks, and yet does not act and that Church which does not dare to think, cannot speak, yet acts"[57].

An important consideration in the church's adoption of a prophetic stance vis-a-vis the state concerns the often-repeated declaration that the church has no business with politics: the church should stay out of politics. To buttress this contention the proponents of this idea quote copiously from

---

[53] Ibid., 54, 57; BOESAK, *Walking on Thorns*, 41.
[54] BOESAK and VILLA-VICENCIO, *A Call for an End to Unjust Rule*, 147, 151.
[55] BOESAK, *Black and Reformed*, 30.
[56] Ibid., 49.
[57] BOFF, *The Church: Charism and Power*, 49.

Romans 13: "Everyone is to obey the governing authorities, because there is no authority except from God and so whatever authorities exist have been appointed by God" (Rom. 13:1). Two points are important in this regard.

First, there needs to be a clear understanding of the meaning of politics. Here Boesak's distinctions are very useful: "Put very simply, *politics* is the ordering, the organization of the political, social, and economic life of people within a state, in order to create and maintain a society which is as meaningful, just, and humane as possible"[58]. He continues: "Because this is so, and because politics has to do with people who are created in the image of God — people for whom he has in mind a life full of meaning, abundance, joy; people for whom Jesus Christ had given his life — therefore politics is also, very much so, the business of the church. The political responsibility of the church is to witness to God's demands for justice and peace, for a meaningful life for his people in the world"[59]. To carry out this responsibility, the church is guided by the norm of the kingdom of God, which "speaks to our total human condition and offers salvation that is total and complete"[60].

Secondly, regarding Romans 13, only a seriously flawed *eisegesis* can use it as a justification for passive obedience to unjust and repressive systems of government. An authentic exegesis of the text sees in it the basis for a transforming social action, rather than a compromising docility. Precisely, as Boesak argues, this action is not *"in spite of* Romans 13", but *"because of* Romans 13": "Romans 13 is the foundation for Christian action and resistance to governmental powers who do not want to acknowledge that their authority is from God, and that they therefore have to reflect the power of this liberating, just God"[61].

---

[58] BOESAK, *If This is Treason*, 13.
[59] Ibid., Boff arrives at the same conclusion by drawing a distinction between Politics and politics. *Church: Charism and Power*, 26-29. See also PENOUKOU, *Eglises d'afriques*, 57-79.
[60] BOESAK, *If This is Treason*, 13.
[61] BOESAK and VILLA-VICENCIO, *A Call for an End to Unjust Rule*, 148, 151; see also Boesak's 'A Letter to the South African Minister of Justice,' *Walking on Thorns*, 58-65.

Conclusion: The Kingdom as a Symbol of Hope For Africa

This essay on the idea of the kingdom of God in African theology is not an exegetical disquisition. It is primarily a theological interpretation of the central symbol of the public proclamation of Jesus of Nazareth as documented in the Synoptic Gospels. Consequently, several issues traditionally connected with the kingdom debate have not been treated extensively. One of the issues is the contentious question of 'realized' *vs.* 'futurist' orientations of the kingdom of God. I take for granted that Jesus' proclamation of the kingdom of God announced the impending end of the world through the imminent arrival and instrumentality of God's definitive reign over all creation. Nevertheless, sufficient evidence from the Synoptic Gospels shows that the imponderable *eschaton* is not without implications for *prevailing* socioeconomic and political structures.

Similarly this essay avoids the question of whether or not the church that Jesus intended is to be identified with the kingdom of God that he explicitly proclaimed, in which case the church is the actualization and realization in time or in anticipation of the *eschaton*[62]. Nevertheless, the major thrust of the final section of this essay sufficiently argues the point that mission, as constitutive of the church, lies at the intersection of the relationship of the kingdom of God and the churches in Africa. Therefore, I have argued that the churches in Africa have a vital role in actualizing the three principal components — annunciation, denunciation and transformation — of the idea of the kingdom of God in an African context. The basis for this argument is that Jesus' proclamation of the kingdom of God goes from annunciation, to denunciation and transformation. It is not only proclaimed in words. It is actively lived in deeds. The idea of the kingdom of God bears decisive implications for the real-life situation on the continent of Africa. In the present context of Africa, one important criterion for

---

[62] It is perhaps important to note here that there exist some prophetic churches in Africa who clearly identify themselves as constituting exclusively the privileged kingdom of God, and where the leader(s) subsequently become(s) the 'savior'. See ISICHEI, *A History of Christianity in Africa*, 292, 316, 349.

judging any community that lays claim to the title 'kingdom community' will be the degree to which it effectively adopts the three-tier kingdom praxis outlined above.

One of the aims of this essay is to make a contribution to the understanding of the Christian message, at the core of which lies the idea of the kingdom of God. Recently African theologians have capitalized on the so-called 'southward shift of Christianity's center of gravity'[63]. If this is the case, then a unique African interpretation of the fundamental symbols of Christianity, like the kingdom of God, is not only warranted; it must also become one of the regulating norms of theological reflection in Africa. One is again reminded here of the significant declaration of Paul VI in Kampala, 1969: "You may and you must have an African Christianity".

Finally, however, the fact must be conceded that a theological exploration of the idea of the kingdom of God in African theology does not immediately resolve the complex problems confronting the African continent. Reflection still needs to proceed to the level of praxis, for Africa remains a bleeding, suffering continent, whose survival is ceaselessly jeopardized by a conspiracy of internal and external circumstances. In this situation, I suggest that the most important component of the idea of the kingdom of God in Africa be *hope*: "In Africa today we are in great need of hope. Despite all the very demoralizing and frustrating propaganda, we need to affirm that tomorrow need not be like yesterday"[64]. Therefore, for this continent whose light is dimmed, ill-equipped to face the challenges of the future, the kingdom of God is highly and ultimately a symbol of hope. This dimension of hope is amply illustrated in the *Message of the Synod* and the Final Exhortation, *Ecclesia in Africa*. In this latter document the word 'hope' features as one of the most used terms, occurring thirty-three times[65]. Thus, beyond the de-

---

[63] This notion is one of the principal presuppositions on which is founded Kwame Bediako's thesis in *Christianity in Africa: The Renewal of a Non-Western Religion*. See also ELA, "The Church-Sacrament of Liberation", 131; MERCY AMBA ODUYOYE, *Hearing and Knowing: Theological Reflection on Christianity in Africa* (Maryknoll, New York: Orbis Books, 1993), 76.

[64] MUGAMBI, *From Liberation to Reconstruction*, 161.

[65] *New People* (Magazine), #39 November-December, 1995, 3.

spair and discouragement that stare Africa in the face, the kingdom of God looms large in the horizon like a mural of hope, inviting it to cross the precarious and shadowy threshold of time into the dazzling promises of the twenty-first century. This hope is neither a gift nor reward proffered at the end of a gloomy historical tunnel. It is a task and a mission that take effect within the unfolding history of the African continent.

BIBLIOGRAPHY

ACHEBE, CHINUA. *Things Fall Apart.* New York: Anchor Books, Doubleday, First published in 1959.
BEDIAKO, KWAME. *Christianity in Africa: The Renewal of a Non-Western Religion.* Maryknoll, New York: Orbis Books, 1995.
BOESAK, ALLAN, A. *Farewell to Innocence: A Socio-Ethical Study of Black Theology and Power.* Maryknoll, New York: Orbis Books, 1976.
—, *Coming out of the Wilderness: A Comparative Interpretation of the Ethics of Martin Luther King Jr. and Malcolm X.* Kampen, Holland: Kampen Cahiers No. 28, no date.
—, "Reconciliation and Liberation in Black Theology". Toronto: Ecumenical Forum of Canada, 1979.
—, *The Finger of God: Sermons on Faith and Responsibility.* Maryknoll, New York: Orbis Books, 1982.
—, *Walking on Thorns: The Call to Christian Obedience.* Geneva: World Council of Churches, 1984.
—, *Black and Reformed: Apartheid, Liberation and the Calvinist Tradition.* Maryknoll, New York: Orbis Books, 1984.
BOESAK, ALLAN, A. & Villa-Vicencio, Charles, ed. *A Call for an End to Unjust Rule.* Edinburgh: The Saint Andrew Press, 1986.
BOESAK, ALLAN, A. *Comfort and Protest: The Apocalypse from a South African Perspective.* Philadelphia: The Westminster Press, 1987.
—, *If This is Treason, I am Guilty.* Grand Rapids, Michigan: William B. Eerdmans Publishing Co., 1987.
BOESAK, WILLA. *God's Wrathful Children: Political Oppression and Christian Ethics.* Grand Rapids, Michigan: William B. Eerdmans Publishing Co., 1995.
BOFF, LEONARDO. *The Church: Charism and Power.* New York: Crossroad, 1985.
BROWN, RAYMOND E. *An Introduction to New Testament Christology.* New York/Mahwah: Paulist Press, 1994.
CHILTON, BRUCE. *Pure Kingdom: Jesus' Vision of God.* Grand Rapids, Michigan: William B. Eerdmans Publishing Co., 1996.
DAVIDSON, BASIL. *African Kingdoms.* New York: Time-Life Books, 1966.
ELA, JEAN-MARC. "The Church-Sacrament of Liberation". In *The African Synod: Documents, Reflections, Perspectives.* Africa Faith and Justice Network, 131-138. Maryknoll, New York: Orbis Books, 1996.
FRANCIS MICHAEL K. "The Church in Africa Today: Sacrament of Justice, Peace, and Unity". In *The African Synod: Documents, Reflections, Perspectives.* Africa Faith and Justice Network, 119-130. Maryknoll, New York: Orbis Books, 1996.

FUELLENBACH, JOHN. *The Kingdom of God: The Message of Jesus Today.* New York: Orbis Books, 1995.
GOLDBERG, JEFFREY. "Our Africa Problem". *New York Times Magazine*, March 2, 1997, 34-77.
HEALEY, JOSEPH AND SYBERTZ, DONALD. *Towards an African Narrative Theology.* Nairobi, Kenya: Pauline Publications Africa, 1996.
HIERS, RICHARD H. *The Kingdom of God in the Synoptic Tradition.* Gainesville: University of Florida Press, 1970
HILLMAN, EUGENE. *Toward an African Christianity.* New York/Mahwah, New Jersey: Paulist Press, 1993.
ISICHEI, ELIZABETH. *A History of Christianity in Africa: From Antiquity to the Present.* Grand Rapids, Michigan: William B. Eerdmans Publishing Co., 1995.
JOHN PAUL II. *The Church in Africa: Post-Synodal Apostolic Exhortation.* Nairobi, Kenya: Pauline Publications Africa, 1995.
MAIMELA, SIMON S. "The Twofold Kingdom: An African Perspective". In *Theology and the Black Experience: The Lutheran Heritage Interpreted by African and African-American Theologians*, ed. Albert Pero and Ambrose Moyo, 97-109. Minneapolis: Augsburg Publishing House, 1988.
MARTEY, EMMANUEL. *African Theology: Inculturation and Liberation.* Maryknoll, New York: Orbis Books, 1993.
MEIER, JOHN P. *A Marginal Jew: Rethinking the Historical Jesus*, Vol. II. New York: Doubleday, The Anchor Bible Reference Library, 1994.
Message of the Synod. Nairobi, Kenya: Pauline Publications Africa, 1995.
MONROY, JUAN G. "A Church Committed to Justice and Peace". In *What Happened at the African Synod?*, ed. Cecil McGarry, 115-130. Nairobi, Kenya: Paulines Publications Africa, 1995.
MUGAMBI, J.N.K. *From Liberation to Reconstruction: African Christian Theology after the Cold War.* Nairobi, Kenya: East African Educational Publishers Ltd., 1995.
New People (Magazine), #39 November-December, 1995.
ODUYOYE, MERCY AMBA. *Hearing and Knowing: Theological Reflection on Christianity in Africa.* Maryknoll, New York: Orbis Books, 1993.
PENOUKOU, EFOE-JULIEN. *Eglises d'afriques: propositions pour l'avenir.* Paris: Karthala, 1984.
PERRIN, NORMAN. "Jesus and the Language of the Kingdom". In *The Kingdom of God*, ed. Bruce Chilton, 92-106. Philadelphia/London: Fortress Press/SPCK, Issues in Religion and Theology 5, 1984.
SHILLINGTON, KEVIN. *History of Africa.* New York: St. Martin's Press, Rev. ed. 1995.
SHORTER, AYLWARD. *Christianity and the African Imagination: After the Synod Resources for Inculturation.* Nairobi, Kenya: Pauline Publications Africa, 1996.
UZUKWU, ELOCHUKWU. *A Listening Church: Autonomy and Communion in African Churches.* Maryknoll, New York: Orbis Books, 1996.
WALIGGO, JOHN MARY. "Christianity and Liberation in Africa: Some Obstacles". In L. Namwera, A. Shorter, *et al*, *Towards African Christian Liberation* (Nairobi, Kenya: St. Paul Publications-Africa, 1990.

Asante Culture and the Kingdom of God

RT. REV. PETER K. SARPONG

PREAMBLE

This brief article is meant to be a kind of Asante Theology of the Kingdom of God. Much of what is said is obviously applicable to other parts of Africa, but I dare not presume to speak for Africa. Indeed, I do not know whether what follows can really be called a theology. It is more or less an attempt to identify the attitudes in Asante (African?) culture that run counter to some of the key values of the Kingdom of God but which, all the same, could be turned to good use in the interest of the Kingdom. I try first to give an idea of the Asante culture; then I move on to give a kind of definition of the Kingdom of God. From there, I identify four cardinal values of Asante life that could, if not properly expressed, oppose the actualization of the Kingdom of God. I end by explaining how these counter values could be made to serve the Kingdom.

1. BEGINNINGS OF THE ASANTE KINGDOM

The Asante people in present-day Ghana developed a very powerful kingdom, especially at the end of the 17th century. This kingdom not only conquered its neighbours to the north, south, east and west, but also fabricated quite complicated monetary, political, religious, social, legal and military systems.

Many African kingdoms which were as powerful as, if not more powerful than, the Asante kingdom have gone out of existence, but in spite of the many social and political vicissitudes of recent times, it has been able to keep its ethos almost entirely intact.

Asante has lost all the territories it gained in war but has kept its identity, and the present king, a London-trained lawyer, is held in high esteem by Ghanaians and non-Ghanaians alike. Exhibitions on the "Asante Kingdom of Gold" have been mounted in Europe and America, and interested journalists, anthropologists and ethnologists all over the world look out for occasions when the king is celebrating a great feast to come and witness it.

The kingdom of Asante can be said to have been founded on a dislike, if not hatred, for injustice. In the 15th and 16th centuries, Europeans came to the coast of present-day Ghana. They had been attracted by the gold that the indigenous people produced, for which reason they called this part of Africa the Gold Coast. They traded with the indigenous coastal people, but the bulk of the gold came from Asante which then was only a conglomeration of different separate chiefdoms — Mampong, Kumawu, Adansi, Kokofu, Essumeja, Bekwai and Kwaman (later to assume the name Asante which was then adopted by the confederation of all these chiefdoms). The point was that these did not have direct access to the Europeans to whom they sold their gold. They had to use the middle men of the coast. In the process, naturally, they were and felt cheated. So when the occasion presented itself, they fought and conquered the coastal chiefs in order to be able to reach the market themselves. In short, they wanted justice.

But before they could ward off the injustices mentioned, they had to be united. They were undergoing another type of injustice. The chief of Denkyira, very powerful at that time, used to send emissaries to the chiefdoms that later on formed the confederacy to become the Asante kingdom, to collect the gold dust and the favourite wives of the chiefs. It was during the time of Osei Tutu that the chiefdoms united to fight the Denkyira. Osei Tutu relied on the advice of his trusted friend, Okomfo Anokye, by profession a traditional priest, who has been described as a political wizard comparable to Cardinal Wolsey of England.

Having joined forces and overcome their enemy, the Denkyira, the confederation became stronger, and was thus able to overcome the power of the coastal chiefs.

Injustice

The establishment and the consolidation of the kingdom, therefore, were due to these two sets of unrelated injustices being perpetrated against the Asante — the injustice of having to pay tribute to another chief and the injustice of being deprived of access to the gold market. Realising its power, Asante then began to fight all other chiefdoms which they thought were their enemies; so they spread north, south, east and west into Togo, Ivory Coast and the northern territories of present-day Ghana.

One significant aspect of the Asante conquest was that they never annexed any territory they conquered. They fought only to get rid of external aggression. Therefore, the Asante aim at justice. A foreigner among the Asante will not take long to notice how kind, hospitable and gentle they are. One can make the Asante slaves if one knows how to handle them. But when the Asante realise that one is taking advantage of them and cheating them, then you see their worst side.

Convergence

If in *Ecclesia in Africa* the Pope singles out justice and peace as the hallmarks of the Kingdom of God, then indeed the Asante kingdom, in this respect, converges with the Kingdom of God. *Ecclesia in Africa* states: "The mandate that Jesus Christ gave to His disciples at the moment of His Ascension into heaven is addressed to the Church of God in all times and places. The Church as the Family of God in Africa must bear witness to Christ also by promoting justice and peace on the Continent and throughout the world". (No. 105)

Church's Witness

It is clear that the Church's witness must be accompanied by a firm commitment to justice and solidarity by each member of God's people. This is especially important for the lay faithful who hold public office because such witness demands an abiding spiritual attitude and a way of life consistent with the Christian faith.

Values of the Two Kingdoms

The Preface of the Feast of Christ the King states clearly that the Kingdom of God is eternal, it is a Kingdom of truth, of life, of holiness, of grace, of justice, of love and of peace. These are the values that the kingdom of Asante has tried over the centuries to attain. The kingdom wants to be strengthened and consolidated; it wants its values to be carried through, and that is why all Asante, no matter the level of their education, are true lovers of their culture. Asante has not allowed the trends of modernity to invade its kingdom. The good elements of the kingdom abide, while the evil elements are gradually eliminated.

Truthfulness is probably the most cherished value of the Asante. A liar is to be feared, indeed dreaded. At the naming ceremony of a baby which takes place on the eighth day after its birth, three drops of water (*Nsuo*) and three drops of wine, for example, palm wine (*Nsa*) are put on the baby's tongue, with the words, "When you say *nsuo*, it must be *nsuo* and when you say *nsa*, it must be *nsa*. (*Wose nsuo a na nsuo; wose nsa a na nsa*).

The significance of this ritual is that the children are now becoming members of the human society and what is expected of them is that they speak the truth all the time. Truth here does not refer only to saying what is in your head but seeing to it that what is in your head corresponds to the reality. *Nsuo* and *nsa* resemble each other in pronunciation. Careless persons can easily say *nsuo* when they should say *nsa*, or *nsa* when they should say *nsuo*.

Probably the most dangerous persons in society are not those who say *nsuo* when they know it is *nsa*, or *nsa* when they know it is *nsuo*. The most dangerous persons are those who say *nsa*, convinced that it is *nsa*, when, in fact, it is not *nsa* but *nsuo*, or those who say *nsuo*, convinced that it is *nsuo* when, in fact, it is *nsa*. To be an asset to society, you must say *nsa* and you must mean *nsa* and it must be *nsa*, and you must say *nsuo* when you mean *nsuo* and it must be *nsuo*. One must take care that what one says is what actually is.

Life is highly cherished by the Asante which is a matrilineal society. Every woman would like to generate life that is honourable and useful. A woman without a child is said to have refused to communicate life, and is rejected.

The Asante regard for holiness is to be seen in the fact that, at least in the past on the day of the week on which one was born, there was a ceremony of purification *(kradwaree)*. A man or woman born on a Tuesday is by that fact called Kwabena or Abena. On every Tuesday, they had to cleanse themselves by some ritualistic device that was meant to make them holy. The king of Asante unfailingly does this even now when almost no other Asante, apart probably from traditional leaders, do it. The king does it in the name of all the members of the kingdom since he is its personification, the embodiment of its members.

We have just spoken about the Asante dislike for injustice. The Asante wants peace which he calls *Asomdwoee*. He does not want trouble; when he appears to be violent, it is paradoxically because he is pursuing peace.

Love is a universal value but the difference between the love of the Asante and the love of the Kingdom of God is that the Asante restrict their love to friends, and to those who are kind to them. The Kingdom's love, on the other hand, is unrestricted. It embraces even the enemy: "You have heard how it was said, You will love your neighbour and hate you enemy. But I say this to you, love your enemies..." (Mt. 5:43-44).

Gratitude and kindness are the results of love. Grace is a value that would normally not be found in Asante religious thinking. The idea of God actually helping you to perform an act would be alien. God helps everybody in general to exist and to act; but that God gives grace to make us holy (sanctifying grace) and grace to enable us to act at a given moment (actual grace) is not clearly articulated among the Asante.

For this reason, it would appear that the Asante concept of a kingdom, even if it is a mundane one, approaches the Christian concept of the Kingdom.

2. The Kingdom

But what is the Kingdom? Throughout the ages, many millions have professed faith in the lordship of Jesus Christ. Millions have venerated His name. But on close examination, it is found out that few have understood Him and probably fewer still have tried to put into practice what He wanted to see done. His words have been twisted, turned, misinterpreted and misconstrued to mean everything, anything and nothing. It seems that Jesus has been more frequently honoured and worshipped for what He did not mean than for what he meant.

Hence, even though there are many Christians in the world now, the system in which we find ourselves appears to be self-destructive. On the one hand, it appears impossible to persuade a human being to limit his excesses in order to serve his own future, and it is even more difficult to convince him to do so for his fellow man. On the other, the world abounds in men and women of goodwill who would do anything to help. The system cannot resolve injustices. From the economic point of view, the system produces wealth and poverty at the same time.

Worse still, the system is now pressing its demands and defending itself with more and more violence. We have found ourselves in a situation where many of those who are trying to fight the system have no alternative but to resort to institutional violence. Institutional violence leads to revolutionary violence, which in turn leads to more institutional violence in the form of riot police, detentions without trial, torture, military governments, political murders, thuggeries — to counteract which there should be more revolutionary violence. The circle becomes more and more vicious.

Organized religion can help enormously in this paradox of violence, but it can help only when, in emphasising the supernatural, there is an equal stress on the need to be concerned about the future of the world and all its people.

This is exactly what Jesus set out to do. Three passages from Isaiah, which the Gospels tell us Jesus read, are relevant: "The deaf, that day, will hear the words of a book and, after shadow and darkness, the eyes of the blind will see. The lowly will rejoice in God even more and the poorest exult in the Holy One of Israel" (29:18-19); "The eyes of the blind shall be opened, the ears of the deaf unsealed, then the lame shall leap like a deer and the tongues of the dumb sing for joy" (35:5-6); "The spirit of the Lord has been given to me, for he has anointed me to being Good News to the poor, to heal the broken-hearted, to proclaim liberty to captives, freedom to those in prison" (61:1-2).

Those described as deaf, dumb, blind, lame, poor, broken-hearted, captives and down-trodden are simply the oppressed. Hence, what is to be achieved for them is liberation. The Good News is to be understood as a form of emancipation.

This is how the teaching of Jesus Christ is to be understood. The basic prophecy of Jesus is contained in those passages of the Gospel which we call the Beatitudes (Lk. 6:20-21). It appears therefore that the Good News of the Kingdom of God was news about a future state of affairs *on earth* when the poor would no longer be poor, the hungry would no longer be hungry, the despised would have their dignity recognised. Time and time again, Jesus would refer to this: "The Kingdom of God has arrived; the Kingdom of God is among you".

Worldly Values

Jesus describes the Kingdom as a place devoid of wretchedness. Jesus preached and fought vigorously to bring about a radical transformation in the state of affairs here on earth. He was concerned about domination from outside; but He realised that there were more injustices and oppression within Israel itself than without. Dominated by the desire to be rich, the struggle for power, the pursuit for prestige and crude insularity, Israel, far from being the People of God, had not allowed itself to become what it was meant to be: the Kingdom of God.

Money

Money has caused a lot of evil in the world. For many people, money is more important than human beings. It is, therefore, no surprise that the sayings of Jesus about money and possessions are regarded as among the hardest in the Gospels. Jesus made it abundantly clear that the important thing about the Kingdom of God is not that it was near, but that it would be the Kingdom of the poor. The rich, so long as they remain such, would have no part in it (Lk. 6:20-26;

Mk. 10:25). When Jesus talked about it being easier for a camel to be threaded through the eye of a needle than for a rich man to go to the Kingdom, it so astounded the disciples (Mk. 10:24-25) that they asked who can be saved.

Jesus' answer needs looking at properly: "For men it is impossible, but not for God because everything is possible for God". God can work a miracle in man, but it will not consist in letting the rich man go into the Kingdom with all his riches. The miracle will consist in getting the rich man to renounce his riches in order to enter the Kingdom. This is what the rich man in the Gospel was asked to do (Mk. 10:17-22). There will be no place in the Kingdom for those who refuse to share. This is depicted in the parable about the rich man and Lazarus (Lk. 16:19-31). It follows, therefore, that subscribing to the Kingdom of God and setting one's heart on its values entail the radical decision to sell all one's possessions. Indeed, Jesus expected his followers to leave everything — home, family, land, boats and nets (Mk. 1:18-20).

Luke has the final convincing word on this: "The Pharisees, who loved money, heard all this and jeered at him. He said to them, 'You are the very ones who pass yourselves off as upright in people's sight, but God knows your hearts. For what is highly esteemed in human eyes is loathsome in the sight of God" (Lk. 16:14-15). In other words, any society which is so structured that some suffer because of their poverty and others have more than they need is part of the kingdom in which people are ruled by their master: money. Therefore, they cannot have a share in a Kingdom ruled by another Master: God, who always shares even his very divinity with us.

Prestige

In the society in which Jesus found Himself, the value of money came second to prestige. As a rule, in the oriental world prestige is more important to this day, than any other factor and people will commit suicide gladly rather than lose prestige. In the society of Jesus, ancestry, wealth, authority, education and virtue accounted for status. They determined the way people dressed, by whom they were entertained socially, and so on.

Looked at closely, status was a kind of religion, just as it was part of social life. Jesus contradicted this vehemently. He saw it as one of the fundamental structures of evil in the world, and dared to hope and labour for a kingdom in which such distinctions would be totally meaningless: "Blessed are you when people hate you, drive you out, abuse you, denounce your name as criminal ... (Lk. 6:22). Woe to you when the world speaks well of you ..." (Lk. 6:26).

Jesus criticized the Scribes and Pharisees not for their teaching, but for their seeking prestige and admiration given by other men. "Everything they do is done to attract attention, like wearing broader headbands and longer tassels, like wanting to take the place of honour at banquets and the front seats in the synagogues, being greeted respectfully in the market squares and having people call them Rabbi" (Mt. 23:5-7).

The same is said of their religious practices of alms-giving, prayer and fasting. They do these things ostentatiously "in order to win the admiration of men" (Mt. 6:1-6, 16-18). Jesus describes it as no virtue whatsoever but hypocrisy (Mt. 6:2, 5, 16). Hypocrites like the rich have no place in the Kingdom. They have had their reward. The admiration they sought and got is their recompense for their work.

When the disciples came to him asking who would be the greatest in the Kingdom of heaven, He said: "I tell you solemnly, unless you change and become like little children, you will never enter the Kingdom of heaven" (Mt. 18:1-4).

Jesus loved those without status — children, women, those afflicted with dreadful diseases. This, of course, did not mean that He did not love others, but it was clear that for Him, the Kingdom of God would be a society in which there would be no prestige, no status, no division of people into inferior and superior; all would be loved and respected not because of their education or wealth or ancestry or authority or rank or virtue or other achievements, but because they are human persons.

False Solidarity

Solidarity is a subtle word; yet, it is found everywhere. In itself, there is nothing wrong with it. It becomes faulty when it turns into insularity. It then becomes false solidarity, and takes on a negative connotation.

Besides money and prestige, the Jews of the time of Jesus sought solidarity. They grouped themselves into clans and societies and associations. Solidarity was especially practised within such elitist groups and sects as the Pharisees, Essenes and the Zealots.

Solidarity becomes evil when it is exclusive and selfish. In that case, it discriminates, selects and leaves out. God's Kingdom is based upon the all-inclusive solidarity of the human race. No one is excluded from it. All are called to it, and given the means and aid to answer positively. Christ said: "You have learnt how it was said, You must love your neighbour and hate your enemy. But I say to you: Love your enemies" (Mt. 5:43-44). Nothing could be more radical than that. This teaching must have shaken the Jews to the core. Jesus extended the concept of one's neighbour to include one's enemy, because He wished to embrace all human beings in His solidarity.

Group solidarity, loving those who love you, is no virtue. A good turn to one whom we like or love may, in fact, be concealed self-gratification. After all, there is the strongest type of solidarity among thieves and other rogues who are a menace to all. Often solidarity looks for rewards or some other gains. Jesus fought this type of solidarity. He appeals for an experience of solidarity with all mankind. He appeals to us to practice a solidarity that is not exclusive. He abhors and warns against an experience of solidarity that is dependent upon reciprocity. Jesus himself abandoned the solidarity of the family in favour of those around Him whom He made into brothers and sisters and mothers (Mk. 3:31-35). Whoever welcomed one of them welcomed Him and whatever was done to the least of them was done to Him (Mt. 10:40; 25:40).

Jesus' solidarity was universal even though He often had to speak against the middle class. Love does demand frankness and fraternal correction. Love understood as solidarity is not incompatible with anger and indignation. Those who are genuinely concerned about people as such will be indignant if they become painfully aware that they are suffering.

This was the situation in which Jesus found Himself and which He had to correct. His correction did not thereby exclude those who displeased Him. His whole aim was to envisage a Kingdom that would include countless numbers of Gentiles from everywhere — north, south, east and west — who would sit down with Abraham, Isaac and Jacob at a great banquet from which many a Jew would be excluded (Mk. 8:11-12; Lk. 13:28-29; 14:15-24).

Power

Another worldly value that is clearly contrary to the values of the Kingdom of God is power. The issue of power and its structures is what politics is all about. At the time of Jesus, politics was, in the first place, about who would be king if Israel were to become a kingdom. In that set-up, power was mainly kingship. It is necessary to realise that the concept also means the approach or coming of a divine political power. The prophecy of Jesus meant that the divine political power would be in the hands of the poor and the little ones: "Blessed are the poor because yours is the Kingdom of God" (Lk. 6:20); "I confer the Kingdom on you ... You will sit on thrones, to judge" (Lk. 22:29-30); "There is no need to be afraid, little flock, for it has pleased your Father to give you the Kingdom" (Lk. 12:32).

The implications of such teaching are dramatic, indeed, revolutionary. There is going to be a reversal of fortunes. The rich and mighty who have wielded influence and power are going to have to relinquish their positions to the poor and lowly: "He has pulled down princes from their thrones and raised high the lowly. He has filled the starving with good things, sent the rich away empty" (Lk. 1:52-53).

These words from the mouth of Our Lady predicted the type of Kingdom her Son was destined to preach and establish. Jesus Himself would say: "Blessed are the poor ... Woe to you who are rich" (Lk. 6:20, 24). The contrast is purposeful because it is true and serious. This is precisely what will happen in the Kingdom of God: "Everyone who exalts himself will be humbled, and the man who humbles himself will be exalted" (Lk. 14:11).

Christ could not have explained better the nature of the Kingdom of God than He did. Humbling oneself or exalting oneself or being poor or rich are all happenings of this world. Therefore, it is not unreasonable to suppose that Christ preached a present state of affairs. In other words, he wanted the present political world to change, to accommodate the underprivileged in a more human manner, as a prelude to our fuller union with His Father on the last day.

Jesus was not against power *per se*; He was against the use of power for the wrong reason. For Him, power and authority were to be used as service; they were not to be used to dominate, suppress or repress. In His own inimitable way, He expressed it thus: "You know that among the Gentiles those they call their rulers lord it over them, and their great men make their authority felt. Among you this is not to happen. No; anyone who wants to become great among you must be your servant, and anyone who wants to be first among you must be slave to all. For the Son of man himself came not to be served but to serve, and to give his life as a ransom for many" (Mk. 10:42-45). Here is spelt out for us the two quite different ways in which power and authority can be understood and exercised. It is the difference between domination and service.

For Jesus, therefore, power in the Kingdom of God is to be functional. In that Kingdom, domination and servitude of whatever type will be out of place.

3. Asante Culture & Money, Prestige, Solidarity and Power

Now, when we look at the Asante culture, we notice that on the face of it these worldly values and others predominate. The Asante like to have possessions. Superficially, they do not appear to have an idea about the evangelical vow of poverty. So long as one can get money, the means (unless it is blatantly evil, like armed robbery) is irrelevant. A rich person is called a "real man" (*Obarima paa*), a "man of means" (*Ebo ne ho*), "He is there" (*Owo ho*), He is "heavy" (*Ne mu ye du*). For the Asante, it is better to die than to be disgraced. The Asante want honour and fight for it. Their desire for prestige is expressed in many ways.

Similarly, the Asante want power. A proverb says: "If you see power being sold, sell your mother and buy it so that after you have bought it, you can use it to liberate your mother". For the Asante, a mother is the greatest person in the world. She is the epitome of the family. A proverb says: "When your mother is dead, your matrilineage is finished". To offend a mother, let alone sell her, is unthinkable. But when it comes to power, one could have no qualms over selling one's mother because in doing this one is not losing the mother; one is only placing oneself in a position where it would, paradoxically, become impossible for one's mother to be sold or bought. With power, you can do anything. You can liberate your mother whom you yourself have sold; you can protect her and all others dear to you from any form of aggression. You can acquire prestige; you can be wealthy. Everybody is at your beck and call.

Solidarity too is a value that could run counter to the Kingdom of God. The Asante tend to be insular, thinking of their own. They might even support their own members when they know that they are wrong. Bribery and corruption, nepotism and favouritism are to a large extent due to such solidarity.

And yet there is no doubt that the same values could be used to construct a theology of the Kingdom that is valid and acceptable. A juxtaposition of the four values against the Kingdom, and an attempt to have the four values converge with the Kingdom will make this clear.

Negative Merits

Wealth, prestige, power and solidarity, therefore, in reality are the four legs of the same ugly creature. They are cultural values which seemingly are opposed to the solid building of the Kingdom of God. They engender the spirit of pride. They result in some persons looking down upon others and not treating them as human beings.

The Kingdom is for equals. We are all children of God with an equal nobility and dignity. In it there is no difference based on wealth, power, fame or human alliance. The only tickets to it are love, compassion, truth, holiness, justice, the spirit of peace and unity. These are within the reach of every person, no matter how lowly-placed. Any values that run counter to any of these can only serve the cause of evil.

Positive Merits

However, there is also something termed ideal culture: What people should think and do. This may sound a little theoretical, but it is important. People may not be doing what is expected of them in actual life. But they can be told that they are going off the course, that their behaviour is not in conformity with expected conduct, if there is a cultural argument to support this. This, I think, is the case with the four values. That their negative effects on the Kingdom are enormous is indisputable. But this is so only in actual life. In the ideal situation, the story appears to be different. Therefore, we are not in any way saying that they cannot be canalized to the advantage of the Kingdom. We may be indulging here in idealism, and every ideal is hard to attain. But with determination, it is not impossible to achieve. From the ideal point of view much could be achieved by utilizing the four values in the interest of the Kingdom of God.

Money versus the Kingdom

We have seen that the Kingdom is expressly said to be for the poor, and the humble. The type of inordinate desire for money that is exhibited by our culture would appear to nullify our desire to be part of the Kingdom. The imperatives of the Kingdom would force us to remember our less fortunate brothers and sisters, if we are rich. This is a duty imposed by justice to one's own humanity, and to the dignity of the poor. Yet our cultural dictates would force us not to consider such people our responsibility. One act of charity done to one of them should suffice. One has one's own people to look after. In any case one cannot afford to die impoverished because of the laziness of others who refuse to work! When one dies everybody would like to know if one left a big fortune behind, and how much.

The amount of wealth bequeathed to one's progeny is the best index of one's success in life. It is the surest way to "leave a name" behind, and how many would not like to immortalize their name?

Money, we have seen, can be the cause of fierce acrimony, and divisive litigation. Not to engage in the fight for money to which you are entitled to lay claim is sheer madness. Some people have been known to break their blood relationship with their relatives because the latter refused to be rich dishonestly when the golden opportunity offered itself! All these and other attitudes can be defended culturally. When, therefore, we contend that African culture should be utilized in our evangelization processes, we do not by any means want to advocate this principle unconditionally. If we did, the pursuit of money would easily become one of the justifiable preoccupations of the Church.

When one begins to talk about nothing but money, there is much to be desired. If the desire for wealth were not the result of selfishness, one would not have much cause for worry. After all, it cannot be unchristian for people to want to improve their lot in life, or to desire not to be destitute. But underlining this cultural obsession is a subtle desire to be better than the others. If in the effort to demonstrate one's dominant position, others suffer, it is bad, but there is nothing you can do about it, really. In a sense, therefore, cultural pride is exhibited through the premium we place on money and possessions in general.

Money and the Kingdom

All this notwithstanding, money could be compatible with the Kingdom. There is nothing wrong with wealth as such. We must live; we must secure our future; we must look after our dependents well. Money helps us to do all that. It is with money that we support noble causes, including projects of the Church. Wealth helps us to give alms — one of the corporal acts of mercy. With money one is able to establish a business, and give work to the otherwise unemployed. These are all praiseworthy acts which foster the spirit of the Kingdom. The Kingdom is against the hoarding of money for itself, the inability or refusal to respond meaningfully to the hardships around us when we have the financial means to do so. This attitude makes money a kind of god whose servants we become. It deprives wealth of its meaningfulness.

The ideal Asante culture too insists that money should be used to assist others. A kind-hearted person is appreciated by all. A well-to-do person is expected to be kind-hearted, to "give when not asked", and to "give to mother and child" (*Woammisa a oderema wo, Ama ni ama ba*). A rich man who is generous is said to have "beautiful" money (*Ne sika nya ye fe*). A rich man who knows no generosity is described as having "ugly" money (*Ne sika nya ye tan*). A rich generous person has a "flexible" hand (*Ne nsa mu go*). The heartless one has a "stiff" hand (*Ne nsamu ye den*). Indeed the former is a true human being (*Oye nnipa dodo*). The latter does not act like a human being (*Onye ne ho nnipa*). He has a "hard head" (*Ne tiri mu dennennen*). Such a person may be seen to be wielding an influence in society, but he commands very little respect in reality. Hence when wealth is accompanied by generosity, justice and mercy, it is worth pursuing. A kind rich man becomes a point of unity for his people. An unkind one divides them. The former, by his benevolence, always extends the ambit of his family. He is the father of all, and is remembered long after his death as "the giver" (*Okyeadee*).

With the proper application of the norms of ideal culture, therefore, the pursuit of money could be in perfect consonance with the values of the Kingdom. After all, it was never the intention of Christ that we should all be poor. On the contrary, it was because He did not want destitute people in his Kingdom that He attached himself to the poor, and assured them that He would establish a Kingdom in which the oppression and iniquity that caused poverty would be blotted out for ever. He wanted the poor to be rich, rather than the rich to be poor. If He was often annoyed with the rich, it was because, while they were in a position to help Him achieve this end, they refused.

If our people would follow the dictates of ideal culture, such a situation would be completely wiped out from our societies. All would enjoy a degree of good fortune. Poverty is condemned by our culture. It is human weakness which, in practice, prevents us from taking the logical step. The rich, therefore, become richer and the poor poorer against the ideals of their own culture.

Here the imperatives of Asante culture coincide with the imperatives of the Kingdom of God.

Prestige versus the Kingdom

That the Asante cultural stance on prestige is opposed to the sentiments of the Kingdom should need no more convincing arguments to prove than what has already been said. A culture that places vainglory over and above life itself is not to be accepted without a grain of salt. Glory may mean anything for the Asante. To refuse to return an insult, a blow or an injury may easily be described as inglorious. Vendetta of the type attributed to other African peoples may not have been institutionalized in Ashanti, but in everyday life, vengeance is practised for the sake of prestige. A child hits another child; the latter will be urged on by his parents to return the blow, so as not to disgrace them. That, in fact, he may have been the cause of the fight would not be the first consideration. Who is at fault can be decided legally when scores have first been settled physically. Yet, for the sake of the Kingdom we are told to offer the left cheek.

What is greatly worrying, however, is how we have allowed prestige to infiltrate the structures of the Church. Often we see one society or organisation in the Church competing shamelessly with another. There is such a thing as healthy competition. But in this case the rivalry is often founded on lies, misrepresentation of facts and misinterpretation of intentions. It easily engenders animosity in the Church. The community that the Church is supposed to be becomes disintegrated. It ceases to be a sign in a world torn apart by hatred. It becomes a lie. Instead of building, it destroys the Kingdom of God.

The idea of prestige has totally overshadowed the concept of service that should motivate many of our Church leaders. They are more interested in the title given them by reason of their appointment to certain posts, than in doing the work that goes with them. Nor would they realize, much less admit, their inability or negligence. Even to suggest that they be helped is to wound their pride. Many notice this and react, setting in motion a chain reaction which can only increase discord.

In recent times, the youth of the Church have been vocal in their opposition to the appointment of wealthy personalities to chair ecclesial functions. They argue that, even if these functions are specifically meant to generate money for worthwhile projects, the presence of people whose sole aim is to enhance their self-image is destructive of any Christian advantage to be derived from the occasion. These persons, leading a life of prestige seek such occasions to enhance their own glory.

There is indeed much to be said against the way money is collected in Church or for its use in general. Names must be mentioned in public. Otherwise donors are humiliated. Some would not give anything until they have taken the microphone and given a speech, which advertises themselves. To tell Catholics to give in such a way that the left hand does not see what the right hand is doing is to order them not to give at all. We have at times had to give in to the demands of Catholic communities from two villages, less than one mile apart, for separate worship centres. Neither considers it dignified enough to be attending the liturgical services of the other. When it is a question of building a school or a dispensary, each would insist that the project go to a completely new location rather than lose the fight to the other. The least that can satisfy both parties is to place the project exactly mid-way between the two communities — even if it is not always physically possible.

A wholehearted adoption of a culture that breeds such inconsistency in Christianity itself can never be advocated. But that is not all. Bigotry born of prestige-seeking has found its way into the very centre of Catholic life.

Unbelievably this attitude has eaten its lethal way into the offering of Mass stipends. For many, asking for Masses is a singular chance to hear their names mentioned in Church. They come to Church eagerly waiting for the priest to announce that they have offered so much money for Mass to be offered for such and such an intention. He dares not forget this, or else he has committed a deliberate sin of omission. Some will be so furious that they may decide to terminate their membership in the Church, at least for some time.

Yes, prestige has caused and continues to cause havoc in the Church. It has helped, in no small way, marriages to break down, parents to force their children to go to the seminary, people to leave the Church, murders to be committed, and priests to abandon their pastoral activity. There appears to be no value more at variance with the building and maintaining of the Kingdom, than prestige — a very cultural value.

Prestige and the Kingdom

On the face of it, it would appear that the pursuit of prestige can never be compatible with the values of the Kingdom. But this is far from the case. Hard work is extolled by the Kingdom. To help your neighbour or the Church or society is a noble task. In normal cases prestige is the result of an ethical life. The Latin proverb says: *Bonum diffusivum sui* (Goodness diffuses itself). One can never be virtuous without gaining fame. The Asante say that "Salt need not praise itself" (*Nkyene nkamfo ne ho*), and "Good beads make no noise" (*Ahwene pa nkasa*). The good Samaritan is famous.

Prestige that is not sought after deliberately but comes to us as a result of the shining example we give by living morally is neither bad nor avoidable. It is the deliberate effort we make to enable people to see our good deeds and sometimes to value us more than we deserve that cannot find a place in the Kingdom. Christ, who preached the Kingdom, was praised. He gained fame all over Judea for His wonderful deeds. But He did not seek it. He even strictly forbade His disciples to speak about some of His deeds. But the more He did so the more His renown spread.

That is the prestige that we find in the Kingdom. It is, as the two proverbs quoted above indicate, the type of prestige which our ideal culture too would like to find in a great person. A man who brags annoys everybody (*Okyere ne ho*). A humble, unassuming leader is made the example for children. He is modest (*Obre ne ho ase*). He is "cool" (*Odwo*). His silence about his qualities are more eloquent than the boastful person's loquaciousness.

We have already pointed out how prestige-seeking could be turned into the virtue of magnanimity: the burning desire to accomplish some great feat for a good cause one believes in. There can be no cause more worth fighting for than the Kingdom of God. If the cultural ideal for prestige were to be transformed into a magnanimous striving for the Kingdom, a sense of justice would be brought to bear on Ghanaian life.

In short then, prestige is not intrinsically opposed to the Kingdom. A thing that God promotes cannot be essentially evil. Angels praise God everyday. God is famous. He is adorable. He is worthy of receiving thanks.

Power versus the Kingdom

The Kingdom is built on the strong foundations of compassion and love. Worldly power eschews these values. The Kingdom demands sacrifice and selflessness. Power is essentially selfish and greedy. It only thinks of itself; and nothing satisfies it. Herein lies the difference between the cultural pursuit of power and the Kingdom's ideal of "weakness". This "weakness", says St. Paul, is what the Christian's strength consists in. It does not consist in the type of arbitrariness and totalitarianism which have become characteristics of many traditional leaders. In many instances such exhibition of power is a cover up for human cowardice and fear. Above all, it shows evidence of sin. An irreproachable person need not surround himself with the machinery of security that keeps him in power and perpetuates his authoritative position. It is significant to note that popular leaders are carefree. As they do not offend their subjects, there is no reason why they should not go near them. They hardly make enemies whom they should keep at bay by the show of power and might.

The callous use of power, therefore, is often the manifestation of fear caused by the evil choices of a person. A thief robs with arms in order to defend himself from capture. An honest man needs no arms. His might is his just life. A power-drunk leader dares not come near his subjects. He does not know their problems. He only listens to those who, because they want to remain in his good favour, will tell him what he wants to hear. This often contains inaccuracies about the actual situation. He gets more suspicious of everybody, and becomes insecure. To protect himself, he intensifies his repressive measures which, in turn, breed dislike for himself and his policies. Threats that may initially have been imaginary now become real, providing sham evidence for repressive attitudes and actions. The leader and his subjects get themselves entangled in a circle that is indeed vicious in more than one sense. Attack and counter-attack, intrigues and counter-machinations become the order of the day.

Only some dramatic event is able to break the circle. In the African political scene this has taken the form of coups d'etat. Unrest after unrest follows. There is chaos. The ordinary people become confused. Those who can, profit of the situation to enrich themselves and gain further prestige, creating more ill-feelings among the populace.

As the Kingdom of God entails peace and understanding, holiness, truth and concord, power in the last resort is its worst enemy. Power can have no place in a Kingdom in which there is no spirit of domination.

The irony is that worldly power is in fact weakness. It reveals failure to communicate with others in human terms. Power is used to cover up human failure in regulating one's life and governing according to prescribed regulations. It is a subterfuge for vice and sinfulness.

It has been said that the best defence is attack. One cannot afford to let one's wicked deeds come to the fore. Therefore one does all one can to hide them under the dirty cloak of power. When in due course the cloak is removed, as it almost always does, the incredible powerlessness of the person in question is patent to all. He becomes a completely indefensible, miserable and pathetic figure, more to be pitied than condemned. Those whom he attempted to suppress become suddenly powerful even when in actual fact they do not hold a position of authority. "The humble are indeed raised by their life. In the Kingdom, the Lord casts the mighty from their thrones, and raises the lowly". This is the Kingdom which will give a sense of nobility and dignity to the millions of people who are languishing under the yoke of the domination of a tiny minority of their compatriots who are (or should one not rather say, appear to be) "powerful".

Power and the Kingdom

Domineering power is adverse to the Kingdom. It is also against ideal culture. Power is conferred so that one may use it to deliver one's people from servitude and prevent such servitude from happening. One of the main functions of a leader is to defend his people. He is also to use his authority to prevent cheating and oppression among his subjects. Power as such is not objectionable to the Kingdom. It is strength and goes hand in hand with authority.

God is powerful, and there is nothing wrong with that. However, His power appears to us as weakness. While He can strike us dead when we sin against Him, He looks on apparently unconcerned. The power of the Cross of Christ consists in its seeming impotence, but that weakness shows the tremendous power of God. Who indeed apart from God, can make use of a thing as despicable and disgraced as the Cross to overcome the whole world, and in fact all history?

This is the paradox of life. Those who appear to be powerful are in fact powerless. Their "power" is endowed them by others. To keep themselves in it, they distribute power to their subjects to "protect" them. Without the loyalty of their powerless subjects they are nothing. In the end it is those to whom power has thus been granted who have strength. If they unite, their collective strength is irresistible. This is the rational behind the success of coups d'etat. The political leader gives guns to soldiers to keep him self in power, no matter how oppressive his rule is (or is it not because his rule is oppressive?). The soldiers thus become capable of easily ousting him.

However, not all the really powerful elements do unite. They choose to maintain the *status quo* because of ignorance or selfishness, fear or pride. So just as in reality the seemingly powerful are powerless, the seemingly powerless are powerful. This ties in with the conditions of the Kingdom wherein the weak and feeble are indeed powerful and strong. This power of the "lonely" does not refer actually to positions. It is an attitude of mind. It can be possessed as much by those in conspicuous positions as by those who hold no position in life. God often makes use of it to promote the cause of the

Kingdom. It was David whom God thus made use of in order to expose the ridiculous vulnerability of Goliath, to reinforce his sovereignty over his people Israel, and to announce to the Gentiles his dominance over nature and history.

This is the type of liberating power which ideal culture would preach. Power, therefore, is not necessarily opposed to the Kingdom. Only the evil, oppressive use of power is.

The Kingdom versus Solidarity

From the description of cultural solidarity, most inadequate though it has been, it should be evident that a certain circumspection is called for when the Asante talk of their celebrated sense of community. It is quite true that they have a sense of community, cherish communal life, friendship and togetherness, and act as one when the occasion demands it. Individualism is foreign to their societies. Everybody, no matter how lowly placed, was, in the past, the object of concern for the Asante. No one went hungry or completely without the necessities of life. Worship was communal, festivities were collective, decisions were corporate.

All this is true, but there is an inconspicuous way in which this collectivity could be very detrimental to the pursuit of the Kingdom. This sense of solidarity was expected to exist among members of the nuclear family, the extended family, the village community, the chiefdom or the tribe as the case might be. It all depended upon the matter in hand or the occasion. When the discussion concerned the family, all others were left out. In fact the discussion could be against other members of the village community. There would be solidarity among the community to plan war or other subversive action against another community. So long as this benefited the particular community, members did not have to worry about justice and the rights of others. In the same vein, a tribe might solidly rally behind its leaders for selfish motives. It was solidarity and communal living, but not the type that was compatible with the Kingdom. The Kingdom takes in everybody. It does not discriminate. Asante culture does not necessarily take in everybody. It does discriminate. Altruism is the mark of the Kingdom, egoism that of culture.

Therefore, it would appear that in extolling the virtues of Asante communitarianism, one would do well to be very cautious lest one, albeit unwillingly, support the worst type of solidarity that is pernicious to the spirit of the Kingdom. In Asante culture, there is no such thing as love of the enemy. The enemy is to be hated, shunned, detested. Asante traditional prayers are never complete without some maledictory wish for the enemy, whether he is a personal enemy or the enemy of the family or the enemy of the tribe.

The Kingdom of God knows no enemy. All are the children of God, and in Him all are brothers and sisters who form one family. The sorrow of some is shared by all the others just as much as their joy. All pray for the aberrant persons within the fold and try lovingly to correct them. The one who cheats or in some other way offends Christians is precisely the one they should be concerned about. The Kingdom of God broods over no injury, harbours no grudge. Its solidarity is universal.

Christians who discriminate or have no respect for persons are a contradiction in themselves. They serve a Kingdom whose rules they are not prepared to follow. The Kingdom would appear to be at variance with Asante societies, because they are divisive, and the Kingdom is uniting. Compassion is the hall-mark of the Kingdom. It should extend to all.

Solidarity and the Kingdom

It cannot be denied that the kind of solidarity that divides and discriminates would be against the Kingdom. But should solidarity always divide? No! Culturally, people who have common interests come together to fight for a good and dispel an evil. When there appear to be no interests in common, the problems created by solidarity begin. To serve the ends of the Kingdom, a good or an evil should be presented as common and of interest to all. For example, if a Government were able effectively to convince the whole nation of the collectivity of all blessings and hardships, solidarity would promote national unity. The whole nation could be regarded as one tribe or family. Solidarity therefore would be an asset to the Kingdom.

It may be of interest to note here that, in spite of its insistence on the universality of God's paternity and of human fraternity in Him, Christianity has helped in no small manner to create individualism in Africa, if only unwittingly.

In the first place, it appears that the concept of individual salvation is widespread. If I have to appear before God and be responsible for my actions on earth, then there seems to be no point in my worrying about what others are doing so long as I am in the good graces of the Lord.

Secondly, Christianity has historically been a divisive religion in our culture. But this need not be the case in the future, since Christianity preaches the universal nobility of all human beings. If Africans emphasise that this is against individual salvation, they will be able to make the best use of solidarity to further the interests of the Kingdom of God. The Kingdom itself is discriminatory; it discriminates against vicious people; it discriminates against greed and pride. In the African setting, these things are basically eschewed; hence it would appear that a thorough examination of the values of solidarity and of communalism on the ideal level of culture would reveal attitudes which are in complete conformity with those of the Kingdom.

Conclusion

From these reflections, the Asante theology of the Kingdom of God should be at least apparent. The Asante would understand the Kingdom of God to be ruled by God Himself who is perfect in every way. He does not seek possessions; He has everything. He does not seek prestige; all honour belongs to Him. He does not seek false solidarity with anybody, since He is one with all His creatures and He cannot act against any person or group. He does not seek power. He has all these values in an infinite way and He uses them for the good of His people. His Kingdom then is a Kingdom that the Asante, in an ideal manner, would like to have.

The king of Asante must try to be of service to everybody. His wealth must be put at the disposal of all. In the ideal situation, he should see to it that no one cheats another. The sort of thing that goes on in Ghana today with regard to the acquisition of money would be condemned in the true ideal kingdom of Asante.

The Asante concept of the Kingdom of God would thus contain no injustice, violence or domination. It should be a Kingdom of peace in which there is no strife, violence or antagonism. It should be characterised by the love and care that the king of Asante traditionally should have for his people. The ideal Asante Kingdom is one in which people are humble, including the king; a kingdom in which great feats are expected to be done for the good of all.

The Asante kingdom, in the ideal situation, should be a kingdom of unity whose source is the Golden Stool, that mysterious object that was created by the founder of the kingdom, the great Osei Tutu, and his close collaborator, Okomfo Anokye, 400 years ago. In the case of the Kingdom of God, these virtues would be not only abundant but also immeasurable.

The Asante theology of the Kingdom of God would view God as a King of splendour, majesty and dignity, whose doors are open to all His subjects. He would not let anybody suffer any want. He would be fatherly, loving and provident. The Asante theology of the Kingdom could not envisage God trying to get rid of an aggression, external or internal. This is because God is all-powerful, and everything and everybody comes from Him.

In short, the Asante theology of the Kingdom would make it clear that false values have come on the ascendancy only because of human beings' weakness and not because in reality the people desire them. For, at the end, the Asante seek compassion, submission, security, peace, true solidarity and love. These are pillars upon which the Kingdom of God is built. True kingship should be about these, and that is why God is, indeed, incomparable and credible.

Finito di stampare il 27 giugno 1997
Tipografia Poliglotta della Pontificia Università Gregoriana
Piazza della Pilotta, 4 – 00187 Roma